Flesh and Spirit

FLESH AND SPIRIT

Confessions of a Young Lord

Felipe Luciano

EMPIRE
STATE
EDITIONS

AN IMPRINT OF FORDHAM UNIVERSITY PRESS

NEW YORK   2024

Photographs by Michael Abramson are reproduced with permission from *Palante: Voices and Photographs of the Young Lords, 1969-1971* © 2011 Haymarket Books

Fordham University Press has no responsibility for the persistence or accuracy of URLs for external or third-party Internet websites referred to in this publication and does not guarantee that any content on such websites is, or will remain, accurate or appropriate.

Fordham University Press also publishes its books in a variety of electronic formats. Some content that appears in print may not be available in electronic books.

Visit us online at www.fordhampress.com/empire-state-editions.

Library of Congress Cataloging-in-Publication Data available online at https://catalog.loc.gov.

Printed in the United States of America

26 25 24   5 4 3 2

First edition

*This book is dedicated to my mother, Aurora Luciano;
my eighth-grade teacher, Miss Ethel Shapiro;
and my friend and mentor, Jacqueline Kennedy Onassis.*

CONTENTS

PREFACE

FOR ME, BEING alone is painful. Writing a memoir honestly is excruciatingly torturous. Years ago, Norman Mailer told me the only way to write was simply to write and continue to write, to craft the sentence, to squeeze the nectar out of the words. The syrup wouldn't necessarily be sweet. Mailer, looking at me coldly, without sympathy or patronage, said flatly, "Be prepared for isolation and hemorrhoids; ya' gotta' sit and write and write by yourself. It's the only way."

So why do it? Why show my wounds to the world, why admit my mistakes and failings to a world where optics is the Holy Grail, how one looks and sounds and smiles?

The past, the old patterns of thought and behavior, began to affect my spirit, began to affect my relationships with my children, women, friends, and family. Metamorphosis of spirit had not occurred. The world had drastically changed and I had not. The charge of "old school" and "old-fashioned" were being hurled at me, and what I thought was honorable and chivalrous in speech and behavior was now close to being viewed as criminal.

The past, something that for me was just the other day, became a weight I no longer wanted to bear. As friends began to die early and my kids began to chide me that I was lazy and refusing to look at a new reality, the mind fog began to intensify. Since physical courage was no longer the immediate option, was I still a warrior? My instincts were, in the main, still sound, but the impulse to jump into a battle with institutions, enemies, or women could be dangerous, destroying credibility and even life itself. Who was I?

Personal truth was to be chained and restrained because there were those who would take even a sliver of confession to discredit you. So, I began to write "The Book."

I wanted to free myself of the demons, demons I had made peace with over the decades. They were starting to smell like unwashed bodies, like rancid meat. The way to change, to move forward, was to admit that Miles Davis and Ornette Coleman were right. Drop the chains, venture out, and be afraid again. And fearless. Tradition is just a springboard to be catapulted into a new birth, a rain of cleansing, self-forgiveness, personal power, and sober analysis.

Everything that happened yesterday is what has made me today. My political thinking about America, born of demonstrations and fighting police, had changed. What was my true ideology, and how do I explain my amorphous thoughts to young people?

I'm gratefully alive for whatever time I have left on this planet, grateful that I've survived the lustful forays of flesh and the spiritual rapids of vacillation. I chose them and I don't cry about cultural habit or coercion.

As I look back, the journey has taken a toll, and that's the reason for this book. The metaphorical scars are to remind me that there are consequences for being an artist, a fool, a revolutionary, a man. I want future generations to understand exactly who they are and what they're facing.

This book is my joystick into the future, a chronicle of the gantlet and the odyssey. And may it help deter descents into Hell and inspire ascents into the heaven of self-acceptance.

Flesh and Spirit

Chapter 1

Know Thy Codes

I didn't kill him but I certainly wanted him dead. He shouldn't have touched my family. That was the unspoken deal between our gangs. No matter what the beef, regardless of the hatred between us, families were sacred and not to be harassed or assaulted, physically or verbally. He broke that deal by beating my younger brother into unconsciousness on Saturday. Now, I had to fight this asshole the next day, on a Sunday so beautiful Satan himself would've kissed God and signed a peace treaty . . . .

In the stank, empty wine bottle–smelling, smoke-filled second floor pool-room, Larry ruled the floor. Wouldn't even turn his fuckin' head to validate my lightweight status on the block or the Canarsie warriors who had just invaded his turf. I anticipated he would try to chump me, ignore me. I knew I was not a tough guy. I loved being loved, and in those days, and sometimes now, I would do anything, be anything, to be loved, to be touched, to be hugged bear-like, in the arms of anyone who saw the possibility in me, an iota of goodness, maybe even a sliver of greatness, because, well . . . I couldn't. But to blithely ignore the Black, battle-toughened young men I came in with was a big mistake. Their scowls permeated the casual banter and raucous laughter that filtered through to us as we walked quietly up the narrow stairway to the wide, semi-lit poolroom. Cigarette casually tucked behind his ear, Larry focused on his shot, oblivious to the lack of noise and the changed, suddenly quiet atmosphere in the joint.

I was trembling. My knees were so weak I thought I would buckle if he turned to me or screamed. Somehow his cohorts knew this was a different ballgame, a different confrontation. No one moved forward to challenge us. The people I came in with were about cashing wolf tickets, calling people's bluff. And their courage was so great, they would walk into your project, your block, in front of your hangout, and wait for you to come down and prove that what you said—the threat you issued publicly— had substance, had merit, and that you could back your shit up, win, lose, or draw.

These were Canarsie Chaplains, outcasts as far as the Chaplain gang mainstream was concerned. While other chapters reveled in the glory of their project bases—Fort Greene, Marcy Avenue, Albany Avenue, Breevort, etc.—these motherfuckers lived in the asshole of the world. Surrounded by an Italian community, Canarsie was still farmland. You could hear the cows, smell the shit. The subway stop was primitive. It had a clanging bell with a fifteen-foot toll arm that came slowly down when the train pulled into the 105th Street stop, and when it rained you had to squish your way through the mud because there were no goddamn sidewalks.

It was the Black Gulag. The Brookline Projects were never any family's first or second choice on Housing Authority applications. In fact, for most it wasn't their third or fourth choice. It wasn't close to Black or Puerto Rican communities, was a long, long ride from factory jobs in the garment center, and had a Sicilian core that was serious about preserving "neighborhood integrity" and proved it by dumping dead bodies in new cars amidst the tall, reeded marshlands of Flatlands Avenue. No, you didn't choose Canarsie. You got exiled there. You fought every day against kids whose fathers were "made men" in organized crime. These guys had guns, cars, beehive-hairdo girlfriends, pocket money, and bravado. If you were Black or Puerto Rican you had to develop a serious gang fraternity because the cops were useless: sometimes they worked for the gangsters, most times they identified with them, so there was no reason to have faith in their authority.

What Larry couldn't have known was that their outcast status had forced the Canarsie Chaplains division to get past the ethnic, nationalistic, skin-color question. The bonds for this gang were born of a desperate need for protection, and it didn't matter where you were born or what language you spoke in the house, Gullah or Spanish. What mattered was your heart, your loyalty, your skill in fistfighting. This was a generation of Puerto Rican mothers who only spoke Spanish, cooked with Crisco lard, homemade *sofrito*, and *tocino*, who baby-sat Black children until their parents came home from work. The same is true of those of us raised with Black families. My second mother was Kathryn Keeles, a beautiful Geechee from Charleston who praised the Lord and cooked like the devil. All over Brooklyn and Manhattan these bonds were developing, and they evolved into a ride or die love. This was more than "necessary, united-front coalition-building" political bullshit. This was family, this was blood. So when my cousin Jose, president of the Li'l People Chaplains, told the guys in Canarsie that my brother Pablo had been pummeled into semi-consciousness, there was no debate. They knew my family. And even if they didn't, their loyalty to my cousin superseded all doubts.

How was Larry to know all this shit? He thought these guys were a hastily put-together crew. That's why he acted like this was a corner neighborhood squabble. He couldn't pick up on the fact that these Chaplains exuded an attitude of I don't give a shit. I've been to Hell, live there now, so unless you're God, your ass is mine. Larry kept playing pool, never taking his eyes off the cue ball, never validating the presence of the Chaplains, even as they took strategic positions around the room so no one could leave. An eerie silence descended on the place where minutes before there had been loud back-slapping, five-hand-slapping noise before we entered the space. The men I was with were not the kids Larry was used to bullying. These were warriors: kangaroo shoes, pressed chino pants, Blye knit sweaters, leather coats, toothpicks in their mouths. There were no smiles, no unnecessary conversation and ashiness on their knuckles. Their shiny and wavy hair was matted down with Dixie Peach pomade and stocking caps covered by stingy-brimmed hats that they blocked perfectly. The Jade East cologne on their cheeks offered the only pleasant-smelling oasis in this shithole. The ritual was that you took your hat off only to hurt somebody and then you had to make sure your hair was "tight" and wouldn't get messed up in a fight. The fight should end in three minutes. Any longer than that, you're wasting time or getting your ass kicked, badly.

Didn't Larry know? These were not your normal run-of-the-mill, dilettante "colored guys." They were young, but they were Black men, forged and tempered in gang battles. Slowly, I walked over to Larry's pool table. He didn't move, didn't speak, continued to cue up his next shot. I made the mistake of approaching him from his right side where he could've easily swung the thin part of the pool cue into my face. I sensed I had blown the approach, so I closed the gap between us. On the streets this kind of proximity meant war. "Why'd you . . . uhmm . . . why'd you beat up my brother?" I said squeakily. His crowd in the poolroom laughed at my cracking voice. My guys glowered at me, their eyes burning into mine. But they didn't intervene. I had to do this on my own—that was the code. They'd back me up, but I had to challenge and follow through. Moose, an obsidian black, heavyweight master street fighter, who had been looking at the floor all the time but was really watching the hip movements of everybody in the joint, raised his head in genuine amazement. In seconds, the rage that clouded his face scared me. He wanted to do Larry right there. Looked at him, then looked at me, his jaws tightening. He cradled his left fist with his huge right hand in front of his genitals. That was the signal. It was time to get this over with.

I was still shaking. I was still scared. But I had to do something to save face, to let my group and Larry know I was going all the way. Quickly stepping forward, I pushed my hand down hard onto the middle of the pool cue and said softly, "There's gonna be no game today, Larry. We gonna talk." Larry, angry, confused, spat out the word "motherfucka" and tried to pull the pool cue up. It didn't move. Somehow, my right forearm, sinewy but strong, didn't give out. Letting go of the cue, he backed up a bit and started to come toward me. I expected him to swing, and I just waited deadlocked in time and space, looking straight at him. Out of nowhere, it seemed, the manager of the joint—a short, semi-balding, middle-aged, brown-skinned man with moles all over his face—jumped in between us, grabbed the cue I had my hand on, and yelled, "Y'all take this shit downstairs. I don't want no shit up in heah. Y'all deal with it downstairs, ya hear?" Larry and I stared at each other for a few seconds. He was trying to figure out where the fuck I got the sudden burst of courage. I was simply holding on to my mission of asking him why he beat up my brother, possibly fighting him, hopefully eking out a draw, and never having him mess with me or my family again. Then, it seemed the entire pool hall clambered down the stairs by the sound of the rumbling feet on that sunny spring day. The crowd surrounded us on the corner—my guys in the inner circle, his people on the outer. It wasn't lost on me that none of his folks tried to muscle in for a better look. There was a gut-churning silence.

And then I spoke, a little firmer, a little louder, but still trembling. I was really scared of this guy and hoping beyond hope that a miracle would occur to end this confrontation; maybe he would say he was sorry or something to that effect. I could call him a bunch of *motherfuckas*, threaten him with murder if he touched my family again, and leave. He would save his life, I would save face, and our mediocre lives would continue unabated. It wasn't to be.

"Why'd you beat him up, Larry? He's just a kid. He didn't do anything to you. He doesn't even know you," I said calmly.

Larry's face exploded in anger, and he started to point his finger in my face as he screamed, "Fuck you, nigga. I fucked him up because I fucked him up. That's all there is to it. He shouldn't have been there. I don't have to tell you shit."

Larry was in a bind. The beating was senseless. I had been told that by Shorty, who was with my brother when he was beaten (and didn't raise a hand to protect him). After I smacked Shorty and bounced him off the wall a few times, he blurted out that Larry and some of his boys had wandered downstairs from the house party the night before and decided to bully three Puerto Rican men coming home late from work. The teens were drunk. The older men were sober, and they fought well, fending off the gang attack and beating the kids with their fists, fair and square. Shorty told me the 'Ricans simply walked away, no cops were called, no weapons drawn. But the humiliation lingered, and the young toughs burst into the house party looking for Puerto Ricans, knowing that the only one there was my fourteen-year-old brother, Pablo, who then paid the price for their loss of pride. You see, by beating up my brother, Larry had violated an unspoken, unwritten street code. It was simple. You don't beat up an innocent person because you lost a fight that you started!

The protocol was gang members would even protect the families of opposing gang members, who were innocent. My brother should have been safe with Larry that night—Puerto Rican or not. Larry and I had a low-flame, simmering conflict since I moved into Bushwick. He didn't like me because, though I lived within his gang borders, I didn't join his crew. Most of his guys were thuggish bullies, directionless, always fighting. The group I joined had dreams, sang doo-wop well, went to school, and dressed nicely. In those days, they called guys like us "cool breezes," guys who would fight hard if forced to but would rather look good, go to school, and talk to the ladies. Everybody also knew I had always stood on the Black side of the "'hood," even when the Puerto Rican gangs tried to recruit me. It was common knowledge that where you lived is where your loyalty lay. And I always lived on the Black-hand side of every neighborhood.

If beatings came, they resulted from being on the losing side, but not because I was Puerto Rican. Larry knew he couldn't explain his racism without losing the support of even his own guys. Whatever anger Larry had toward me should have been directed to me—personally—not my brother. The same gang code applied to women. No matter what beef you had with someone, what fight you had or were going to have, women were never to know—especially women of the opposing group. Mothers, sisters, and girlfriends were sacred. If you saw your enemy's mother on the streets struggling with groceries, your job was to carry them upstairs for her and never, I mean never, accept money. If you were high or drunk and that same woman passed by, you sobered up immediately or acted sober and made sure you said, "Yes ma'am" and "No ma'am" to all her enquiries, regardless of your reeking breath or unsteady gait. Some folks today think that those codes applied to people you were connected to in friendship, but that wasn't the whole of the matter. It applied to all elders and family members of opposing gangs as well. It was street chivalry, the warrior code. By beating my brother to within an inch of his life, Larry had violated that code.

My inner circle started to get impatient. Their way of fighting was quick, fast, efficient, very little talk. I was taking too much time. Moose stared me straight in the eye and then issued the challenge, dryly. "What you gonna do with this dude, man?" I was shocked into reality by those few words. This was neither a movie nor a game. Somebody had to go down, something had to happen. I looked away from Larry and said, "I'm gonna ask you again, why'd you beat my brother?" Larry saw the redundancy of the question as a sign of fear and weakness. It was. He spat out his answer. "I told you I fucked him up 'cause I felt like fucking him up and if you keep this shit up, I'll fuck you up, fuck your mother up, your sister . . . ." I saw his lips moving, but I couldn't hear anything. A bomb went off in my head and the punch started from my right toe, went through my knee, ripped through my hip, flashed through my lats, flooded my shoulder, strengthened my forearm, and granitized my right fist. It stopped Larry's bravado and shattered the afternoon standoff.

He fell down in stages, crumpling the way metal cans do when the air is sucked out of them. I kept on punching and screaming and kicking. He fell and stayed on the sidewalk, his legs spread awkwardly on the concrete. Clumsily, he raised himself up on one elbow, shaking the fogginess out of his brain. Clarity must have seeped through the cobwebs quickly; within seconds, he jumped to his feet and began to run. He never looked at me or my guys or his gang. I'll never forget the fear in his eyes. He had not only been knocked down in a fair fight, he had been knocked from power and there was no refuge. He had no plans for loss. He had no plan for failure. No backup. And his minions were not jumping to his aid. So he ran. And we ran after him. I can't remember who grabbed him first, but I do remember screaming, "No! He's mine." My breath control was well known. I could stay underwater for almost two minutes and I could chase anyone, staying a yard behind them, for a long, long time. Larry was not going to escape.

Bloodlust had overtaken me, and all I felt was the pulse of the hunt. I was no longer prey. I was predator. He tripped and fell. I pounced on him, taking aim, hitting him square. He couldn't protect himself anymore and while he tried in the first few seconds to block the blows, he gave up and I saw his head recoil with each punch. And then my guys caught up and I almost felt sorry for him, sprawled backward on the pebbled concrete. This beating was going to be quick, painful, and methodical. "This is to remind you of who not to fuck with next time," Moose spat out as he punched Larry in the jaw, hard and fast. "And this, motherfucka, is for acting like you had heart . . ." shouted Moose, the sweat trickling down his face from under his fedora, "and the bitching up. Take this, you punk ass!" Moose's size 12 alligator shoe heel collided against Larry's light-brown, almost reddish head. All of us stood back for a minute as we let Moose beat him up for a while. Then we jumped him again.

It lasted no longer than fifteen minutes, us shouting, punching, and kicking the gangly kid, humiliating him by throwing garbage cans on top of him, all in front of his so-called gang of friends, not one of whom stepped up to help him or even beg us to stop. We might have listened to that. And then the hurricane of hate stopped, just like that. Five of my guys instinctively stopped hitting Larry, stopped shouting, and ran down Broadway, quietly. Larry was still alive. The Canarsie Chaplains were professionals—cool, methodically dangerous. The only ones left around the victim were John and I, the unprofessionals. The knife came out. John stuck Larry twice, once in the lung, once in the heart. I heard the death rattle, saw his eyes go blank, saw life leave Larry as I punched him for the last time and realized I never wanted it to end this way. I never even saw the knife go in.

I remember looking up at the pearlized, iridescent sky that April afternoon in 1964: a soft, salmon-pink sky with pastel baby-blue streaks running through it and small puffs of white clouds hanging like bright, bleached underthings on an invisible, celestial ghetto clothesline . . . .

I remember looking back down into Larry's small, frightened, pukey yellow-brown eyes and screaming, "What happened to all your heart, motherfucka?," punching him squarely in the face while he was on his back, again and again, until his squirming stopped.

I remember wondering why he wasn't fighting back, viciously. He was known for his brutality. I figured he knew he deserved this ass-whipping. "*Wasamatter, man? You beat my brother's ass last night, but now you punking out, huh?*"

I remember wondering why his gang, about twenty of them, wasn't jumping in. Ten yards away and not one of them moved a muscle to protect his skinny ass. They must have felt the same way. They quietly watched Larry get his ass kicked. Either they felt he deserved the beating or they didn't jump in to help because . . . because they weren't ready to die that day.

What I didn't understand was why there was this strange guy next to me throughout the fight. A guy I didn't know, had never met. I knew the other guys, had hung out with them, drinking fifths of cheap Twister wine and grinding to slow ballads with sweet-breathed, full-lipped, shapely sisters in basement parties with blue lights right above the door. But this guy? Never present. I found out later that on that particular Sunday, for some unknown reason, "John" had volunteered to be part of the Chaplain gang division from the Brookline Projects, recruited by my cousin Jose, to avenge the beating of my brother the night before. According to Jose, John was never an official member of the group.

I vaguely remember the long, arching punches John threw at the guy's chest. Even in the heat of battle, I thought the blows were ineffective and wouldn't hurt. They were graceful punches, almost surgical. I never thought my new "friend" John was stabbing Larry. I grabbed Larry's shirt, near the open collar, to pull him up and punch him again when I noticed John, knife in hand, standing, almost trancelike, staring strangely at the body. His shoulders stooped, his back bent, his legs trembling. He looked like Dracula—a long, black leather coat draped over his boney shoulders and a longer belt and buckle hanging from the coat loops, coiled along both sides of the coat, almost touching the concrete sidewalk, like a serpent. He looked like an undertaker, like the spirit of Death come to visit Bushwick, Brooklyn, right under the tracks of the "El," dead smack on the corner of Halsey and Broadway. The bloody knife was in his hand. His mouth was open, but no sounds were coming out. I knew, he knew, that he had killed Larry. Suddenly, I remembered how John had let me scream and punch until I let up for a second, out of sheer exhaustion. That's when he got a piece of him. And that's when it all came together. The soft arc of John's arm going into Larry's chest and his back, just two times. That's all it took . . . I let the body drop.

I remember looking at Larry's lifeless face, his eyes almost shut, his mouth half-closed. It was that semicircle of light that bounced off his iris that shattered any veneer of vengeance or victory I might have harbored. It was the grotesque way his mouth looked, lips locked frozen around a black hole as if he were in freeze-frame caught in the middle of something he was about to say or snarl. Throughout the entire beating he had not uttered a word, only grunts. It was as if his pride, his manhood, his ego would not let him give us the pleasure of hearing his screams of fear or the possibility, the very real possibility, of his losing this battle. The cops came within minutes of my stepping off the body. Of the original seven combatants, five had already fled down Broadway and turned left on Eldert Street. To this day I don't know whether they saw John stab the boy or felt the beating was over and it was time to split before the police arrived. John was in the aftermath of bloodlust—a state of shock after one has killed or seriously hurt someone. It was as if he was possessed.

I remember looking up again, thinking what a beautiful day it was and how, maybe, it was just a hint of what the summer of '64 would be like. Balmy wind, pearl-like sky. Damn! What a way to spend a beautiful spring-like afternoon . . . . Immediately, I knew the cards I was being dealt. Nothing was going to be the same. Ever. It was going to be dark for a long time—dark, different, deranged, a bad dream. And as I rose from the body to gently take the knife from John's bloody hand and hide it under a corroded metal garbage can, I knew I had taken that huge step into acknowledgment of consequences. And on that Sunday, on that day of worship, punishment was meted out, whether I was ready or not.

Chapter 2

A Tale of Two Beatings

The red strands of bloody mucus hung, suspended in air, from my mouth to my knees as I bent over hugging my ribs. I couldn't breathe through my nose anymore. My eyes were swelled shut. I begged them to stop but what came out of my mouth was more blood, more spit, a hoarse gurgle. I wasn't giving the cops what they wanted. I kept hearing this soft, soothing voice inside telling me to just let go, just sleep. I wanted to so badly . . .

I had heard that voice before, heard that music when my mother had beaten me four years earlier on a Friday night in early June right before my sixth-grade graduation. She first used the strap, then the mopstick. She was going to beat the demons out of me, she said, because dancing was an excuse for sex. I had reveled the day before in the fact that I was going to my first prom dance at P.S. 170 on West 112th Street in Harlem.

At about 1:30 A.M., Mom had slipped into the darkened bedroom I shared with three cousins, my brother, and my sister and whispered in choked breaths that God had come to her that night and warned her about this dance and the ensuing demonic flesh rituals that would take place during and after. I kept my eyes closed as she tearfully implored me not to attend. Hell, I had been waiting for this "bacchanal" all year. Just the thought of it had kept me up all night.

My mother had a different revelation. She had dreams that the prom was just an excuse for boys and girls to kiss and touch each other in private places, forbidden places. She was Pentecostal, the "Chassidic" branch of the fundamentalist, evangelical Protestant denomination. Everything normal was a sin: baseball, movies, jewelry, makeup, money and . . . sex. "Philip, God spoke to me, clearly, just like I'm talking to you. You can't go to that dance. You'll be sinning, defiling your body, and God doesn't want that. He wants you pure and clean, a perfect vessel for Him. He can't use you if you're dirty." I knew she was looming over me in her flannel nightgown, I knew she was terribly upset, but, without opening my eyes I answered her in as measured a tone as possible, "Ma, this is not God, this is what you want. *You* don't want me to go to the dance, the same way you don't want me to have girlfriends. C'mon, Ma, I'm twelve, I'm growing up. You can't stop me from living my life. Ma, I'm going to the dance."

There was a long, uneasy silence in the bedroom and suddenly I felt the long, warm stream of my brother's urine against my backside. We slept in the same bed. He was terrified. He knew what was coming. So did I. You didn't disobey the "word of the Lord" in my mother's presence. She was the interpreter of His will. Willful disobedience was reason for harsh punishment, brutal beatings with anything she could lay her hands on. "So you know what to do with your life better than God?" From an early age I knew my mother's heaven-sent pronouncements were nothing more than her fear of losing me. After God, I was the light of her life. My father had darkened her existence by leaving her for another woman, nine years before. She wasn't going to let that happen again. She couldn't control him, but she damn sure was going to control me, or so she thought. She was lonely, broke, and on welfare. And she was frustrated. There was no man/woman intimacy, no fleshy, sweaty thrashing of thighs and bodies. God was her husband, her only Man. The church was her only community, her only solace. And she obeyed all their rigid rules, religiously. Spare the rod, spoil the child. "Okay," she whispered as she backed out of the room, "Okay, I'll be right back!" She waited. I waited.

The loud rummaging sounds in the bathroom were meant to scare me, crush my spirit, make me think of surrendering to her and her version of God. Upon hearing those sounds, my brother and sister would always confess to whatever lies they had conjured up, whatever unruly behavior they were responsible for. I refused, had always refused, so I got beaten the worst. I heard the mopstick being popped out of the coiled spring handle, heard her hand swishing over the top shelf of the outside closet for the wide, black Garrison belt she kept there. I kept my eyes closed one last time, to gain strength. This was war, "spiritual" and physical. Forget about winning; I just wanted to survive. There was no warning, no negotiation, no quarter asked, no quarter given. My mother just rushed into the room and started flailing away, first with the belt in her right hand, and when she saw I protected myself with the bed cover, she used her left, pummeling me with the mop-stick. It didn't matter to her where the blows landed; she usually aimed the belt buckle at my head or my balls. I had learned not to run; that was senseless and enraged her even more. I developed a method of bobbing and weaving, avoiding the blows to my face or head, lifting my legs to protect my penis and scrotum but allowing her to place the blows to my thighs, back, and arms, all the while talking to her calmly, asking her to stop.

She was my mother; she didn't have the answers for her rage. I knew how confused she was, how angry. She left the poverty and rigidity of her mother's house in her late teens, dropped out of high school in the tenth grade, and placed all her hopes on a streetwise, handsome boxer and mambo dancer named Joe Pepito, a.k.a. Lucky. And now, after his abandonment of her, nine years and three kids later, she had to deal with her oldest, who exhibited the same cockiness, the same charm with girls, the same independence and rebellion. At twelve years of age, I knew she loved me, though she was never that physically affectionate unless I first threw my arms around her. But I also knew there were times she hated my intelligence, my questioning atti-tude about everything from God, the Church, my father and sexuality, questions to which she had no adequate answers most of the times. There were times, even during these regular monthly beatings, I really felt sorry for her. She just dreamed of raising her kids and loving her husband. Not being alone. She never asked for this.

"Ma," I hissed, "why are you hitting me so hard? That's not God, Ma. That's just you. You need help, Ma. Why don't you go see Daddy? Talk to him. Hug him. Sleep with him. But don't beat me anymore." And the lashes continued with even more ferocity. I had broken the code by bringing to the surface something I should have only thought and kept to myself. And now she had to kill me.

She told me so. "I can't believe what you just said," she sobbed hysterically. "The devil has entered this house, but I will beat him out of you."

And for the next hour I thought I was going to die from the pain. That was the first time I heard that voice telling me to sleep, the voice I would hear in the police station. I crawled into a fetal position in that Harlem project bedroom and just screamed until I fell silent. I felt every blow. I just didn't have the strength or the spirit to resist anymore. My mother flailed and grunted and lashed and exhaled heavily until she got tired, threw the belt on the floor, and ran out of the darkened bedroom, crying. I stayed on the floor a long, long time, until dawn. I survived. I didn't heed the call to sleep until much later. I didn't go to the dance. My welts were too thick, too noticeable.

And now here I was, four years later in a police station, getting beaten again. Why wouldn't I just stay down? I resisted even more. Each time they crushed my shins with their nightsticks, each time they slammed into my back with a bat, each time they opened my scalp with their gun butts or punched me in the face I'd fall and then slowly pull myself up, clutching onto that dirty gray metal desk with the brown stained circles of coffee cups. I wanted to die then too. The cops, like my mom, wanted to kill my spirit. I didn't listen to the voice, didn't follow that nice white light. It was a death call. These cops and detectives were huge, burly men, hated the neighborhood they were assigned to protect, and hated the people in it. These were the great-grandsons of those Irish immigrants who were considered the scum of Europe, the refuse of the British Isles. They were purposely starved by England during the Potato Famine and forced to leave their emerald homeland to come and get beaten by German and nativist Scotch-Irish police on New York City streets. They became politicians, boxers, actors, and criminals. They were also wife-beaters, drunkards, prostitutes, absentee fathers and charity cases. And as they slowly climbed out of the ghettos of a country that loved their cheap labor and hated their guts, these great-grandsons of some of the finest human stock I have ever encountered developed cultural amnesia. They forgot their poverty, their pain, their rejection, their self-hatred. They imposed the same negative stereotypes that once shackled their progress onto the lives of the new slumdwellers. And they did it with a vengeance.

I was a skinny, 5′7″, sixteen-year-old Black Puerto Rican who belonged to the All City Chorus, who loved history and music, and who had just helped kill someone. A voice pierced the fog.

"All right, kid. We're gonna ask you again. Where were you the night before you killed this guy?"

I was delirious. But I knew their game. By talking about your whereabouts you were automatically admitting guilt. Somewhere, in the back of whatever consciousness I still had, I was holding on desperately. I tried speaking but I couldn't pronounce the words properly. My lips were too swollen. I started to cry. "Ah din't kill him."

More slaps. More punches. They were having fun. I couldn't distinguish one from another. They were coming in shifts, some Black, some white. And they hit me all the time, with whatever they had in their hands or on them. "So, if you didn't kill him, who did?"

"Ah 'own know, man."

One detective, one of the guys who booked me and had been quietly watching the ass-whipping, just walked up to me and punched me straight in the mouth. On his right ring finger was a silver wolf's head with two ruby eyes that embedded itself in my upper lip. Flesh ripped when he pulled his fist back. "This fuckin' guy bleeds like a pig," he said to no one in particular.

The gaping hole in my upper lip, the exposed flesh and the blood made him stop for a while. I knew it wasn't over. The detective suddenly took something out of his pants pocket—some keys and a small gun— and laid them on the table. I jerked backward, but he grabbed my blue mohair sweater, pulled me toward him, unlocked the handcuffs, and quickly walked to the sink and began to wash the blood off his hands. The gun was a foot away from me. All I had to do was jump, grab the piece, and shoot. And though my vision was blurred, at that distance I was not going to miss. What the hell, I was being accused of murder, I figured I was never getting out, and the pain was unbearable. All they could do was kill me, but one of them was going with me. I straightened myself up and began to rub my wrists as much for relief as to see how alert the detective was. With all the loud talk and laughing outside the room, he'd never hear or see it coming.

The man immediately jerked his head up and looked at the small mirror right above the sink, his right hand sliding toward the butt of his snub-nosed Smith & Wesson .38. I stared straight back at him, motionless. He bent over again to wash his face and that's when I looked hard at the gun. The bullets inside the chamber didn't have conical shapes; they were flatheads, powder charges used by referees in athletic events. The gun was a starter pistol. This motherfucka had purposely unhandcuffed me and left a gun on the table near enough for me to reach it. Any movement toward that gun would've been suicide for me, justifiable homicide for him. Thank God I had heard about this cop psych game in the Brownsville Projects: "They beat you senseless, then leave a phony gun near you, hoping you go for it." It was not my day to die.

Drying his huge hands with a brown paper towel, the detective from the 83rd Precinct walked toward me as if nothing had happened. I remember thinking maybe he'll stop, he's a human being, maybe even he can't stomach the brutality. He lowered his head so that his eyes looked directly into mine.

"You're a fuckin' liar. We know you did it, cocksucker. Just say it!" he barked, and I knew this was the second round.

As the blood dribbled down my chin, as my legs wobbled like a woman whose water had broken against the door of that small, smelly, dirty room, I kept thinking, how can these humans do this to me? So what if they were white? How could they continue punching me so hard in the face? Couldn't they see the blood spewing out? Couldn't they see my eyes had disappeared into balloons of flesh? The detective continued, but his voice was changed. He sounded rational, almost soothing, like a counselor. With his face still close to mine, his hairy, muscled arm leaning against the flaking paint of the police-green wall, his right hand on his hip, next to his gun, just in case, he explained what the real deal was from a police perspective and, in some ways, the very human perspective I was hoping for.

He looked away for a few seconds and began. "You know sump'in? We knew this kid. He was a motherfucka . . . known to us. Bad seed. But we never killed him. We busted him a few times, busted him up a few times, but we never fuckin' killed him. Maybe he was gonna be an asshole and do the shit that most of these niggers around here do. He coulda turned out okay, y'know. But you and your fuckin' merry marauders stopped the process. Who fuckin' gave you the right to kill him? Who died and made you God?"

I couldn't believe this torturer, this human piece of shit, was talking like this. He knew Larry, and by the tone of his voice, he even liked him. Larry was the reason he was getting paid and feeling good about himself. Cops like him helped Blacks see the path of hard work and family, or they murdered them. Now, I was not only in pain, I was confused and devastated. "You coulda broken his knees, coulda put the fuckin' guy in the hospital. Or you coulda given him a fair fight and beat the crap out of him. But, no! You guys killed him. And he never had a chance. That's why you're here, asshole. You killed somebody. You didn't just beat 'im up, you murdered him. And you want me to fuckin' believe that you were listening to classical music the night before. Whaddaya think, I'm stupid?" He backed away, rolled his sleeves up, and said, "Now, let's go over this again." He had done this many times before. I could feel it.

There was a polite knock on the door. I was relieved, but the voice was not directed at me. "How ya doing?" the voice said matter-of-factly.

"Okay," the detective said looking directly at me, "I think we're gonna get somewhere."

My spirit dropped. Whatever hope I had for the end of this torture session faded quickly. "Lemme in there for a second," the voice commanded.

My hope rose again. Obviously, whoever was outside that door was a superior officer who, maybe knowing the rules of proper procedure, would stop the beating. The detective, wordlessly, grabbed a handful of my sweater sleeve, pulled me away from the door, and motioned for me to stand in the middle of the room.

It was rectangular, wood-floored, dirty, and it had two long rectangular civil service–type gray metal desks and one small wooden desk against the wall. If it weren't for the sink, the mirror, and the industrial brown paper towels, it would've been a large closet. There was no light. The windows, two on the street side, had wrought-iron guard rails on the outside. I had often passed this precinct laughing to myself at the stupidity and paranoia of the 83rd. Who the fuck would want to break and enter the second story of this rathole police station? What scared me were the long, dark-green shades pulled all the way down. Even though I saw slivers of sunlight peeking through the sides of the shades, it was perpetual night in that room. You could hear the soft rumble of traffic and the elevated train, sounds of normalcy in our world, but nothing else. No voices, no kids playing, no adults greeting one another, nothing. It was a place of torture.

The detective opened the door and in walked an elegant silver-haired, square-jawed, handsome Irishman. I noticed a professionalism about him, a cold professionalism, businesslike, impersonal. "What you got?" he said to the underling, bending his head to light a half-smoked cigar while checking me out. "What's his story?" With military precision, the detective quickly turned to me and barked, "All right, tell the Sarge what you told me."

Was this a sick game they had played before with other prisoners? Or was he trying to kiss up to his superior officer for not having extracted the confession yet? I suddenly felt like a captured alien under the spotlight—naked, defenseless, scared. The detective was acting like a schoolyard bully who'd been caught by the principal before for beating kids up for no reason, but now, having caught a purse-snatcher, could redeem himself.

"Get a load of this, Sarge. Where were you the night before you stuck this kid, what's his name. Larry, right?" For some strange reason, I nodded my head, agreeing with him.

"Yeah, Larry."

"Tell the Sarge!" he said. I was hoping beyond hope that this head honcho would stop the game. I was badly beaten, my lips were grotesquely puffy, my mouth full of blood, I was terrified of spitting on the floor.

"Ah wuz at Congee Hall . . . lissing to moosik" was all I could muster.

"And tell the Sarge, what kind of music was it, you fuck?"

"Gregor'an chants . . . Renahsance." The detective got a kick out of this, a nigger with culture. The sergeant said nothing, just continued squinting at me through the cigar smoke.

"You hear that shit, Sarge?" the heavyset detective said incredulously. "He's a fuckin' psycho. Listens to that fuckin' music, whatever it is, and then kills people the next day. What a piece of work."

He must've imagined the headlines with my picture and his name attached to the lead story of Monday's dailies, "Thug Attends Classical Concert, Then Murders."

He punched me into a wooden chair directly behind me. I fell over, hit the floor backward. And then, in front of the sergeant, he started to scream. "Get the fuck outta my chair, you spic bastard. Think you're better than me, huh? Think you're smart?"

The other officer did nothing to stop him, just puffed on his cigar quietly. As if this was a well-rehearsed drill, the detective took a few steps toward me, picked me up by my sweater as if I were a rag doll, made me stand straight, and with a putrid breath of chocolate bars mixed with coffee and cigarettes, his mouth almost directly in my nose, said menacingly, "You're going to tell me what I want to know. And you're going to sign this confession."

Through my puffed eyes all I can remember seeing were his crooked yellow teeth and the sweaty, humid smell of fear emanating from his body, his ass, his underarms, the whole of him. What the hell was he afraid of? I knew. My God, a Puerto Rican, a black Puerto Rican smarter than him, loving a musical form he had never heard of, liking something he was never taught, having attended a concert in a place he had never been—Carnegie Hall—and having rubbed elbows with upper-class folks, something he could only dream of. He had to break me down, look good in front of his boss. As he raised his hand to strike me again, I cried out, "Yes. Yeah. Yeah. I'll sign it, anything."

Two-and-a-half hours of having my face used as a punching bag, my body used for batting practice, I had had enough. I felt defeated, ashamed that I was ratting out John who was seated, handcuffed, just outside the door, listening to everything. There was no joy, no songs in my head, no memories of laughter, no pretty girls, no family, no God—only a formless darkness swirling through my head and my being. If there is a Hell, I was there.

There was simply no hope in that place. I collapsed in front of those men. I was hoping I could just die, just dissolve, or waft into the atmosphere before I signed anything. It was the only time the sergeant moved. Quickly, roughly, they picked me up, held my body upright and placed their thick hands over mine to steady my trembling fingers. I signed my name to a confession I didn't write on a green-lined yellow legal pad. It was over. They hung me like a tanned hide in a bullpen, a cage for prisoners, inside the larger detectives' room. My arms were raised way over my head and they cuffed me again, on my tiptoes. If I let my heels down, the cuffs cut into my wrists. I heard them bring John inside the same little room. I strained to listen, but with the noise outside and my tiredness inside I didn't hear much of the details of the conversation. What I did hear was some muffled commands, two or three smacks, a body hitting the door and falling to the ground, and then silence. They dragged John out minutes later. He had given up quickly and confessed that he stabbed Larry. Even in my pain, mouth swollen, eyes shut, I wanted to kill him. Why hadn't he come forward earlier? He heard my screams; he knew what they were doing to me. Why the fuck did he let them beat me for hours when all I was trying to do was protect him for having helped me?

When I raised my eyes from the filthy floor through the bullpen bars and squinted at him, my heart broke. He silently mouthed "I'm sorry" to me. I looked and then hung my head. He had heard my screams and that was enough torture for him. Years later, I realized that was the purpose for their beating me . . . to get to him. They knew I hadn't stabbed the guy; a witness probably told them John did it. But they needed us to say it. And they worked the brain game. Beat me up bad, so John could hear . . . and fear. It worked. Hours passed. I would fall asleep and then the pain in my wrists would jolt me awake. I couldn't see her, but I heard the cops addressing my mother when she finally came to the station house. I heard her scared voice as she asked, respectfully, to speak to the commanding officer. Some of the cops answered deferentially, others nastily. She passed right by me. I knew it was her, her smell, the timbre of her voice, the shuffle of her gait. She didn't recognize my face. That's when I knew the cops had really done a job on me. "Where's my son?" she asked fearfully. One of the nasty voices shot back an answer. "That's him hanging over there." What came out of her mouth was a bloodcurdling scream and it didn't stop. They had beaten me. They had beaten my mother. She screamed for me. I moaned for her. Sounds came out of our mouths for a long time . . . until the tears came.

Chapter 3

Confronting Demons

AFTER THE ARRAIGNMENT I was transported to the Brooklyn House of
Detention. It was a horrible jail, smelling like disinfectant and unwashed
bodies. Mothers who came to see their sons waited on long lines and broiled
under the summer sun for hours. During winter snows, their feet froze in
those cheap, clear plastic rain boots they'd wear, their hair and ears protected
by gaily colored nylon kerchiefs bound tightly under their chins. Those
mothers, some of them overweight and plagued by high blood pressure,
others, too thin with anemia and worry, all of them with sleepless eyes, were
the human womb cradles that had given birth to the detainees inside. Those
mothers—Black, brown, and white, huddled together in the winter to stay
warm praying and exchanging stories about their "babies."

During the first few weeks of my detention, I noticed an anxiety about
my mother, an emotional cloud around her. I kept asking what was bothering
her and she'd shake off the question, preferring to spend the time asking
about the conditions inside and how I was faring.

"What's the matter, Ma? What's going on? Is anything bothering you?"
"Well," she said haltingly without looking at me, "you remember that loud
boy you said was your friend . . . the one who always used to greet me with
hugs and kisses on the streets near my church?"

"Oh, you talkin' about Lippo," I said flippantly, "the guy from Cooper
Street? What happened?" And then my mother breathed that sigh that said
I-don't-want-you-to-get-involved; this-is-a man's-job-and-I-wish-your-father-
were-here.

"The day after the beating of that boy . . . the stabbing . . . Lippo came up to me, followed me after church with his gang, and showed me the knife he said you used to kill his friend. Philip, I started to scream. He put it right near my face," my mother said, her gaze losing clarity through the bulletproof glass.

"I saw the blood and everything. He said Larry was his boy and that we were going to pay for this. Baby, I just screamed and screamed and thought about your sister Margie and your brother Paul . . . and then I fainted."

My skin got cold and prickly. It wasn't anger, passion, or impulse. It was murder. Lippo had to die, as quickly as possible, as soon as possible. He had crossed the same gang boundaries his dead friend had, but now he had moved into the no-exit, no-return area, the threatening of mothers. It was not a question of who would kill him, or how, but when. My decision to murder was not a long, conflictive process. I simply knew what had to be done.

I returned my attention to Mom. She was not afraid of anything, anybody. She was a true prayer warrior, praying daily as many times as my Muslim brothers inside. This woman had prayer calluses on her knees from praying so much. Aurora Luciano believed "no weapon formed against you will prosper" and instilled in her kids a strong, strict, visceral, down-here-on-the-ground, faith in God's love and protection. It wasn't mystical. I heard her heartfelt prayers throughout my life; through the hollow sheetrock walls of the tiny one-bedroom tenement in Bushwick or the solid concrete cinder block walls of whatever lower-income project development we were assigned. This woman was strong!

Two years before, when I was fourteen, I had watched my mother do battle with screaming demons who possessed my Aunt Tina, my mother's oldest sister, one winter afternoon. Aunt Tina, a very dark, voluptuous Puerto Rican woman, liked white men who worked hard, played hard, had cash money, and liked to share. She was dating Charlie, a Syrian Jew, who sold costume jewelry in a small store on Broadway under the El. Charlie was a mensch. He loved to talk, sell, philosophize, and fight. He also liked to drink a lot. So did Aunt Tina.

One weekend when he was out on a buying trip, Tina drank more than usual and fell asleep at the kitchen table. She hadn't quite gotten that drunk yet, but she was cursing the family out, mentioning all kinds of personal secrets.

And then she began to beat us, hard. My cousin Jose and I were used to it. But when I heard two voices coming out of her and saw her spinning in the kitchen near the open window, I called my Mom, "Mommy, Aunt Tina's possessed." My mother pooh-poohed it for a minute and questioned my ability to diagnose demonic forces. "Oh, c'mon now, Philip. You know Tina gets drunk like that sometimes. Don't leave her alone and put cold compresses . . . ." I cut my mother off quickly. "She's dancing real fast in the kitchen and the stove's on, Ma. She's talking in tongues. Her body's jerking and the window's wide open. This is serious, Ma. Get over here, quick." All my mother ordered is that I ". . . turn off the stove and bring the windows down just a little bit. You need the air. And keep her there, no matter what you hear or what she does to you. I'm getting my holy oil and my Bible right now." And she hung up.

My mother was right. Aunt Tina grabbed me by the shirt and thrashed me about, screaming, "You are nothing. Your father is nothing. You're shit. Your mother's an asshole for marrying that creep." That kind of stuff I could handle. Then it got serious. Aunt Tina's eyes became slits and as she put her mouth next to my ear she rasped in a guttural voice, "You think you'll succeed? Never. I'll make sure of it." Her body had suddenly turned as hard as a man's. She grabbed me again, her forearms swelling with muscle, pulling me toward her pelvis, her body pushing into mine. "We could do this, you and me. You'll be mine, forever. Feel me. Go 'head. Touch it. I'll teach you things you never read about." Jose, embarrassed and terrified, grabbed a knife and approached his mother from the side, screaming, "Who are you? Leave my cousin alone, motherfucka. I'll cut the shit out of you."

Aunt Tina's face turned to me, the spittle trickling down her mouth. "Who is this? How dare he approach me? I will kill him in less than a second." Judging by the strength she was using on me, I felt she was telling the truth. "Jose, stay back. This is not your mother. This is another spirit. Stay away from her. She'll hurt you. Stay away from her!" And that's when my aunt's creature-like eyes narrowed and turned colors. "Oh, you know about me, don't you?" she said roughly. And then she loosened her grasp on my shirt and said it softly again, "You know who I am. And you think because you're Aurora's kid, you're protected?"

I had never seen evil incarnate before. The devil was real and now I was shaken because I knew I didn't have the spiritual tools to fight this kind of enemy. The pounding on the door jarred the moment. Jose ran for the door and my aunt leapt after her son, barely missing him. In one motion, he unlocked the door, flung it open, and crouched behind it as my mother confronted her sister. I had never perceived my mom to be a superhero, but that day she was Super Woman and Wonder Woman, all in one. The fight in her face, the light in her eyes, the way she stood firmly facing this "thing" shocked me. "Get out of my sister, demon," my mother shouted. "I will not," it screamed back. "I'm taking her with me." My mother jumped right in front of Aunt Tina, not touching her, but not allowing her sister the space to move. "You're not taking anyone, tonight. You're a liar. You've always been a liar. And you are not going to destroy this family. I plead the blood of Jesus on you," my mother shouted, and she repeated it. "The blood of Jesus, the blood of Jesus, the blood of Jesus, hallelujah. There is victory in this house because Christ overcame Death, and you, Devil, have no power. Let my sister go, now!" The demon in my aunt growled, "I'll kill you, bitch. You can't stop me. Who the fuck do you think you are? God?" And that's when my mother, quoting all those verses and prayers she learned in church, put the Bible right between my aunt's breasts and shouted, "We are more than conquerors" and "I am the head, not the tail," and "I rebuke you in the name of Jesus. Devil, you have no power here because we walk in the Shadow of the Almighty."

My aunt began to back off, making the most horrible noises. And then suddenly, Tina leapt at my mother, grabbed both her arms, and snapped, "I'll never let her go. She's mine. She told me so." Aunt Tina closed her mouth suddenly and when she opened it again, a forceful stream of vomit hit my mother's throat and breast area, thick, smelly, and pellet-filled. In one motion my mother placed the Bible under her left armpit, reached into her pocketbook with her right hand and opened the flask of holy oil, pouring some of it on her palm and smacking the shit out of Tina's forehead, intoning, "We are children of the Almighty. You have no power here. Now let my sister go. Leave now, in the name of Jesus, in the name of the One who died for our sins and whom we call on to fight our battles." Aunt Tina screamed, "Noooooooooo" and collapsed on the bright white linoleum floor of the dining room. I rushed toward my mother, but she raised her arms, and said with her eyes closed, "Start praising the Lord, now, Philip. Start praising him and thanking him for this miracle. He protected you, me, and everyone in this house. Praise Him, hallelujah, hallelujah, hallelujah." And once my mother started softly speaking in tongues, peace returned to the house, a peace that felt and smelled heavenly, like wildflowers in a pasture. It was over. We had won. The forces of evil had taken no one.

Imagine me looking at my mother's tired face in the visiting room of 275 Atlantic Avenue—the age lines etched deeper than ever, the bags under her eyes blacker, and hearing her now saying she fainted from a punk like Lippo who showed her the murder weapon? He was as good as dead, and I would utter no Bible verses after him. He would go where he had to go . . . real fast. With no apologies. "Mommy, I'll take care of it." I said, with the breezy confidence of a Miami drug trafficker who just knows who he's going to whack when he gets out. "I don't want you to worry. I'll have some people talk to Lippo. They know him real well and he respects them. It won't happen again." My mother got up slowly, too slowly. There was no bounce in her step as she walked away, no cheery laugh. "Oh, I forgot to tell you something. Tina is blaming you for getting Jose in trouble," she blurted out. "She wants him out of jail, Philip, immediately. And she wants you to tell the court he had nothing to do with anything that happened."

I fell back against the metal partition, shocked. "Ma, Jose is Prez of the Little People Canarsie Chaplains. He organized the gang that Sunday. And anyway, it's out of my hands. There's nothing I can do. It's up to the D.A., who leaves and who stays."

"Look, Philip. You're my oldest child. But my sister only has one child. I know you. You're going to handle this because you always do. I'm not so sure about Jose and neither is Tina. And then she said something that really hurt me, *papi*."

"What did she say, Ma?" I asked coldly.

"Well, it's not really that important, you know, but it hurt me . . . ." my mother said in that cool, impersonal victimized tone she used when she felt her love was not being reciprocated. I shouted loudly, so loudly through the telephone that my mother recoiled. "Ma, we don't have that much time! You know visiting time is over. What the hell did she say, Ma? Stop beating around the bush."

"Tina told me I owed her my life. That she was the one who pulled me from that stove fire on Front Street in Brooklyn when we were kids and got burned in the process. And then, Philip, and this I couldn't believe, she pulled up her left sleeve blouse and made me look at the scars on her arm. 'You see this?' she said. 'You didn't get burned, baby, I did. My sleeve caught on fire saving you. No scars on you. Just on me. And all I'm asking from you is to show some mercy and get my son out of jail. Philip started this whole thing. He's the one who called Jose and got him all riled and now look at him: in jail for murder. No, I want my son out. He had nothing to do with this.'"

I couldn't believe what I was hearing. Jose was president of the gang, always in fights. He hit and stomped Larry at least as many times as I did. It was just a matter of time and luck that he hadn't been arrested before this incident. "Ma," I said softly, trying to caress her eyes, her soul. "Listen to me carefully. Did Jose say he had nothing to do with it? Is that what he told his mother?"

"I don't know, baby. I don't know if she's saying it, or he said it. All I want you to do is get him out."

It was no use arguing; time was up and I was really tired. "Okay, Ma, I'll see what I can do," was all I could muster. Now, Aurora pressed her face against the bulletproof window, nose to nose, eyes to eyes, and spoke firmly into the phone. "No, Philip. You're not going to see what you can do; you're going to do it . . . please. I know you can, okay?" And then she stopped and what I saw on her face was the darkest veil I had ever seen over her, the veil of fear, of defeat, of resignation. "Did you do it, Philip? Did you kill him?" "No, Ma. I could have. But I didn't stab him. I've never lied to you." My mother looked at me for a long time. Then she smiled for the first time and said, "I understand," and left.

Two weeks after my mother's visit, all six of my crime partners, including John (who had stayed very quiet throughout our stay) and I were together in the bullpen of Brooklyn Supreme Court for another appearance before the judge for the murder of Larry. It sounds callous, but after the tension and anxiety of jail, being with people you know, people you've grown up with, people you're related to by blood, block, or geography, is heavenly. You forget for a few precious seconds the severity of the charges against you and all you focus on is the camaraderie. We hugged, I kissed my cousin Jose, and all seven of us slapped five and exchanged street news and gossip. I announced to the group I had something to say. I was not considered by the Canarsie Chaplains to be a leader. I was Jose's cousin, a schoolkid, a church kid. But in the small window of time during our detention I had gained a modicum of respect, because I stayed close to John after he stabbed Larry. I didn't run. The fact that I hid the murder weapon and took a brutal ass-whipping by police for two hours stood for something.

Moose, the most sensitive of the Canarsie Chaplains, looked up at me while the laughter between the guys was the loudest, and silently, by picking his chin up repeatedly and opening the palms of his huge hands, asked me what was wrong. I stayed quiet just looking at him intently until he motioned for everyone to be quiet. "What's on your mind, little brother?" Moose asked respectfully. I tried to sound cool, logical, lawyer-like. "The assistant D.A.

hinted that not all of us were going to do a bid, right? What if the D.A. is right? Remember what he said? That maybe four of us would be cut loose but three of us would have to do time. The way I figure it, I'm definitely going upstate. So is John. That leaves one more."

The guys avoided my eyes and began to look at one another nervously. This was their decision. I wasn't a Chaplain, they were. The air got thick and I knew why. Everyone was expecting Jose to throw his lot in with me. Jose said nothing, choosing to look at his shoes. I waited for a few painfully embarrassing seconds and spoke again.

"Look, fellas! I don't know how you gonna deal with this, but I'm gonna let it out. I don't want my cousin to do any time. I'll take the weight for him. Makes no sense two members of the family doing time for the same shit. Somebody has to stay out to take care of our families. Jose jumped up from the metal bench and started his bullshit: "Hell no. I'm the one who fucked him up too, so I'll do the fuckin' time. I ain't no punk."

I wanted to slap the holy shit out of him. What hypocrisy. His voice didn't even sound convincing. It took all my strength not to blurt out that he probably begged his mother to get him out. As Jose babbled on, I flashed back to how many times he had copped out on me. I thought with age he would change. It never happened. Nobody in the group paid him any mind.

Finally, Carl Riley spoke. "I'll do the bid with you. Fuck it. I have nothing to lose." There was a stunned silence among us. Carl was the quietest warrior, tall, dark, good-looking, Asian-shaped eyes, crowded teeth, unnervingly polite and extremely gifted in the fight department. I loved the way he shifted his weight, bobbing and weaving to avoid fists or weapons. His hands were really fast, too. Trying to hit Carl was like trying to hit a ghost. Very few people could tag him. The only problem was that Carl had not touched the deceased. He was there to watch my back.

I was dumbfounded. "You don't have to do this, man," I whispered. "You never even touched the dude." Carl looked at me with the most compassionate eyes and said, "Yes, I do. I was there. I'm just as guilty as everyone else. And anyway, I don't want his mother to suffer."

But what about *his* mother, Mrs. Riley? Years later, he confessed, she did suffer . . . horribly. The deal was done. Jose hung his head, eventually thanking Carl Riley for taking his place, promising to visit and send him packages (which he never did).

The group stayed unusually quiet until they called us to court. Through my public defender, I asked the court to allow me to join the Marine Corps. I was only sixteen but had heard on the streets that if your mother agreed to it, they would add another year to your age, hastily train you, and ship you out to the jungles of Vietnam. Upon hearing my request, the judge leaned over and, looking squarely at me, said, "You've just helped murder a man. The armed forces of this country do not need a man of your character. Denied." Of the seven of us arrested in April 1964 for the murder of a gang kid called Larry on Bushwick and Broadway, three of us eventually did state time, and four of us walked out of the courtroom free men, including my cousin.

Chapter 4

Living under the Sign of DEATH

I can't forget the utter humiliation of prison. What is done in the darkness of those metal cages leaves an emotional scar so indelible, so deep that it corrodes hope. It creates a murderous cancer of hate and vengeance. You will get back at someone for having gone through this gauntlet of depravity and the stripping of your soul. Sometimes, you get back at society. But, all the time, you get back at yourself, ashamed of having had to undergo this rape of spirit—and at having collaborated with the jailer just to stay alive. Yes, you hate yourself for not having died or been killed. And you live with that ugly truth for the rest of your life. Until forgiveness reigns, forgiveness, and redemption.

I've tried for decades to get beyond the intellect, the rhetoric, the epidermal metaphysics of what it must have been like to be a slave—powerless, frightened, defeated, bewildered, and shackled—and nothing ever came as close as being an inmate, a Black inmate in the United States of America. I will say this clearly and sternly and I don't give a fuck about the political correctness of multicultural diversity or people-of-color bullshit the Black man in prison—yes, I'm talking about the African American street-blood you see in your home, on your block, in your church, or in your face—that Black man has a sign on him in every prison that reads "DEATH." And the blacker you are, the quicker the sentence, the more brutal the punishment.

Summer, 1964. I was sixteen. I had gone through the initial arrest process, arraignment, and trial, where I had been convicted of attempted manslaughter in the second degree. Each borough had its own county jail. I was sent to 275 Atlantic Avenue, the Brooklyn House of Detention. I was interrogated by an ignorant white boy they called a psychiatrist on the tenth floor. After he figured out I wasn't a sociopath and I didn't want to fuck anybody in my family, I was transferred from the psych ward to the hardcore recidivist adult ward on the ninth floor. For a few days, I played whist and pitty-pat with some of the toughest criminals in New York. Because I was a young-blood, out of his element, they took care of me and took pride in doing so. They wanted me to stay on their floor, and they told the officers on duty. They knew what was in store for me if I was transferred out. I remember the officers just shrugging their shoulders and putting their eyes down as inmate after inmate argued with them about my situation. It was futile.

For the two weeks I was on the ninth floor I had put up a good front, adapting to a regulated life. I tried to be cool, nodding my sixteen-year-old head slowly, wisely, at the horrifying tales of murder, madness, and thievery, all of which I had never experienced. With adult inmates I could forget. I could hide behind my age and excuses for being in jail in the first place. I could impress the elders with my speech; my memory for information; my ability to explain abstract concepts in theology, philosophy, history, or science. I wasn't one of those teenaged thugs, I told myself. And I tried to project that idea to the older guys. The adult men on the ninth floor, even some who may have suspected I was bullshitting about my violent life, went along with the façade. I suspect they saw themselves, from a long time ago, in me. Some of them, from other benches in the dayroom, would turn around slowly at my hooting and hollering when I won a game of cards. They'd squint their eyes and smile at me. I was their kid, their grandkid, and while they protected me and plied me with long harangues about not following in their footsteps, they took tremendous pleasure in teaching me the finer points of the emotional con games and the nuances of the honor code: You see nothing, you hear nothing, you say nothing. They taught me that most people don't get murdered—well . . . someone does actually kill them, but what I mean is that they bring it upon themselves. The law is inviolable. You play, you pay. You don't, you die.

The transfer day came. The law stated that a minor could not house with adults. I was moved one floor below, the adolescent floor. The kids·on the eighth floor were off the hook, totally out of control. Between the unbearable noise, music, and sudden movements of bodies flashing by as they ran toward a fight or away from one, it was all I could do just to keep my sanity. My cool façade clanged to the floor like a metal bar hitting a concrete sidewalk. I couldn't keep it together. I locked myself in the dark, narrow slop-sink closet and wept and wept, stifling my moans with my cupped hand so those outside wouldn't hear. Most of the guys in the dayroom took no notice. The radio was blaring, whist was being played on yellow Formica tables, kids yelling out their desire to go uptown or downtown in the card game, "making books," as they called it, with noisy knuckle slaps on the table surface. The remaining teenagers were motherfucking each other. It was bedlam and nobody gave a shit.

When you are locked up it is dangerous not to judge a book by its cover. If it looks evil and looks like it wants to hurt you so much that the stench of pain reeks from its body, nine times out or ten you'd better leave him alone. How you look, your skin color, your head shape, your hair texture, your body size, your hands and fingers, your ass, your biceps, your knuckles, your forearms, your thighs, your eyes, and the look you decide to wear on your face every day, all of that plus your tone of voice will determine how you'll be treated in jail by the correctional officers and the inmates. Since your demeanor and the aura you exude is the way you're treated, rare are the opportunities to get beyond the rage in any prisoner's eyes.

There was a sudden knock on the door of the slop-sink closet. I quickly opened the cold-water faucet, slapped water on my face to reduce the puffiness of my eyes and answered gruffly and as quickly as I could, "Who is it?" The voice came back as if the lips were pressed against the crack of the door, calm but authoritative, "Motherfucka, this is my dayroom. And you in my closet. You know who the fuck this is, and if you don't know you'd better open this door and find out." I splashed more water on my face and flung the door open. I didn't even look at him, just tried to take a step past him to scurry away into a corner. He wouldn't move. I kept my head down and just stopped dead in my tracks. To have gone farther I would have had to deliberately push him out of the way and even I knew that would've meant instant death. He didn't budge. We stayed motionless like that for a long, long time: me with my head down, sniffling softly, him, glowering at me, not saying a word.

Slowly, the snap/slap of the cards on the tables subsided, then the laughter, then the curses, then the casual conversation. All I remember was Little Anthony and the Imperials singing, "I'm on the Outside Looking In," as the radio blared away in a tense, dead-silent dayroom in the middle of a May afternoon in Brooklyn with thirty guys watching. The song ended softly and this motherfucka wouldn't move, didn't utter a sound. The guards, anticipating violence, had cut off the radio and were watching anxiously, perversely curious as to the next move on the floor. Silence. Stillness. I had to do something. I finally looked up at the guy. I had never seen such a beautiful face—handsome, honey smooth, even-toned complexion with no scars, beautifully even teeth, sculpted jaw, broad, intelligent forehead, stocking cap, perfect hair with symmetrical waves, massive shoulders, even more massive arms, a full, sensitive mouth, and clear hazel eyes. Shit, this was no killer. This was a warrior/king. I felt I had met my next gang prez. And it was obvious he had never been looked at with pure admiration. He moved back so quickly, I recoiled. Quickly snatching the nearby metal mop wringer out of the bucket, he lifted that thirty-five-pound machine away from his body like it was a wand, pointed it horizontally toward me. His arm didn't even tremble.

"What the fuck are you crying about, nigger?"

Sniffling, my head down, I whispered hoarsely, "I got zip-five for a murder I didn't even commit. I didn't think my boy was gonna kill the dude."

His voice boomed at me. "The next tear comes out of your eye, I'm gonna bust your ass with this wringer. Who the fuck do you think you are crying over some bullshit like that?"

I stood there, shoulders slumped like a chump, and answered feebly, "But, I've never been to the joint, man. I got five years, *five years!*"

He stepped back as if to get ready to swing. His eyes got cold and vicious.

"Shut the fuck up. I don't want to hear a fuckin' sound out of you. You think you different than everybody else in here, nigga? Everybody got time in here. Deal with it, motherfucka . . . crying over some bullshit five years you got. Take it like a man. A motherfucka's dead and you were there, right? You led the ma'fuckers, that's what the papers said, right? Answer me, punk! You do the crime, you do the time. You don't cry, you hear me? Now, go 'head, let me see you bitch up on me, so I know the kind of faggot I got to deal with."

I stiffened. My jaw tightened and my eyes bored into his. I didn't care anymore. He had stepped over the line. He had betrayed me by taking my admiration and turning it into a sick play in front of his psychopaths. He must've seen my face change. I slowly took my eyes off his and looked for the opening to take him down: the third button from the top of his shirt. But I needed a sharp instrument. With enough speed and force I could stab this motherfucka right through the heart. He wasn't that much older than me. With darting glances, I looked around the dayroom for anything I could use to take this guy out. I hadn't killed Larry, but I was definitely going to kill this guy in front of me.

"Don' even think about it," he said softly, confidently. "Better niggas than you have tried and died. But at least your heart ain't pumping Kool-Aid."

And just as quickly as he turned the venom on, he turned it off, laughing heartily. I was livid and trembling. I refused to budge. I said nothing. Just stared at him.

He now pointed the mop wringer away from me and in the general direction of the main area of the dayroom where mouths of the detainees were dropping in disbelief. And then he spoke, this time his voice bellowing, bouncing off the cream-colored semi-gloss bricks of the room where I would spend some "quality time" for the next four months, "Five years ain't shit, you hear me, yella boy? Ain't shit! Every motherfucka here got busted for the same shit, d'ya know that? Know how much time they got?" Without taking his eyes off me he screamed, "Epps! How much time you get?"

"Twenty-five to life," Epps screamed back.

"Did you do it?"

"No."

"Rice? How much time you got?"

"You know how much time I'm gonna do! They ain't lettin' me out of here. Twenty-five to life, easy."

Around the room he went, calling the names of the detainees, asking how much time they got for murder, manslaughter, attempted manslaughter, felonious assault. Not one of them had less than seven-and-a-half to fifteen; most had twenty-five to life. I felt like shit. He didn't stop.

"The next time you feel like going into your little room and crying about the 'pound' [five years] you got, remember these niggas' faces. And most of them got busted for the first time, just like you. But they didn't have teachers kissing judges' asses and priests writing letters and white folks calling up behind the scenes like you did."

I was shocked. I didn't know all this had happened for my case. Before I could open my mouth, he screamed, "Shut the fuck up, I said! You didn't know but we did. We heard about your funky ass before you even got sentenced. So, the next time you even mention your sentence or shed a tear over it, I'll lay your ass out. 'Cause I hate you, ya hear me?"

I looked at his eyes again. He didn't mean it. Everything in his face showed that he wished that he could be in my place. "I'm sorry," I said softly.

"Don't tell me, tell them."

"I'm sorry, fellas. I really didn't know."

The leader mocked me in a white boy accent. "'I'm sorry, fellas. I really didn't know. I was a Boy Scout 'til I got busted. Then, when I hit the joint, I found out I was a Negro. Still, I thought I was special, a Spanish guy, a *mira-mira* ma'fucker 'til they gave me five years. That's when it hit me and I started to cry. And now . . . you colored guys are threatening to take my booty and possibly injure me. I mean gee whiz, golly fellas, I'm shitting in my pants right now.'"

The impersonation was pure *Leave It to Beaver.* Thirty teenagers laughed so loudly and slapped five so hard they called extra guards up to the eighth floor. For fifteen minutes the detainees pounded tables, fell on the tiled floor in hysterics, mimicking me, mimicking the leader. I could only smile wanly. The tension was broken. The pressure was off.

While the laughter was at its peak, the leader looked at me, winked, and threw a left cross, which I deflected. "Aw, shit," he said, "This motherfucka thinks he's good."

And while they laughed, paying us no mind, the leader and I boxed and bobbed and weaved. I slipped most of his punches and trapped his hands a few times. He punched me on the top of the head, hard, several times, letting me know this was survival fighting, not the play fighting I was used to on the streets. To top it off, when he threw a wide left cross and I stepped in and met him face-to-face, he kissed me on the cheek, jumped back, threw two light blows to my head and then stepped on my left toe so I couldn't move back.

"Nice!" I said.

"Not nice, motherfucka. Pretty. Won't be so pretty if you get caught like that upstate." Then he put his arm around me and talked to me all the way to my cell.

"You wanna know sump' in, brother? You got the glow. You gonna be all right. Ain't nobody gonna fuck with you . . . here or upstate. I just hope you remember our asses when you get out."

"I'll never forget you, man," I said reverentially. "You're an angel. By the way, what's your name?"

"Diablo!" he said softly, and walked away.

My pain was so deep, my fear so obvious, my need for love, for an embrace, for someone to tell me it was all right, that it bewildered the seasoned dark

men in the Brooklyn House of Detention. I was so ignorant, so scared, so goddamned naïve and downright stupid that I'm still amazed I wasn't raped or slashed the first day I began to serve time. I was beyond frailty. I was a baby trying to walk, falling down every few steps and crying for its mother or anyone else who could calm the terror and explain the night. I can only say that God stepped in. His angels came in the form of Black men—some young, some old—who hugged me, wiped my tears away, and vowed never to leave. Yes, I'll say it again. My angels were Black prisoners, many of them Muslim, who took my hand and guided/guarded me through two years of confinement.

Chapter 5

Prison Pedagogy

Most kids who get locked up for the first time fall into three categories: prey, pawn, or powerful. The institution forces you, aggressively or benignly, to make a decision about your classification in their house. You learn that hands, nails, knees, feet, forearms, elbows, heels are all weapons, capable of tremendous damage and, in extreme cases, death. Preparation involves working on a series of moves I call jailhouse katas. As I was escorted down the tiers of the eighth floor to my cell, I stared straight ahead; looking into someone's cell could be construed as an insult. My peripheral vision caught young men in steel cages, grunting, as they punched, kicked, and grappled with imaginary enemies, some taunting and talking out loudly to the ghosts in the potential scenarios they might encounter once the gates of their metal boxes opened for meals or yard time.

In jail you learn to be predatory, paranoid, and possessive. Leap first at your enemy, hit hard, draw first blood; even if you lose you'll be respected. Trust no one, listen to everyone and everything. Unless you run the tier, speak as little as possible and certainly make no threats you can't back up. And finally, know what you have in your cell and where you have it. Police shakedowns for contraband were sudden and inevitable. Pornography, razors, homemade knives, and maces were always seized. Those inmates caught were put into solitary confinement, the "bing." But better solitary for two months with nothing but tea, bread, and no mattress than having your house ripped off by another inmate or getting stabbed with your own shiv. In a strange way, robbery of another inmate was considered a worse

crime than rape. I hated thieves, and I hated robbing. It was the one thing
that signaled total disrespect toward the victim and yourself. It was the one
thing that could get you killed quickly.

In my sixteen years I never took the time for self-reflection. In jail I found
my essence. The external stress and pressure forced that within to rise to
the surface. I had to fall back on values instilled in me from birth. I had to
make decisions based on who I really was, and what I wanted to be. Even
with the constant screaming, the raucous laughter, the loud verbal bantering,
the horrible sounds of colliding bodies, there was free will. I had to make
the choice to live, languish, or die. And I was tested. Many of my peers
tried to break me through getting right in my face—because I chose not
to be part of the asylum. In a strange and miraculous way, those who
witnessed my decision to be myself defended me and put their lives on the
line to keep this kid "pure." They seemed to see in me something they
wanted to preserve.

A few days after my transfer to the eighth floor and my confrontation with
Diablo, an older guy befriended me by offering Pall Malls every time I
turned around. I was nervous, still scared, and I smoked them, thanking
him all the time. Diablo had kept his distance, not uttering a word to me
for three days. On the fourth day he motioned for me to come over to his
spot in the dayroom, a long bench and Formica table way back in a corner
of the brightly lit dayroom. I walked eagerly toward Diablo, excited to be
called over by "the Boss." I felt honored. His eyes registered disgust with
my innocent enthusiasm.

"Motherfucka, do you have to jump like a fuckin' rabbit when you're
called? Slow down, nigga, 'foe' one of these motherfuckas gets stupid and
tries to take you off. Start learning, man!"

Again, he looked disgusted but sounded caring. I crossed my arms like
I saw the big guys do, spread my legs, and said nothing. He looked me up
and down with that "You can't be serious" look and burst out laughing hysterically. Then in the matter of a few finger snaps, he stopped, popped up
from the bench and said, "Take a walk with me."

We passed the older guys' group and my newfound cigarette benefactor
stuck a hand out in front of Diablo and offered a cigarette, smiling warmly.
Diablo, having to stop his momentum, caught the older guy on the left side
of his face with a right forearm smash. I heard the guy exhale forcefully,
saw him spit out blood. Diablo's left hand, with its thick, powerful fingers,
circled the thin guy's neck and tightened, cutting off his air supply. With
his face real close to the guy, Diablo whispered so low that only we three

could hear: "The next time you offer him a smoke will be your last. This simple motherfucka don't know what you doin', but I do. Do we have an understanding?"

The guy was wincing, gasping, the snot and blood bubble dripping from his nose to his mustache to his chin.

Diablo said it again. "Do we have an understanding?"

Wordlessly, the man nodded slowly, his eyeballs bulging. Desperately, he looked my way and mouthed the words "I'm sorry."

Diablo stopped him quickly. "You not sorry for shit, punk. You and your homos would have fucked him in the ass if you had the chance. Get the fuck outta here. I don't want you on this side of the dayroom no more. And if you see this punk anywhere, move away."

Diablo let the guy drop like a crumpled rag doll. Whether the guards saw the lightning-fast assault or not, I'll never know. What is certain is that they never moved or turned around. Then I saw why. The confrontation had taken no longer than thirty seconds, maybe less, but in that tiny window of time, Diablo's people—tall, huge brothers—had encircled their leader protectively like silent ninjas, as soon as he slammed the guy to the floor. I've never seen anything like it again. These warriors didn't think, didn't hesitate. They just moved. They were just there—*Bam*—no audible directions, no footsteps heard, no grating noise of benches being pulled back, nothing. The guards must've thought it was one of those daily inmate meetings.

Diablo picked up the conversation, barely breathing hard. "Where the hell did you grow up, stupid? You take nothing from nobody in here. You take it, you pay for it. A few more cigarettes, then he and his crew were gonna ask you to pay up. Cash or your ass. And nobody here was going to do anything to stop him. Learn, nigga. I ain't gon' be around all the time."

Diablo was my orientation program. He taught me survival. Little did I know he had an agenda. I didn't pick up on the clues immediately. I'm pretty sure it unfolded for him as he saw me avidly reading everything I could get my hands on: the guards' newspapers, the Bible, the Quran, magazines, anything. Diablo was illiterate and took pains to hide it from the other inmates. His natural intelligence allowed him to deduce what the words in the papers meant once he saw the printed news photos alongside the text. I'd secretly see him watch television news with total absorption. Then, Diablo would argue brilliantly about who got busted and why, the culpability of the perpetrator and the victim, and take bets on how much time the arrestee would receive. He was rarely wrong. Diablo would've made a great trial lawyer. He just couldn't read.

Slowly, Diablo let me into his vulnerability and trust. If I abused it, I knew, he'd have to kill me—reluctantly, but kill me nonetheless for exposing his weakness to his fellow inmates—predators who he kept at bay through head games and brilliant fighting skills. I saw him break guys down mentally even before a fight began. If you robbed inmates or collected protection money he would offer honorable options like his taking two cartons of cigarettes rather than six for an alleged offense against his rules. There were those youngbloods who had their own robbery scams going on the floor, thereby challenging Diablo's authority. The whole floor knew a battle would be in the making. A low din would permeate the dayroom, a voyeuristic air of expectancy floating through the jail cells for hours, sometimes a whole day. Diablo would not attack desperately. He'd wait. Make you wait. And then, after a visit from your girl or your mom, when your guard was down, he'd announce the shit was on—not by speech, but by movement. He'd walk over to his opponent, get close to his ear, and throw down the gauntlet without his body telegraphing the move. Everyone knew the shit was on, but no body telegraphed, no one moved. Then, Diablo would trudge back to his corner spot, sit down, and just survey the dayroom. The brazen kid would get up and plant himself in the center of the dayroom issuing threats and thunder. Diablo, feigning fear and emotional tiredness at having to defend his kingdom again, would slowly, painfully, raise himself from his roost. He would walk to the back of the room, his shoulders hunched like an old man's, his slippers slapping the floor. He'd take off his shirt, look at the tile floor, and then ask the young cub, "Do you really want to do this?"

When there was a resounding "Fuck yeah" or serious silence, Diablo would turn around. Inevitably there'd be gasps.

Diablo created masterful theater, designed to create awe among the inmates. No one but me knew that secretly Diablo would do extra sets of exercises, especially pull-ups, so that when he moved his shoulders back and forth to loosen up, his back looked like an enormous rippling tortoise shell. Diablo's form seemed to grow larger before every battle, a chiseled, muscled African sculpture, more impressive than any Greek sculpture I'd seen at the Metropolitan Museum of Art. Every once in a while, I noticed the challenger's fear and shock when he saw Diablo's massive back, thick neck, rippling triceps and shoulders accentuated by a thin waist. He never took his shirt off in the dayroom. Only in these *pas de deux* of pain would inmates catch a glimpse of the upper torso of the ruler of the eighth floor. But at that point it was too late for the opponent to back out, and in a slow dance of well-placed blows, Diablo would humiliate his challenger, instructing him verbally, matter-of-factly while connecting to face and body, how the guy fucked up and why he was getting fucked up. I'd be mesmerized. Diablo loved my worship and would wink at me in the middle of battle.

Over time, my opinion mattered to him, and it seemed clear that for the first time in a long while, he was beginning to feel . . . and trust. He was my older brother, the protective father I never had. And he loved the responsibility of caring for his kid and showing what could/would happen to those who crossed the line. While I was passing his cell one afternoon, he called me in. I stood in the doorway to his cell, respectfully, quietly.

"I want to write to my old lady, but I don't know what to say. Give me some shit to write," he said gruffly, pencil in hand, his head low over the legal pad like a little schoolboy.

I didn't move or show emotion as I spoke. "Just tell her you love her and you can't wait 'til you come out so you can be with her all the time," I said softly.

Diablo nodded his head vigorously. "Yeah, that's good. That's good." he said and made some slow, scratchy moves on the pad. He was embarrassed and wouldn't look up, afraid to tell me to leave, afraid to admit that he couldn't write and needed help. And only I knew. I had to do something quickly. Beads of nervous sweat began to appear on his forehead and his writing hand began to tremble slightly.

"Look," I said without missing a beat, "I'm not good at just talking stuff. I've got to write it down myself. That's the way my mind works," and without thinking I walked into his cell, something no one ever did, snatched the pad out of his hand, and started writing a love letter. It was corny, but it saved the moment.

I scribbled a schoolyard poem down furiously, anything that ended with *you, blue, Sue.* Diablo stood up, nervously watching the doorway to see if other passing inmates would catch me writing for him in his cell. It wouldn't look right. Nobody came through the tier that hour. I read the simplistic rhyme/love letter to him and asked what else he wanted to say in the letter. Looking at the tall windows facing The St. Joseph's Orphanage, his huge body looming in the doorway, in a voice hardly audible Diablo squeaked out, "I wish I knew what to say. I . . . umm . . . I . . . don't know . . . how to . . . ."

My response had to be quick. I had to show that I saw his dilemma but not his frailty. "I know, man. I know. And I'll help you. It ain't that hard, brother."

Exhaling hard, Diablo's head turned to me, "You knew all the time, didn't you?"

"Yeah," I said.

"Think you can help me?" Diablo asked in a voice so pure, so innocent, it forced tears from my eyes, down my cheeks.

"Every day, man," I said. "Whenever you want to, I'll show you. I love this stuff, Diablo. You'll catch on real quick." We both wiped our tears away in that cell, and that summer afternoon, two warriors bonded to save each other's lives . . . or die trying.

In four months, Diablo learned the fundamentals of how to read and write. If Diablo kept me safe on the eighth floor, the Harlem Six kept me sane. They were six young Black men arrested, allegedly for killing a white store owner on 125th Street. Ham, Turk, Rice (Malik), and Raheem are the only names I can remember. Their ideology was Black nationalism. Their religious persuasion was the Nation of Islam. They didn't need to join a gang or build a crew. They brought gang loyalty and faithfulness to credo with them, something most of us admired secretly. They stuck together in a fashion rarely seen inside the joint.

I needed to stimulate the brain. I needed to debate. With all the physical and psychological games I had to endure, my brain was deteriorating. So, when an opportunity arose I argued, always respectfully, about the contradictions in their Black Muslim theology of Yacoub, the mad scientist, expelled from paradise, who created the original white man. They called him the Devil and declared he had deceived the Asiatic Black man through a system called "tricknology." I had to use every educational tool, every piece of literature I had memorized from the Bible to a smattering of articles on Darwin's "Evolution of the Human Species" to *National Geographic* in order to dispute their claim that the Black race was created 66 trillion years ago and that we were inherently superior to white folks.

"Y'all worship Jesus as a white man," Turk would declare loudly in the dayroom to anyone within listening distance, "but the truth is Jesus is Black, Moses was Black, and all the so-called prophets were Black. How can you love and worship someone who does not look like you?" Of course many of these loud polemics were exacerbated when we were served bacon, sausage, pork chops, or Jell-O, which they despised and gave away, to our great delight. "But hold up, Turk," I'd protest, with food in my mouth, "I believe Jesus and the prophets were all Black or at least brown, if they came from that part of the world, brother, but, melanin has nothing to do with their message."

"You see, my brothers, Philip is a perfect example of how the Devil uses Black men," Turk would crow. "Smart and usually light-skinned. Nigga, you been brainwashed and we just trying to show you the way." The whole day-room would erupt in laughter.

"How was it possible for the Black man to have existed 66 trillion years ago," I would ask, "when all the anthropologists, Black, white, or polka-dot, traced the beginning of man to 2 or 3 million years back?"

Rice, the most serious of the Harlem Six and the one who spent more time in solitary for infractions, would lecture me seriously about how white historians had lied and distorted the true history of the Black man in order to keep us down. But he would never just shut me up or put me off. He loved the debates and I loved him for allowing me to even question his theories on white people, even though he believed that Puerto Ricans had the blood of the devil in them and couldn't be trusted. Privately, he confided that the reason I was allowed to debate was that at least I identified as a Black man—confused, but Black. Rice believed that a race war was inevitable unless Black people could separate within the United States and build their own nation. He was talking about reparations in 1964! His estimate was that with inflation and cost of living adjustments over 300 years, America owed Black people billions of dollars. Rice was small and had a peanut head, long arms, and large eyes, but he wasn't afraid of anybody—guards or bullies. He'd jump right in your face during an argument about reparations, real close, and say, "We are owed at least that much. They didn't give us 40 acres and a mule. And if they that serious about segregation why don't they just let us go so we can build our own shit."

Inevitably, I and some of the other inmates would debate the concept of traditional Christian love versus the Nation of Islam's brand of political religion and anger. "Y'all just can't go around hating all the time. You fuck yourself up. Your family too. Look where we are today from hating. Look how many of us are in here. In the end I'd argue, 'You gotta love.'"

"You gotta love *yourself*," Rice would answer. "Do for self. Take care of your own shit first. We out here loving everybody else but ours. That's what has us messed up."

Turning to all the inmates playing cards, Rice would preach with loud encouragement from his crime partners, who'd shout, "Go 'head, brother, speak on it. Tell the truth." Then, Turk would stand up and begin his theory of why the white man had taken away our innate ability to fight, to defend ourselves.

"What does any animal do in the jungle when attacked?"

The whole dayroom would scream, "Fight back!" and above their cry, Ham would rise and scream, "Take the Devil's head! Have no love for someone who hates you. Take them to the cross, y'all." It was a revival meeting, Nation of Islam–style, with applause, call and response, and a lot of laughter. But you got the message. White folks and anyone connected to them were to be despised and not to be trusted. That's why what happened within one month of my being on the eight floor was so shocking and revealing.

On a sweltering, summer day, the heavy metal door opened suddenly, and a short, white Puerto Rican guy was thrown in. There was blood all over him. It looked as if every bone in his body had been broken, including all his teeth. The police had hurt this boy real bad. The pain waves we saw coming from his body unnerved even the toughest inmates. His moaning was heartbreaking. For minutes, no one moved. Rice, slowly strode over to the spot where the guy was dropped, gently picked him up and put him on the table. Never taking his eyes off the kid, Rice ordered his group to get some hot water and whatever white cloth they could get. Then he cradled the Puerto Rican kid in his arms, almost cooing to him, "It's all right, brother. We got you now. Just lay back. Let us hook you up." And as Rice was handed the pieces of cloth dipped in warm water and salt, he would dab at the wounds on the guy's face, shoulders, and arms, slowly cleaning the poor guy up. He even went into the guy's mouth, cleaning the gums and swabbing whatever teeth were left. When the guy finally opened his eyes and looked at Rice's face, he began to sob.

"I didn't know the guy was a cop. I stabbed him, but I didn't know. He had no uniform. I thought he was trying to rob me." And Rice continued to swab him down, listening to him intently, never taking his eyes off the new guy. Finally, even the guards offered some more absorbent gauze pads through the door. When Rice's eyes met mine, I saw love. He never uttered a word about the Devil, the system, or white cops. He just loved on this kid and stayed with him for hours until it was time for us to lock in. Rice left him on the table. We never knew how they got him to a cell. But for the next three weeks, Rice fed him, gently placing the tin cup of tea next to his mouth so he could drink as he tended to his wounds. During that period, there was no loud debate, no pontification; sheer humanity reigned.

The kid recovered nicely, and Rice was the reason. Once he could walk and talk again, he gravitated to the Puerto Rican table but would always smile at Rice when he caught his eye. Rice would never smile back. He'd just nod wisely. Rice never brought it up in conversation, and neither did we. Love is what you do, I learned, not what you say, and Christians don't have a monopoly on it.

Music was another sanity component. I had the best of both worlds, doo-wop and big band jazz blaring through the loudspeakers of the jail. When they were in a good mood, the officers would turn to those stations playing Martha and the Vandellas, Shep and the Limelights, Little Anthony and the Imperials. When we acted up with fights and noise, they'd abruptly change channels to William B. Williams, the Chairman of the Board on WNEW AM and play Sinatra, Bennett, Sammy, Andy Williams, and Eydie Gormé. I wouldn't tell the guys, but, truth was, I loved the Great American Song-book, still crazy about Sinatra and Sammy. I mean, who could sing my theme song in jail, "What Kind of Fool Am I?" better than Sammy Davis Jr.? When the guys got raucous, I'd find a corner of the dayroom, make believe I was napping, and see myself as a normal American white teenager with sports letters on my sweater, a jalopy, and pretty girls. It's amazing what comic books like *Archie* can do to impressionable Black Puerto Rican children. They were times that were so boring inside that I'd almost wish somebody would start rumbling so they could change the music. I loved doo-wop and was part of a street corner group in Bushwick called the Sunny Boys, made up of Caribbean teenagers who happened to be my best friends. Hector Rivera ("Frenchy") and I were Puerto Ricans. I sang first tenor, Frenchy sang second. Sebastian Sinclair ("Sabu") was the lead singer, born in Panama. Frederick Morgan ("Rat") was the baritone, born in Jamaica, and Wesley ("Jazz"), the bass voice, had a Southern mom and a Caribbean dad. So I was thoroughly immersed in the '50s/'60s culture of music and dance. Those songs, those street corner melodies, sometimes sucked my bones dry, remind-ing me too much of home and so little hope of ever getting there. Imagine being locked up and listening to "A Sunday Kind of Love" or "Daddy's Home" or "Dancing in the Streets." The Flamingos and their hit "I Only Have Eyes for You" was pure torture and could drive a freshly incarcerated, skinny sixteen-year-old like me to want to escape. Even I noticed that the guys got a little wild when our street music came on. They were hurting inside, too. (The consequence of crime hits you only after you're locked up.)

Jazz music was my first love. I loved its harmonic complexity and rhythmic inventiveness. I always had an ear and excellent pitch inherited from two parents steeped in Afro-Cuban jazz and bebop. Aurora Olmo and José

Luciano met in the Park Plaza, a popular dance club on 110th Street and Fifth Avenue, while dancing to Machito, Tito Puente, Tito Rodriguez, Marcelino Guerra, and José Curbelo. My father leaned more toward rhythm swingers like Count Basie, Machito, Cortijo, and Jimmy Smith, all Black men with no slack in the beat department. Mom's music was more lyrical, more romantic. She loved harmonizing and singing whole choruses of Frank Sinatra, Billy Eckstein, and Ella Fitzgerald, especially while she was cleaning. If you add that to the fact that I was raised in a Puerto Rican Pentecostal church with a born-again Black Dominican former jazz drummer named Braudy who knew Billie Holiday, played like Philly Joe Jones, and sang like Louis Armstrong, it's not surprising that I grew up loving music in general, jazz in particular. The moment the guards switched to the big band station because of the noise or the potential for violence in the dayroom, there'd be loud curses from the inmates but quiet prayers of appreciation from me.

Music saved my life, was the healing balm that cleansed my soul and allowed us all to get through the rough hours of the bricks and bars of jail. Though many of the inmates would talk about how much they hated white folks and their vapid, funkless culture, they'd force me to sing the corniest songs to them at night until they fell sleep. Diablo heard me singing the Andy Williams version of "Moon River" one night in my cell and asked me to sing it again. I did, he loved it, and so did the whole cellblock. The fellas loved it so much, they wouldn't let me stop. They wanted to hear the same song over and over again. They did the same with the song "Maria" by Johnny Mathis. Finally, I got tired and refused to sing. I simply stayed quiet. I heard the inmates calling for me, but I refused to answer. Hell, I had to sleep too. They started really getting loud and a little threatening. One voice cut through the din. Diablo's.

"My man," he said deeply, "I think you better re-think your strategy and sing the fuckin' song. Don't mess with niggas' sleep. You hear me, Philip?"

I don't know what the hell got into me, but I refused to answer. It was disrespect.

He knew I wasn't sleeping. And then he would bellow so loud you could hear it through the upper and lower tiers, "Nigga, you must be out yo' moth-erfuckin' mind. Sing the song!" Which I proceeded to do immediately.

The inmates laughed themselves silly. The hooting and catcalls lasted almost as long as the song. "Ma'fucker may be stupid," they shouted in the dark, "but he ain't crazy. He don't wanna die."

If by chance I'd sing myself to sleep or fall out from sheer exhaustion, the inmates would yell so loudly that the night officer would turn the lights on to check the problem and leave them on so that no one slept. So, I sang other songs, like "Whistle a Happy Tune" from the Disney cartoon *Snow White*, which became their favorite; "Getting to Know You" from *The King and I*; "When I Fall in Love" by The Four Freshmen" and "Will You Still Love Me Tomorrow" by the Shirelles. Until there was stillness on the cellblock. Every night for almost four months, I sang my people to sleep until they snored. With all the fronts and façades they put on, they dreamed like I did, they were kids like I was, they were scared like I was, they missed their homes and moms like I did, they wanted to be held like I did. I was never afraid of them again. I had newfound status. I was Diablo's mentee; I wrote letters for everybody, I sang them to sleep. In short, I had power. I had also learned to follow Diablo's lead and do countless push-ups, pull-ups, and sit-ups. My body had taken on a new form.

Several weeks into my stay at the Brooklyn House of Detention, the guards announced they had a new detainee for the eighth floor. When I turned around to see who was coming in, I saw Lippo, the guy who had threatened Mom. I immediately stood very still, very quiet, at attention, placing my hands, one over the other in front of my crotch. I didn't want my face or my body to betray me. I wanted that motherfucka inside, deep inside. The look of terror that crossed Lippo's face when he realized it was me was priceless. He recoiled as if he had been shot with a .44 Magnum.

And as he back-pedaled he began to scream, "No, I'm not going in there. Fuck it. Kill me. I'm not going in there." There were two correctional officers on either side of Lippo, and in his quest to get away he inadvertently back-handed them in the face. They proceeded to whip his ass. Diablo's people quickly stood to the left and right of me and made believe they were simply watching the spectacle.

Under his breath one of the guys said, "Is that the punk who showed the knife to your mother?" I just nodded my head.

"Do nothing, brother. Stay still. If he lands here, that's his ass. We'll take care of it."

"No," I said, without turning, "I will." I was surprised at how easily my brutality slipped out. Lippo's histrionics and the ass-whipping they gave him got him off the eighth floor. They pulled him away with ripped clothes and a bloody face. I never saw him again. They say he got out eventually. Ran the streets for a while. They told me somebody killed him. Just like that.

Chapter 6

Every Block Has a Story

I spent 4 months in the Brooklyn House of Detention; 4 months of stomach-churning fear that forced God and some primordial warrior code to the surface. My case was dismissed on some technicality, and I was home free. I was released. I remember that exhilaratingly brisk fall day when the steel doors of the Brooklyn House of Detention opened up. I couldn't get out of Brooklyn fast enough. I had enough of its violence and brutality. Ghetto Brooklyn of the '60s was dreamless, visionless, intolerant, and blatantly myopic. I had enough of rarely seeing whites or Asians, of only dancing to doo-wop, of a futile, self-destructive pattern of masculinity that gave you only one option: kill or be killed. I was going back to Harlem where my mother had fled with Paul and Margie after Lippo threatened her, where Spanish was spoken proudly, loudly, not in hushed tones. I was returning to the land of bebop and mambo, Machito and the Count, Pacheco and Jimmy Castor, the beautifully crazy Black/Latino gumbo that everyone cooked and everyone tasted. A hodgepodge soup that was not based on potluck. It was love. It was family. It was Harlem. Harlem always had a smile on in those days. 125th Street was part party, part barbershop, part classroom, part church, the major artery of the village. We lived right on it, right above a second-hand furniture store, on the second floor of 20 East 125th Street, between Fifth and Madison avenues.

At the corner of Fifth Avenue and 125th, Butterfly McQueen, who acted in *Gone with the Wind,* used to scoop ice cream for us in a luncheonette she worked at for years. And directly across the street, closer to Madison Avenue, Olatunji, the master Nigerian drummer, had his loft and performance space. Every Sunday morning I would lie on a little brown-and-orange fuzzy-fabric sofa bed and enjoy the classic sounds of Blackness: the stomping, heartrending, Down South gospel shouts and organ riffs from the Pentecostal storefront church across the street mixed with booming African drums played with sticks and long verses of Nigerian chants from Olatunji's space. The air was full of sound: car radios and Sam Cooke, old ladies screaming for Jesus, and an overmodulated mike carrying a preacher's plea to "throw ya'self on the altar befo' it's too late"; all that rhythm plus Egyptian musk incense drifting in trails of smoke to my nose on the second floor.

I was home and it was good. I didn't need a preacher or an imam to teach me Blackness. I was in the sea of negritude, pure, folksy, street, and scholarly. And I loved it because they loved me, no questions asked. It didn't matter that I was Puerto Rican. It didn't matter that my momma and my family were on welfare. It didn't matter that I just got out of jail. I was family. And I could wander anywhere, from 110th to 135th, and no one gave a shit or batted an eye. I was just another nigger and I liked it that way. From Oscar Michaux's Tree of Life bookstore to the Apollo Theater, four blocks north, Black culture pulsated with life on 125th Street. You could spend hours browsing through books, perusing art and sculpture, perfecting your debating skills with some of the finest Nationalist speakers, or learning new dance moves from the kids who seemed to live for the moment the record store owners would place large speakers on the sidewalk and crank out the latest R&B 45 discs. You could live your whole life in Harlem and never need anything else.

Though we were living on 125th Street, the major artery of Black Harlem, I found myself drawn to Spanish Harlem. The language, the music, the smells, the incredible passion, good and bad, of the people. I would walk from 125th Street and Fifth Avenue to 112th Street and Fifth, looking for familiar faces. C.C., Charlie Cameron, my fourth-grade friend, was now an established numbers man. My older brother, Lucky, and my friends Richard Battle, Gary Keeles, and Al Smith had gotten hooked by the drug game and were dancing in the daze of heroin. They were still solid friends with character and a fierce loyalty to me and those they loved, but their dreams, their day-to-day existence, were wrapped around how to escape the inescapable— their color, their poverty, the childhood violations of body and spirit, their addiction. The disease wouldn't/couldn't allow them to dream or lead. I needed more because I was bursting with ideas for how to re-invent myself after jail. I went looking for fellow dreamers, those who hadn't lost hope or faith. I was in a state of euphoria.

I was free. I was home and I walked through the streets of El Barrio with an authority that makes me laugh now: chest out, posture erect, smile on my face, and a hearty hello to anyone who stopped to chat. This was my Barrio. I owned it. My family owned it. We were the pioneers. The Lucianos planted their flag on this piece of real estate in 1920. We were part of native royalty, the ruling clans consisting of the Manguals, the Maristanys, the Maderas, the Marquezes, the Berrios, the Sabaters, the Bobos, the Oquendos, the Rodriquezes, the Grillos, the Palmieris, the Moraleses, the Puentes, the Pantojas, the Encarnacions, and the Torreses. We had stock. We paid the price through gang fights and prison; through crime, blood, and salvation; through intermarriage, children, grandchildren, memories, and music. We had stock. We earned it.

Each block had a story, a character, an adventure, a lesson, a memory. For example, there was Tula, the "yella-skinned" *jaba* prostitute and madam den mother who directed the johns and sailors to the working girls' apartments on 111th Street between Fifth and Lenox avenues. She would sit on her throne, a wooden milk box, leaning back against the black-painted aluminum front of a Puerto Rican restaurant, directing the street players with the sternness and authority of a village chieftain. Even then she looked old (I met her in 1957 in her thirties) and had a sad, wrinkled face with even sadder eyes that made me think she had seen enough of the rawness and brutality of human nature—the drunks, the addicts, the sexual freaks, the violent men who came to hurt rather than release. She could read character in a nanosecond and either approve or reject a buyer of flesh and sex. She knew the good cops, the tolerant ones, and she knew the assholes trying to make a name for themselves. With a bandana wrapped around her head, African style, and a loose dress whose bottom part she would fling out repeatedly during the summer to air out her private parts, showing her large panties to anyone willing to watch and saying loudly, "*San Lorenzo, echa viento*," Tula held court daily and would be consulted by the drug dealers, the bookies, and the working girls. Without looking at them, but keeping her eyes straight ahead, watching the streets like a sentry, she would dispense directions, warnings, and wisdom.

When I was young she would always greet me with a smile, a whistle, and an air-kiss, calling me *chulo* and *lindo* with the charm of a young girl, watching me as I passed. My mother hated her, and when we had to pass her, she would call out to me, like a woman calling her customer, "oye negro lindo, mi cielo, como tu estas?" And as my mother smacked me on the head repeatedly, she would roar with laughter in that husky voice of hers, knowing she had gotten my mother's goat and pierced the Pentecostal veil of the holier-than-thou attitude that so many Evangelicals in the ghetto exhibited. "How does she know you, do you talk to her?" my mother would scream, making Tula almost fall off the milkbox with gusty laughter. I'd answer, "That's Tula, Ma, everybody knows her." To which Tula would scream, "She knows me too" and laugh until we turned the corner from Fifth toward Lenox.

Tula was the early-warning system for the entire block. If there was going to be a raid, a gang fight, or a righteous ass-whipping, she knew about it and would determine if there was to be intervention or not based on her consultations with cops and gangsters. Eventually, she bought a candy store that was a front for numbers and solicitation. According to the kids on 111th, she was the nastiest store owner in the area, always screaming for the kids to buy their shit and get out. What did they know? All they wanted was two-for-a-penny Banana Splits, Squirrel Nuts, and Dubble Bubbles. All Tula wanted to do was sell numbers and pussy. There was definitely a conflict of interest and "a failure to communicate."

I never saw Tula hit a kid, but when she hit a man, she threw solid punches to the face and balls, or *macanazos* to the head with a miniature bat she carried. I'm sure the humiliated john wished for death rather than this rather public degradation. She would curse a motherfucker out like a sailor, fight like a professional bouncer, and fling you around like a rag doll. No one—no one—messed with her, and I loved the theater she provided and I loved her. My Tula. May she rest in peace.

Then, there was Fifi, the first proud, gay Puerto Rican man on Madison Avenue between 111th and 112 Streets who walked in tight bell-bottoms, pointed boots, and flowery shirts with billowing sleeves in the winter and tank tops, short shorts, and open-toe sandals in the summer. Fifi was short, light-brown-skinned, with the flat features of Mexican Indians rather than the sharper features of Tainos and the thickest, most luxurious hair in the 'hood, which she primped to perfection. She was also the loudest person on the block, and I suspect she knew more about the private lives and fantasies of the so-called serious husbands in the neighborhood than their wives or their priests.

Fifi wasn't just gay; she was a diva and she sauntered around the block like a reigning beauty queen, taunting, flirting, and, believe it or not, inspiring wives and lovers to do more with their miserable lives than sit there and cry over "a worthless Puerto Rican man," *un desgraciado.* "Leave the motherfucka," she would scream to the sobbing women, "He's not worth it. Leave the kids with me. Lose some weight and go to work, bitch. There's a man out there for you. You'll see. Now come over here, mama, and let me do your hair. Do you know who I did last night . . . ? Nena, you wouldn't baleeve it. Yeah, that *papi chulo*! And, he's *guuuuud*, too. He rocks it, baby."

To mistake Fifi for a punk was a fatal error. I saw her punch and kick a little teenaged gangster's ass right on the avenue and then get super mad when the kid messed up her hair. The kid had beaten the young mother of his child the night before, and she was pretty bruised up. Then, in a perverted act of forgiveness, he gave her money to "do her hair." She said nothing as she sat waiting for her turn in Fifi's chair at the beauty salon, even when peppered with questions from patrons. The girl sat, head down, refusing to answer, shaking her head and steadfastly maintaining that everything was okay at home. Everyone in the shop knew her little gangster "man" had marked her up. Apparently, he had a rep for impulsive violence. That Saturday afternoon, she took too long to return home from the beauty parlor, and guess who showed up outside the door.

"Oye, vamos," he commanded, like a little dictator. Fifi hadn't finished taking the curlers out of the young girl's hair after the dryer. As the trembling young girl started to rise, Fifi pushed her down into the chair and shouted with just as much authority, "Quedate aqui. No termine. I ain't finished with you and you know I love to comb out your hair, girl." Fifi totally ignored the bully. He went ballistic.

"Bitch, what I tell you to do," he screamed at the doorway.

Fifi, never taking her eyes off the girl and looking directly into the huge mirror in front, said, cooly, *"Ella se va quedar aqui hasta que yo termino con ella. Lo que tu tiene que hacer es esperar afuera o irte pa'l carajo.* (She's going to stay here until I'm finished with her. What you need to do is wait for her outside or go to Hell.)"

The kid made a bad mistake. "Fuck you, faggot. Mind your own business before I come in there and tear your ass up!"

Fifi smiled in the mirror and told the girlfriend, "Ohhh, my goodness. He likes to fight. *Coño*, so do I," and she placed the long, black comb with a very sharp-edged handle on the counter, took off her earrings, quickly smeared Vaseline over her face and ran right at the kid, knocking him down.

Fifi waited for him to get up, slipping her countless rings off her fingers and shouting to him, "I don't want you to say I bum-rushed you, *cobarde*. I want to beat you fair and square so everybody could see this faggot kicked your little macho ass. Now get up." The little gangster scrambled to his feet, and once he put his fists up and took his stance, Fifi proceeded to methodically whip his ass. Lefts, rights, uppercuts, never using her nails or elbows. We knew she could fight; but not like this. This was a professional beating and Fifi took the boy to boxing school. His light-skinned face began to swell and bruise, much like he had done to the mother of his child the night before. And then he made another classic mistake, pulling on Fifi's perfectly coiffed, perfectly still, sprayed hair. It came totally undone: a mess. With a perfect counterpunch Fifi knocked him onto the sidewalk. "Oh, your ass is mine, now, *pendejo*. You fucked with my hair, *maricon*" and proceeded to whip this boy's ass again while he was on the ground, bending down to hit him repeatedly in the face and ribs. Once she let up, he clambered to his feet and ran away. Everyone was laughing. Fifi, however, was no joke. She hid guns, hid guys running from the cops, had tremendous heart, was more man than most men, and never, ever touched my ass or disrespected my person but, God, did she love hugging and kissing me.

She was the best babysitter on the block 'cause she would let the kids vent their feelings and maybe even smoke, but you could not verbally disrespect your mother or father. For that, she would sting you with a quick slap and an admonition never to say those things again. We loved her, though she couldn't cut nappy hair to save her fuckin' life. She tried with me. When she finished her version of the buzz cut, I looked like a cancer patient from *Pirates of the Caribbean*. She thought it was divine.

"That's the shit, babee," she said as she handed me the hand mirror to look at myself. I was crestfallen. Half my 'fro was up, the other half down, and the back was sheared off.

"*Tu no cree que se ve lindo?*" she asked the women in the beauty shop. They all nodded their heads in agreement without saying a word but looked at each other, hands over their mouths, dying to burst out laughing. I hated them.

They didn't want to face the prospect of not sitting in Fifi's chair anymore. It wasn't that she was the best hairdresser. It was that she was the best psychologist, comedienne, priestess, sex therapist, and gossiper in the 'hood. A day at Fifi's was entertaining, informative, uplifting, and funny as hell. Who would want to mess that up by contradicting her? Fifi was Liza Minnelli before Liza Minnelli, bilingually. Fifi died in the early '80s, from AIDS. She was one of the most honest and loving persons I have ever met.

Now that I was out of jail, I needed a job. Ironically, it was the Police Athletic League that found me work at a stationery store on 75th Street and Lexington Avenue. The store was owned by an elegant, very white, prematurely old

French Jewish man, Mr. Kaufman, with skin so thin I could see the veins running through his face and jaw. His lips were thin and purple, and he inhaled Gauloises as if they were magic sticks. He was a character out of an old French movie, dark beret, scarf carelessly wrapped around his neck, rumpled overcoat and all. He loved fountain pens and good stationery. I discovered that there are folks who buy fine pens for the pure art of it. They love the art of writing and they'd rather do it with a precision instrument. Mr. Kaufman would gingerly remove a Mont Blanc case from the display shelf for a customer and then gently lift the individual pen from the velvet packaging as if it were a priceless diamond brooch. He would discuss the finer points of weight, balance, feel, font, and stroke with them. When he finished the presentation, you wanted to make love to the damn thing. Slowly, he would wrap the gift up, and, if they so chose, he would promise them delivery at an appointed time. That meant me. God, I loved it. I got to peek inside incredible apartments on Park Avenue, living rooms that dwarfed my family's whole apartment, emanating smells that reeked of luxury. They most certainly were not the familiar Old Spice/Avon/Clubman good grooming street smells that I had become accustomed to; these smells were light, nuanced, dancing between citrus, light baby powder, and musk. I was in a different world, delivering pens and stationery to rich matrons in opulent apartments with art, plump furniture, and fragrant smells. Whether it was pedigree and upbringing or consciously learned behavior, I felt extremely comfortable in it and around it, and I knew the boundaries.

Outside this enclosed world, however, things were different, very different; and the crossing of boundaries, real or imagined, could carry deadly consequences, as a young junior high school student named James Powell learned in late July of 1966. It was a terribly hot day in the city, and the Harlem kids who had been bused into Robert Wagner Jr. High School on the Upper East Side were playing with an open hydrant, spraying water on one another. Somehow, the super of one of the luxury buildings got involved in the horseplay, and when plainclothed-off-duty police officer Thomas Gilligan arrived on the scene all he saw was a group of Black kids chasing a building superintendent into the lobby of the building with a water hose. So he shoots one of them. Dead. Tells his superiors and the media that the kid came after him with the hose. He was charged and acquitted eventually, but not before Harlem erupted into one of the worst race riots since World War II. That police officer's attitudinal perceptions about Black kids, about Black kids in a white neighborhood behaving like all giddy kids do on city streets in the sweltering heat of summer, resulted in the loss of two lives, injuries to hundreds, arrests of thousands, and millions of dollars in property damage.

As customers walked into the stationery store to recount their varying stories of what happened, I kept going back to my exhilarating experience on that same street. James Powell was shot to death. It could've been me gasping for air on the sidewalk and finally being forced to let go of life. I wouldn't change places, no. I loved what I'd experienced, but I realized that no matter how blessed, how fortunate I was, reality and racism still lurked around the corner. I was alive, James was dead, and there were only two years between us. New York City was in a fear grip. And Harlem, the mecca of Black culture, had the first urban riot of the '6os in America.

I asked Mr. Kaufman to take off early, and the old French gentleman grabbed my shoulders firmly, looked long at me with those sad eyes, and said, "Of course." Harlem was on fire for several nights, the flames leaping from the buildings like thick lightning going up rather than coming down. The acrid smoke of burned stores and the produce inside, the maddeningly high-pitched sirens of police cars and fire engines, and the occasional bursts of gunfire didn't frighten me, it depressed me. I wasn't afraid of going out to the streets, wasn't afraid of the cops or the rioters. I simply lay on the living room couch watching the reflections of the flames, hearing the noise, knowing that this was not the Harlem I loved, not the Harlem I wanted to be part of, not the Harlem I wanted to stay in. I didn't have to. A few months later, detectives arrived at my door with handcuffs and ankle chains for a long train ride to Elmira Prison in upstate New York. The Legal Aid attorneys had not told me that the technicality that allowed me freedom was only temporary.

Parnell Hargrove, my "older brother" from Brownsville, had come to visit me. He had tremendous courage but knew there was nothing he could do. He watched sadly as they cuffed me and marched me downstairs to the waiting car. Everything I knew, everything I took for granted, was going to be tested, harshly. Elmira Prison was the filtering house for New York state prisons, the place where they tested and analyzed you for three months before shipping you out to an "appropriate" correctional facility. If you had potential, intellectually, if your crime was not too violent, you were sent to Wallkill. If you were of average intelligence, a first-time offender, a teenager and were convicted of a major felony—murder, armed robbery, etc.—you were sent to Coxsackie, a reformatory as vulgar as the sound of its name. The state called it a Correctional Institution, but its walls, its barbed wire, its armed sentry posts, its smell, and its vicious, organized racism had adult prison written all over it. But, first, you had to pass through Elmira.

Chapter 7

Crossing the Lines

I was still in a state of shock and disorientation. Whatever mindset I was supposed to settle into had not jelled. I simply did not believe I was a criminal. Yes, I was the ringleader, as the news article called me, and, yes, the gang fight resulted in a fifteen-year-old's murder, but, the fact that I had to do the time for the crime was a horrible discovery. Couldn't they see I wasn't a born loser? Couldn't they feel I wasn't a killer? How many times had my looks, my syntax, my carriage, my total recall of Western European history gotten me out of trouble with cops, teachers, preachers, gang members, and neighbors? I was always forgiven. I was a kid, dammit! Why were they treating me this way?

The state saw no wayward minor, no cute teenager with a preppy camel-hair jacket with suede elbow patches, a yellow Oxford button-down shirt, and Fred Braun shoes who was going places. 14524. That was my number. I was another asshole gone haywire. In the state's defense, they had accomplished a minor miracle. I was given only a five-year bid. With good behavior I'd be out in two years. I was an accessory to a murder. Attempted Manslaughter II was the final conviction, and, no matter how I deluded myself for years, emotionally, I knew it was a serious felony. God had blessed my ass from my nappy head to my ashy toes by not sending me to a down-and-dirty traditional prison, but I still couldn't shake the leaden weight of truth: A human being was dead, and I was responsible. Though I had promised Diablo in the Brooklyn House of Detention that I would never cry over my fate again, once I saw the cages of Elmira, stacked one on top of another, I became hysterical. For two weeks I cried every night, howling into my pillow, trying to muffle the sound, but it was heard.

John, my crime partner, who somehow had already internalized the fact that he had stabbed and killed someone and gotten only three-and-a-half to seven years (another blessing) was like a compassionate father. "Philip. Philip. Please take it easy, brother. It's gonna be alright. I'm with you. I'm going to stand by you. Philip . . . *Philip! You hear me?*" I would whimper back some half-assed choked-back response and John, bless his soul, would continue to talk to me from his cell. Every night, every afternoon, every time we were locked in, he wouldn't let up. "Don't cry, Philip," he would say, and then *he* would start to cry, "Don't cry, brotha, I love you, man." For fourteen days, the guy I took the ass-whipping for, after the initial arrest, the guy whose spirit got entangled in memories of a cruel childhood and bloodlust that murderous afternoon in April, stood by me like a courageous, understanding, compassionate friend. He pulled me through and never once ratted on me or ridiculed me in front of others.

One day, as we locked out of the three floors of cages they call the "Flats" to go to chow, some guy, looking straight at me and pointing me out to his buddies, made whimpering sounds, exaggerated sobs. His high-pitched laughter was cruel, so cruel that his friends simply looked my way apologetically. The "joke" fell flat. But something had to happen. I had to put closure to this or be stigmatized with the rep of crybaby, sicko, or worse. Something as simple as a joke can lead to death or rape in jail. I was crushed. I had no response. For seconds, I stared at the inmate, too cried out to act. I wanted to jump him. I wanted to bite his ear off and spit it out. I couldn't. I was done in.

John stepped quickly toward the group, the freckles on his light-skinned face seeming to pop out, his thick forearms hanging almost too casually at his sides. He had a habit of bunching up his shoulders when he got mad and sticking his neck out like a drill sergeant. Without missing a beat, I walked to the right of him. And I never looked at the other guy's face. I just watched his hip. I stared vacantly at his stomach and lost all sense of where I was. I started to hum. My skinny body was twitching ever so slightly and I simply continued staring at this guy's stomach, looking away every so often to see if the hacks were watching. They weren't. It was time to do it. And at that time, I didn't care anymore. We were in for one body, might as well make it two. I had snapped and John sensed it. He quickly grabbed my forearm, real hard, and looked directly at the group.

Then, he spoke. Real softly. "You know . . . I love this guy. I mean, I really love him."

No one laughed. They knew he wasn't talking "homo" shit.

"And after I stabbed that motherfucker and everybody ran, he stayed with me. He knew I didn't know what I was doing. He knew I was in shock. And he took the bust with me. So . . . I love him. You know what I mean?"

All the guys in the group, except the Big Mouth, murmured their approval. Then, John's face took on a vicious, glacial frigidity as he looked into this guy's eyes.

"If you don't know what it is to lose your mother, your brother, your sister, and every good thing going on out there, then the best thing for you to do is shut the fuck up. Yeah, he's crying. He's hurt. And I've been crying, too. But I guess you're too much of a man to say you're scared, right?

The wise guy shrank in stature as his buddies shrank back from him. He was alone. "Hey, man, I was just goofing. He can't take a joke?"

"Answer my question, man. You never cried before?" John whispered, putting his face even closer to the dude.

The inmate hung his head. And his eyes teared up. Not from fear, but from communion with a feeling. John had touched his soul. "I'm sorry, man," he said and reached out to shake my hand. I grabbed it firmly and clasped his forearm with my left hand. I said nothing. John stuck his hand out to the group. "My name is John. My partner's name is Philip. Can we let this shit die right here?" I never heard those guys mention the incident again.

After the "adjustments," I began to like Elmira. The short walks from one building to another filled me with reverence for things like fresh mountain air, regional accents, and rural white people. Christmas, that year, was actually joyful; the snow didn't turn black as it does on city streets and the radio seemed to play an endless stream of traditional carols. It was Dick and Jane–ish, but I liked it. I needed it. And, I wish I could've stayed longer, talking theology with the pastor and discussing world politics with the counselor. But the day came. Ship-out time. Coxsackie became the new adjustment, the new testing ground. I suffered separation anxiety after leaving Elmira. Instinctively, I must have known it was going to be a long two years.

Before I stepped into the Big Yard of Coxsackie, the inmates already knew who I was, what crime I'd been convicted of, and how much time I was facing. The Puerto Rican crew told me later they were waiting for me, another addition to their small, respected collective. The informational network in jail is organized, secretive, and very efficient. They knew what had happened in the street, in the court, in detention, and they knew when I was supposed to arrive. How the hell they amassed that much intelligence on me I'll never know, but it wasn't unusual. What helped is that my older half-brother, Lucky, had already served time there.

If there was ever a physical replica of the old plantation South in the "new" North, this was it. As I stood on the inside porch facing the inmate population, I became nauseated, not from fear, not even from rage, just from disgust at what the New York State Corrections Department allowed to exist in order to maintain control. It was dehumanizing.

The New York State Institution for Men at Coxsackie was a rectangular building built around an inside patio or courtyard. And you were allowed to lean against the walls of that courtyard only if you were part of a racial grouping: a gang. From the porch of the administration building and to my immediate left, there was "Spain," the Puerto Rican section. Following a horizontal line all the way to the end of that wall, at a right angle, another wall, all controlled by white boys from cities I had read about in Edith Hamilton's book on Greek mythology: Troy, Schenectady, Utica. Their territory extended halfway around the yard. It stopped at the final wall of the rectangle, the North Wall. That was Black territory. And then, you were back to the porch. That belonged to the administration. There was another grouping, multiracial, integrated (I was the first Puerto Rican in it), and totally lacking in jail honor or respect. It was called "The Middle," and that's where it was, smack dab in the center of the yard, reserved for creeps, those rejected by gangs for not following through on a contract to hurt somebody or for being a rat. Throughout the year you stood with no wall support or sat on the asphalt ground. Any infraction of group rules could mean banishment to creepsville, the Middle. There you stayed, isolated, alone, and exposed.

While huddling close to the wall provided some kind of buffer from the fierce Catskill mountain wind in the winter and shade from the intense upstate sun in the summer, the opposite was true of the "Kack" gulag, the Middle. You froze in the winter and fried in the summer. And, unless you did whatever the gang wanted you to do—stab, slash, or pummel—you were never allowed into the family business, holding up the walls of the prison that held us captive. It was pitiful. We were already in jail, yet we imprisoned ourselves even further, all with the tacit agreement of the guards and the authorities, warden included. One tall, heavily muscled Black inmate, part of the inmate crowd watching the newcomers but staring at me, put his bent right forefinger in his mouth and exclaimed loudly, "Oh God, I'm in love."

I turned to the new guy behind me and said stupidly, "Are there girls behind us?" The new inmate, not even laughing, said. "Hell no. He's looking at you." I paid no attention to the comment.

Several days later, I was lifting weights in the prison gym and was losing control of the bar. My arms were trembling and it was a choice between having the bar hit my throat or chest. Either way I'd be dead or seriously injured. That same inmate, who I had been warned was a flaming homosexual, crossed over my lower torso with short-shorts and no underwear. I could see everything . . . everything.

"Need a spot?" he asked softly.

Now was the moment of truth. I could hold on to my homophobia and die or be saved by the gay Black Hulk. I chose the latter, thank God.

"Yes," I gasped. "Take this shit off me," and in a flash, the guy lifted the bar as if it were a feather and placed it back on the rack.

"Whew! Thanks, man," was all I could muster.

The guy looked at me strangely. "You know, you're the only guy who didn't have a problem with my helping them. You know I like boys, right?"

"Yep, they told me. But I had to choose whether I wanted you to help or have my throat crushed. It wasn't a hard decision, you know?"

The Black Hulk laughed. "You're alright. I ain't gonna bother you . . . and nobody else will, ya hear?" And, that's the way it stayed for the next two years.

But, that first day, squinting into the sun, hand over my eyes, I finally stepped off the porch and walked briskly to the Black territory, the North Wall. I had recognized a familiar face from the Brownsville Houses in Brooklyn, a good friend and sort of a street mentor, Craig Coleman, a.k.a. Chain. Though I had great, wholesome friends, like Parnell Hargrove, Milton, Frank, Denise Revels, Juanita and the only other Puerto Rican brother on my side of the projects, Moses, I gravitated toward gang life.

Chain was one of the humblest, bravest, and most protective warriors on the Dumont Avenue side of the Brownsville Projects. There were two other guys like that: Parnell Hargrove, a Black satin, handsome brother, whose apartment at 345 Dumont Avenue I almost lived in and whose ethics and loyalty stood heads above everybody else's. Then there was Milton, the only boy in a sea of sisters. He had a bad eye and an even worse temper, if you crossed him. But Chain was the unchallenged leader. He played the silent role and relished a bully's challenge. His punches were super-hard. The impact of his body blows could be heard fifty feet away. He never, ever started a fight, but pity the person who started one with him. Though he was of medium build, slim, sinewy with Afro-Cherokee features, his arm strength and vise-like grip were legendary in the projects. I looked up to him. And, I was elated to see him that day. But was it really him?

As I approached the North Wall, I started to walk faster. It was him. My eyes weren't playing tricks on me. It was Chain, my man. I was safe. But why wasn't he rushing to greet me? Everyone in the yard noticed the new jacks coming in. Well, I thought naïvely, maybe he didn't recognize me. After all, it had been more than two years since we last laid eyes on each other.

"Hey, Chain," I screamed in childlike glee. "Chain, it's good to see you, man. We didn't know where you were."

As I spoke, I stepped over a painted yellow line that served as some sort of border. I felt coldness from the group around him. Chain, his face sullen, put his forearm against my chest. I had seen that look before. It scared me.

"Philip, you can't come in here, man. You see that line you stepped over? That's the Black line. Now, if you knew better, I'd fuck you up, but this is the first time, so, I gotta tell you the rules."

I stepped back over the line in horror. This was not the man I knew, the happy, neighborhood older brother who never allowed us to stray too far or be abused too much by the older guys. This was not Chain, my friend. The person in front of me was a hardened inmate, a robot.

"Chain," I said, choking back tears, "When the fuck did I ever care what was Black or what was Puerto Rican? We're homeboys, man. You helped raise me. What the fuck are you talking to me about this Black shit for? I always bugged with you, Chain. When did I ever deny I was Black, man?"

Chain looked at me sorrowfully and then, quickly, lowered his eyes. He kept the same intensity and physical attitude, but his voice returned to normal. It was the voice of the brother I loved years ago. But he refused to look at me.

"Philip, I don't have much time to say this. I had to change in here. Jail is different from the outside. Here, I'm Black, you're Spanish. Get it? You belong in Spain with those dudes over by the porch. Now, if you come into the Black side, you're gonna have three enemies: the Puerto Ricans; the white boys, who'll try to 'Jap' you; and the guards, who want to keep things nice and simple. I'm maxing out and I know it. You gotta make a decision right now. Do you want to max out? 'Cause that's what's gonna happen if you step over that line again and become Black. Listen to me, Philip. Keep your nose clean, do two years, and go home. Now, turn around and go to Spain . . . and don't look back. See you, kid."

Tears blurred my vision. I had been "saved" by being rejected . . . by one of the guys I loved most in the world. The walk back to "Spain" took seconds, but it felt like hours. The Puerto Rican inmates waited for me, arms folded across their chests, contempt on their faces. The prodigal child had returned and they would never let me forget it. I slid into Latino territory without saying a word. To their credit, the guys said nothing . . . that day. But Chino, the darkest one, had it in for me. I could tell by the sneer on his face. As for Chain, I never spoke to him again though our eyes would meet in the Big Yard from time to time. He wouldn't nod, nor would I. The hurt I felt I never forgot, though I forgave him, later in life, in my heart. To this day that rejection pains me, and every time I meet a person, cultural nationalist, activist, academic, or project dweller who professes Pan Africanism, the love of all Blacks in the diaspora, I ask questions, probe gently, but mainly watch, to see whether the love they profess includes Latinos, especially Afro-Latinos. The proof is not in the rhetoric; it's in their relationships and behavior. Chain taught me a brutal, vital lesson. Loyalty, ethics, love have to supersede circumstance if it's to mean anything.

For forty-eight hours there was a truce in Spain with regard to me. Most of the Puerto Ricans made casual conversation, but nothing intimate, certainly nothing inclusive of me. I was confused, nervous, a bit scared. I kept real quiet. I had to listen and learn the laws, the pecking order, the expectations. Archie, a freckle-faced white kid whose claim to Latino heritage was that his stepfather was 'Rican and who identified more with Latinos than with his own Irish heritage, had been allowed to join Spain. Archie had a limp, a lisp, and a hearty laugh. He took a liking to me.

"Hey, man, cheer up," Archie told me excitedly with a huge grin. "It ain't so bad. At least you were accepted. I've seen guys get sent right to the Middle for pulling what you pulled."

"You know something, Archie? I didn't even know about this shit—Blacks there, Puerto Ricans here, white boys everywhere else. This shit is crazy." Archie's answer was brutally honest.

"Yeah, well, the streets are the streets and the joint is the joint. You here now, so you better get hip, quick."

Archie was being real. And thank God, someone was showing me the ropes. After Archie broke the political silent treatment being accorded me, others in Spain loosened up. Jokingly, they recounted how I fucked up by going first to the Black Wall but that, hey, everybody's allowed one mistake and tomorrow is another day. I began to like Spain. I saw a camaraderie, a spirit, a gang-like loyalty that I hadn't noticed. Things were very different in the Latino territory than in the rest of the Big Yard. Here, brothers were touchy-feely, combed each other's hair, kissed and embraced warmly in the traditional Latino way, watched each others' backs without too much back-biting. It wasn't that the same rituals didn't occur in the other gang areas of Coxsackie; it's just that the depth and fullness of those feelings were light-years ahead in Spain. We, the Latinos, were men, yet there was a maternal incandescence that emanated from our group as opposed to the rough, gruff behavior that posed as masculinity with the other gangs.

There were those in Spain who forgave me, attributing my indiscretion, my lack of judgment, to ignorance of the jail system. After all, they would say, it was my first bust, my first time in the lockup. Within a week, the guys were talking and smiling with me, patting me on the back and asking real questions about the world I had just left, the streets of New York City. There were geographical tests: names of streets and locations of prime points of teenage interest in places like El Barrio, East New York, Bushwick, and Brownsville.

"Where can you buy the best Spaldeen in East Harlem?" and "What store in Brownsville has the best comic book selection, the best egg creams?" These tests would get detailed, and before long I'd have a throng around me roaring approval as I struggled for answers.

"What year did the principal of Junior High School 210 commit suicide by throwing himself off the roof of the school?"

"Where's the hole in the fence around Betsy Head Pool in Brownsville?" 'What blocks did the Viceroys control in El Barrio?"

"Where were the loudest Pentecostal storefront churches in East Harlem?" It was huge fun and I thrived on the verbal exams. Though it proved, to some, that I was a real Puerto Rican, what I loved most was the thrill of competition, the gathering around of the group, the communal laughing or shouting down of a wrong answer. It was the Roman Senate to me and I had the floor for almost two weeks as I was peppered with questions and more questions. It was Paradise. I missed a few big questions, but I did very well, adding little anecdotes to each answer, stories that only I could know, coming from the "world." And, every once in a while, those anecdotes would be confirmed by a visiting family member of a Hispanic inmate. I was floating on clouds.

The second level of questions centered on events, groups, and personalities—that is, intimate knowledge of historic gang fights, inclusive of strategy and tactics, gang politics and sociology and a breakdown of the Who's Who of gang presidents and war counselors. This was my forte. I would sit for hours on the streets listening to the older guys discuss the pecking order of gangs, both in Brooklyn and Manhattan.

Some gang leaders I knew, most I didn't, but I made it sound like I was connected to every housing project gang that ever existed. Peppered with questions on the intrigue, the plots, the betrayals, the blood, the ultimate revenge and battle victories of gangs like the Chaplains, the Frenchmen, the Corsairs, the Stompers, the El Quintos, the Jolly Midgets, the Mighty Bishops, and the Roman Lords, all from Brooklyn, I launched into long tirades on who did what to whom and what the consequences were. Then I would volunteer information on the "fine wine" groups from Manhattan: the Viceroys and Dragons and the Turbans from East Harlem, the Tiny Tots and the Imperial Knights from Central Harlem, the Sportsmen of the Lower East Side and the Italian Redwings from Pleasant and First avenues in East Harlem. I only had bits of information about the Fordham Baldies from the Bronx, an Irish gang that allegedly got its name because one of its leaders had head lice and had to shave his head. In deference to their Prez, all the members shaved their heads. To my knowledge, the Fordham Baldies were the first gang to really integrate their membership with Blacks and Puerto Ricans, a sign of things to come.

Chino wasn't the best fighter in Spain; he was just the nastiest spirit. The most he could work up in terms of a smile was a partial opening of his mouth to show some large horse-like teeth with the ends of his mouth struggling to stay up 'cause it just wasn't natural. He had an Afro-Indio face, high cheekbones, and slanted eyes that I thought could've been softer if he would only allow himself a decent thought. Instead, Chino's eyes looked menacing. They never smiled. And they were watching you, all the time. He had a sharply angled Arabic nose with a wide flare to his nostrils, large lips, a small expanse of forehead, a small head, and what my mother used to call Dixie Peach hair—tight, nappy curls that would relax and open up only with gobs of Dixie Peach pomade and water, matted down with a stocking cap so you could produce wavy hair that looked like a process hairdo. He was a short, barrel-chested teenager who looked much older than the seventeen or eighteen they said he was. I didn't want to psycho-social this guy. He was just mean and ugly, like those illustrations of Atilla the Hun in the grade school history books. I didn't want to go any further into figuring out what made him tick. I avoided him, deftly, diplomatically. I just stayed far away from his force field.

Chino and his cohorts had made up their minds that I was a Black man who happened to be Puerto Rican. They supported their theory by pointing out my Black accent and my inability to speak Spanish fluently. It didn't matter that I understood Spanish perfectly or that I had passed countless jailhouse tests conducted by Puerto Rican inmates whose sole goal was to trip me up. As I regaled Spain with stories, I kept my eye on Chino. I was relishing the victory of having won the group's acceptance. Puerto Ricans had accepted me for once, something that had never happened completely in the outside world. Acceptance brought with it a sense of peace, a tolerable attitude toward prison life amidst the sheer deprivation of freedom inside those three-foot-thick walls. I wasn't alone anymore. I wasn't an outsider. I actually remember being happy.

There was a price I'd have to pay for joining the gang. Eventually, I'd have to pay the piper: do something horrible to someone, probably against my will or better judgment, but I flung those thoughts away. Today was the only important reality, I remember telling myself; enjoy the moment. The euphoria didn't last long. I was becoming the *de facto* head of Spain, and Chino felt it. It was only a matter of time before he made his move. Chino was plotting. He wasn't stupid. He knew my Achilles heel was my love for Black people.

In the months to come, he would try to crush that love. Eventually, as new inmates brought new information, my stuff became old, stale news. I had to re-adjust; I shut up and watched my back. Noticing the shine beginning to dull on my "newness," Chino began his hatred campaign. Wherever I stood and engaged in conversation, he would pop up and start a raucous, vulgar, curse-filled, violent, racist diatribe, the butt of his jokes, the object of his poison: Black inmates in particular, Black people in general. The few 'Rican inmates he gathered around himself would roar in laughter as he pointed out Black prisoners with parted front teeth, long heads, very dark skin, and large lips. As certain Black inmates passed by, Chino would jump and grunt like a baboon, his flunkies roaring with laughter. For a month, he continued this madness and as the groups around him got larger, he physically moved away from me, stopped stalking me, so as not to be charged with envy or jealousy. But people were beginning to notice. And whisper.

He was playing brinksmanship with people's lives just to stay king of Spain, and the dead-eye stares he was getting from Black inmates did not stop him. Chino was setting up a war inside the joint, a war between Black and brown inmates simply because he was losing power. He knew he was losing ground, even with the small crowds he was attracting, including some of the officers who would join in the laughter. I would overhear some of his ignorant shit and tremble. I hated this motherfucker. I hated his stupidity, his ugliness, and his ability to draw a crowd to his venom. I literally thought of killing Chino. The jokes, the racial lies passing as pseudo-scientific knowledge, the put-downs, the same bullshit I heard coming from white Puerto Ricans growing up in East Harlem. It was usually directed at me and my family.

As I'd pass Chino's groups, he would raise his voice. I never looked at him. I never laughed.

The sad part of it all was that Chino was the darkest Puerto Rican in Spain. His lips were more "African" than most of the Black American inmates on the North Wall; his nose was just as flat, and his hair, without the aid of a stocking cap, was just as kinky. What finally stopped his racist antics was that one of the white Puerto Rican inmates blurted out, as he was doubled up in laughter, that Chino looked more like a monkey than any of the brothers on the North Wall. That statement ended the freak shows. The sad part of it all was that, even at sixteen, I knew Chino hated himself and would do anything to distance himself from the truth of his own Blackness. And, in a strange, perverted island code of mores and customs, Puerto Rican inmates superficially accepted Chino's dark skin but rejected the color of other Black inmates and the African connection binding us all. It was clear, especially in jail, that color was not the sole criterion for rejection of American Black folks by Puerto Ricans; it was culture as well.

And Chino used the cultural differences between Afro-Americans and Puerto Ricans to hurl insults. It didn't stop. Every day that we were outside in the yard, he would bring up how close Puerto Ricans were as a people and how divided and "disloyal" Black folks were to one another. From my perspective, putting down another culture in order to upgrade your own was bound to be a short-lived philosophy. After three months, even those who laughed with him in Spain began to feel uneasy, nervous, and fidgety, putting their heads down in embarrassment and casting quick, furtive looks at me to gauge my reaction. I didn't give them one.

There were Black inmates I had really taken a liking to: Philly, a short Latino-looking guy with horrible skin and a great voice. Coxsackie was for inmates from sixteen to eighteen and he looked much older. He lived to sing and knew every song in the doo-wop repertoire, '50s and '60s: "Wind" by the Cadillacs, "Why Do Fools Fall in Love" by Frankie Lymon and the Teenagers, "Shimmy Shimmy Ko-Ko-Bop" by Little Anthony and the Imperials, and "Will You Still Love Me Tomorrow" by the Shirelles. I heard from the guys who bunked in his division of the prison that he would go to bed singing and come out of his cell singing in the morning. He had an appreciative audience among the Black inmates and it was I who would look longingly at the backs of the brothers who would encircle Philly, two and three deep, in the North Ward as he sang his heart out to their loud roars of encouragement and appreciative applause. Even the guards would applaud a skillful rendition of an old tune. Music soothed the Big Yard, tempered the beast inside, and made us forget for just one moment in time that we were locked up.

There was Itchy, a lanky, light-skinned, brown-haired, dimpled, Gerber-looking baby of a teenager who got busted on some dumb robbery charge and never should have been sent to jail, according to the jailhouse lawyers. It was a joy going to chow 'cause you knew Itchy was going to ladle out the food, tell you honestly whether it was tasty or shitty, and do it all with a joke. He was the senior guy on the kitchen staff, well respected by inmates because he had earned his position through hard work. He would be scouring those stainless steel mixers and soup vats long after it was time for him to stop. Their surfaces would sparkle in the morning and afternoon light, and we took pride that he took pride, hoping one day when he went home one of us would replace him.

And then it happened. For ninety days, even with the Chino controversy, I lived a fantasy in which I was on vacation in some upstate boarding school. I ignored the officers, the watchtowers, the rifles, the barbed wire.

One afternoon, as my division, A2, marched into the cafeteria to eat lunch, Itchy, normally on the food line, was working at stirring the huge soup vat, his back to us. His boss, a tall, burly, cruel-faced correctional officer who often laughed with Itchy as they prepared the food, who trusted him with everything—the staff (Itchy was in charge of new officers in the kitchen as well as inmates), the food, and the ingredients—was nowhere in sight. Suddenly, this officer strode into the food-preparation area behind the serving line and for no apparent reason smacked Itchy hard on his back. I stood transfixed, holding my tray, trembling.

Itchy whirled around quickly and in one motion dropped the long-oared soup ladle and right-crossed this officer square on the jaw, knocking him down, almost knocking him out. He didn't have time to think. In jail, you react quickly to unexpected touch or end up scarred for life or dead. As soon as Itchy realized it was the Boss Man, he immediately bent down to apologize and offer the officer a hand up. "Man, I'm sorry. I didn't know it was you, Boss." The officer's face was purple with rage and embarrassment. It had happened in front of the entire inmate population and the few officers on chow duty. The transformation that occurred in this white man's face and body was demonic. After all the kidding around between them, after all the work Itchy had put in to become first boy in the kitchen, after all the Boss had invested in him, teaching him the ins and outs of the food trade, nothing mattered now. The hatred, the pure venom toward Black people flooded this former dairy farmer's face and he proceeded to pummel Itchy into unconsciousness, screaming, "You nigger bastard, you nigger bastard" again and again as Itchy fell under the soup vat holding his arms over his head. No one moved in the cafeteria, not the guards, not the inmates.

All of us were in shock. Finally, the Boss, not content with having beaten his best student to the ground, lifted the big soup ladle and flailed at Itchy's almost-lifeless body until all the inmates started screaming, "Stop. You're killing him."

That afternoon and all night we speculated at what would happen to Itchy. Most of us speculated he'd be thrown into solitary confinement and lose his first-boy status. The older inmates, the ones who never smiled, the ones who had dark spirits, told the new jacks it was over for Itchy. The administration couldn't allow him to stay in our jail after he hit a guard.

The next day, we saw them drag Itchy, a guard on each side of him, his limp arms over their shoulders, to a waiting van to be transported to a prison for the criminally insane. They had broken both of his legs, destroyed the bones in his face, and they made sure they took their time as they trudged to the van. I had never seen brutal, vicious racism, even with my own beating by the police. Somehow, witnessing Itchy's torture confirmed what I had been told by the Muslims in the Brooklyn House of Detention: the white man was the Devil and there was nothing you could trust in him, not his word, not his friendship, not his contracts. There was only one solution: *war*! And that's when we began to organize the hunger strike.

It started as a rumor, secrets whispered among Black inmates, that it was time to take action. Though the whites were also traumatized by Itchy's beating, they stayed neutral, goaded by the officers who had an interest in keeping the status quo. That same week, however, two Italian kids, identical twins, were beaten badly for cursing an officer. It's amazing how an ass-whipping can radicalize you, make you Black, even if you're white. I don't know how the inmate leaders got together, but it was decided we would refuse food for a day, a fairly serious decision for prisoners for whom food is sometimes the only activity to look forward to. The final piece was for the Puerto Ricans in Spain to agree to join the protest. Chino took his time, time we didn't have if we wanted to make an effective statement quickly.

For the first time in the history of that institution, Blacks and whites were of one mind, ready to move, but Chino reveled in his newfound power over all Coxsackie inmates. You could feel the stares, the anger directed toward the Spain area as inmates from New York City and towns all over New York state glowered at us. We as Puerto Ricans couldn't take action until our leader said, "Go." The guards were nervous, mistakenly thinking the growing bubble of emotional tension was about race. Nothing was further from the truth. Chino laughed and cavorted as if nothing was happening, as if we had all day. Privately, I lobbied for the strike, explaining to the guys in Spain that this was the first time we had achieved any sort of unity among inmates and that this could be the beginning of something good for all of us. Chino sunk to new depths.

"Why the fuck should we care about some 'cocolo' they beat up? If the shoe was on the other foot" (and then he stared directly at me) "niggers wouldn't do shit."

I lost it. "Fuck you, you racist bastard. Can't you see if they did it to Itchy they could do it to any one of us? This guy was top dog in the kitchen and they almost killed him. Who the fuck do you think you are, white? You're as Black as any of those guys on the North Ward and either you're blind or stupid. Either way, you're a fuckin' ass. Motherfuckers are waiting for a decision and you're standing here, bullshitting. Time is not on your side, Chino. Make a move, punk."

I meant make a political decision. Chino interpreted it as a personal threat, which of course it was, and he lunged at me. The guys in Spain, who loved me, quickly restrained him, talking into his ear about how bad it would look if we began to fight against each other right now. The whole yard was looking at us. The guards began to take notice now, really thinking there was going to be a race riot. Chino's eyes were bulging, foam appeared at the corner of his mouth as he struggled to get loose, but they locked his arms and wouldn't let go.

"You Black motherfucker, *molleto*, *maricon*," Chino screamed hoarsely. "You wanna do this shit? Okay, I'll do it. But after this strike, it's me and you, punk. We'll see where your fuckin' heart is at."

And then he stopped struggling, told the guys to get the fuck off him, and issued the command "The shit is on!"

The decision was relayed throughout the yard and it felt like heaven that afternoon. The inmates lay back against the brick walls of Coxsackie—white, Black, Latino, Native American—smiling at one another in the confidence of coalition. We knew something the guards didn't. We were together, and nothing could stop us. If we won, fantastic. If we lost, fuck it. It was a good day to die.

The next morning there was an eerie silence throughout the halls of the institution—no jostling, no curses, no horseplay as we entered the eating area, the correctional officers, holding their wooden batons up, hitting their palms repeatedly and nervously looking in every direction. They were not smiling; we were not talking. Even the jailhouse rats kept their mouths shut. We picked up the metal trays. We picked up the spoons and forks. We shook our heads no when asked by the kitchen staff how much food we wanted. And then we walked to our tables with empty trays. Complete and utter silence.

Some guys were pushed around as guards yelled in their ears, warning them of consequences if they didn't eat. We didn't break. We all stared straight ahead, scared but determined. It was a very tense, very hushed confrontation with hundreds of grim, gray-uniformed inmates and blue-shirted correctional officers milling around, conferring with one another and trying to figure this one out. Finally, at the end of meal time, a sergeant shouted, "All right. You guys don't want to eat, fine. How you're going to get through the morning, I don't know, but it's your damn stomachs, not mine." And then, turning to the other officers, snapped, "Let 'em go."

Each division of the prison with a discipline I had never seen before or since rose from those metal benches like trained troops, not even looking at one another, just at the back of the head of whoever was in front of them. I can't vouch for what happened to the farm crews or the rockpile crew, but in the classrooms, nothing was said about the strike. It was as if in discussing the collective action we would break the spell. So we just answered our teachers mechanically and performed our classroom duties of reading and writing by rote.

I was hungry. My stomach was grumbling. But I had set my mind the night before to go through with this, no matter what. All of us were secretly observing one another, and since I had advocated in favor of the hunger strike, I couldn't let my comrades see me sweat. Lunchtime arrived. We had refused the breakfast meal. We had two more to go, lunch and dinner. And then, thank God, it would be over. It would be breakfast—a new day, a new victory, a new sense of unity, regardless of race, nationality, or what city we came from. First, we lined up outside by housing division and then marched into the cafeteria. I was already seated with the guys from my housing unit, looking straight ahead, when I heard Chino speaking in a normal tone to the guys in his division. Because no one else was talking, everybody heard Chino's vocal betrayal. "Listen, man. I'm hungry. We already proved our point by not eating breakfast. They got the message. Shit, I'm not about to lose another meal, and they got porkchops today? Hell, no. I'm eating."

Too many guys on his line were laughing too hard for me not to see this was a setup to break the hunger strike. By the smiles and smirks on the hacks' faces it looked as if Chino had already made a deal. When he got to the serving line, he commanded, "Lay it on me" and the staff piled his tray with mounds of steaming mashed potatoes and gravy, five big porkchops topped with sautéed onions and more gravy, and a small hill of stringbeans. "That's the way you do it, my man," Chino chirped to the guy serving him as he bopped to his table, forearms straining to hold the weight of the food. First, one Puerto Rican and then another, and then another, took the food, avoided our eyes, smiled at their trays, and dove in as soon as they sat down. There must have been a deal. We never got porkchops and red Bermuda onions for lunch. It was a dinner item and served maybe once a month. The warden and staff knew that Puerto Rican and Black folks were raised on pork. It was a definite comfort food, meant to calm anxiety when times were rough. Spareribs, bacon, pork loin or porkchops—it was all meant to bring back memories of home. They used Chino to test the waters, to break the strike, promising him God-knows-what, maybe more food he could bring to his cell at night. The fragrance of the meat wafted above our heads, floated to our nostrils, until I was almost beautifully dizzy. The warden and staff knew what they were doing. And as soon as some 'Ricans broke ranks, so did the brothers and then, of course, the whites. A few Black men, based on their own ethics, refused to get up to get the food. And I (and I'm ashamed to say this even today), after watching three-quarters of the inmates happily chow down, got up and piled the food on my tray. There was a small cheer from the room as I succumbed and ate and ate. Was happy, for the moment. Sad, for the rest of the month. We had our opportunity and we blew it. Chino had given in. And, so had I.

For days I walked through the jail like a broken horse: head down, sad eyes, slow gait. No one intruded on my space other than to offer the normal pleasantries of "How are you?" and "You okay?" I always answered in the affirmative, but the guys knew I was taking this defeat personally. Chino was in his glory—not gloating, not preening, just quietly taking back his power. He would give commands and people obeyed without question: We were back to the way things used to be. He knew better than to order me to do anything. A wounded animal is better left alone.

I went back to the Middle, sat on the ground, and observed the inmates. The routine of everyday life, racist and brutal as it was, was comfortable. They were used to it, so why change? The image of Itchy's broken body had faded. So had the anger. And as long as you went along with these idiots in power, well . . . you could get by; do your time, breathe, eat, shit, and laugh from time to time. It was the first time I actually noticed the innate passivity of most Puerto Ricans, the fearful resistance of going against authority. Talking was fine. Cursing those who assaulted your being, your loved ones, your culture, your right to live was fine. But breaking the patron's face was out of the question. Killing the man who was trying to kill you was out of the question. However, killing each other never seemed to be a problem. Self-hatred ran rampant.

I watched how the Latino inmates interacted with the same guards who broke Itchy's face and legs, the same guards who would offer racist jokes about Blacks, Puerto Ricans, and Jews and guffaw loudly, smacking their thighs at their own comic relief, while the most self-deprecating 'Rican would just smile benignly at the vulgar humor and stay there, continuing to talk to these motherfuckers. I watched how we rubbed our bodies and spirits around these enemies like cats looking for approval from those who warehoused us like animals and offered a bowl of milk only because it was the law of the land; how so many Puerto Ricans admired their oppressors and hated any leader who offered them a way up and out, threatening their welfare status: a bowl of soup, a bone with some meat on it, a cot, some song and dance and a pat on the head from the white man.

I vowed never to give in to the nihilism of prison again. No matter what the price, I would hold on to my character, my values, my faith in the Creator. Slowly, it dawned on me that I needed this experience, needed to be tested in the prime of my adolescence: that passing this gauntlet of pain would prepare me for whatever was out there in the world. I didn't know yet who I was, what I would turn out to be, or what challenges I'd face in my adult life. All I knew was that I had to pass whatever tests came next.

It didn't take long. Chino was stalking the corners of my daily existence and while even he knew better than to brag about having capitulated to the warden, day by day his voice got louder, his racial references cruder.

There were some Black inmates, conscious even then of the racial turmoil occurring in America, who felt that the Puerto Rican group was as much the enemy as the whites. I had suffered this argument before in the Brooklyn House of Detention with my Muslim buddies and didn't take personal offense. Part of the argument was quite true, especially in light of how 'Ricans caved during the hunger strike. It was also true that too many Puerto Rican families viewed "*cocolos*" as inferior and prone to crime and poverty. Woe to any Latina who fell in love with a Black man, regardless of his character and educational attainment. 'Rican families would entertain him for one day with smiles and coffee. But that evening, once the brother stepped out of the apartment, the girl would be told under threat of physical beating that she was never to bring a Black man to the house again.

"Imagine," fathers would scream, "bringing a child into this world darker than you. *Queremos adelantar la raza.* (We want to advance the race.) Y *con esa gente no se puede.* (And with those people you can't move forward.)."

So, to some degree, the Black cultural nationalists in jail were correct. The problem with the supposition was that it was all-inclusive, smeared all Puerto Ricans with the same racist brush. And while I had grown up witnessing how my culture did everything short of painting themselves white so as not to be identified as Black American, I knew there were too many notable exceptions, starting with my Afro-Rican mother and father.

When Chino got wind that the brothers on the North Wall were blaming him for the failure of the strike, he stepped up his racial baiting and nationalistic rhetoric. He knew that by making it an all-for-one, one-for-all battle, it would be an all-out race riot. He also knew if he was assaulted by Blacks, white inmates would either stay neutral or join Spain.

"Fuck those niggers! They don't have shit to say to me," he would scream loudly in the Big Yard, holding his crotch and spitting while looking toward their area, making sure they saw and heard him. "They haven't done a fuckin' thing to help us since I been here. Chicky, they ever help you? Roberto, they ever help you?" Chino would ask the lightest-skinned 'Rican inmates, guys who looked Italian or Irish, guys you wouldn't know were Puerto Rican unless you heard them speak or saw them dance or fight. Of course, they would shake their heads No to Chino's questions, which would goad him on to new oratorical anti-Black tirades. And there was always one Puerto Rican, wanting to curry favor, wanting to be the leader's aide-de-camp, who'd reiterate the threats he heard second-hand.

"Well, I wasn't there, but someone who was there said they were thinking of 'Japping' you [giving an unannounced ass-whipping]." Chino would go ballistic, speaking so quickly he was unintelligible, almost incoherent.

"We gonna do one better. We gonna fuck 'em up before they have a chance to get to us, you dig? Y'all down?"

There was a half-hearted response, but it was a clear declaration of war against all Black inmates. Then Chino, seizing the power of the moment, strode toward where I was sitting and threw down the gauntlet. "You with us or not?"

I got up quickly and we were eye to eye. I was no match for him physically. Same height, but he was thicker, wider, and much more muscled.

I answered, "First of all, did you personally hear anything said about you? Or are you just going off on some bullshit that somebody heard from somebody else? And anyway, they don't like you. Has nothing to do with us."

I stared right back at him. Without missing a beat and without taking his eyes off me, he gestured to the guy who claimed he heard the threat against

Chino. "This motherfucker is calling you a liar. He says you didn't hear what you heard."

The little lapdog was caught. He had to back up whatever he said he heard, true or not, or be branded untrustworthy, forever. The little punk started yapping in my face. "I heard what I heard. Who you to question me? You just got here, punk. Yeah, that's right. I'm talking to you."

I didn't take my eyes off Chino, but I did say to the little guy, "Get the fuck out of my face."

He was empowered now and had the attention of everyone in Spain and the rest of the Big Yard, so he kept yapping. If I broke concentration and whipped his ass it would be seen as a bully move since he was a shrimp. I gained more respect standing up to and fighting Chino who was known as a dirty fighter. I don't think Chino was terribly afraid of me. What he did know is that it wasn't going to be an easy, 1, 2, 3, battle. It was definitely going to be a bloody tussle. He took the more devious way out. Continuing to stare straight at me, he curled his mouth, bared his crooked teeth, and hissed, "Are you with us or against us, my man?"

It was time to take the stand I promised myself I'd take after the hunger strike debacle. "Neither," I said softly. I was surprised at how peaceful I felt, how confident. Breaking the gaze, I bent down to pick up my books. "Fuck you and fuck them," I spat out gesturing to the Black Wall. "If I can't be in any camp, I'll stay by my goddamn self," I said, and walked into the Middle.

The wide-open space in the middle of the Big Yard where there was no shade or shelter from the elements and where the only occupants were guys who couldn't fight, or gay guys, or those who had been rejected by the gangs for infractions or disloyalty. I represented a new category. Spain was in shock. Never in the history of Coxsackie had anyone voluntarily chosen banishment and isolation. For two years I suffered the searing heat of the summer sun and the jagged winter bite of the Catskill wind, but I didn't break. I got to know myself, God, and how far my faith could take me when everything in the physical world pointed to failure.

For weeks, Spain was disoriented. Everything was off-kilter. From where I stood I could see the pained expressions, the stooped backs of men who looked defeated, the quick looks at me and then the rapid turning away. They were hurt, embarrassed, and depressed. Spain had lost its baby brother, a Puerto Rican who chose a public solitary confinement rather than the safety of the group. The sense of family between Puerto Ricans is so thick, so primordial, that losing someone has physical as well as emotional manifestations. We get testy, anxious, and extremely quiet or angry, sharp-tongued, abusive, and violent. Sometimes, we just sit in corners and cry, especially when we know that the missing partner, family member, or friend is correct about his or her reasons for leaving and we don't have the fortitude, courage, or common sense to stop or change the negativity in us, among us. Rather than consolidate his position, Chino weakened himself and the collective by not softening his position. Spain lost its greatness and reputation after the hunger strike. It became known as a hole in the wall for Latinos, a place to hide, not a place where warriors congregated and waged battle with whoever challenged our way of life.

I made it clear I couldn't live under the current system of ignorance in Spain. It had reached crisis level and I wanted no part of it. I didn't advocate they revolt because I knew they wouldn't. They simply didn't have it in them to take Chino out. But they loved me and I felt it. They were decent young men who couldn't take a stand. I would see this pattern among many 'Ricans later in my life, time and time again—the unwillingness to confront. The solitude I imposed on myself was maddening for the first three months. All eyes were focused on me. Would I break? How would I break? Which modality of release would I choose: mental breakdown, a knife fight with Chino, suicide? I chose none, thank God, save school, books, and prayer.

Having some incredibly gifted, neurotic teachers with habits and facial tics that probably kept them from teaching in the regular school system in Greene County, New York, helped a lot. Take Mr. Francis, my music teacher, for example, an overtly gay, obese, and highly intelligent man with a tendency toward flamboyance in dress and cologne. His candor, his wit, his slicing sarcasm, and his dry humor made him an object of derision or admiration, among inmates and correctional officers alike. He was Black, spoke impeccably, and sweated profusely. Hated ghetto language, ghetto values, and ghetto behavior, and if he perceived either in class, you were a candidate for harsh disciplinary action, including solitary confinement. The man was graceful, obviously loved young boys, especially Puerto Ricans, and truly loved teaching composition, performance, and theory. (Joe Bataan, one of the defining forces in Latin soul/boogaloo music in the United States, studied with Francis also. He made both of us aware of our natural musical gifts and cultivated it by exhorting us to be great and requiring us to listen to the beauty of classical music and harmonies that were not so "street." Joe Bataan was released from Coxsackie and built a thriving music career as a singer and bandleader.) Francis loved my singing voice and suggested I take up an instrument. The alto sax became my favorite, and I labored long and hard to play well. I worked on "Desafinado" for the annual talent show with squeaks, squawks, and cursing. I never could approximate the cool sound of tenor saxophonist Stan Getz.

The show came, I failed. Played the first sixteen bars competently, then destroyed the improvisation. I just wasn't ready. There was slight applause. I left the sax business and never went back. Trouble started when I was given an "end date" at my first parole board hearing, meaning I had nine months before I'd be released. Mr. Francis tried to teach me all he knew, every bit of his musical knowledge, within that nine-month period. That's all the time he had. I didn't understand his frustration. For me, nine months was a lifetime, so . . . sometimes I was receptive to the lesson plans, other times I wasn't, too busy with the very real business of prison in the present and worried about what I would do when I got out. Francis would roar at me in almost operatic style.

"How dare you take a talent so lightly. You must apply yourself, you must be diligent, you must be committed," and then with a flourish, pre–Luciano Pavarotti, he would whip out a huge pocket square reeking of his cologne; wipe the beads of sweat from his face, neck, and bald head; and in a dramatic finale, head down, would exclaim mournfully, " . . . and you must sacrifice."

Sometimes, we would burst into applause, which he might have taken as a compliment, but for us it was pure theater. We appreciated it. Hell, all we needed was popcorn. At the six-month juncture, Mr. Francis approached me with the strangest proposition that I felt was a thinly veiled sexual overture: "Would you consider staying here for another year, voluntarily?" with my only prison job being the formal study of music.

With my best acting instincts, I turned and quietly said I'd think about it. I was repulsed, revolted. He had to be insane to even consider the thought that I would put my life on the line for another year in order to learn music. When I asked him for outside contacts to pursue my musical studies, he said no one would understand me and he felt he was the only one who could teach me. I knew the rejection had to be timed perfectly, or I'd bear the brunt of Francis's rage. I went over the rejection speech at least one hundred times, word by word, syllable by syllable. If I told too many people, Francis would be humiliated and I'd be seen as a rat. What surprised me was that while the inmates I confided in were in agreement that freedom was more precious than education, they told me I should really think about it, that it was rare that anyone would take that much of an interest in an inmate like me. Returning to the streets, they said, was not going to be a festive event for too long: no job, no friends, no future. I had to be clear about my goals, they told me, or end up back in the joint. I lied to them. I wasn't clear about goals, but I sure as hell wanted to get the fuck out of Coxsackie.

It took me a few days, but finally I mustered the courage to talk to Francis one on one. It was late afternoon, rest time, right before dinner. I marched into Francis's office and without pleasantries, without letting him own the space or the moment, I told him I had made the decision to go home. I thanked him for the offer. He was visibly shocked by my almost physical approach. He ground his teeth, his jaw muscles bunching up and then relaxing, methodically, steadily, like a musical beat.

Francis sat quietly, not looking at me, and said he understood, then looked up again and asked, quizzically, if I was sure. I paused for emphasis, inhaled slowly, and then exhaled, "Yes, Mr. Francis. It's my final decision, and I'm very sure."

"Okay," he said softly, "you're dismissed!"

I can tell you the war of wills didn't end that day. Francis tried the worst trick, bottom of the barrel stuff, to get me to assault him. It didn't work but, it almost got me sent to solitary.

There was a coolness, an almost perfect professionalism, in Mr. Francis's demeanor when I walked into our next session. When it started getting serious, I started getting scared. He would order me to do the most menial tasks, tasks that were traditionally the job of the new guys in the class.

The unwritten rule was that seniority, good musicianship, and behavior brought you privileges: private tutoring at the other end of the room with Mr. Francis, where he would let his mask down and magically show you how to resolve chords, how to breathe from the diaphragm in chorale pieces and reach the seemingly impossible notes, how to articulate so that the audience could hear the consonants; the man was a genius. I was denied these perks and suddenly thrust out of the inner sanctum. At this point, the guys in class knew something was up.

Each day became more and more torturous with Francis making fun of every mistake I made in class, sarcasm dripping from his lips with derogatory comments on my height, my culture, my "lack of application to the task at hand." Smiling and laughing good-naturedly was an effective antidote for the first few weeks, but when he started digging into Puerto Rican culture, its "backwardness" and lack of formal music, I started answering back, curtly, nastily. And he responded in kind. He loved to talk about how little I was, how short, cute but no real threat to the outside world. How did I ever get to Coxsackie? There must have been some mistake.

I lost it and shot back, "Yeah, I ended up in the company of professional misfits." That did it.

Francis rose from his stool like an inflated dragon, eyes flaming, sweat popping from his brow like molten lava, screaming in a basso-profundo thunderous voice, "How dare you? How dare you speak to me in such a manner?" and in one lunge grabbed my shirt, pulled me out of the chair, and proceeded to bounce me around the room with his enormous stomach. The guys were laughing hysterically. After all, it wasn't a jailhouse ass-whipping; it was a Mr. Francis move, meant to establish discipline and nothing else. But they weren't watching his face, convulsed, and getting darker by the second. I wasn't about to play into his sick psycho-sexual shit, his belly punching into mine repeatedly as he pinned me against the wall. He was not going to fuck me, not that day, not any day. I felt I was back in the sixth grade with a gay teacher who threatened me with physical harm and I reacted the same way. "Get the fuck off me. You touch me again, I'll kill you." He looked at me, startled. I looked at him, coldly. I meant it. Something snapped. He knew it.

Francis had crossed the line. There was no turning back. He whipped around quickly and screamed to the class, "Call the Captain . . . now!" and then he retreated. I stayed in the corner, my eyes never leaving his face, my body tense but ready. No fists balled up, no fighting stance, just ready. It was over—the lessons, the relationship, the fun of the class, the joy of learning music. The guards came and quickly put me under the clock in the lobby, a move meant to humiliate an inmate and scare everyone else into submission to the rules. I didn't give a shit. I had stood up to the tyrant. And while they left me there during the entire lunch break, the brothers and the whites tried to figure out what the hell happened to the "smart kid."

After six hours, I was escorted to the Captain's office.

"What happened?" was all the Captain asked, dryly, as soon as the door was shut.

He had a kind face, but the lines around his mouth and eyes made it clear that he had seen enough lies and liars to discern between what was real and what was bullshit. I waited for a minute, studying him. Had seen him in the yard, from time to time, crisply pressed white shirt, hat always on, blue uniform pants with razor-sharp creases, official issue patent leather, shiny big black shoes with thick soles, and no expression. He was no-nonsense and he wasn't about to play games with me. So I told him the truth, everything. He listened to every detail without looking at me. Then he said, in an almost sympathetic voice, "This is jail. You do what's told, you understand me?" I nodded assent and then, remembering my manners and jail protocol, said, "Yes, sir." He then issued his decision. Sent me to the worst detail in the joint—the rockpile.

It wasn't the worst turn of events; I wasn't sent to vegetate inside a solitary cell but to an outside work crew to sweat, to smell the sweetness of new grass and the pungency of wet earth, to laugh with guys comfortable in their own strength, a strength born of swinging 16-pound sledgehammers at granite boulders that stared stupidly at you and dared you to tear them apart. We obliged. Every day. And slept well. And nobody, I mean, nobody, messed with us. We were sledgehammering ass kickers. We broke rocks for a living. Imagine what we could do to a rib, a jaw, a human body.

I was in heaven, in heaven with my half-brother, Lucky, who had been to Coxsackie before and had been paroled. Worried about me, he purposely got busted on some simple-ass charge and manipulated the system to end up in the same joint I was in.

We loved each other on the outside but traveled in different circles. We made up for lost time. I was his chisel man, the guy who slammed the iron pike into a cleft of the wall of rock, held it steady with left or right forearm, turned my face away, secure in the knowledge that my partner, my brother, would hit the head of that sucker straight on, drive the spike further in until it stuck, at which point both of us would take turns beating on it, two separate sledgehammers spewing huge chips with rhythm. *Click clang, click clang* all day long. Now, there was always the chance the person swinging the sledgehammer would lose focus, turn his eyes away, angle his swing wrong, not plant his legs firmly in the ground, lose his center of gravity, or the worst, laugh at a joke. That simple misplaced loss of concentration, that one incorrect exhalation of breath or false movement sent men to the hospital with split heads, broken arms, smashed cheekbones, disfigured faces. It happened from time to time. You couldn't think about it. You had to trust the swing man to hit it head on, sparks and all. He had to trust you not to shift the spike in fear of the velocity or the possible burn to head and neck.

I treasured the camaraderie my brother and I shared during that time. When we were children, my father convinced Lucky's mother to let him live with us. Pablo, Margie, and I jumped for joy, they because they had a new sibling who wouldn't beat on them as much as I did, and I because I was relieved of the burden of being the strict older brother. It didn't last long—he missed his mother, and she, though poor and still very street, pestered my father about returning her child. Eventually, my father gave in and returned Lucky to his mom.

While I had always viewed him as a tough gang kid, this time around I saw his beauty, his dedication to family, to protecting me at any cost. He eventually served his time at Coxsackie and was released. On September 16, 1988, Jose "Lucky" Luciano was stomped to death by his "boys" for not sharing the profits and the drugs gained from robbing a local drug dealer. He died on East 111th Street from a ruptured spleen in front of the local Boys' Club in East Harlem. Now, I was alone, and while my newfound status in the rockpile fraternity accorded me a certain respect in the general population, there were still those individuals who had a "thing" with me. They were not bigshots in their jail gangs, but they felt they had a right to bully the "weaklings" in the Middle.

Insults were hurled in passing and a certain amount of grab-assing was par for the course as the inmates would move from their territories in the Big Yard to line up for chow or the march back to the cells. I had avoided most of the crap that passed as fun for most of the year and a half.

I was told, however, by those who knew jail ritual, that the nine months before my release would be trying. There would be those who might try to get me to act out violently and, in turn, lose my chance to go home. Those guys were seen as harder to rehabilitate by the parole board either because of the severity of their crimes or the nature of their personalities, which in essence meant they made a bad impression on their first appearance before the commissioners of the parole board. You always knew who they were. After their rejection, they would slowly walk into the Big Yard, sullen, too quiet, faces twisted with rage, ready to explode because they had been denied freedom.

Fields was like that: a tall, wide, muscular kid from Yonkers who had worked his body down from chubbiness to a comfortable fighting weight. He was strong, fast, quick with the quip and verbal comeback; kept his hair tight and had all his teeth, which meant he had won most of his fights. But with all of that going for him, he wasn't top dog in Coxsackie; he wasn't admired. His physical attributes belied the fact that he had no heart: looked big, sounded big, but when push came to shove, when confronted with a real street dude who liked hurting people, he backed off. So he would mess with the guys who couldn't or wouldn't defend themselves. And then he tried me.

It was a simple act, really. A schoolyard prank that would be laughed off in the city. But we were not in the city or on a playground. We were in jail, and simple acts can stigmatize you, even get you killed. Fields had grabbed my ass on a sunny, uneventful day as I was walking toward my group to line up in the yard, just felt he had the right to reach out, grab me, and say luridly, "How you doing, baby?"

I whirled around, too late to stop him or jump in his face. He was already in line and to have jumped him there would've been an infraction. I did turn around and barked, "Fuck you, you stupid motherfucker" and then stood very still, looking ahead but watching out of the corner of my eye to see if Fields would break rank and come after me. He didn't, but out of the corner of his mouth made the threat slowly, with emphasis on each word.

"No, not fuck me, little boy, I . . . want . . . to . . . fuck . . . you!"

His whole division hooted and laughed until the officer told them to keep it down. The officer didn't hear, didn't care. To their credit, my line stood firm, not laughing, not even smiling. They knew the move on me was a move on them. It could've happened to any of them since my division was known as "the goody-goodys," guys who would probably go home early.

"First of all, you big doofus, your dick is too small," I hissed loudly. "Your mama told me. She said you like boys 'cause you can't do girls. So you can't fuck anything, sucker. You can get fucked up."

Both lines of inmates cracked up, smacking five at the wit of the quip. Fields had been beaten at his own verbal dozens and wasn't about to let it go.

And then he issued the words all inmates hate to hear, "On the lockout, motherfucker. It's on." And then there was quiet. Everybody knew what that meant: a fight to the end, a fight with no quarter asked and no quarter given, until maybe an officer would come across someone's body, unconscious or dead. I mustered up enough courage to whisper loudly, "I'll be waiting for you. Bring your best shit!" but, my legs were trembling and I almost defecated on the spot.

I had three hours to prepare: There'd be lunch, some rest time in the cell, and then the Big Yard and the fight. I was numb.

This guy was huge and powerful. Even blocking his punches was going to hurt. I decided there was only one strategy: Spar for a minute, try to figure out his style, and, before I lost heart, attack with ferocity.

It was a long, torturous three hours. No one said anything to me, no words of encouragement, nothing. And then, we were ushered into the Big Yard. I knew, everybody knew, we had to wait for at least thirty minutes until all the inmates were in the yard, assembled and accounted for, before any action took place. By that time, the guards would relax, take out their cigarettes, talk to each other, and take their eyes off us. Fields and I just watched each other, a weird game of who can unnerve who, who can win before the punches are thrown. We circled each other about fifteen yards apart while the other inmates secretly watched the guards to then give us the signal to go at it.

One of the older inmates, a guy I hardly knew, stayed suspiciously close to me. I was watching him out of the sides of my eyes when, with his head down, he said, in a slow, deep voice, "That nigger just had an appendix operation. He's in no shape to fuck with anybody. Spar a little bit and then hit him with all you got right above his hip, ya hear me? Don't go for the face and don't hesitate. Take that motherfucker out!" And then he disappeared into the crowd. I didn't follow him with my eyes. I would've given him away. His directions were so damn clear they had to be true. Anyway, it was all I had to go on.

Suddenly, a voice barked, "It's on" and Fields approached me like he was in a heavyweight bout at the Garden, head down, moving side to side, street style, knees slightly bent, hands up against his cheeks, and no more smiling. He was not going to grapple. He wanted to rain down on me, get it over with, quickly, painfully. I played the pawn, the sucker, and deflected two strong jabs and one powerful right hand to my chest but, that's all I needed. Grabbed his forearm, held it tightly, and punched the shit out of his rib cage, three, four times, each time putting all my power into it, from my thighs to my hips to my lats, to my shoulder, digging my fist in and up, exhaling hard, the mucus running from my nose, my eyes tearing up. Fields just stood there, didn't move, didn't fall. Just stood there, on his toes, mouth open, eyes bulging, as if he had been shot. When I backed off, I saw the blood seeping through his shirt, slowly spreading from a small circle to all over his stomach. I must've busted his stitches.

Inmate code was total silence when a fight took place, which made the whole scene more eerie. He trembled in freeze-frame and then began to wince and breathe heavily. To his credit, he didn't cry, he didn't scream, he swayed, now flat-footed, one arm holding his ribs, the blood seeping heavily through his fingers, the other hand up to repel the next attack, the final kill. It never came. I backed off, turned around, and walked back quickly to the middle of the yard. There were no whistles, no pandemonium, no drama. The fight was over.

Immediately after that incident, a real new jack, wide-eyed, ignorant, and oblivious to reality came into the joint and was thrown in "The Middle": Steven Zapolsky. He was Jewish American, gawky, uncoordinated, couldn't fight, and loved Asimov science fiction. He was red meat to the predators. I felt I had to defend this guy. The reason was simple—if they attacked him, it would only be a matter of time before the haters came for me . . . again.

Steven was one of maybe three Jews in Coxsackie at the time and it seemed he had been rejected by his own. The others had joined white gangs for survival and took up the cudgel of racism. Just by looking at him, you knew Zapolsky was not a street kid. When he entered the Big Yard he looked like a deer caught in headlights, scared and trembling. Somebody suggested he talk to me.

"Is your name Philip?" he squeaked out.

"Yeah," I answered. "What are you doing here? What did you get arrested for?"

"Homicide," Steven sighed, and it was an exasperated sigh. He had obviously gone through these questions before.

"This guy tried to rob my house and when we told him no, he tried to hurt my little brother, my family. So I killed him."

I didn't react. Just stayed quiet for a minute looking away from the kid.

"Me too."

"You too?"

Steven had no fuckin' jail etiquette; God, was he ignorant. Whatever came into his mind, he blurted out.

"So what happened, you actually killed somebody?"

I had to laugh. Zapolsky was not the sharpest knife in the drawer, but he was refreshingly honest. "Nah. Somebody beat my brother. I beat him. One of my guys stabbed him and he died. End of story."

Steve looked at me admiringly, like I was some kind of Mafia don.

"So, you didn't kill him. The other guy did it. So, why are you here?" Steve persisted. "Because, schmuck, I was involved, I was an accessory, I was the ringleader. So . . . since I organized the whole thing I got hit with an attempted manslaughter charge."

As he began to open his mouth with another dumb thing to say, I told him to shut up, " . . . and stay close to me. With your fucking 'brilliant' questions, you're sure to attract the wrong kind of attention here. Just shut up and watch your back."

So now I was a caretaker. But, why not? Diablo did it for me in Brooklyn. And I was just as scared as Zapolsky. I thought to myself how weird life was. Muslims defended me in the Brooklyn House of Detention and now I'm defending a Jewish kid in a state reformatory. The Harlem 6—Malik, Raheem, Billy, Craig, Turk—all of them would've been dumbfounded if they knew what I was doing. But maybe not. They were the ones who taught me that humanity has no color.

Anyway, I took a liking to Steven. I don't know what it is with me and Jews; I just love the culture, the food, the humor, the sense of family and scholarship, Judaism itself. I just love it. Always have. I mean I walk into a Jewish deli or bakery and I'm home. I swoon over the smells, love the accents, the arguments over Torah or Israel and the Arabs, love Myron Cohen and I'm crazy about Menachem Schneerson, the late Rebbe of the Lubavitch Clan from Crown Heights. He had the gentlest eyes and smile, looked like

Santa Claus in black clothing, and gave dollars out. How could you hate somebody like that?

For the next few months, Steven bored me to tears with his rendition of the plots of Issac Asimov science fiction novels. I tried to teach him how to make a hard fist, how to punch, where to punch, to no avail. He just wasn't a fighter. He taught me a little of the Hebrew alphabet, general Jewish history, and Jewish diet customs. But jail was not for him. They busted him all the time for masturbating, even during the daytime. Berated him a lot. Laughed at him, ridiculed him. He was the institutional oddball. A few months later, he was transferred out of my division, suddenly. He had some measure of safety in division A2 and he had me. Leaving our group didn't bode well for him. He broke down and wrapped his hands around a scalding-hot pipe one winter day. Didn't cry out. They found him too late. They smelled the flesh, they said. Burned half his hands off. Steve got his wish; he was transferred out of Coxsackie. I felt it was my fault. Why didn't I catch the signals? I went over and over our conversations. All the telltale signs were there; why didn't I do something about it? I did nothing. Just protected him physically when what he needed was an internal defense system, one that would lead him to believe in himself, to fight back if attacked.

I felt personally responsible and took to walking endlessly around this imaginary track inside the prison, eyes down, hands in my pockets, not speaking for a week. It was obvious to everyone in the Big Yard that something was up, but I felt no need to vent. Just wanted to process the events, figure it out and try to forgive myself. MacArthur, a young, light-skinned, heavily muscled inmate friend of mine, would defy the rules of the Black Wall and come out of the boundary lines to walk with me, silently.

Usually "Mac" would give me a pat on the back before he left the track to go back to his friends. But I noticed a lingering of his hand, as the days wore on, an almost passionate grabbing me around the neck and shaking my body. I felt uncomfortable, queasy. And then, one day, as he left to go back to his group, he looked at me straight, and said, seriously, "I love you, brother."

Now, there were two ways to look at this: a warrior declaration of bonding and loyalty or a budding gay love, not unheard of in jail. By the soft look of his gaze, by the increasing pressure of his embrace, I knew MacArthur was falling in love . . . with me! And he didn't care who knew about it.

Diablo had warned me about this. "You can't even look like you dig somebody in here and you can't be somebody's homo dreamboy, ya hear me? You'll be labeled a faggot, the rest of your life, inside and out."

I had to put a stop to the friendship. It would be hard on Mac. I'm not sure he even knew what he was feeling or doing. But it had to end.

For a few days, I purposely avoided Mac, hard to do in a closed environment, with everyone attentive to details and nuance, pecking order and power, disrespect, and relationships. Finally, to his credit, after a few days he crossed from the Black territory line into the Middle and approached me.

"What's going on in your head, brother?" I knew that though my instincts were right about his "love" for me, still, he was a good friend who would kill or die to protect me. In jail, that kind of warrior-love is priceless and I'd be throwing it away by telling him our friendship was over because I felt he was gay and how that would look to the other men in the jail.

"Mac," I said, "we've gotten real close in the last year. You're my boy and you kept me from almost going insane. When no one else stood by my side, when people thought I was crazy for leaving the gangs and the walls, you walked with me and dared anyone to jump . . . ."

Mac was looking hard at me, his face serious beyond his sixteen years. He knew. "And?" he asked as we walked around the track the third time.

"You've been too physical with me, brother, too lovey-dovey, and people are beginning to look at us funny."

Mac looked at me with incredulity. I had defied the tradition of racism in prison. He had defied his race by crossing the invisible boundaries to hang with me, a pariah. *And now I was concerned with what people thought?* I could see every one of those questions on his face. "Fuck these niggers! And fuck what they think! You do your own time in here. You're my brother and I don't care whether these Black motherfuckas like it or not. They can kiss my Black . . . ."

I stopped him in mid-sentence as he began to look around for the culprits, his eyes glowering. "Mac, it's not them, man . . . it's me. I'm beginning to feel funny about it. And I know you love me, brother, but the hugging and shit is getting a little too personal. I love you, blood, and if anyone fucks with you in here, I'll be right beside you, but for now, we've got to let each other go. I don't want anyone to get the wrong idea and . . . really . . . I don't want you to hurt anyone and lose your parole." It was a lame excuse, but I had tears in my eyes as I was explaining and I think he emotionally cut through the bullshit and felt my conflict. We walked in silence, around and around the track the fourth time, until it was time to line up to go back to our cells.

He turned me around with his huge hands on both my shoulders. Now his eyes were full of tears.

"Is this what you really want, baby? Really?"

I told him the truth. "Yeah, Mac. Yes."

"I respect that," Mac said and suddenly pulled me into his chest, hugging me hard, "And I respect you."

Before turning away for the last time, he grabbed my hand, shook it warmly, and said it again: "I love you, Philip." And walked away.

My time was up. The waiting, the anxiety was nerve-wracking; never knowing if the parole board would deny my freedom.

The last ninety days in Coxsackie were hell, and I stayed quiet, vigilant, and neutral. No gossip, no offhand comments about jail or inmates.

As I was walked out the doors of Coxsackie, a German American correctional officer, one who professed Christianity and would talk through the open porthole of my cell door for hours about Jesus and the benefits of salvation and forgiveness, said, "You'll be back. They always come back."

I didn't even turn around. And I didn't answer loudly for fear of being remanded back to that place in Hell.

As I walked briskly to the state car in an ill-fitting suit, state issued brogan boots and some subway money to report immediately to my new parole officer on Gold Street in Manhattan, I whispered "Don't hold your breath."

I never returned.

Chapter 8

||||

Culture Shock

MY MOTHER HEARD the knock on the door, flung it open thinking it was her younger son or daughter, and went back to cooking the afternoon meal in the tiny kitchenette stove of the one-bedroom apartment at 20 West 125th Street. I have rarely seen my mother cry. She's old school, like her mother, used to confronting life with a scowl and a terse comment. When she saw her firstborn in the doorway, she dropped the greasy fork she was using to fry the chops and simply stopped moving. We just looked at each other. She started to tremble as the tears rolled down her cheeks, those usually active arms and hands that beat me and caressed me hanging limply at her sides, as if she were paralyzed. "Hi, Mom, I'm home," was all I could say.

I was afraid she would fall so I rushed toward her. We both collapsed into each other's arms, my mother sobbing uncontrollably and praising God loudly, me grinning broadly, eyes closed, reveling in the smell of my mother's neck and hair, then putting my right ear on her chest to hear her heartbeat, the way I used to do when I was a child, she continuing to kiss my hair, my left ear and cheek and then pulling my face up to kiss my forehead, both cheeks, her tears streaming down now as she loudly thanked God for my return. I had never seen her like this. In an instant, I realized what she had suffered during the last two years, the indescribable pain, the profound suffering, the loss of her eldest son, her confidante, guide, and protector.

Until the age of sixteen, I guided her through bad dreams, welfare regulations, my father's vacillation, interpretations of the Bible, Pentecostal Christianity, and the streets of our lives. In defending my brother, in defending

84

my family honor, I had left her alone to fend for herself, with no one to back her up. My brother and sister were too young, and in those days, she didn't reveal too much of her inner conflicts to them. With me, her oldest, she was real and admittedly scared a lot of the time and said so. But we held hands and forged ahead through promises of checks from my father that never arrived and ignorant, racist welfare investigators who pried into her personal life to see if she had a man or a TV in her home so they could cut off the welfare checks and the allotments for clothing. She would show me her secret writing and I'd exhort her to send the pieces to *Reader's Digest*. She never did. Never felt she was a good enough writer. She was. In that one tearful embrace, I felt the entire history of this woman, Aurora, my mother: her poor childhood, her abandonment by my father, the fears of inadequacy of being a single mother, the temptation to just leave everything and live her own life, and the faith and extraordinary discipline that kept her going. It all came out in that one embrace, and I just kept telling her I would never go to jail again. For anything criminal.

Coming back to Harlem the summer of 1966 was pure joy; it was the family I loved, my birthplace, the village where I felt most secure. Here the guys could hang together, goof off, love the girls, get high, and dance to each other's rhythms with no hang-ups, no cultural barriers. It wasn't Brooklyn with its hard-edged gang ethic of "take no prisoners," "let's see if you can kick my ass" attitude. It was a multicultural summer soul dance with soup made from South Carolina butter beans and Puerto Rican pernil. I was home again . . . but while being back home was wonderful, I had to do something, had to find work.

Before releasing me, the New York state prison system demanded that I have a promise of a job. I don't know how my mother got HARYOU-ACT, a Harlem anti-poverty program, to offer me a job upon my release, but that promise got me out of jail. My mother confided in me that my incarceration gave her much-needed relief, some breathing room, a break from the constant worry that something tragic might happen to me in my triple life as son, student, and gang member. My younger brother, Pablo, courageous but not as talkative as me, stepped up his game and became the Luciano standard-bearer while I was away; he became one of the leaders of the Franklin High School Student Movement along with future Puerto Rican poet Victor Hernández Cruz. Benjamin Franklin High School had recently transitioned from having a predominantly Sicilian student population to one that was Puerto Rican and Black.

The neighborhood was changing, albeit violently, and both the old guard Italian neighbors and some of the teachers and administrators at Franklin couldn't stomach the new wave of dark-skinned Spanish speakers and southern sharecroppers. So, my brother and Victor fought them back with walkouts, protest assemblies, student strikes, and hallway confrontations. The mission had given Paul authority; he was more serious, less prone to horseplay and irresponsibility. He took the job of protecting Mom and Margie seriously and made sure there was food and money in the house outside of the welfare monies we were provided by the city. He never minded working hard.

I now had to do my part. I noticed, however, that after the initial joy of arrival, Paul became moody and retiring. I had taken the top spot in the family again. He was back to being the middle child, not the man he wanted to be. And I, giddy with freedom, spoiled with being the first child and self-absorbed, noticed but never brought it up.

I walked into a wide second-floor office space of HARYOU-ACT, gave my name, and waited. Within half an hour, a short, attractive, energetic, Black woman with a closely cropped Afro strode toward me.

"My name is Miss Francis," she said authoritatively. "What can I do for you?" I quickly checked her out as I walked behind her, beautifully muscled legs connected to perfectly proportioned hips and butt, V-shaped back and nicely defined arms and shoulders. In jail I had learned to size people up quickly. Turned out she was a dancer and took classes in her spare time. When she turned around I looked into a pure African face: broad forehead; wide, confident eyes; a cute pug nose with a slight flare; fat cheeks; and a mouth accustomed to laughter. Her teeth were straight and beautiful. And I just stared . . . for a minute.

I hadn't seen or been close to a woman in two years.

Apparently, she was used to this type of scrutiny from paroled male offenders and wasn't fazed. She stared right back.

"You finished?" she asked boldly. "Do you want a job or don't you?"

"Yes, ma'am," I stammered.

"Well, what can you do?"

"Uhh . . . I can type."

"How fast?"

"Umm . . . about 50 to 60 words a minute."

"Really?" Miss Francis said in a genuinely surprised tone of voice. "Well, let's see: I want you to go into that corner office over there, sit down, and type these letters for a few minutes," she said as she stood up and handed me a book of business letters and memoranda.

"I'll be checking for mistakes," she said curtly, "Go!"

I walked into an empty office, ran through the exercises with no white-out or erasure tape, and plowed through it, typing even more than I needed to in the time allotted. Got up, walked into her office, plopped the pages on her desk, and declared, "Finished."

"Um hmm," was all Miss Francis said, then proceeded to redline the work. Every word she circled or crossed out was like a knife slashing my flesh. I was crestfallen. I had blown it. My jail typing probably was not up to par with industry standards. "Hmm," was all Miss Francis muttered under her breath. "Sit down, Mr. Luciano." I sat gingerly on the edge of the wooden chair, ready to be rejected, ready to walk out quickly and mentally beat myself up on the way home.

Miss Francis looked up at me from the typed papers, leaned back in her squeaky chair, and just looked at me expressionless.

I couldn't bear it. Why didn't she just say what she wanted to say? Why the suspense? There was no need to torture me. I put my head down, my confidence broken.

"Look at me," she barked. "You did well. Do you know that? I'm surprised. I gave you difficult business letters and memos. The vocabulary was intense . . . and you know what the funny thing is, you typed the difficult words correctly. Where you messed up was in spacing and some punctuation which I'll attribute to nervousness. Do you know the meanings of these words?"

I had won at something. It didn't matter if I got the job or not. "Yes, ma'am," I answered softly. "Every one of them."

"I believe you. I'm not even going to try to test you on them. Tell me something. Have you ever thought of college?"

My eyes hardened, my jaw stiffened. She wanted to humiliate me. I came in looking for a simple gig and she was talking fantasy.

"No, ma'am. I just need a job. Nothing else."

Her eyes bored through me as if she needed to know something deeper. And then she started preaching.

"You are more than this," she blurted out. "I'll get you a damned job, but something tells me you're meant for more. I don't know why I'm saying this, why I'm feeling this, must be the ancestors, but you need to go to school. Come with me, I'm gonna test you myself!"

She took me into another room, a classroom with those Formica desks attached to chairs, walked out for a minute, came back in, and plopped a sheath of exam papers in front of me.

"I'll be back in an hour," Miss Francis said professionally. "Do as much as you can and leave nothing unanswered. Anything you skip will be counted as a wrong answer, you understand?"

Of course, I fuckin understood. Why was she leaving me alone? Why was she doing this? I never really thought of college, well . . . maybe some jail dreams of me on a campus with a white cardigan, a red letter on its breast and blondes around me. But that was Archie, Betty, Veronica shit, straight out of the comic books. Nothing real. No one in my family ever talked about college, no one had ever attended college. This sudden exam was bullshit when all I wanted to do was get a job and stay out of jail. I finished the exam early and waited in the room, staring at the white walls with no pictures. In precisely an hour, Miss Francis showed up, picked up my exam, and told me to wait in the lobby.

Thirty minutes later she rushed out of her office toward me, excitedly shouting, "Do you know what you did? Do you know what you did?"

What the hell was wrong? Did I not follow instructions?

"You aced this exam—multiple choice, essay questions, everything. You don't belong in an office, you need to go to college!"

It was summer, 1966, so she found me a temporary job with the Shakespeare Recording Company doing some filing. That fall I entered Queens College under the auspices of the CUNY SEEK (Search for Education, Elevation and Knowledge) program. It was the beginning of my revolutionary period, a paradigm shift from streets to school, ideology uneasily weaving itself with religion, critical thought tempering impulse. Getting admitted to college, however, wasn't that easy. Miss Francis sent me through the CUNY system. City College said no. Brooklyn College said no. They gave me all kinds of excuses. Would I act out on campus? Was I really ready for college-level courses, the stress of exams? It boiled down to no one's wanting to take a chance on a paroled ex-con. And then, the real question, the gut-churning fear of administrators: Did they want a parolee convicted of attempted manslaughter to touch shoulders with white middle-class kids who knew nothing of guns, gangs, and jail? Miss Francis, bless her soul, didn't give up. She heard about an experimental program at Queens College, one that took chances. And off to Flushing, Queens, I went. That fall day changed my life.

Getting off the subway at Continental Avenue in Forest Hills was a cultural shock: neat homes and apartment buildings, clean streets and folks who seemed to walk without fear. I felt like a tourist on the Q25-34 bus to the campus, craning my neck to watch the private houses with yards and tall trees, people going about their day and no police cars. It was a scene out of *Father Knows Best*, the old '50s sitcom, fathers and mothers taking their kids to school, taking out the trash, picking up their newspapers from the front yard. Was I in Connecticut? It was just too normal, no visible drama. On that bus, I immediately relaxed, the tension drained. I was home. This is the place I dreamed of, where I wanted to be.

As the bus approached the campus, it was like looking at the proverbial city on the hill, heaven. Some modern tall buildings mixed with large bungalows, Spanish-style houses, grass, and quiet. I asked a few students and professors where a certain building was and there were no stares, just smiles. There were no Black people in sight.

After some confused meandering, I got to the building, walked into a basement office, and waited to be ushered into the office of the man heading the SEEK program, Joe Mulholland.

He was a bruiser, built like a fireplug, short, a bit paunchy, but powerfully built. His smile was genuine but cautious.

Sitting down, finishing a conversation on the phone, he motioned for me to sit down. Hanging up, he hit me hard!

"I'm not one for small talk. I'll assume you're here because you want to learn something. And you just got out the slammer so you're still adjusting. I've convinced these college people that former convicts would make great students. I've got four on campus already. We've got one slot left and it's yours, if you want it." I stammered some corny, grateful response and Mulholland cut me off quickly. "Don't thank me just yet. I hate bullshit and I'm going to shoot it to you straight. You'll be the guy with less time served in the joint which means you may or may not have learned your lesson. You fuck this up and I'll ride you to Hell on a motorcycle. You will study and if you need help, I'll get you remediation classes and tutors. But you better be honest with me. This is not going to be easy. There are a few assholes out here who don't want ex-cons on campus and relish the thought of you failing. This will not happen, understand?"

I nodded my head, said nothing. We stayed quiet, staring at each other. I liked this working-class, thick-necked, burly motherfucker. He spoke my language. Finally, I spoke, keeping my eyes on him. "How the hell do you know so much about us?"

"I'm a former parole officer. Somebody gave me a chance to get an education. I'd like to give somebody else a chance. Are you ready?"

"Yep" was all I had to say.

"Good, you've got some papers to sign. My secretary will guide you through it. Be here next week, on time."

When he struggled to get out of his chair, I figured it was his weight. He bent down and placed one of his legs in an upright position, used the desk as support, and literally pushed himself up to see me to the door. It's when I noticed his leg. It was useless, paralyzed, had a heavy steel brace attached to it. He hobbled toward me and I instinctively rushed toward him to help steady his body. He waved me away. "Polio. Caught it when I was a kid. Lived with it ever since. Went through hell. School, bullies, society. And I beat 'em all. So I know about the cards being stacked against you."

And then he gave me the biggest bear hug a man can give another man and I instinctively kissed his cheek, Puerto Rican style.

"Good luck," he said softly and I closed the door behind me.

I was in. I was a college student.

That semester I suffered from adjustment problems with study habits, carried big books, and took courses with names like Aesthetics, Political Science, and Physics. I was so overwhelmed I wanted to quit; it couldn't be true. Dreams just don't materialize that quickly.

The women on campus were gorgeous: curious, inquisitive, excited by the potential danger of a walk on the wild side with a former convict. There were stares in the cafeteria, some hostile and overtly racist, but the majority of looks were purely curious, as in 'Who the hell is this Black guy?' I loved it and soon was talking and laughing with fellow students as if I had been born a Jewish New Yorker and lived in Forest Hills. I met their moms, their bubbes, screwed in their bedrooms when we were supposed to be studying, and developed a real love for their culture.

My Pentecostal upbringing was so Old Testament Orthodox, the students, marveling at my grasp of the Torah, thought I was Jewish anyway. They rarely asked, I rarely told. But the fact that I knew more about Judaism than they did impressed them. My mother believed that the Jewish people were truly God's Chosen Ones. They were blessed with the original Covenant with God, a convenant which stated that while God would punish Israel for wrongdoing and not keeping their part of the spiritual/religious bargain, they were His people, His beloved, and He would always love and ultimately protect, rescue, and prosper them. He would never forsake them, and woe to their enemies.

From Sunday school to evening services, seven days a week, three times on Sunday, Puerto Rican Pentecostal Assembly of God parishioners were regaled with the stories, the heroes, the judgments, and the tragedies of the Old Testament. And while David doesn't receive as much recognition in modern Judaism as does Moses, we were fed the David and Goliath story from the breast through the rest of our lives. Like David, we saw ourselves as underdogs. It was the Puerto Rican response to discrimination; colonization; racism; sheer urban brutality by cops, teachers, bosses, and welfare workers; and just being marginalized. Sampson and Samuel, David and Daniel, Joseph and Jonah, Solomon and Sheba, Issac and Isaiah—we were bombarded with the stories of the glories of obedience to God and the horrible consequences of betrayal of oath.

To this day, you will find very little anti-Semitism among Puerto Rican fundamentalists. It is a sin. We were taught to admire and emulate the Jewish people and their religion, to remember their role in history and to bury, deep in our hearts, the fact that Jesus, the son of God, came from their lineage, their tribe. And whether they believed in Him as Messiah or not, they were not to be messed with, for the wrath of Heaven would descend upon those who mistreated them. I just never felt uncomfortable in a Jewish setting, home, shul, or school. And Queens College was their school.

I took an instant liking to four teachers: Sol Resnick for political science; Joan Meinhardt for English; Erna Sensiba, who, though not my teacher, identified with Black and brown students, having suffered the ravages of the Holocaust in a displaced persons camp in Europe after the war; and John McDermott for Contemporary Civilization, who taught Aesthetics, an honors course in philosophy.

Sol was the proverbial thinker and worrier, always twirling a strand of thick black hair around his finger as he lectured, pacing nervously in front of the class. He wore dark suits, teacher suits, but they were always rumpled. He never smelled, he just didn't care about superficialities like clothing. His was a ruggedly handsome oval face, always in need of a shave, long nose, sad eyes that almost forgave you for betraying him and his ideals, small, thin lips that betrayed his total generosity and love, a manly forehead that he often squinched when he didn't get the answer he wanted in class, large ears, and beautifully imperfect teeth with canines a little larger than usual, but clean. Sol rarely smiled, and when he did, it looked like a sneer. I know he didn't mean it, but I guess no one ever told him that when smiled he looked menacing. And he was mercurially temperamental with his peers. I saw him screaming down conservatives and assholes right on campus. He wasn't afraid of too much, which was pretty amazing for a scholar.

Sol Resnick had a tall body that looked like a coiled spring. You never knew when he was going to pop up and catapult into your face. Students, faculty, and administrators steered clear of him unless they had to engage. Sol was not about small talk or flattery. And the Black and brown students adored him, because he was real. He never patronized us, never assumed we couldn't do the work, and though it seemed at times he was conversing with himself, head down, eyes to the floor, he knew who had read the material and who hadn't. He would jab his finger at me and almost yell, "Why do you believe Marcuse? Because he's in a book? Because he's a professor? Question him. Does his thinking make sense to you? Does it jibe with what you know and what you've experienced?" Sol Resnick refused shoddy thinking. "Think," he would scream, "your brain is all you've got."

It was Sol who started me on the road to revolution with his fiery lectures on the French Revolution and Rousseau, the American Revolution, and Tom Paine, Herbert Marcuse and *One-Dimensional Man*, C. Wright Mills and *The Power Elite*, Hans Morganthau and *Politics Among Nations*, Karl Marx. I became addicted to political science. I saw reasons for poverty, racism, oppression, and read everything, no matter how contradictory the messages were: *The Federalist Papers* and Fanon's *The Wretched of the Earth*; Wilhelm Reich on orgone energy and Sigmund Freud on dreams and sexuality; Sidney Hook, the Marxist theoretician, and Adam Smith, the capitalist apologist; *Asylums* by Erving Goffman; *Growing Up Absurd* by Paul Goodman; *Technics and Civilization* by Lewis Mumford; everything, including Che Guevara, Fidel, Kwame Nkrumah, Sékou Touré, Stokely Carmichael and Charles V. Hamilton's trailblazing *Black Power: The Politics of Liberation*, Malcolm X, John Williams, the amazing books and essays by James Baldwin, the fierce writings of Richard Wright, Susan Sontag, Jean-Paul Sartre; it was exciting, exhausting, and filled me with enthusiasm for each new day.

Sol's passion for truth, for justice, for scholarship infected/affected me profoundly. There was one slight difference between him and me: I wanted to change the world *now*, to begin armed struggle immediately, first by educating, then organizing, then fighting. Sol thought I was a bit mad, and when I'd come to him, my face flush with the excitement of battle, after a rally or march against the war in Vietnam that was attacked by police, he'd look at me and shake his head sadly.

"Why are you doing this, Felipe?" he'd ask in the quiet of his classroom.

"Because you taught me, Sol. You opened my eyes. You can't shut them, once you see what's going on, Sol. You taught me to fight."

He would look at me with those sad, rabbinical eyes, wrinkle his nose, take off his glasses, rub his eyes wearily, and say, "I taught you to think, not to die."

There were many times I'd pass him in the hallways, screaming at another professor, "You're an idiot. I don't know why I'm even talking to you" and then mutter to himself as he hurried to his next class, "What a schmuck!"

I never laughed openly in front of him, none of us did. The one time I innocently asked what seemed to be the problem, he whirled around and shouted, "It's none of your fuckin business. Why are you listening to my conversation? Get to your next class and you better have read the materials. On time, Felipe, on time." That was Sol. Beneath that rough, take-no-prisoner scholarship, he was one of most compassionate, tolerant men I've ever met.

I fell in love with his colleague and friend Joan Meinhardt, my English professor. After weeks of her helping me work through an application for Cornell's School of Industrial and Labor Relations, a school in which I was almost guaranteed a seat, thanks to Miss Leahy, a speech therapy teacher, I asked Joan if she had any romantic feelings toward me. It was a bold move, a student asking a teacher if she cared for him, not to mention the color/culture question.

I was aware that this kind of crossing-the-professional-line relationship was taboo. I was prepared for rejection, having spoken for hours to my best friend, a decorated Vietnam corpsman, Hector Rivera, a.k.a. Frenchy, who had several affairs with older women under his belt. "Fuck it," he advised me. "You have nothing to lose. You think she's spending her precious spring break helping you with this application to Cornell because you're bright? She likes you, dummy . . . a lot. You gotta find out how much, so . . . pop the question. If it works out, you got your woman; if not, say you hope you didn't offend her and go back to being student and teacher."

So, there we were, Joan and I, in the back of Caffe Reggio on Bleecker Street, drinking black coffee and munching on Italian pastry, when I let it all hang out. "Joan, I like you. I've liked you from the moment I walked into your class. Look, let me stop right here . . . I'm in love with you and I need to know if you have feelings toward me, not teacher/student . . . man and woman."

Joan took her eyeglasses off, pursed her lips, clasped her fingers under her chin, looked me straight in the eyes, and whispered, "Felipe . . . sweetheart . . . why did it take you so long to ask? Couldn't you tell? I spend all my waking hours with you. Yes, I'm in love with you, have been for a long time. All my friends know, Sol, Erma . . . ." I was really taken aback. "Sol knows?'

"He's known for a long time."

"And what did he say?"

"He told me to go for it. He thinks you're wonderful."

Heaven happened on Bleecker Street during spring break in 1966; my angel was in front of me, holding my hand, the other angels were singing and my favorite professor, Sol Resnick, approved of the relationship. If I had died that day, that moment, I would've fulfilled my destiny, to find love, the right love, tantamount to connecting with God Almighty. Nothing was more precious. I was in love. And I never sent the application to Cornell.

I adjusted to the collegiate mode of dress instantly. On the streets, during the gang days, I was known as a Peter Prep boy, which meant I dressed in the uniform of a private-school kid; chinos, blazers with elbow patches, button-down shirts, Brooks Brothers diagonally striped ties, Fred Braun shoes and belts, duffel coats in the winter, and a splash of Jade East or Canoe to carry the image to the bust. It helped me escape police dragnets more than once after a gang fight.

Because of my dress and vocabulary, my escapes from the police were a source of anger, envy, and humor on the block. The older guys admired the smoothness of the strategy; some close friends tried to imitate it but couldn't quite replicate the script or the role. My enemies inside the gang just seethed with repressed anger. But they never ratted me out.

There was an ethic, a gang code in the '50s and '60s that went beyond ego and personal vendettas. If you were part of the collective, you were family. And you never turned on family.

If you were the only one of your gang caught in a gang fight, you accepted the consequences. You prided yourself on not snitching, not turning others in. To this day, I feel twinges of guilt for having broken that code, telling police that John stabbed and killed Larry. It doesn't keep me up at nights but does stick in my memory like a piece of white lint on black velcro.

While dressing collegiate was easy, scholastically the transition from jail to college was difficult. Command of the language and verbosity were not enough in the classroom. One had to translate abstract ideas into written compositions, and while I could think and speak of my ideas about the subject matter, it was quite another matter to compose the readings and classroom lectures into class papers. I also had to cram those ideas into my head for exams. I hated them, feared them, and I would spend anxious days before the exams agonizing over whether I had the stuff to pass or not. That year, 1966, I passed my exams, with a D plus in Physics and an A plus in Philosophy.

I moved into Joan's large studio apartment at 100 Bank Street in the West Village.

The lifestyle was liberating, easygoing: books, scholarly debates, casual strolls through the labyrinth of narrow streets in the Village, hand-in-hand, lunch at the Chez Brigitte, Greenwich Street off Seventh Avenue South, dinners at the Peacock Café on West 4th Street off Sixth Avenue, the Sunday-morning ritual of almond croissants and black coffee and reading the *Times* at Sutter's bakery on Greenwich Street, an occasional chamber music concert and passionate lovemaking throughout with Joan teaching me how to satisfy her slowly, how to make love lying down rather than standing up in the rushed and selfish style of the project hallways.

The relationship with Joan Meinhardt colored everything—my deciding not to go to Cornell, my present and my future. I realized we'd never have kids; she was fourteen years older than I and that as we got older I'd probably have to take care of her, if she took ill, and, after a graduate degree, assuming I did well as an undergrad at Queens College, I'd probably go into teaching college English or political science. I was so enthralled with college life and new learning that I wanted to share it with other students, Black and white. I asked the president's office for and was given permission to teach a non-matriculation political science course on campus. Once a week, I took Sol Resnick's passionate, red-hot dialogue and excellent syllabus and McDermott's cool, laser-like philosophical logic and turned it into a revolutionary Black Power course. The classroom was packed every week.

I was eighteen, Joan was thirty-two, and my mother hated the relationship. At one point, during my student activism, detectives or federal agents visited my mother and said they wanted to talk to me about schools and scholarships.

Mom, never suspicious of anybody, gave them an old address, the only one I gave her, purposely. I knew Mom would accidentally, on purpose, give up information to the authorities to keep me safe: "Better to have you safe in jail than dead out here on the streets."

Deep down inside, and she told me this later, she wanted strangers, cops, teachers, whoever they were, to report this "illicit relationship" to the college authorities. Apparently, the authorities, whoever they were, were not interested in my love life but in my political activities, activities that were becoming more radical the more I listened, the more I read, the more I learned.

I was ripe for revolution after jail; ripe and ready to fight. The Vietnam War was the central organizing point for all races and classes. We all felt the war had to end. My mother cared nothing about global affairs; Jesus was the central tenet in her life . . . and me.

She wanted this affair to end and didn't care how she accomplished that goal. It did end eventually, but the "secret" of my illicit relationship never got out beyond our little professional circle at Queens College.

With Joan, I experienced another quality of life, scholarly debates with dry humor rather than with raucous arguments ending in fistfights or worse; summer vacations in New Hampshire rather than at Riis Beach or Orchard Beach or Coney Island, beef bourguinon rather than carne guisada, tweed jackets rather than denim, and a mental process that required thoughtful deliberation rather than an automatic, emotional response.

The only conflict I had with Joan and my new liberal friends was racism and how to fight it. They believed strongly that education and the electoral process were the way to combat discrimination and the murders of Black and brown activists and children in America. I argued forcefully for revolutionary organization and self-defense. "No people, no culture, no nation has ever been given its freedom by an oppressor," I would shout over the guitar strains of Max's Kansas City's new bands or the conversational din of the new restaurants we'd discover.

"America did it, Israel did it, why not people of color?"

Joan would get livid and scream, and then, eventually, her face would drain and she would say softly, "I don't want you to die." It was the one issue that eventually broke us up.

Chapter 9

East Wind and The Last Poets

SINCE GETTING OUT of jail in mid-1966, I instinctively knew I needed something besides college and clerical work. I needed a creative outlet. Victor Hernández Cruz, already a published poet of a now-famous book called *Snaps*, suggested I visit a loft called the East Wind on East 125th Street run by a group of Black wordsmiths called "The Last Poets." In August of '68, I walked from the Gut Theater where Victor was resident poet on 102nd Street to 125th between Fifth and Madison avenues. And there I met him, one of the most brilliant, creative, crazy, eccentric minds I've ever encountered, a soul who would have an indelible impact on my life, a giant of a yin/yang genius, Gylan Kain. Man, was I in for a ride.

The musty-smelling building was of weird construction, with a large L-shaped loft on the second floor. Climbed the stairs, knocked on the door, heard a menacing shout of "Come in!" and there he was, sprawled out on a bridge chair, in the dark, on a makeshift stage, by himself.

"Waddaya want?" he spat out, his eyes piercing even in the dark.

"I heard you're looking for a poet, someone to join your group."

"Who told you that?"

"Victor Cruz," I whispered nervously. Maybe he didn't know him.

"Oh, yeah. Victor . . ." and then Kain smiled that fuckin' smile that's both demonic and heavenly.

"Yeah, I know Victor. He's a good poet, very lyrical; I've read his stuff. So . . . .?"

"Well," I gulped, "he thought I could work with you . . . uhh, you know, write, help around?"

"So, what the fuck can you do? You got some poems, where've you read?" And then he paused. "Who the fuck are you?"

I jumped into my rehearsed soliloquy. "My name is Felipe Luciano. I just got out of jail for murder. I got a chance to go to Queens College. I read my ass off. I like Plato and Nietzsche and fighting. I'm a Black Puerto Rican who was raised in the Pentecostal Church and got real, real problems with their repressive shit. And if I don't find something to do real quick, I'm gonna go crazy in this motherfucka. This is not the Harlem I remember."

Kain stared at me for a long time, in silence. Then, he started to cackle and laugh, bending over with glee. "You, busted for murder, in jail, a gang-banger, in college, a hallelujah motherfucker, Puerto Rican and you call yourself Black? You couldn't make this shit up." And he laughed himself silly for another minute.

Then, straightening himself and getting suddenly serious, he bellowed, "What can you do? Did they teach you anything in the penitentiary, carpentry, anything, 'cause what I need is a set designer and carpenter. Can you build, like, a self-standing doorway, right here, in middle of the stage?"

"Of course, I can," I lied through my teeth. (Abiodun, one of the original founders of The Last Poets, told me he was there at this meeting and knew I was lying.) I was so bad in carpentry in JHS 263 in Brownsville that the shop teacher told me he'd pass me with a 65 if I never came back to his class. I passed.

"Well, come back tomorrow and we'll start. The lumber's right here. Yeah, you'll do, you sick motherfucka. I like you."

And that's how I started with The Last Poets.

Harlem's 125th Street was a hotbed of Black nationalism in the '60s. There were two schools of thought: cultural nationalism, in which every thought, every word, every action, every manifestation of style and aesthetic was boiled in a cauldron of Afro-centric consciousness: we revered our ancestors. We believed all our schools and colleges were to teach Black history and culture, and we aimed at building our own institutions and patronizing them. All things consumed should be produced by Black people, we would marry Black and support the Black family, all people of color would declare and accept their African roots. We were not anti-white; we were pro-Black. We believed in the BlackArts Movement and declared that we hear, see, feel, and think differently from whites, and, finally, we were owed reparations for slavery.

Then, there was the second school of thought, revolutionary nationalism, wherein thought and action, though steeped in Black consciousness, was tempered by a Marxist class analysis. The thinking was that critical analysis had to be applied to race and class, the two concepts that have bedeviled Black folks and America since its foundation. Most of the Black '6os revolutionaries cut their teeth in cultural nationalism, but some of us eventually saw its limitations: like corruption in the newly liberated African nations, like co-optation of the Uncle Toms in America. Revolutionary Nationalists wanted an end to capitalism even if it meant armed struggle for liberation and the establishment of Black socialism.

On 125th Street, from Fifth Avenue to Morningside Avenue, there was always a parade of people in dashikis and geles, sandals, and walking sticks, long skirts in brilliant patterns, and intricately woven African reed hats, all exuding scents of fragrant musk oils bought from street merchants, all enmeshed in swirls of exotic incense burning freely on the main drag. Aided by the constant drumming on the street, I had transported myself, at warp speed, into a new Africa, an urban mecca of new dreams and freeform thought, à la John Coltrane. It was not the careful, methodical, cadenced thought processes of the liberals in the Village. This lifestyle was immediate, passionate, in-your-face; there was no ambiguity about the identity of the enemy. The object of our hatred was whiteness: for the cultural nationalists, the white man; for the revolutionary nationalists, the white capitalist system; for most common Black folks, the whole fuckin' thing.

Unconsciously, I followed the same trajectory as LeRoi Jones, the brilliant Newark-born poet, who left the Bohemian lifestyle of coffee shops, love-struck white girls, and abstract metaphors of the Village on the Lower East Side to start the Harlem Black Arts Movement in 1964. Changing his name to Amiri Baraka after the murder of Malcolm X, he also proposed a game-changing thought system.

"Suppose I told you that Black people see beauty differently than white folks; we hear music differently, we use language differently, we pray and play and lay out our thoughts differently. We are *different*! That's why America is in conflict."

Even after 400 years of slavery, Amiri seemed to say, "Our African DNA will not allow us to be anything but Black. And, because of ignorance, miseducation, and institutionalized racism, we still don't get it. We think we're inferior, we're the bad guys, the poor guys, the ones who never quite made it to the top."

Amiri's exhortation was "Look at the genius we've produced, even in the pit of hell: Louis Armstrong, Duke Ellington, Count Basie, Charlie Parker,

Thelonious Monk, Miles Davis, John Coltrane, Dizzy Gillespie, Ella Fitzgerald, Sarah Vaughn, Billie Holiday, Nat King Cole, Cab Calloway, and Billy Eckstine. God, the list is endless.

"How could you ever think you are worthless?"

During my re-immersion into Harlem, my initiation into The Last Poets, my body throbbed every day with the newness of the Black Arts theory. If Black people had an instinctively different aesthetic, it had to be true of brown people, too! We were the first Blacks in the so-called new world of the Americas, brought to the Caribbean in chains, 111 years before Jamestown. We sang original African chants, still worshipped African gods, played original African drums with rhythms so fierce that people dropped to the floor writhing with the spirits of the orishas; we produced Chano Pozo, Arsenio Rodríguez, Tito Puente, Rafael "Cortijo" Hernandez, Pedro Flores, Daniel Santos, Candido, Mongo Santamaria, Julito Collazo, Francisco Aguabella, "Patato" Valdes, Cachao, the great Machito, Mario Bauza, Tito Rodríguez, Miguelito Valdes, Beny More, Vicentico Valdes, Bobby Capo, Orquesta Aragon, Graciela, Celia Cruz, Johnny Pacheco, La Lupe, Joe Cuba, Jimmy Sabater, Willie Bobo, Ray Barretto, Pete "El Conde" Rodriguez, El Gran Combo, Hector La Voe, the incredible singer Ismael Rivera, and the genius of Eddie and Charlie Palmieri. I saw the light, or, better, the dark.

The prime mover of The Last Poets, the daddy, Gylan Kain, didn't hate white people: he hated what white people did: the vulgarity of their violence, their refusal to see Black scholarly genius—Du Bois, Richard Wright, Baldwin, Ralph Ellison, Langston Hughes—and America's co-optation and diluted imitation of every raw piece of artistry we'd ever spawned. I deduced that when whites couldn't originate, they'd imitate. When Little Richard first sang "Tutti Frutti" and caused orgasmic pulsations in the panties of pony-tailed, saddle-shoed, southern white girls the recording industry came up with the vanilla corniness of Pat Boone, singing the same song with no funk in the arrangement and making millions. When James Brown shouted triumphantly, "This Is a Man's World," the vulture culture vinyl producers, realizing that Elvis couldn't/wouldn't be Black enough, they found a Welshman named Tom Jones to pop his polyestered penis in womens' faces while they tore their bloomers off and flung them unto the stage. Eartha Kitt oozed sexiness and sensuality; but it was the white imitation of Blackness, Peggy Lee and the song "Fever," that was marketed heavily in the '50s (don't forget the sultriness of Nancy Wilson and Carmen McRae), and, of course, in the late '60s when the Jackson 5 convinced America to love the innocence, the pure beauty, the celestial talent of young Black males from middle America, then up popped the Osmond Brothers straight out of Bumfuck,

Utah, with Donny desperately trying to match the dance magic of Michael Jackson (we knew he wouldn't even try to match the vocals).

Kain hated it all, viscerally. As the days turned into weeks, during the fateful summer of '67 I was introduced to the members of The Last Poets: David Nelson (co-founder and mystic spiritualist), proletarian pop poet and meistersinger Abiodun Oyewole, and intercultural renaissance drummer Nilijah (who wouldn't unsheath his congas if he didn't feel your poetry, if it didn't ring true). The truth of their progressive consciousness seeped into me. Not once did they question my Blackness, not once did they bring up that my being Puerto Rican might hurt their popularity with Black youth, and not once did they question my dedication or courage. What they did question, in the beginning, was my corny poetry.

As per Kain's instructions, I finished nailing together a rickety door frame. It was laughable. Kain finally realized I didn't know what the fuck I was doing but let me stay on primarily because he liked the long, intense conversations we had on religion and philosophy. We had a lot in common: strict, orthodox Pentecostal mothers with no husbands; an almost incestual relationship with them amidst the love, loyalty, and hate tales about their fathers; an intellectual capacity that got us into trouble with church doctrine; severe whippings; and a real questioning of who and what God is or was. Add to that our mothers' dreams that we would become famous preachers and vindicate the suffering and sacrifice they endured, and you have a perfectly dysfunctional childhood with the eldest boy being husband, father, confidante, therapist, pain-cushion, and young child. Some days you had adult rights and responsibilities—you could come and go as you pleased and answer your mother back forcefully; other days you were severely punished and/or whipped for exercising those same rights. So, you retreated into your intellect; not even your brothers and sisters could help; you saw them as brainwashed loyalists, sycophants who groveled at the feet of an uneducated, brutal woman who made it her business to break the independent man-spirit you exuded.

As we exchanged notes, Kain and I would howl and slap five at the similarity of our bathed-in-the-blood-of-Jesus church upbringings with its lack of tolerance and hypocrisy. The church hated gays, preached vehemently about the sin of homosexuality, but allowed active, flamboyant gay men in the choir (usually leading it); they condemned violence, but beat the crap out of their kids; they hated illicit, unmarried sex, but every year there was another freaky sex scandal between a minister or a bishop and a congregant. And since most of the storefront churches were packed with abandoned Black and brown women with frustrated sexual desires under the spell of a charismatic preacher whose sermons swayed their passion and played with their fantasies of a strong, virile leader, sex was bound to happen somewhere, in the church or out of it. It was a hen house, and the minister was the rooster.

Kain and I rebelled in different ways; he became a child preacher, speaking in tongues and becoming a major contributor to the family's finances with his "guest" preaching. But in irregular fits of anger his mother would humiliate him by forcing him to play the role of baby boy. His extraordinary intelligence and command of language, his growing sense of manhood and responsibility, meant nothing as she would berate him verbally. At one point, during a tirade against violence, she threw two of his six-gun cap pistols down the project incinerator. Kain loved those guns. Something broke in him, he told me. He was never the same again after that incident. He stopped preaching, became sullen, questioned God's existence, and, as soon as he could, left home and started poetry . . . and drinking. He tried college; he was brilliant at math but eventually dropped out. And he drifted into the world of Bohemia, doing as an adult all the things he was forbidden to even think about as a child. I, on the other hand, joined gangs and battled my demons away. The gang provided me with sanctity, sanity, and sanctuary. My intelligence was appreciated, and the need for family was understood by all; we all wanted it and pledged to each other our undying loyalty that sometimes resulted in death and, often, resulted in jail. I, too, became a rebel, a cock-hound who hated women, had rough sex with abandon, followed by words of love and culminating, eventually, in an impersonal, cruel abandonment. I was following in my father's footsteps.

In 1968, the East Wind became the focal point of Black art and thought in Harlem. Sun Ra and his Arkquestra were regular guests, blasting their dissonant, prophetic twenty-first-century music through the roof; gentle, gangly Nikki Giovanni started her poetry career in our loft; Amiri and Amina Baraka and their entire theatrical ensemble called "The Spirit House Movers and Shakers" made regular sojourns to the East Wind, as did Bob MacBeth of the New Lafayette Theatre; Black theater producer Woody King (who eventually managed us); Stokley Carmicheal and H. Rap Brown of the Student Non-Violent Coordinating Committee; the revolutionary family of the Shakurs—Assata, Zayd (who presented me with my first dashiki and aunk), and Afeni—who gave birth to the genius of Tupac Shakur; the newly organized New York City chapter of the Black Panthers; the lyricism of Askia Muhammed Toure; the in-your-face honest poetry of Marvin X; playwright Ed Bullins, the chronicler of the Black family; avant-garde tenor saxophonist Albert Ayler; drummer extraordinaire Sonny Murray; elder griot poets Ted

Joans, Larry Neale, and Sonia Sanchez; the deceptive elegance of Jayne Cortez; the deadly serious poet Don L. Lee from Chicago; and comedian Jimmie Walker, who eventually reached stardom with the sitcom *Good Times*. We were happening, we were the Harlem hot spot and whether you were the Ahmed family of the Harlem Youth Federation; Oona, owner of the Liberation Book Store, the only leftist bookstore in Harlem; or Barbara Ann Teer of the National Black Theatre, the East Wind is where you met and networked and launched your artistic vision and organization.

Kain became my big brother and my father-surrogate; I could tell him everything and anything. He knew the world and had the wisdom of the sages of ages past. In those days in Harlem, poets would physically battle one another over meter, history, ideological content, and whether the metaphors matched the actions and behaviors of the individual poet. I always sided with Kain in arguments, following him the same way I followed gang presidents. In battle, dissension is out of the question, and as far as I was concerned, we were at war in America. As cultural warriors, our job was to inspire the troops, no questions asked. It was life or death. We knew who we were; we knew what we stood for and were willing to fight, to die for, a dream, a code of ethics, a poem.

We, The Last Poets, would spend endless hours of the day and the night, arguing content, intent, and the consequences our people would bear, if they took our battle cries to heart. I spoke of armed struggle, of blood that had to flow to cleanse the land of madness and injustice. David would close his eyes and intone about the ravaging of our own humanity if we took lives, any lives. His ethereal metaphysics and poetry did not always mesh with the radical blood and guts ideology of the day. Abiodun emphasized the need to educate our folks before we picked up the sword. And Kain would look at us all and say, "You can't say a fuckin' thing in your poetry if you are not living it. Truth is what matters. Poetry resonates when you live it."

That thought haunted me for months. It was one of the reasons for my co-founding the Young Lords Party of New York City. I wanted to go beyond the rhetoric and even the lyricism of Black and brown poetry. I wanted drumbeats and rifles. It wasn't the Devil or the Panthers that made me do it; it was a guy named Rap Brown. I noticed that anyone could tell a story on stage with tales that brought out the fury of injustice and raise the people to a fever pitch; I wrote several early poems like that. It was quite another thing to take that same idea and make it a piece of art, make it ring with beauty, make people think, dig deeper, shower them under a metaphorical fountain where beauty, elegance, and truth cleansed their consciousness so that they saw not only the enemy but also the in-a-me, those ideas, habits, perceptions, language, and behavior that negated success and victory.

It was during this incubation period I wrote "Jibaro, My Pretty Nigger." It remains one of the most popular poems in my repertoire as it speaks of the beauty of three cultures, Taino, Puerto Rican, and Afro-American, from a position of pure admiration and historical connection. As I walk the streets of New York City, when strangers can't remember my name, they shout out "Jibaro" and I know they know that I know that we know what time it is. The poem is a vow of unity within Puerto Rican culture and a written bond of love between Blacks and Puerto Ricans. I organized a political workshop at the East Wind based on the academic curriculum, and I ran it like a college course complete with assigned readings and verbal tests. You had to read. You had to think out of the box. And you had to back your analysis up with empirical evidence, not just anecdotal information or subjective experience.

The attendees loved Rap Brown's participation. They loved this tall, Louisiana-drawled brother who could play the dozens and rank on you in the best street tradition. "C'mon now," he would chide a dark-skinned Puerto Rican man who insisted he was racially Puerto Rican, "Puerto Rican is your nationality, brother, not your race. You Black. Try going down South and running that game. Those crackers will whip your ass as fast as they will a brother. You just a nigger with a Spanish accent, fool!" We would howl in laughter at Rap's rapier wit. He could slice you comically and dice you historically until you came to your senses, until even the subject of his humorous derision would have to laugh out loud. Harlem and El Barrio loved him.

My poetry got better through osmosis. Just hanging out with The Last Poets, listening to their rhythms, their style, the substance of their poetry, lit a flame under me. I had to gain their approval, had to kill them with my words, make them shout with approval. Yes, there was competition, the good kind, iron sharpening iron. In the East Wind, you had better come with your metaphorical "A" game or keep quiet and listen. While we were gaining a national audience with our college tours, tension was mounting in The Last Poets. While I loved Kain's fatherly leadership and direction, Abiodun was chafing internally at Kain's criticism of his poetic style and manner. Kain was steeped in the classics and demanded that while our powerfully raw message of Black empowerment was substantially different from other Black poets, we should not throw out traditional literary forms. He loved Whitman, Frost, Ezra Pound, Ginsberg, Garcia Lorca, Neruda, Guillen, and Amiri Baraka. He detested the rhyming method that Abiodun used to convey the message. (Abiodun was way ahead of the rappers on this one; he was using rap before rap blossomed.) Kain hated the simplicity of it, called the form "mediocre." But there was something else seething in the background. Abiodun simply didn't appreciate Kain's assumption of the father role in the group. He didn't have the best relationship with his stepfather and didn't need another critical surrogate dad. Things came to a head when David decided to leave the group to be part of an entrepreneurial company called "New Breed." Abiodun and I, having had some musical training, handled the vacancy pretty well, singing harmony in conjunction with Nilijah's intricate poly-rhythms. The transition was smooth and the money was better. We divided it four ways instead of five.

A year later, when David's business venture hadn't fared well, he asked to be let back into the group. It was a weekday afternoon when we met to discuss the issue, something I thought would be a simple matter. Kain opened the conversation by saying he wanted David back in; he was an original founder and should be given a chance. I, always agreeing with Kain, felt the four of us would have even more poetic impact. Though I truly enjoyed the synergy between Kain, Abiodun, and me, why break up the family, even though David had left us flat with no real explanation or concern for our future or feelings. Abiodun disagreed vehemently.

"David left the group. He didn't care about us. He was only thinking of himself and the money he could make. I love the brother, but, no, I don't want him back in. We're doing fine as a trio. ['Dun and I sang better without David; he couldn't carry a tune well.] Why go backward? Let's move forward and think of some new shit!" Abiodun declared.

Kain was visibly angry; he wasn't expecting this strong a backlash. For him, this was a matter of simple rubber-stamp approval; he was just letting us know to be polite. He and 'Dun argued for about an hour, and it became obvious this was not just about David but also about leadership of The Last Poets.

"You can't just come in here and make decisions for us, Kain. We're all part of this group and since Felipe just entered, the decision is really between you and I. And I say no!" Abiodun shouted.

Kain countered with, "David is one of the founders. He coined the phrase 'The Last Poets.' You can't arbitrarily freeze him out. As the leader of this group, I say we take him back."

Abiodun became furious.

"You see, that's the fuckin' problem. You think you're the father. You see the vision, you choose our direction. I'm a grown fuckin' man and I don't need and don't want a daddy. Had enough of that shit growing up. You wanna make decisions for Felipe, fine. Not for me. You don't tell me what the fuck to do or say."

Kain stood up and screamed, "I found this loft, I agonize over the bills, not you. I do the bookings. And after the crowds are gone, I do the cleanup, not you." It got hot.

It got nasty with voices raised, and the potential for violence very thick. Chairs were thrown, and though I was there, I still can't remember who motherfucked whom or who threw the first chair. I was paralyzed. My family, my father, and my brother were fighting and I was immobilized.

"Please stop!" I screamed. They didn't.

Abiodun stormed out, never to return, and as I write this, I still feel the pain. I felt we broke up the best Black/Latino cultural grouping in Harlem since Machito, Mario Bauza, Dizzy Gillespie, and Chano Pozo in 1945. It was my only gang at the time, my only family, and the answer to so many young Black folks' hopes of a group that could speak their language, in a loft where dreams could be spoken of, examined, and actualized. I hated what became of us, after. We almost killed each other. War was about to begin . . . with disastrous consequences.

Abiodun formed another group with two students from the East Wind poetry workshop, Umar Bin Hassan and Jilal Mansur Nurridin. On the surface, it seemed like a natural thing to do. What caused a scandal in Harlem was that Abiodun called his group "The Last Poets" and they began putting up posters of upcoming concerts that he booked. Kain and I felt totally betrayed. The gnawing in our stomachs, the in-your-face treachery of counter-programming whatever concerts we had planned in New York City by using our group name and confusing the public, was a call to war. By appropriating the name "The Last Poets," Abiodun was throwing down the gauntlet. In the Black and brown world of the streets, if you leave the gang, you leave, start your own gang, if need be, but never, ever steal the name of the original grouping. You could get hurt for less, but you could definitely die for taking the name without permission.

Kain didn't want to go after them physically. And since I had already joined the Young Lords, I had the backup to make it happen, make it hurt. Kain obtained the services of a lawyer who explained that since Abiodun was an original founder, under American jurisprudence he had a right to the name "The Last Poets." Kain and I had no legal case. The lawyer patiently explained the case of the famous '40s singing group the Mills Brothers, wherein one of the brothers defected and formed another group with the same name and when sued was vindicated by the courts. As an original member of the ensemble, he had as much right to the name as those siblings who stayed in the original group. Kain and I were devastated. Every day we were approached by Harlemites who wanted to know what the hell was going on, why the break in the group? I wanted to pursue and destroy. I called Umar and told him I was coming for him. I meant it. Umar retorted, "Bring it on."

Kain felt it would destroy our philosophy of Black revolutionary love if we killed our own the moment there was a disagreement. So, finally, we relegated ourselves to being called "The Original Last Poets," and David Nelson, Kain, and I performed under that name for the rest of our collective poetic careers. Thank God, Kain won me over. I would've participated in the murder of two poets, Jilal, now deceased, and Umar, now a dear friend. It was bad enough having our faces rubbed in the Harlem streets because of the confusion as to who were the "real" poets, the original group, but what made matters worse is that Jilal and Umar started aggressively gunning for us. As long as we were around, they couldn't claim total ownership of the title "The Last Poets." Abiodun was never involved in the hunt for us. He was busy organizing a student/citizens group of Black radicals in South Carolina called the Yoruba Society. In an attempt to bail some of his arrested members out of jail, 'Dun robbed a Klan gas station. Fortunately, he was not gunned down. He was busted and served two years down South. I admired his decision to put his life on the line, especially because he, Umar, and Jilal had just garnered national attention for their first recording on Douglas Records called "The Last Poets" with poems like "Niggers Are Afraid of Revolution." He could've just basked in the sunlight of fame but instead turned the poems into bullets. His poetic partners didn't share his commitment. Abiodun says he was never sent any money from the royalties of the hit record while he was incarcerated.

During the breakup, Kain, David, and I stayed passive, to my consternation. Kain demanded we stand firm and continue performing. Jilal and Umar confronted David, punches were exchanged, and he was knocked to the ground. There was a nose-to-nose staring match with me and the aforementioned two poets on 125th Street. Threats were hissed, no punches were thrown, and we walked away from one another. And then, the unthinkable . . . Kain said they were calling, threatening to kill him; his young wife, June; and stepson, Khalil, whom I adored. One night, they appeared at his building in the Bronx and began issuing threats toward his upstairs window. Rather than call me, Kain decided to go downstairs and confront them alone, a ballpeen hammer in hand. He was no match for them.

More than fifty years later, the details are still fuzzy. Kain ended up on the floor, bleeding profusely from his forehead, beaten with his own hammer.

Kain called me and in a slow, raspy voice told me what happened. He would stop the narrative, intermittently, to tell me, in his all-too-familiar, therapeutic manner, what he did to cause the ass-whipping. I was incensed. I was hysterical. Hung up the phone and called some of the Ministry of Defense members of the Young Lords Party, old heroin addicts who loved Kain and knew how to execute orders and people . . . literally. I put them on standby. Kain made me promise to call him before I did anything.

"Kain, it's done. My people will start looking for them now. I suggest you take the family and leave town for a minute. Don't tell anybody where you're going and I'll call you in a few days after this is all over. Bye . . . ."

The scream was audible as I was hanging up the phone.

"Wait, motherfucker . . . you can't just kill people because of me . . . because you want them dead. You're not GOD! I was flabbergasted and pissed.

Before I could respond, Kain started to scream again. "Motherfucker! I am the one who was beaten, I'm the one who decides who lives and dies, and I say No. No. Nooo! You are not to decide for me, you understand?"

I stayed very quiet, waiting for him to finish his dramatic soliloquy so I could just give the guys the word and get this hit over with; it was a street matter and Kain was decidedly not street, especially now. He was still playing Hamlet, still playing the arrogant victim. Fuck him, I thought, he's hurting himself, threatening his own family if he doesn't take these guys out. If I called off the hit because of his bullshitty Black Nationalistic compassion, I'd certainly ruin my street rep. You don't get guys hyped out to do a job for you out of love and loyalty, have them oil the guns and work out supporting alibis, and then call it off. You're never trusted again. Kill 'em, I thought. I'll deal with Kain's remorse later.

Kain's voice on the phone softened. He knew how pissed I was. He started to speak *sotto voce*. "C'mon, baby boy, please don't do what you're about to do. It's going to hurt you, it's going to hurt me. It ain't worth it."

I was silent, breathing hard.

"Are you there, bro . . . Felipe . . . Felipe . . . are you there? Talk to me . . . Felipaay!"

I answered curtly, brusquely. "What the fuck do you want from me, Kain? Want me to connect the dots between Kain and pain for you, motherfucker? Want me to listen to your tales of woe and punishment and not feel anything, not do anything? I ain't Christian that way, Kain. They fucked you up, brother. Now, I'm not going to sit here and discuss what *you* did wrong. That's not the Puerto Rican way. I wouldn't ask my sister why she got raped, God forbid. I'd find the motherfucka and kill him. Case closed. No cops, no discussion. Done deal. I moved the same way when they hurt my brother, Kain. You know what I did, and I never felt remorse. So why the fuck do you keep recounting this dumbass story to me? Do you like torturing yourself? I love you, Kain, but let me tell you something. You call this off and I don't want you bringing this shit up again, ever. I mean it. If you're not going to retaliate, shut the fuck up and cry by yourself. I don't want to hear it anymore. Look, I've got to go. I have to tell my guys to stand down and forget about it. They love you, Kain, and they're not going to understand your Pentecostal shit; it's too dark." And I hung up.

During this period of uncertainty, there was a group of Puerto Rican students from State University New York at Westbury on Long Island who started coming to the loft to attend the political workshops I conducted. I knew one of them, Micky Melendez, had seen him on the Queens College campus. He had since switched to Old Westbury. I was surprised. With the exception of a tall, strapping, straight-talking, Asian-looking Puerto Rican City College activist named Henry Arce, very few 'Ricans attended the workshops regularly. Some would come, listen, ask no questions, and never come back. Henry didn't give a shit how "Black" the sessions got; he stuck with it, always bringing up the "Puerto Rican" question. Why was the class ignoring Puerto Rican participation in the Black struggle? Why were Black students claiming they were the only victims of America's war on people of color? Why didn't Black people view Latinos as natural allies since Blacks lived and worked right next to them?

There were times he was challenged by the group, sometimes verbally, sometimes physically. Emotions ran high in the East Wind loft as Black men swathed in traditional African robes or jeans would rant, "This is a Black thing. Spanish people, Puerto Ricans, whatever, have to build their own movement in their own communities. Why the hell should we care about others when we have enough problems of our own? That's our problem; we care for everybody else instead of loving ourselves. You have no right to tell us how we should act or fight."

I remember having to go toe-to-toe with these activists, using their own words and historical data. "So, you proclaim yourselves Pan-Africanists, you say all of us are Black, but when you have to deal with Latinos on a real tip, when you have to construct a real community-wide strategy for victory, when you realize you have to fight just as hard for a Puerto Rican and Latino Studies Department as you do for an Africana/Afro-American Studies Department, you suddenly back off and want to do your own shit. That's exactly the kind of divide-and-conquer move we've been dealing with for centuries. What's the difference? We came in the same ships, just landed in different ports and ended up speaking different languages. The slave masters separated us in Africa. You don't know if my mother is yours, or your mother, mine. We got all mixed up and yeah, a lot of us were raped and have different skin tones. Is that a reason to separate our struggles? We're all oppressed, we're all suffering! When did Black people become more superior than Latinos?"

At that point, rather than battle with me historically, the brothers would turn on Henry as he explained the strategy and tactics for taking over City College because of their lack of academic inclusion and diversity.

"Man, you talk too fuckin' much. Who do think you are?" they'd scream.

"A Puerto Rican!" Henry would bark back.

This warrior never backed down. If they came at him he would stand straight up, facing whomever, with whatever threat and bark, "Bring it!" No one ever did. Henry gained Black folks' respect the hard way and became one of the trusted members of my political workshop out of which emerged "The Committee of Ten," architects of the City College student takeover that won the right of open admissions for all CUNY colleges, the establishment of Black and Puerto Rican Studies at CCNY, and the hiring of more Latino and Black professors.

It was all planned at the East Wind Political Workshop right on 125th Street. This new group of Puerto Ricans coming to the workshops wouldn't go away. They would listen intently to my lectures, looking at one another with incredulity. After a few visits, they approached me. There were four students I remember, Micky Melendez, Robert Ortiz, Denise Oliver, and David Perez. After a few pleasantries, Micky got directly to the point: "We're building a Puerto Rican student movement." I said nothing, just looked at him. I was sweaty and exhausted from teaching. It had been a particularly trying two-hour session on Nietzsche's "Thus spoke Zarathustra" and the need to build a new movement free of old morality and rancid ideas.

Micky continued, "We don't just want to build a movement around student issues; we want to start attacking those issues that affect our people: racism, police brutality, poor schools, poor housing, poor hospitals. And we want to do it on the streets where we live."

I looked at the clean-cut group, felt their good intentions, but coming from jail, where talk was cheap, I didn't place much faith in their words, but I continued to listen.

"We'd like you to join us. Our movement needs people like you!"

I scrutinized their faces. Micky? Too serious. Did he understand balance? Denise? Too runway-model beautiful. Would she be willing to get her face bashed in? David Perez? A real country-looking, light-skinned *jibaro*. How

Black was he? The only face I trusted was that of Robert Ortiz, a brilliant, bearded, mulatto heroin addict and student at Old Westbury with small, piercing, suspicious eyes, a pockmarked face, large teeth, strong hands, veined, sinewy forearms, prominent Taino cheekbones, and an Afro. His lips were pressed together tightly, like he was dying to tell me something. He had a nervous twitch, a street twitch, the kind of twitch I had often seen in jail right before short Puerto Ricans stuck much larger, much taller Black inmates in the gut with any sharp object they could find. The assault was always wordless, no trash talk, and it always came from a 'Rican who was deceptively quiet, not a great English speaker, one whom the brothers would belittle daily. The shock on the Black brothers' faces while they held their guts in place told the story: Don't fuck with Puerto Ricans and don't take them for granted. I told Micky and the group that I'd think about it, told them I didn't think the Puerto Rican community was ready for militant confrontation or armed struggle.

Everything I had read, everything I had experienced was that most stateside Puerto Ricans had a severe distaste for violence against the state and a voracious appetite for violence against each other. A notable exception was the Nationalist Party, whose members stood up courageously to the U.S. government including having a shootout in Congress while unfurling a Puerto Rican flag and screaming, *"Que viva Puerto Rico libre!"* and trying to assassinate President Truman at Blair House. While many of their island counterparts had been fighting for independence from the time the Spanish brutally raped the island in 1493, many who emigrated to the United States were too *"ay bendito,"* too passive, too accommodating, too apologetic for everything from their color to their culture. I understood how they kept their mouths shut just to put food in ours, how they sacrificed their dreams so we could achieve ours, how they laughed at the racist jokes and comments of their bosses while seething inside, but why didn't they revolt at some point and kill the people who treated them as subhuman?

The only heroes in my barrio were the gang members who defended my family's honor against Italians, the Irish, Jews, and even Black Americans. They didn't go to school, they weren't educated, but they had a fierce pride in being Puerto Rican and defended our community to the death, even against the cops. I marveled at the gang members' fighting skills, the way they would practice fighting, cigarettes dangling from their mouths, dodging and weaving powerful punches while tapping the neck, heart, and stomach of their opponents, letting them know where they could've stuck the knife had this been real, all the time exhaling smoke from their nostrils and laughing heartily. They were Viceroys and Dragons, Spanish Romans and

Corsair Lords, Sportsmen and Flaming Satans, Shing-a-lings and Jolly Bishops, Chaplains and Turbans, Stompers, and Copasetics. They seemingly had no fear of death or defeat. And they walked, talked, and acted like that. Jail was just an occupational hazard, and when these guys came home they were treated like royalty with wine, women, song, and smoke. Very few ratted out their countrymen. They took the ass-whippings from cops like warriors, losing teeth and gaining scars. Most were Puerto Rican, and, in my day, that stood for something. Robert Ortiz smiled beatifically after my little rejection speech. Turning to his little college group, Robert yelped, "Yep, I told you guys, come correct or don't come at all. This motherfucker ain't about bullshit." And then he swung around, came close to my face, and in a sincere, respectful tone, said, "Can I talk to you on the side?"

Robert opened his mouth, pointed his finger at me, and then froze in mid-sentence, his mouth still open, his finger still pointing at me. And then he started laughing, a hoarse, pot smoker's raspy, half-cough laugh.

"Excuse me, brother, no disrespect intended, but I gotta tell you the truth. These ma'fuckas don't have a clue. You're right! They don't know what the fuck they want or what they're doing, but you know something . . . ?"

His eyes narrowed and his face took on a nasty, killer look and his tone indicated I was about to be given some highly classified information.

"I like these fuckin' kids, Felipe. Yeah, you and I have seen some nasty street shit and we pride ourselves on heart and what we did, but what the fuck are we doing now for our people, huh? What the fuck are we doing for 'em? At least these kids are trying. I hang out with them all the time. I know their hearts. They're scared, Felipe, but they're down, they're ready. They need you, and you wanna know something? You need them too. You've been away from us too long, man. C'mon home. That's all I gotta say."

We walked back to the group and then Micky started in on me, same theme.

"Been thinking about what you just said. You're Black. We know that. But you're Puerto Rican, too. You owe your people something—your skills, your brain, your talk. We're dying out here and nobody, nobody is coming to our aid. We've gotta fight back, Felipe, we can't be silent witnesses to our people's murder. What are you doing here on 125th street, when we need you in El Barrio? Don't answer now, we'll come back next week. Think about what I said." And then they left.

Kain had been watching from afar and sauntered up to me after they walked downstairs. "So, what did they have to say?" I told him everything in detail while he alternately stared at me and then looked out the back window.

"Can I tell you something? This day was bound to come; you've been avoiding it by throwing yourself into the Black thing and I understand it. You've been hurt by your own, man. You chose Black and they didn't and now they're coming up to you looking for the very things they hated in niggers—loudness, in-your-face shit, heart. Truth is, you're looking for acceptance, brother. I see it, I hear it every time you talk to me and curse 'em out. You can't say you don't love them, Felipe. They're yours as much as my Blackness is mine."

I got a queasy feeling in my stomach, that insecure, embarrassed churning of the mind and intestines when someone hits you with who you really are, no matter how much you protest to the contrary. At that moment, I hated Kain. Hated him for seeing right through me, for touching my feelings of inferiority around white Puerto Ricans, for hating my not being able to speak Spanish properly, for not being able to throw my straight hair back, for being rejected by Elizabeth, that strawberry-blond pug-nosed white 'Rican in the sixth grade, for touching the rage I felt at all those women in the church and the projects who rejected my mother because she boldly sat with Black women in the front of the building and laughed heartily with them, exchanging stories of the stupidity of their men for thinking their wives didn't know what they were smoking and who they were fucking, for having no family in Puerto Rico that I could visit in the summertime and come home with tales of sandy beaches, *mofongo*, and the bathtub warmth of the Caribbean. I hated those motherfuckers who thought I wasn't good enough because of my lips, my nose, my kinks, the ashiness of my feet, my Black accent. Fuck them, they should die. I screamed at Kain in the most venomous tone, "I'm Black, motherfucker. I am a Black man and fuck whether you or anyone else knows it."

I don't know how he did it so quickly, but Kain leaped across the stage, grabbed me by the throat, and pounded me against the wall, his eyes blazing.

"What color are you, punk?" he bellowed.

"Fuck you," I spat out as he choked me.

"What fuckin' color are you, Felipe?"

I was scared of him, scared of that demon in him, that horrible look in his eyes, the sneer on his face. Tears started to trickle, snot came out my nose. "I'm brown, man . . . brown. Now get off me."

"Fuck you," he hissed. "Tell me right now, the exact color of your skin, punk."

He was hurting me, humiliating me. I wanted to knee him, but he had me wrapped up too close, his knee against my groin, his whole body pressing on me. I had never seen him like this.

"I'm light brown, like light-colored coffee. Get the hell off me." He pressed on.

"Light-colored coffee. That's so fuckin' cute. Look at me," he screamed, "*Look at me!* You know what color I am, motherfucker. I'm black, midnight black, charcoal black, the black that scares crackers. I'm their worse fuckin' nightmare. I know it. I live with it every day. Every fuckin' day. And I have to endure their shit everyday. Their scowls, their sneers, their thinking I'm another dumbass nigger who can't read or think. I can't speak that *mira-mira* shit and get a pass. My hair doesn't straighten like yours with Dixie Peach, I'm a nigger and I've learned to accept it and fight back the only way I know how."

I couldn't look at him anymore. I turned my head.

He loosened his grip, then stepped away. I was heaving, crying uncontrollably. "You've done everything you can here," he said. "You've taught us, you've inspired even me. But your time is done here. You need to go back and educate them, the same way I have to educate and raise the consciousness of my people. Because if you don't, who will, who will? Now, get the hell out of here and don't come back until you make your decision. And it better be the right one."

I ran out.

The only one I could speak to about this matter, the only other person I trusted, was Rap Brown. Though he chastised Black folks from the stage and almost shamed them into revolutionary consciousness through his juxtaposition of American liberal rhetoric and the brutal reality of our daily lives, off-stage, with friends and family, he was gentle and nonjudgmental. I called him a day later, after I had calmed down, and he listened to my lament, quietly.

"You need to get out of the city for a while. Why don't you come with me to Baton Rouge? It'll be good for you."

I quickly jumped at the opportunity to see the South and he told me when to be ready and then hung up. I thought to myself, what the hell just happened? what does Baton Rouge have to do with my dilemma, my pain? Why didn't Rap just comment on Kain's weird behavior toward me? He was up to something. I didn't press him.

Baton Rouge, Louisiana, was a clean, nicely trimmed city that seemed to have come to terms with itself and race. I got no strange looks from white folks and they seemed fairly comfortable in the presence of Blacks. The

Black people I met—Rap's mom, Thelma, and brother, Ed—were truly hospitable and courteous, and they seemed to live a comfortable, easy-going life. The first thing I noticed was Rap's softened demeanor; he walked and talked less suspiciously, laughed more, and his wicked, sometimes sarcastic humor disappeared. I was shocked to discover Rap was actually shy and learned the dozens to defend himself against the bullies. Why fight 'em when you can beat 'em with your brain and mouth, he explained to me.

While we were in Baton Rouge, Rap's old childhood friends played the dozens with him, kidded him about his militancy, all in good taste, and Rap never hit back, never. I realized he knew he was home . . . and safe. But, I now knew whence he got his street-style oratory and his nickname because when he started to verbally rain on them it was like watching Sugar Ray Robinson stick, jab, and dance with his oponents. Another thing I noticed, Rap didn't come from poverty and projects. His family was working-class; his dad worked at an Esso refinery and his mom was a dietitian. Rap was used to a real home and possession of property, which meant defense of that property, if necessary, including guns. Guns were just tools in Louisiana, and everybody had them. It was not some magic stick that spit fire; it was a hunting gun, a home-defense gun, a part of the makeup of a Southern family, Black or white. There was no mystique to the damn thing; it was as natural to have a gun as it was to have a shovel, a pickup truck, or a lawnmower.

Rap's ease with a rifle was a beauty to watch; he wasn't a showboat, it just seemed like part of his body, an extension of his arm. He reminded me of John Wayne and Audie Murphy when he walked with it, though I would never have told him that. And from all accounts he was an excellent shot, which is why I've always questioned his alleged murder rap of an Atlanta policeman and the wounding of another. I was told Rap could shoot a muskrat out of an upper rain gutter at fifty feet. He grew up shooting guns. His father, Eddie Brown, hunted regularly. If in fact, there was a shoot-out with two policemen on an Atlanta Street, near his home with his wife inside, trust me, the two cops would've been dead, not just one. I'm convinced someone else did the shooting, but knowing Rap, if he knew, he'd never tell, ever. The truth is that someone else confessed to the shootout, but it was never admitted as evidence in Rap's trial. He's been in prison since the year 2000.

A few days into our stay at his house, Rap took me to a football game between Southern U and Grambling held at the Black Southern University athletic field. (Though the Louisiana State University was blocks from Rap's house, Black teams were not allowed to play there.) The Southern U stadium was packed, whites and Blacks jostling one another to get tickets, scurrying for seats, and no overt hostility even as people bumped into one another. I didn't watch the game, wasn't interested. What fascinated me was the camaraderie of the fans, slapping five with each other, the loudness of the taunts from the fans of the different teams toward each other with no fear of a fight. Maybe the South had reached a new plateau of racial harmony. Here I was in the Deep South, the old antebellum South, dripping with gumbo, under the drooping branches of Spanish moss, and Blacks and whites were laughing, slapping each other's backs over touchdowns and gained yardage and generally getting along. They had reached critical mass, I thought, and had decided to morph into new consciousness. I leaned back in my seat, watching it all, marveling at the harmony.

Half-shouting to Rap above the din, I said, "It's beautiful to see Black folks and whites getting along so well. This is blowing my mind, brother!"

Rap, standing up while I was seated, looked at me quizzically, then he looked at the crowd, then looked back at me. "Felipe, everybody in here is Black. There are no white folks here . . . hell is wrong with you?"

I figured Rap was pulling my leg, but his eyes weren't smiling. I figured Rap wasn't looking in the right places.

"Look at these people . . . look at those folks over there . . . look at that couple . . . look at that family over there . . . hello? Rap, they're not only white, they're white white. It's them damn sunglasses you got on, blood. I don't know what you seeing."

Very rarely did Rap take off his sunglasses while he was outside. He took them off and stared at me like I was a fool.

"Negro, these are Black people, octoroons, quadroons, mulattos and bloods. And they're probably all related. This is Louisiana. You can't run away from your Blackness here. Niggers will let you know who did who and when and if bloods don't, white folks will. You can think you passing, but these crackers around here will nail you to the cross if you ever think you're white 'cause your skin is light. They know these Negroes and their mommas."

I stayed with my mouth open, in total shock. When I say the folks in the stadium looked Irish, Italian, Jewish, and German, I mean it. But as I started to peer into their faces as they were shouting encouragement for their respective teams, I began to see their Blackness: a fuller lower lip here, a rounder butt there, a hint of knappy curliness to the straight hair. Damn, what an experience! I never thought a stadium could be a sociological classroom. The next day as were just driving around Baton Rouge, I brought up the subject of my reluctance to move into organizing in East Harlem. I gave

Rap all the reasons, calmly, well thought out. Rap kept driving, nodding in assent, to let me know he was listening.

Then, without looking at me, keeping his eyes on the road, he spoke, slowly. "I can't stand some of those chumps we saw at the game yesterday. They bought into slavery with the little privileges their yellow asses could muster. They were brainwashed into feeling lower than white folks and higher than us. House niggers is all they are, is all some of them will ever be. But some house niggers were valuable during slavery; told the field niggers everything about the master, when he slept, when he woke up, when he left, when he was coming back, where the guns and machetes were and where the food was stored. Some were Black, some were blue, some were fair-skinned. But they all had a burning desire . . . freedom; getting this cracker off their backs by any means necessary. Some paid with their lives, they'd whip 'em, cut their Achilles tendon so they couldn't run anymore, or sell them off to other, meaner plantations. What if I decided I wasn't going to organize Black folks because most of them had accommodated themselves to being slaves, to not even thinking of going against the white boy, much less fighting him, huh? Where would we be? Where would I be?"

The silence hung in the car like a wet, floppy blanket. I hung my head, embarrassed to even look at the man I admired. We drove in silence.

"You have a choice, brother. Fight or watch your people die. And, it's your choice. No one will know you bowed out. I know a lot of brothers who just decided to slide through life, pay a little money to the movement, talk shit and raise little boojee negroes to go along and get along. I ain't mad at 'em. That's what they chose. I just won't trust 'em in a fight. But, if they're gonna contribute in some way to our victory, I'll take whatever they got to offer; just won't tell 'em too much. It's really up to you, Felipe. You could continue teaching. Or you could put your body where your mouth is. You're my boy, I'll back your shit up no matter what decision you make, you dig?"

It took all my might not to cry in that car. In his wisdom, Rap slid the knife in silently, without a lot of hoopla. He had brought me all the way to Baton Rouge to see the contradictions clearly, contradictions within the people he had to deal with every day. And he still had faith in them, in the righteousness of Black liberation, in the dream.

It was there, in Baton Rouge, Louisiana, with my older brother Rap Brown at my side, that I decided to become a full-fledged Puerto Rican, an organizer, an orator, a soldier, a warrior. Whether my people were ready or not, on the island or on the mainland, if they needed me, I'd be there; if they called me, I would answer and bring every talent, every skills set, every gun to the fight or die. I lost my conceit, the hatred of my own and gained a new love. The lesson of Baton Rouge never left me, and I have Rap Brown to thank for that. Funny, huh, a Black man who motivated me to co-found the Young Lords. God works in mysterious ways. That day, Rap Brown was His angel, his messenger, and I believed it. I still do.

Jibaro, My Pretty Nigger

Jibaro, mi negro lindo/
                    De los bosques de cana/
Caciques de luz/
                    Tiempo es un cosa comica.

Jibaro, my pretty nigger.
Father of my yearning for the soil/
The land/ the earth of my people.

Father of the sweet smells of fruit
In my mother's womb/
The earth brown of my skin/
The thoughts of freedom
That butterfly through my insides.

Jibaro, my pretty nigga man,
Sweating bullets of blood and bed-bugs/
Swaying slowly to a softly strummed 5 stringed guitar/
Remembering ancient empires
Of sun gods and black spirits
And things were once so simple.

How Times have changed men
How Man has changed time.

"Unnatural," screams the wind,
"Unnatural."

Jibaro, mi negro lindo/
Fish smells and cane smells and
Fish smells and cane smells and tobacco
And oppression makes even God smell foul.

As foul as the bowels of the ship
That vomited you up on the harbor
Of a cold metal city to die/
No sun, no sand, no palm trees,
And you clung to the slimy ribs
Of an animal called the Marine Tiger
In the name of the Father, the Son
And the Holy Ghost, amen?

Jibaro/
Did you know you my nigga?
I love the curve of your brow/
The slant of your baby's eyes/
The calves of your woman dancing/

I dig you/ you can't hide.

I ride with you on subways/
I touch shoulders with you in dances/
I make crazy love to your daughter/
Yea,
You my cold nigga man

And I love you 'cause you mine.
And I'll never let you go.
And I'll never let you go.
You mine/ nigga,
And I'll never let you go.

Forget about Self
We're together now.

And . . . I'll never let you go.
Uh, uh.
Never nigga!

Chapter 10

The Battle of the Brooms and the Founding of the Young Lords

ON THE TRIP home from Baton Rouge, Louisiana, to East Harlem, in the summer of '67, the sun didn't let up. It seemed to intensify every ten miles. By the time Rap and I got to New York City, even the sidewalks were sweating. Puerto Ricans in El Barrio were exuding an uncommon surliness, and it wasn't just because of the heat and humidity. The cops were being abusive, harassing folks for drinking on their own stoops and playing Latin music from speakers on their windows. The people were pushing back, cursing the white cops who couldn't distinguish law-abiding citizens from the real criminals; any living being could've told you the place was a tinderbox and a bomb was about to explode, soon. All that was needed was a match. As soon as Rap dropped me off with a wry smile and a wave, I knew this was it, the moment when one is thrust into history, whether prepared or not. With all my bravado and rhetoric, I wasn't exactly ready. I was scared. I didn't change my clothing, didn't call my mother, and went straight to visit my old friend Victor Hernández Cruz at the Gut Theatre on East 104th Street.

Headed by a revolutionary Colombian, Enrique Vargas, the Gut Theatre had become the epicenter of radical culture and politics in East Harlem. There, I met Reyes Tijerina, the Chicano political land activist who believed that all the Spanish land grants should be recognized by the U.S. government and returned to the proper heirs, the *campesinos*. His vision was to have all the conquered Mexican lands—Texas, New Mexico, Colorado, Nevada, Arizona, and California—under one federation called ATZLAN. I also met Pedro Santaliz, an island-based blond Puerto Rican gay poet and playwright whose dedication to the independence of Puerto Rico impressed me. His sacrifices, his loyalty to the people of Puerto Rico, his love of the island and his hatred of the American imperialists stunned me; he was white and well connected; he didn't have to endure the poverty he suffered if he just played along a little with the lackeys on the island. He refused to do so. I met Shirley Chesney, his benefactor and muse, an indominatable Jewish American spirit who worked for the New York State Council of the Arts and gave progressive artists whatever funding information they needed and then lobbied, often successfully, for the granting of the monies to their neighborhoods. She was the inside "gal" for many of us in the movement. And I met George Rivera, an urban *jíbaro*, a tenant on 102nd Street with a revolutionary spirit that reminded me of Che Guevara. He just didn't believe anything was impossible. His gaze, his actions, his badly accented English, his political vision, his wisdom was so direct and honest it startled people who assumed he was just an uneducated 'Rican. He hit hard, too, fought like Rocky Marciano, Carmen Basilio, Archie Moore, knees bent, shoulders bunched up, hands in front of his face, face serious and coming straight at you with pulverizing body shots, not interested in going upstairs to the head, he wanted to hurt; two of those punches and you went down, exhaling tortuously, crumpling slowly, in stages, in pain. He never smiled. Upon meeting you, he'd give you this deceptively light handshake and then study your body, from feet to head, like an old Puerto Rican grandmother, right in front of you, sizing you up, body and spirit. If he didn't feel right about a person, he'd say to me, in almost unintelligible rapid-fire Spanish, "*Vamonos, este tipo es come mierda.*" And, God, was he homophobic! And he'd tell the gays to their faces. It wasn't always easy being his friend.

George was sitting with Victor when I climbed the stairs to Victor's living quarters. After the introductions, I recounted the trip to Louisiana and what I had discovered about myself and my people. George listened with not a small amount of disdain on his face, looking at Victor's face often to see whether he was agreeing with me or not.

"*Dejame decirte algo* [Let me tell you something]," he spat out. "I don't understand what you're saying, *con to' esa baba que 'ta hablando* [with all that babble you're talking]. It comes down to one thing, *eres Portorriqeño o no?* [Are you Puerto Rican or not?]"

I was stunned at his coarseness, and yet here was the moment of truth, the reason for which Kain and Rap Brown had intervened in my gauntlet of identity, the point of entry into the next battle, the next phase of my life. I could either get furious at the messenger for his rudeness and disrespect and miss the point or say yes to myself. I stared at George harshly; he didn't blink.

"Yeah," I said softly, "yeah, I'm Puerto Rican. But, saying that is not enough. I'm not going to hide behind that title so I can pass for white. I'm a Black Puerto Rican. And when I left El Barrio there was a sense of family and protection. I don't see it or feel it anymore."

The challenge was obvious; George was white, and he wasn't making me feel welcome. The ball was in his court, now. He could rant and carp about why I used the adjective *Black* before *Puerto Rican* or he could see the broader picture. He chose the latter.

"Well, then, welcome home, *hermano*." George said and extended his hand, "My name is George, George Rivera. *Un placer.*"

That fateful, humid, sweaty summer afternoon in 1967 bonded us, Victor Hernández Cruz, the Taino; me, the African; and George Rivera, the Spaniard. We, three Puerto Ricans, were about to embark on a political odyssey that would change our lives. There was no need to preach or teach to George or Victor. Every day that summer brought a new insult from the police or the landlord. One day, George called me to come over to his building, immediately. He never sounded desperate; that morning, he did.

When I arrived at the first-floor apartment on 102nd Street, George swung open the door and looked insane.

"*Entre!*" he commanded, and I followed him into his daughter's bedroom. His wife was crying hysterically, as was his seven-year-old daughter.

What I saw revolted me, and my instinct was to run out of the apartment. Rats had chewed his daughter's legs, leaving open, bloody wounds. George was beside himself and began to scream to his wife, out of frustration, "Stop crying!" which only frightened his daughter and further panicked his wife.

He grabbed my forearm, hard. He was a fearless fighter. If there was a person he could kill, he would do it. But how do you fight rats that brazenly come through your daughter's bedroom from the trash-strewn back yard to feed on her flesh? This brave man was without answers; he didn't know how to fight the system or how to navigate it.

"Let's get her to a hospital, right now!" I said sharply, trying not to look too long at the bite marks or vomit. "She's gonna need shots to prevent infection. Put on a shirt, George. Don't bathe her, don't touch the wounds. Put a blanket around her and let's get her to a hospital."

Can't remember what hospital, but when security saw us rush into the emergency room, they didn't stop us. The nurses saw the raw flesh, gasped, and quickly put her on a bed and rolled her in, only allowing her mother behind the drapes. George, bent down, head in hands, began to cry openly in the waiting room, oblivious to all around him.

"I'm gonna kill that fuckin' landlord. I told him the rats were coming through the window. I told him a million times. All he did was put steel wool in some holes like these were tiny mice. When I heard her scream, Felipe, I ran into the bedroom with a bat, but these things were the size of cats. They didn't move. They just looked at me, Felipe, like I was disturbing them. I couldn't hit 'em without breaking my daughter's legs so I started smashing the crib. They didn't even run, they just walked to the window and jumped out." His body began to shake.

"I couldn't help my own daughter, man. I couldn't help her." And then he began to scream, horribly, from inside a place I never want to visit. That morning, George changed. He wanted to destroy anything or anybody who brought death or destruction to his kids, to his streets. His commitment was not ideological; it was deeply, deeply personal.

We began to organize a revolutionary cell. And then we started to buy guns. George wanted to be independent of any group; he felt whatever we did we should do it secretly, without fanfare, and go back to our daily routines. I wanted to be part of something larger than just us, a group that had a plan, some strategic reasoning, some history, like the Black Panthers. I mentioned to Shirley Chesney that I'd like to meet the Panthers officially. Within a week, she arranged for me to meet Bobby Seale, Chairman of the Black Panther Party, in a brownstone on the West Side.

I was elated, Victor Cruz was cool with it, but George had real reservations. He had problems with Black folks starting from childhood and public school where, because of his accent, ill-fitting, mix-match country boy clothing and boots, not to mention his white skin, he got picked on. He said he never started it, but he definitely finished it and by the time the teachers came over to investigate, the bully was unconscious, and George couldn't explain in English why he knocked the boy out. He was tagged a troublemaker, taciturn and nonresponsive. Though he had a curious, brilliant mind, linear and logical, in frustration he dropped out of school. Our loss.

"We don't need to ask them permission to fight for our own people," he shouted at me when I excitedly told him about the coming meeting. "Look at you, all nervous and shit, like you gonna meet a movie star. He's a man like you and me, *pendejo*. He puts his pants on one leg at a time."

I calmed down, took a few breaths, admitted I was in awe of Huey and Bobby, and then tried to explain why I thought the meeting was crucial. George peered at me, biting his cuticles.

"Why should we re-invent the wheel, Georgie?" I asked. "These guys have already fought it out with the police, they know warfare."

"We do too, Felipe. Why you always putting us down? We know how to fight!"

"Yeah, we know how to fight," I shot back, "Gang-fight, fist-fight. I'm talking about a group getting to the enemy and getting out all in one piece. We need to learn from their experience how to fight as a disciplined group."

"*Ave maria, aqui viene con la mierda* [here he comes with the bullshit]," George said loudly in an exasperated tone. "I'm telling you, you are my brother, we don't need anybody. We can do what we gotta do without asking anybody anything. *Somos 'panas,* we're Puerto Rican, right? You'd die for me, and I'd die for you, right? *No hay mas na'* [There's nothing else to say]."

Part of what George was saying was right. I had always been too hard on my own, always admiring other groups rather than loving the beauty within, the simplicity of honor and loyalty that Puerto Ricans possess. I stayed quiet, thinking maybe I was too critical of my own people. George, still biting his nails, softened his tone.

"Look, if it means that much to you, I'll go with you, but the moment those dudes get stupid, somebody's gonna get cut. I mean it, man. Nobody's gonna put me or my people down, *entiende,* you got it?"

"Thanks, George."

I was relieved. I didn't want to go without my people, my core group.

"Naw, don't worry about it, negro. I love you. That's all that counts. Later!" And he left for home.

That day came, a hot, sunny day, and my group didn't say much other than agreeing to let me do most of the talking.

It was a decent brownstone inside, nicely furnished. I thought: damn, radicals can have a good life, too. The bottom floor was a garden apartment with a real backyard and there they were, Bobby Seale, a guy named Pennywell who looked like a bodyguard, and James Forman, a well-known radical intellectual and member of SNCC (Student Non-Violent Coordinating Committee), lounging, looking relaxed. I liked Seale's eyes—a bit sad, but friendly, compassionate, a wise old southern elder's countenance. Pennywell's face was all war, alert, vigilant, ready. Forman had an aloof air about him. It was obvious he was smart and well read. I just felt he was going to be a problem; he reeked of superiority. George Rivera stiffened a little bit, butting his chest out a little more than usual. I began.

"Glad to meet you, gentlemen. We really admire what you've done on the West Coast. We'd like to start a similar group here for Latinos. You're the Black Panthers, we'll be the Brown Tigers."

Pennywell snickered. Forman laughed. Bobby stayed quiet, just looking at me. Victor was visibly annoyed. George stepped back and put his hands in his pockets. Pennywell got the message and sat straight up, nervously, moving his eyes over the group, waiting. Good! We had gotten the enforcer's attention. This was not kindergarten and we may have been ignorant, but we weren't kids in a sandbox.

Bobby spoke first. "Brothers, I admire your courage, I really do, and we believe that all communities need to organize within themselves to fight these racist honky pigs. Black power to Black people, brown power to brown people, red power to red people. . . . "

I interrupted and intoned, ". . . Yellow power to yellow people, white power to white people." To which I added, ". . . on a revolutionary level."

Bobby smiled and continued. "Look, brother, copying us is not the answer. You've got to take scientific socialism and apply it to the objective conditions in your community. I would think that Puerto Ricans and Latinos have some unique problems that can't be answered with a Black Power program; you've got to find your own way, and that includes your own name. We're catching hell with a picture of a black panther with his teeth showing like he's gonna eat somebody."

James Forman shouted out, "That was the intent, eating somebody's ass."

Bobby ignored the bravado. "But for you to call yourselves Brown Tigers would put you in jeopardy too soon. These pigs would know you came to us and from us. You'd be shut down and killed before you started. Find another name, build another platform, a Puerto Rican platform that answers the shit you're going through in your community. It takes time, brothers, time and patience."

I was crestfallen and so disappointed. I thought we'd be welcomed with open arms. Victor, sensing the emptiness in the air, talked about the conditions in El Barrio. "The cops have gone mad, beating us, harassing us, arresting people for no reason. This shit has got to stop!"

George just looked on, saying nothing, one hand in his pocket, the other now thrust inside the front of his pants, right over the belt buckle.

James Forman, sitting on top of a rock outcropping, straightened up and began to pontificate. "You see, my brother, revolution is a process. You can't just come in here and want to start a war. You gotta read. Understand the ideological principles of struggle against capitalism . . . ."

I knew what was going to happen and I cringed.

George let out an exaggerated sigh and said, "*Otro come mierda, coño. Vamanos ya.*"

Forman, a little angry, very embarrassed, but annoyed that someone didn't respect his authority, spat out, "What he say?"

George opened his mouth to say exactly what he meant and I knew it would only be a matter of seconds before George slashed him. Pennywell wouldn't have gotten to Forman fast enough and we would've had an international incident, not to mention one of us, on either side, dead.

Victor, brazenly and just in time, barked at George, *"Callate ya. Dejalo terminar."*

George backed off a few yards and stood glaring at Forman.

Pennywell, to his credit, said, "That motherfucker's serious, ain't he? I like him. He's down." Pennywell had no idea how "down" George was.

I leapt in. "He's a street brother, very impatient, but he's a good soul, great fighter."

Forman eased up. "Yeah, well, that's the kind of impatience and ignorance that gets niggers killed. Impulsive shit."

I looked at Forman with disgust. Rap had told me about his brilliant thinking and his physical cowardice. He was talking brave because he was near Bobby and Pennywell. Alone, he would have been cool, very cool, and a lot more diplomatic. He was a lucky man that day.

Bobby never moved, never took his eyes off me. "Look, stay in touch, stay strong. If you're serious, if you really want this, we'll hear about you. We got some business to discuss, so we'll have to cut this short, but thanks for coming. Y'all can let yourselves out. Power to the people."

And then he laughed and shouted out to George, "And, power to you, you crazy motherfucker."

It was one of the few times I saw George smile. He had been recognized. Someone knew who he was, and he appreciated it. Without turning around, he waved his hand goodbye to Bobby and muttered to us, *"El me cai bien* [He impresses me]."

It wasn't long before the match was lit in East Harlem. The insensitivity, the stupidity of the police in El Barrio was predictable; all that was needed was the right confrontation, the perfect storm. We were already on edge, having heard of a cop killing a Puerto Rican man on 111th Street and Third Avenue. There was bedlam and rampaging in the streets, but it hadn't hit 104th Street yet. On a hot late afternoon, the Gut Theatre performed a street theater piece on 104th Street depicting the oppression of peasants in South America, replete with beatings of Indigenous people by local militia, the hypocrisy of the Church, and the uprising of the villagers. The neighbors loved it, screaming encouragement to the revolutionaries, and booing the militia. Flash, one of the actors and well known to the community, was basking in the compliments afterward when suddenly he stopped and ran toward Lexington Avenue. His brother, a local wrestler, was being handcuffed over a domestic dispute and arguing loudly, refusing to be "cooperative." Three cops were struggling to put the cuffs on and there was a lot of pushing and shoving. The cops were visibly nervous, having been shipped in to quell any further outbursts. Any incident, even a domestic dispute, was going to be interpreted as troublesome. Now . . . Flash's brother and sister-in-law always fought, and it was always public. No one took it seriously. She would accuse him of misusing their money to go out drinking with his boys, and he would scream back that she couldn't cook, couldn't clean, and that's why he didn't stay home. While on the surface this may have seemed of no consequence, the charges they were hurling at each other went to the core of old school Puerto Rican beliefs of what constituted being a real man or a real woman.

In the old Barrio, a real man could hang, get drunk, fight, and even have a mistress, a *"chilla,"* but he first had to provide well for his family; rent had to be paid, food had to be plentiful, clothing had to be fairly fashionable and seasonal. Kids who had no winter boots and wore sneakers year-round did not lift their parents' standing on the block, whether they lived in the house or not. The wife had to have some measure of pocket money; kids needed popcorn and soda money for the movies, milk and cookie money for school snacks, and the missus had to have money for church offerings and small loans to needy neighbors. A man who had good standing in the community didn't screw around where he lived, kept his mouth shut about local crime and the secrets of other men, and no matter how drunk or high he got, always went to Mass on Sundays and to work the next day. This applied to working men, bookies, dealers, gang members, anybody. Do what you do but take care of your family first or your reputation and respect on the streets would go to the dogs. No one would ever say anything about the brother to his face if he didn't meet this criterion, but radio bemba would secretly pass the word around the block: This man is a shit—has a job, makes a salary, but is totally irresponsible. I saw the destruction of healthy nuclear families by white institutions like the New York City welfare department whose employees made Puerto Rican men jump through hoops like circus dogs just to make sure their kids had a roof over their heads and enough food to eat. These men who simply didn't make enough to get through the year and who reluctantly and with much embarrassment had to appear at the welfare offices with their heads down, eyes averted, would have to explain why they couldn't take care of their families; why their wives and kids needed the checks. These warriors who faced down police, organized crime, bullies, and youth gangs, whose authoritative voices you heard in laughter or anger a block away, were reduced to whispering in Spanglish as they answered the bellicose questions of racist "investigators" who pierced their pride with insulting, rude, humiliating interrogations as if poverty was a crime. I remember vividly the loud disrespect of Puerto Rican men; these "investigators" didn't care who heard.

"Are these your kids? Jesus, they don't even look alike. You sure these are your natural kids? No different mothers or fathers? It says here, you separated for a while. Anything could've happened."

What the fuck did that matter? We were Puerto Rican and came in all colors. In one family, you'd have a son with freckles and red/blond hair and a daughter with dark skin and green eyes. That was totally normal for us. For American whites, it was weird and suggested promiscuity. We were aliens. To us, so were they, with their repressed sexuality, leering looks, and insistence on rules. I saw great men, powerful warriors on our streets, reduced to tears or frightening anger, standing up in the cubicle and cursing out the investigators in mangled English, only to be led out by grim-faced security guards. Yes, the men kept their pride, but they lost the checks their families needed. But no longer would they have to worry about the emasculation of unscheduled home visits in the middle of the night with pimple-faced, newly graduated college students or weary, wheezing old white men with clipboards, trudging from room to room, checking off items that were not allowed. It was the height of humiliation for my mother, for me, for all Puerto Ricans, who had to scurry to hide the black telephones. Telephones were not allowed. They were considered luxuries. Using welfare checks to pay for phones rather than for food and clothing was a no-no. The worse part was the frantic passing of the TV sets from one apartment to a neighbor's apartment, antennas and all, for fear the investigator would find them and cut off the bi-monthly allotments. In the '50s and early '60s, television sets were considered luxury items.

The eligibility criteria for welfare helped destroy the Puerto Rican family in New York City. Lonely husbands in furnished rooms, men who could not visit their families for fear they'd be discovered and blow their family's chance for monthly checks, men who respected the law because it was American, because colonization had produced a people who would rather be "honest" and obedient than crafty—men like that sought comfort in other women's arms, which produced other children, which produced pain, anger, confusion, and separation. Another horrible side effect was the dissolution of compassion within the culture. Some of those brave men decided they wouldn't submit to the humiliation of handouts, worked 80 hours a week at menial jobs, never seeing their kids, losing their humor, never leading a balanced life. Many raised healthy families whose kids became teachers, doctors, policemen, city workers. Others fell victim to the clock and became like their bosses: rigid, hard taskmasters with their children, their women, and their neighbors.

Some of them, proud of their decision to take care of their families (and die young through overwork) became contemptuous of their Afro-Rican counterparts, calling them lazy and immoral, mouthing the same Calvinist principles of the power elite: Hard work and savings would bring success. They never admitted to the overt racism in front of their faces, the marginalization they suffered on the job. Many of them, white enough to slip through the white sentinels of other neighborhoods, developed cultural amnesia, changing the pronunciation and spelling of their last names, anglicizing them. Lopez became Lopes, Rivera became Rivers, and they constantly brought up their Spanish heritage (as if genocide was something to be proud of). I witnessed the insidious alienation with which they greeted their darker-skinned neighbors in the mornings, passing them on the stoop with cheap attachés in hand to hide their doorman uniforms. They dressed in ill-fitting, cheap polyester suits and even cheaper ties as they ran the gauntlet of the block, disguising what they really did for money. There were no heartfelt embraces anymore, no kisses on the cheek, just a quick handshake, superficial enquiries about the family, and they were gone, back to their white world of subservience as doormen and porters on Park Avenue or, worse, pack mules in the Garment District. Yeah, they ate well, secretly bringing home steaks they stole from restaurants in which they washed dishes or bringing home a fancy chair they took from the garbage heap of the luxury building they spent hours mopping, but, ultimately, they starved us of the love.

Those Puerto Rican whites who could move, did. They fled out of El Barrio, upstate or out of state. But wherever you go, there you are. Daughters of these *jibaros* who proudly married the immigrant sons of Irish and Italian workers found themselves in bond-servitude with racist husbands and culturally confused children. Whether it was Yonkers or White Plains; Newburgh or Poughkeepsie; Reading or Allentown, Pennsylvania; Hempstead or Brentwood, Long Island, the alienation produced the same gangs, the same addictions, the same heartbreak, only now they had no societal matrix to fall back on, no community upon whose shoulders they could cry. They suffered in silence. And they died in silence. East Harlem was *la cuna*, the mecca. You can't run, you can't hide. Wherever you go, there you are, seriously and forever. So . . . the accusations hurled at each other by Flash's brother and his wife hurt; they meant something. They both were guilty, they both knew it, and the hurt made them fight. They loved each other, but I often wondered if they really liked each other. Whatever it was, they couldn't or wouldn't change, and their periodic outbursts could be scheduled on a calendar.

We, of course, loved the "naturalness" of the theater, sitting on stoops drinking soda, eating rice and beans and *carne guisao* or standing, slurping our *piraguas* on the street, acting as if we didn't care but listening to all the juicy, intimate tidbits blurted out by husband and wife. This was not a tele-vised *novela* with skinny, thin-lipped, straight-haired, flat-assed white Latinos; this was ghetto theater, with dark-skinned, knappy-haired, pot-bellied men with sleeveless undershirts and big-assed, big-breasted Puerto Rican women with bandanas on their heads. Hell, who wouldn't love it. A real play? A real drama? And free admission? Shit, you knew we were going to be there!

Somebody called the 23rd Precinct. We knew it wasn't the couple. They never called the cops, no matter how physical it got; street people would never call, it's against our ethics and anyway, why make the effort? He'd get locked up for a day, she'd go crying to the stationhouse with friends and family demanding the release of her only love, he'd be let go with a warning, they'd kiss and make up, the whole community would applaud outside the station house and nine months later, out would pop another beautiful, brown, chubby, curly-headed Puerto Rican baby who would cheerfully hear, every year, of how he or she was conceived. The tattletales had to be those damn Pentecostals down the block who tried to drown out El Gran Combo's music with their off-key *coritos* on weekends. It never worked. Those scrawny welfare women with tightly pulled-back ponytails and long dresses who had no man but Jesus frowned on the drinking, the dancing, the loving that took place every summer weekend, twenty feet from their tambourines and American flags.

The cops got belligerent, roughing up Flash's brother, and the crowd got belligerent, too. Victor threw a soda bottle that hit a cop and they charged, knocking people down, pummeling them with nightsticks. We charged back, throwing rocks, bottles, and jagged metal garbage can tops like boomerangs, screaming at them to get the hell off our streets, picking up the women, kids, and seniors who had fallen. Police reinforcements arrived, sirens screaming, and we broke up into little guerrilla bands on the roofs, in the alleys, on side streets, throwing everything but the kitchen sink at them. For the next two nights, cars we didn't recognize were burned, garbage bonfires were lit, white males we didn't know and whom we suspected of being informants were punched; cops became the targets. From what I remember, two people were killed, but loads were beaten and arrested. It wasn't as full scale as the riots in Detroit, Watts, or Newark, but it laid the foundation for the emergence of the Young Lords Party, complete with garbage offensives and running battles with police. People were radicalized on the spot.

A year later, after repeated beatings and insults by cops, Puerto Ricans were ready to support a radical organization, a revolutionary group that stood up and fought back. The spark for the East Harlem riot of '67 was a simple domestic dispute; ignorant cops who, failing to distinguish between a public screaming match and a potentially fatal spousal abuse crisis, provoked a riot by pushing too hard. All they had to do was ask the neighbors or the children of the couple, who were right there, next to their arguing parents, sucking on popsicles. The police had no intel, no Spanish-speaking officers, no experienced beat officers who knew the streets and the players. They had negative perceptions of Puerto Ricans, a real fear of closeness to a people who had no visceral hatred of police. It was their anger at the simple, normal, human resistance on the part of the male arrestee that ended up causing millions of dollars' worth of damage and jail records for those busted. It happens every day in the barrios of America, and, these days, someone usually ends up dead. And usually, it ain't the police.

After the riot and in the afterglow of rebellion, I joined the group that came to visit me in the East Wind, the Sociedad de Albizu Campos (the forerunners of the Young Lords Organization). Jail had given me more than enough time to think; I was ready for action, street-style. My philosophy was simple: Deal through confrontation with whatever injustice existed toward our people. I thought the police were the real problem. The people in East Harlem had quite another thought. When we took the time to talk to them, to ask what they really needed, the answer astounded us: garbage pickup. Time and time again, in casual conversation or in what might be deemed informal surveys, we discovered that while police brutality was an issue, quality of life was foremost in their minds—education, health, housing, and . . . lack of garbage pickup. I was so disgusted I wanted to leave the group, leave the community. Who the hell cares about garbage? What does trash have to do with the oppression of a people? And then I remembered George's daughter and the strip-mining of her flesh, the ugly, bloody gouges on her legs, the tetanus and rabies shots she had to suffer, the images she'd have to deal with the rest of her life—waking up in pain to huge, slimy rats chewing on her body. I was so embarrassed at my arrogance, so sorry I had allowed my anger and vengeance to dominate my feelings. The people of El Barrio were wiser than all of us. They knew it wasn't just the fetid, putrid smell of garbage lying around that was dangerous; it was the disease it could cause, the rats it would attract, the loss of time in school for their children, the loss of pay from their jobs if they had to spend time in hospitals, not to mention their having to leave the other children home alone while they rushed from specialist to specialist trying to heal the injured one. It wasn't only that the bagged garbage was not picked up; the sanitation sweepers wouldn't even appear, and when they did, they would sweep haphazardly, leaving a path of garbage in their wake. Those few sanitation men assigned to East Harlem routes would pick up the metal cans outside the tenements and toss the garbage casually into the truck, leaving half the contents on the sidewalk. When the Sociedad group investigated, we realized garbage was a disaster in El Barrio, but what to do? How do you fight garbage bags and garbage pickups? Who do you attack? What's the chain of command?

Those who were to become the founding members of the Young Lords— David Perez, Micky Melendez, Pablo "Yoruba" Guzmán, Juan "Fi" Ortiz, Juan Gonzalez, Denise Oliver, and I—took matters into our own hands. With the help of tenants and street kids, we started to sweep the streets and bag the garbage. Within a weekend, we realized we needed stronger, sturdier brooms; the little borrowed brooms from neighbors and tenants just weren't doing the trick; they were disintegrating quickly and shredding, totally useless to us. This was East Harlem trash, pungent, sharp-edged, and legion. Summer weekends left beer bottles on the sidewalks, on the stoops, because that's where Puerto Ricans congregated. It was a mess. We tried sweeping just one block, our block, 110th Street, then placing the plastic bags, donated to us by the supers, on the corner of Third Avenue. The trucks passed us by, totally ignoring us. We were starting to get pissed, but the tenants on the block, having been told by the authorities that the reason for lack of pickup was incorrect bagging of the garbage, were incensed. Now that we did it the "right" way, they still didn't pick up the trash? Consciousness takes time to develop, but when the "a-ha" moment hits, it's like an epiphany, a born-again moment; there's no turning back.

After two weekends of sweeping and bagging, we had enough. Someone suggested we visit the Sanitation depot on East 99th Street and borrow some industrial brooms. So, off we went, about ten of us, to ask for the heavy stuff, brooms that wouldn't shred and bags that wouldn't burst. Revolutionary moments are simple. They don't pose themselves as grand or heroic. A sudden burst of energy, a speech, an action, can galvanize a group or a community, can serve as a catalyst, a lesson in power, courage, and character stemming from an inner sense of what is right and what is wrong. It happened that day. The revolution in El Barrio started with brooms. We walked and talked jovially on the way to the depot. It was a good day to be alive, sunny, cloudless, and we had each other for strength; what could go wrong? The pudgy, green-uniformed supervisor was standing at the door when we arrived, a little surprised, but certainly not afraid. I spoke as calmly as I could.

"Hi! Look, we're trying to clean up our block on 110th Street. The sweepers never seem to get there, and the bags are not being picked up. Could we borrow some brooms, maybe get some heavy-duty plastic bags so we could sweep up the stuff and bag it?"

The olive-skinned supervisor looked over our motley crew and dismissed us with his eyes and his tone. It was a mistake.

"Sorry, fellas, these brooms are for official use only. Can't give 'em to you. Sorry."

"But, sir, we'll bring the brooms back. We just want to sweep up the garbage, that's all. The place is filthy."

The man turned surly and in his best street Italian American accent said to my face, "Hey, kid, what did I tell you? The answer is no. No is no, you got me?"

I didn't take two seconds to answer him. It had nothing to do with teaching the group a lesson or grandstanding. He insulted me and I forgot the love of the Italians I knew and had befriended and remembered those Italian men who treated us like vermin, like we were nothing. My arms seemed to move by themselves. I pushed him so hard he almost fell, stumbling back.

"Fuck you," I screamed. "Don't you ever talk to me like that again. Now, we're taking the fuckin' brooms. We came to you nice. Now you wanna be a tough guy in my own fuckin' neighborhood? Fuck you! Try and stop us."

The other sanitation workers stopped dead in their tracks, dumbfounded, open-mouthed, as we rushed in and grabbed as many damn brooms as we could. And we didn't run out, we walked out. No one laughed, no one said anything. We became a unit, instantaneously. As we were leaving, I shouted to the supervisor, "And, like I said, we'll bring 'em back. We keep our word."

It was the most exhilarating feeling in the world, a small act really, but our first victory as a group. We had won. Holy shit, we won. We walked back with our chests out, heads held high. No one was going to disrespect us again. And we swept 110th Street until it was spick-and-span clean. The tenants clapped and cheered; word had already gotten back to the block.

In the following days, the sweepers purposely ignored our bagged garbage, the drivers telling us their orders were to leave us alone to fend for ourselves. That was the New York City Sanitation Department's second mistake. After a week, the garbage was beginning to reek; sun, humidity, and standing garbage do not mix; the smell was nauseating, clinging to your skin and nostrils long after leaving the block. We had won the battle of the brooms. How could we win the war of garbage pickups? The members of La Sociedad de Albizu Campos and the people of 110th Street decided if the trucks were not coming to the garbage, we'd bring the garbage to them. The grating, screeching sounds of metal cans being dragged a full block, from Second Avenue to Third, woke up apathetic neighbors and the spirits of our ancestors. With garbage can after garbage can, plastic bag after plastic bag, we fully covered the wide width of Third Avenue with the smelly containers and just stood and waited. Buses could not move; they blocked the delivery trucks that blocked the cars. Talk about honking horns? The cacaphony of loud horns, low-pitched, high-pitched, could be heard, up and down, for five blocks. Mixed with the high-decibel, ear-busting sirens of police cars trying to push through and not being able to, the sound was that of a macabre carnival gone mad, a Fellini movie being shot in East Harlem. The place was crazy. Cops were running out of their cars for blocks, holding on to their Smith & Wesson revolvers that were bouncing off their thighs, not sure of what was stopping traffic, maybe a shoot-out, maybe a murder, bored barrioites were running to see if the circus was in town. All you could see from the east side of Third Avenue to the west was a phalanx of silent garbage cans and a loud crowd of young and old Puerto Ricans, loving the spectacle. The Fire Department was called out, to no avail. What could they do? There wasn't any fire. Without intention, we had blocked the commerce of New York City—buses, cabs, delivery trucks. Finally, someone got the crazy notion that, maybe, they should call the Sanitation Department. And a convoy of trucks and green-uniformed workers wormed their way through a lane provided for them by the police. They picked up the garbage cans, threw the contents in the smashers, threw the cans back on the sidewalk, and swept up the residue, neatly. We couldn't believe our eyes; the tenants couldn't believe what was happening. We'd won again. The garbage was gone in one fell swoop, just like that. Talk about victory dances— the neighborhood pranced and cheered. It was like a Cuban *comparsa*, with neighborhood toughs using sticks to beat out rhythms on the garbage cans. Alcoholics, dope fiends, gang members, and street folks all came out to dance and celebrate. And no one, not a soul, ratted us out as we, the activists, stood and mingled with the crowd.

We learned another political lesson: collective action in the face of injustice can produce positive results. And as the people partied, we, the Sociedad, smiled and stood dumbfounded. One can read about revolutionary action, but to see the victory, to see ideology transformed from idea to reality, to see what organized, consistent pressure can do to change patterns of institutional behavior left all of us stunned, humbled . . . and proud. And no one died. The pickups went regular for a while and then they lapsed. We tried the same tactic of pulling garbage cans from the front of the buildings to the middle of the avenue, but the cops had already been alerted. There was obviously a police informer in the community group we always included in our strategy sessions. The plan was to arrest as many of us as possible. We outmaneuvered them through our street kids who were our spies and lookouts. They were only eight, nine, ten years old, the oldest maybe twelve, but they would walk for blocks looking for police staging areas. If the kids told us the police were mobile, we'd retreat, knowing they'd be there in minutes. If they were on foot, we'd hit hard and fast, pulling cans onto different avenues, stopping traffic. But the police and Sanitation were adapting, rushing to the scene and quickly disposing of the cans and the contents. We had to change tactics, had to keep the garbage in the press.

One afternoon, it happened spontaneously. Somebody poured lighter fluid on top of the debris and threw a match. It was a brilliant move. Now, we'd engaged not only Sanitation and the police, but the Fire Department as well. It meant a lot of overtime for the city. The uniformed city workers had to put their regular duties on hold: cops had to cordon off the area, the Sanitation folks had to pick up the garbage, and the fire folks had to douse the leaping flames engulfing thirty garbage cans, accompanied by an occasional pelting of rocks and bottles. After all, they were extinguishing the only evidence we had of dereliction of duty. We took our chances of getting arrested; they took theirs of getting their heads bashed.

As La Sociedad gained experience in street tactics, we became more confident, more known to the community. It helped that several of us had been born and raised on these streets. We needed a gathering place, a headquarters. We knew that we needed to formalize our student organization. Our activities had moved us into another modality. La Sociedad had morphed from a study group into an activist unit. The paradigm shift had occurred; internal self-determination led us into a new reason for living: our people, our island, future generations of Puerto Ricans. Immediately, we had to make serious decisions about our lives, decisions that would affect us and our families. It would mean action, action that could get us killed. I was thoroughly immersed in this battle and falling in love every day with the nobility and courage of the Puerto Rican community, especially the street people. For me, college was no longer an option. I loved scholarship, loved Queens College, loved Plato, Nietzsche and Kant, loved Marx, Marcuse, and Rousseau, adored Hemingway, Baldwin, and Dostoevsky, but I knew that I could not be a full-time student and a full-time fighter. The nip in the air told me fall was on its way and so was registration for the new semester. It was not to be.

The last meeting of La Sociedad de Albizu Campos was not a sad affair—serious, but not sad. Denise Oliver, one of the students from Old Westbury who had helped recruit me from the East Wind, was there, along with David Perez, Micky Melendez, Pablo "Yoruba" Guzmán, and Muntu, a faithful Afro-American who looked collegiate, loved his Blackness and saw no differentiation in the struggles of Black and brown people. Muntu was not afraid of criticizing us when we got too stupid and nationalistic. He was scrupulously honest, loyal, and fearless. He looked like a high school student, probably the reason he rarely got busted; he was a bespectacled, pretty Black man who would sit quietly in the corner, filing his nails, until he had something to say. Muntu kept the balance, making us laugh when we got too serious. While we would fall on the floor laughing hysterically at his comical observations, he would stay stone-faced after his criticism of some local official, "Well, am I lying? You know that mothafucka ain't no good. Why y'all bullshitting?" which would convulse us again. We needed him during the early times, the good times; he was so damn real.

After the banter, we got serious. I had made up my mind. In all honesty, I wasn't sure if my decision to leave Queens College was because the courses and exams were getting more intense, my study habits were horrible, and I was anxious as hell, or I had caught the revolutionary bug. Probably both. But I knew I had to serve one mission and one mission alone. I chose the streets. I had to tell the group, and on this, our last day, I let it all out. I started my explanation slowly.

"I've been thinking about this for a long time, this decision. Something's happened to me. I'm excited in the morning. I get up wanting more, more of the streets, more of the people, more of the action. I'm so into it I can't see myself sitting in a classroom talking revolution; I'm doing it. I'm right in the middle of history, right in the middle of change, in a community I was born in. I can always do school, but this moment I'll never get back. The feeling I get when we help these *viejitos* or when those kids follow us because they've never seen anybody stand up to the man, the feeling I got when we got those fools to pick up the garbage, that shit is priceless. I can't go back to who I was or what I was. I'm a servant of the people now, and I love it. I'm leaving school. I'm not going back. I'm staying on these streets. I'm fighting."

The room was thick with unity and determination. One by one, the individuals made their commitment to full-time struggle. We had passed a crucial landmark without a compass. We didn't know what to do next, what to expect next. We did know, at that very moment, that whatever came next would have to face all of us, together. As I looked around the room at my comrades, I saw the nervous, happy energy slowly fade to a sobering realization. We said it, now we had to do it. And we had to tell our parents. Not an easy task. I stopped laughing, too. My mother was not going to take kindly to having to worry again after suffering through gangs, murder, and jail.

I didn't bring revolutionary talk into the house when I went to visit. I told my mother almost everything, but when it came to street stuff, crime, or radical activity, she was safer not knowing. Neighbors, friends, and enemies knew my mother's apartment was barrio neutral (an enemy or his parents could come plead his case for help or a cessation of hostilities). Our mothers were sacred; I protect yours, you protect mine, and shut the hell up. Sure as shooting, the female gossip mafia, knowing I wouldn't touch them, began their misinformation campaign. It was faster and more insidious than anything the FBI could do, short of murder. First came the rumors, whispered to Mom in choir rehearsal, about my being spotted and chased by police. Then came the predictions of beatings and jail, the anecdotal accounts of what happened to some mother's boy, beaten senseless and left paralyzed by big white policemen, who, it was said in whispers, had been looking for him since his release from prison. Finally, they would sit my mother down and, with tears and death wails, "holy spirit" trances and awkward body jerks, sudden shouts and speaking in tongues, prophesize the death of her oldest son, me. Aurora could handle most of the negative buzz about her children with some measure of equanimity, but this information about me was coming in too hot and heavy.

When I was younger, complaints from a neighbor about her children's behavior were handled with a serious slap and an order, "Get your behind upstairs, you got one coming." As we were adults, those tactics, weren't going to work, though from time to time, in crisis mode, my mother would stand up slowly, face me, and hiss with venom, "You're still my child. Don't make me go crazy on you, 'cause you know I will." I believed it. Obediently, I'd sit my ass down to listen to the Puerto Rican Pentecostal *fatwas* she'd issue. They'd always start with "The next time you see '*fulana de tal*' and you brush her off and continue talking with your friends and not say hello, I'll beat you until you turn white."

The very thought of that was hilarious, but I'd learned a long time ago that when Mom was on a discipline trip, the worst thing to do was laugh. Unless you had a serious death wish. This time she called me on a sunny Saturday and said she had to go shopping and needed my help. I thought nothing of it; hey, it's my mother and that's what you do. The only strange part was that she rarely asked me to help her shop. Paul, Margie, and I were living on our own and she had stopped buying large quantities of food.

We walked to the old Safeway on 111th Street, between Fifth and Madison, bought what she needed, and I took the old metal shopping cart with the cheap, squeaky wheels that every mother in El Barrio owned and pulled it slowly as we trudged down Fifth Avenue to her Lakeview complex building on 107th Street. She kept taking sneak peeks at me, not saying anything. I never saw it coming. She was forceful and direct. "I don't want you with that group anymore. They're causing problems and they tell me you're leading it. Somebody's gonna get hurt, Felipe. Somebody's going to jail. And I know you with your big mouth. I can't take it a second time." I stood in the middle of Frawley Circle and 110th Street (now Schomburg Plaza), just stopped in the middle of Fifth Avenue (thank God, no traffic was coming our way) and looked into the pained face of this handsome Afro-Indian, an Ella Fitzgerald–looking queen with lots of hair and a regal aura. But I had to tell her; I had to make my stand, right there, right next to the church where she found the Lord and raised me to stand up for others.

"How many times have you told me, Ma, to stand up for what I believe in? How many times have you said if God puts something in your heart, and you feel it's right, do it, regardless of what people say? Ma, I'm fighting for what I believe in. I'm not doing street, mommy, I'm not selling drugs, I'm not robbing people, and I'm not planning to die. But, Ma, sometimes . . . sometimes in a man's life he has to stand up. Look at how we live, Ma. Look at the garbage, at the way cops treat us, this is not life, mommy. It's hell and I know you know it. I've heard you rail against the way we're treated, how you hate abuse, how you always go to the welfare office, to the Housing Authority, to help people who can't speak English. I'm doing the same thing."

"Yeah," she blurted out, "but you're breaking the law and they're going to try to kill you. Do you know what you mean to this family? Do you? What am I going to do without you?"

She was standing in the street, trembling. Her lower lip was trembling, her arms were trembling. I felt like shit. But this was my time, my decision, my mission.

"Ma, I love you and I love Paul and Margie. But this is something I must do. I don't want to die, but if I have to die, let me die doing something I love, something I believe in. I'm not leaving the group, mommy."

Her chest was heaving now, her voice heavy. "What do I tell them, how do I explain what you're doing?"

In that instant, I realized the pressure she had been under, the barrage of pressure that only Puerto Ricans can impose on an individual to conform. I had to bolster her confidence, give her hope and heart.

"Remember the way the church tried to reject Piro as pastor because he was Black and you stood up in front of the whole congregation and gave that speech about how Christ would be ashamed of them, of how they should be ashamed of themselves? You shouted them down, Ma, you had the fire of the Holy Spirit in you and when they tried to sit you down and shut you up, you defied them. Told them to come and try and sit you down. You were burning, Ma, full of your God, full of what you knew was right. And, if they had killed you right then and there, you would've died happily, doing what you had to do. I feel the same way about our people, Ma. I'm ready to do whatever to change this madness we live in. If I die, I don't want you to cry. I want you to be proud, proud I died doing something I believe in. You've got to say that to those old ladies. Be proud of what I'm doing, Ma, 'cause it's the right thing to do, it's the only thing to do. Don't let them badger you into silence or cowardice, please, Ma."

As we stood in the middle of Fifth Avenue and 110th Street, I saw my mother go through a physical transformation. She straightened her back, pushed her hair out of her face, wiped the tears off, and smiled a smile that only warriors can understand.

"You know, you're right. I don't know how I let them get to me like that, but it won't happen again. You go ahead and do what you need to do."

And that was the end of that. My mother became a supporter of liberation for Puerto Ricans through me. That's when I knew this was a holy war and that if we could get more mothers on our side, this was a war we were going to win.

Now I had to try to convince my friends of the need to join us. George Rivera and Victor Hernández Cruz saw the new group as a bunch of college kids out for an adventure, out to prove they were Puerto Rican and street. George made fun of them every chance he got, but there was some truth to his observations. They were thinkers, not fighters; they were not from El Barrio, and while they may have visited grandparents from time to time, they didn't come from our streets, our projects, our tenements, our gangs. George didn't like them at all and warned me there was a streak of punk in some of them. "When the shit hits the fan, I don't know if they're gonna be here," he warned.

George was also hurt that I was spending more and more time with La Sociedad, rather than simply hanging out on the streets with him. He had simple tastes and saw all the abstract conversations about political science and philosophy as bullshit and a waste of time. Never liking large groups anyway, he slowly began to pull away. George had family in Bridgeport, Connecticut, and we went up there toward the end of the summer just to hang and get away from the city. He was a little too quiet on the train ride. As we wandered aimlessly through the Puerto Rican section, he suddenly asked me to follow him into a store. It was a gun store and we started to talk about hunting, brands of guns, ammo, reloading, the knock-down power of certain calibers. George was a hunter, and, judging by the paper targets we hung in the back yard of his Barrio apartment, he was an excellent shot. No military training, but his bullet pattern was always very close on the bullseye, very close. He was a natural, had an excellent eye, and knew his guns. I had my eye on a pretty walnut stock Marlin .22 and George asked the owner if we could handle it. I fell instantly in love with it, just kept caressing the stock, the barrel; it was beautiful, just the right weight, had a simple open sight, and while it was simply a target or varmint rifle, it fit perfectly in hands. George pulled out a wad of bills and asked the man to wrap it up. I was in shock. What the hell was he doing? Turning, he handed me the rifle case and said, "Felipe, this is for you; it's my going-away present."

I backed off and placed the rifle back on the counter, the manager looking at us quizzically. "What the fuck are you talking about, George? What's wrong with you?" George turned to the owner and in the nicest tone I'd ever heard from him, said, "Do you mind if we talk in private for a minute?"

"Suit yourself," the owner said; "I'll keep the gun by the register" and walked away. "Look, Felipe," George said, looking straight at me, "I've been thinking about this a long time. I can't stay in El Barrio any longer. I'm gonna get killed or I'm going to kill somebody. It's getting crazy with all the cops and the revolution shit. I'm used to doing things alone and I know deep down inside that you need a bigger organization. I already see what you guys have done with the garbage and stuff. But . . . I don't know, I don't trust those guys. Too many people with too much information, I don't know who's who and somebody's gonna rat you out. When it was Victor, you, and me, it was cool. That's the way I thought things were gonna go down. You know I never liked gangs or big groups."

I opened my mouth to protest and he put his finger to his mouth to shush me. "It's not only that, Felipe. After the rat bites, I started thinking, I can't raise my kids in El Barrio. (His wife was pregnant again.) They deserve more trees, man, trees and good schools. I don't want them to grow up like me. And I know, with the shit that's going on there, I'm gonna get more involved and you know me, I'm gonna go all the way and end up dead or in jail for life. I gotta think of my family, *papi*. I hope you understand."

I stood looking at him, speechless. I never expected this. If there was anyone I wanted to fight with, to die with, it was George Rivera. It may sound melodramatic, it's a warrior thing, I guess, but it's a feeling deep down in your heart that only a precious few deserve the honor of your sacrifice and blood. George was that person, and I was losing him. I knew I couldn't stop him. I knew, in my soul, he was right. If it's not about family, what's it all about? I admired his sense of responsibility, his sense of duty. Mine was to community; his was even more personal, his family unit. Neither of us was wrong. George just stood there with me, in the middle of the store, his hand on my shoulder, as I bit my lower lip to keep from screaming. I have rarely held back tears, never understood men who do. I felt totally abandoned.

"I'm here, man." George kept saying. "I'll always be here for you." We walked to the counter, he paid for the gun, we walked out into the afternoon sun. He put me on a train for New York City and I never saw him again.

Victor Hernández Cruz was a loner by nature, a keen observer, a mystical poet whose couplets never rang with the incinerating anger of the '60s; his was the metaphor of hot ice, a word picture that sliced you behind the eye, malleted your toes so you hobbled to truth, all done with an Arabic/'Rican lyricism that stayed with you, that stunned you, after you closed the book. He, too, didn't like large groups, but since it was normal for him to spend days away from us, just writing, I didn't see anything abnormal in the routine until I noticed we hadn't talked in weeks. When we finally spoke, he simply said, "Be careful who you do the do with," a Black way of saying, "Watch your back!" But he never directly criticized my involvement in the larger group, never openly said I was off-base or wrong. I realized a long time ago that 'Ricans have a circuitous way of voicing disagreement. You have to look behind the jokes and silences, the little stories and examples they give to bring a point home. Victor didn't like to argue. He never joined the group. He is a gentle man, not soft, gentle, firm in his beliefs and he goes his own way, seeks his own counsel. He married a Moroccan woman and travels between Puerto Rico and Morocco. Today, he's a well-respected poet, married with kids, and is still a great friend.

La Sociedad de Albizu Campos had heard about a Puerto Rican gang in Chicago that decided to turn from killing rival gang members to teaching people how to fight the system: the Young Lords, led by a charismatic, soft-spoken, blue-eyed, blond Puerto Rican named Cha Cha Jimenez. From what we heard, after a stint in the local jail, Cha Cha was befriended by Fred Hampton, the leader of the Panther Party in Chicago. I discovered later that Cha Cha doesn't make quick decisions. He thinks strategy over and over, like a chess player, painstakingly, so Fred must've taken quality time to drop some science on this Puerto Rican. It must be remembered that Fred Hampton's genius was converting gangbangers to revolutionaries. And he was very successful at it. It was one of the main reasons they eventually shot and killed him in bed, aided by a sleeping potion put in his drink by an agent posing as a Panther. He was the future, the next national leader of the Black Panther Party in America, and everybody knew it, including the FBI. He could convert anyone—gangbangers, Latinos, or white people. Cha Cha was released, eventually, but he was a changed man, serious about defending 'Rican rights in the corrupt political atmosphere of ChiTown. Almost singlehandedly, he turned the Young Lords around. Wisely, he based his operations in a church near Humboldt Park, headed by a white progressive minister, Reverend Bruce Johnson and his wife, Eugenia. Rev. Bruce actively supported the Young Lords as they fought Mayor Richard J. Daley in his land-grab, shock-and-awe campaign against Mexicans and Puerto Ricans. Latinos lived on valuable land, center of the city and lakefront, ripe for white, middle-class empty-nesters who wanted back into the metropolis after their stint of childrearing and good public schools in suburbia. The Chicago political machine played the gentrification card, one of the first cities in the '60s to blatantly condemn whole swaths of land, traditional Spanish-speaking neighborhoods that housed grandmothers and memories, churches and bodegas, social clubs, and block associations. Reverend Bruce and Eugenia were despised by the establishment, but they bravely continued advocating for and inspiring Puerto Ricans to defend their communities against land rape, joining in a coalition of community organizations to stop the land grabs. For their reward, the pastoral husband and wife team were murdered brutally, mysteriously, stabbed seventeen to nineteen times, repeatedly, by an unknown assailant while Cha Cha was in jail. The case is still unsolved, though some of us have strong ideas about who issued the contract.

The Chicago Young Lords Organization was gaining moral influence and newsprint. Imagine Puerto Ricans standing up to Mayor Daley, the maker of presidents, governors, and senators, one of the most powerful politicians in the United States and the bully of bullies! This group in Chicago, the Young Lords Organization, had balls and vision. We had to meet them.

Micky, along with David Perez, who came from Chicago; Pablo "Yoruba" Guzmán; and Hiram Maristany, the official photographer and the only member with a car, decided to drive hundreds of miles in a beat-up Volkswagen to check the group out. I wasn't with them, but whatever happened there was transformative. They came back converted and convinced that the next phase of our development had to be organizing the New York City chapter of the Young Lords Organization. Their enthusiasm was infectious; they bubbled with energy and even brought back a newspaper published monthly. To me, a newspaper meant these guys were serious and disciplined. I listened as David, Pablo, and Micky, related what they saw and felt. Then they dropped the bomb: We should all become Young Lords. There wasn't much to discuss. It was a unanimous decision. We jumped in with all the fervor we could muster.

Now came the rough part, the part that can potentially divide and destroy: the election of leaders. At the same meeting we decided to become the New York City chapter of the Young Lords Organization, we also decided to pick leadership; no need to waste time, we had work to do. There was not much of an election, only two candidates, an activist named Diego Pabon and me. I had the biggest mouth, seemed to handle myself well on the streets, and I came from El Barrio. Diego had courage and intelligence but was a bit more introspective; that, and the fact that he came from the Lower East Side, threw the election my way. Pabon eventually drifted away from us, and I still don't know why. I was now the guy on top. I had never been a gang leader, or a leader of anything. I was always a good soldier, ready to follow my boys to the gates of Hell if need be.

This, however, was different. Egos and gang pride had to take a second seat; everything we did from now on had to point to community and power. Instinctively, I knew we had to affect the bold swagger of young street toughs and the intelligent tactics of seasoned revolutionaries. But first we had to find a storefront office, a headquarters. David Perez, the quiet, unassuming member of our group, started to scour the neighborhood and came up with two great finds, a storefront on Madison Avenue between 111th and 112th streets and a tall, black Panamanian older man named YaYa. He drank too much, talked too much, but damn, he knew everybody in the neighborhood. Add to that, he was quite a handyman.

We were blessed with a twofer: an office right in the heart of East Harlem and someone who could open the place and maintain it every day. We were ready. There were five founding members of the Young Lords Organization Central Committee: Pablo "Yoruba" Guzmán, a bright, articulate Westbury student with a flair for communicating with the press; Juan "Fi" Ortiz, a former gang member who had a way with street youth; David Perez, who seemed to carry the essence of the island with him in everything he said and did, calm, compassionate, and a hard worker; Juan Gonzalez, a brilliant Columbia University student with an amazing strategical mind; and me. I was proud that three of us were definitively Black. We also had the stalwarts from the streets and college who stood with us in the beginning: Denise Oliver, a highly intelligent and very pretty Black middle-class woman who knew the street of El Barrio. Micky Melendez, serious, already married with a child.

There was no hemming and hawing about Africa; our hair was knappy, we wore Afros, were immersed in Black culture, and knew the value of a brown/Black coalition. We were the first stateside Puerto Rican organization to have a majority of Black men in leadership positions. That fact was not lost on our people. We changed the colonial mindset about Black 'Ricans who, heretofore, with notable exceptions like Arturo Schomburg, were seen as happy, passive, and incapable of critical thinking, much less violence against authority. America had carefully cultivated the image of the apolitical Latino: We could be anything, just not revolutionaries. And the thought of Black men leading rebellion had to scare the hell out of those who read and understood history; Touissaint Louverture in Haiti, Antonio Maceo in Cuba, Albizu Campos in Puerto Rico. Be anything, but don't be Black and rebellious. We could be lovers, as in the case of Rudolph Valentino, Carlos Gardel, Cesar Romero, Fernando Lamas or inoffensive comedians like Cantinflas or Desi Arnaz. (Arnaz was one of the visionary geniuses of television, inventing the three-camera shoot and the syndication of the *I Love Lucy* series, along with the development and syndication of the series *Mission: Impossible*, *Mannix*, and *Star Trek*; the introduction of the Spanish language on a English-speaking series; and the bold move of using Afro-Cuban music as the *I Love Lucy* theme song.) Latinos were either greasy, sleazy Mexican bandits or teddy-bear cowboys like Cisco and Pancho, who, in the 1950s TV series, met injustice with laughter, shoot-outs and fistfights but never really killed the bad white guys. The other image was of Latinos as provincial, tribal, alpha-male knife-cutters who sliced anyone who violated their women or their honor: *West Side Story* comes to mind. In Harlem, we often said that the white man took the chains off our wrists and wrapped them around our minds. There is ample evidence of that in how Latinos still negatively look at themselves and their color. To this day in Latino culture, Blacks are only allowed to excel in athletics and music. On television all over the United States, the Caribbean, and South America, you'll see singers and domestics, boxers and baseball players, nannies and musicians, weather "girls" and actors playing *"brujos"* but, with rare exceptions, never an intelligent, courageous, confident Black man or woman as lead actor or lead pundit. We're still ashamed, embarrassed about our negritude, thanks to the Spanish conquest and their insidious method of divide and conquer: one drop of white, Spanish blood makes you white, no matter how Black you are. The effect of this policy has over centuries caused hatred of skin color, hatred of African culture, and hatred of self. I'll rape your mother, your sister, your daughter, murder your men, disembowel your chiefs, but don't worry, the rape seed you carry will be treated better than you because it'll be less Black, lighter, different hair texture, thinner lips, thinner nose. It'll look like the conquerer, the conquistador. It'll have "superior" blood, Spanish blood, and you will be treated more favorably. To cement the matter, the Church required the invaders to marry those they slept with, adding a patina of legitimacy to the charade. Puerto Ricans, Cubans, Dominicans, Brazilians, and the rest of the Black and Indigenous peoples of South America were forced to accept this contract. And those who drank the cultural Kool-Aid could say they were related by blood to *"la madre patria,"* the mother country, avoiding the reality of being born Black or brown. To this day, when given multicolored dolls to play with, most Latina children will pick the white, blond dolls. Their racial sensibility comes directly from parents who come from a sick and colonized culture. In every poll and survey, too many Latino adults in America identify as white, no matter how dark they are. It is changing, but that view still predominates.

For the time we existed, the Young Lords shattered those stereotypes in America. We were young, Black, brown, white Latinos articulating our grievances, challenging the state, and giving young Latinos the heart to develop a political voice, precisely because they were people of color and oppressed. So, we had a Central Committee that was diverse and a national organization, so what? I knew, we knew we had to prove our worth on the streets. The old Viceroys, rulers of East Harlem's streets, viewed us with a mixture of puzzled amusement and apathy. We were young and brash, but could we really change things? And, in the end, the litmus test for acceptance was, could we fight, could we take an ass-whipping, get up and fight again? It took the local barrio gang, the Viceroys, a year before they fully bought into us to the extent that the older gangsters began to join. They soon found out we were not playing schoolyard games; this was not a sham battle. This was revolutionary armed struggle. This was war!

The Sanitation Department gave us an easy reason to keep fighting. After the first few garbage offensives, they again stopped the regular garbage pickups. Institutionally, I don't think they could've helped themselves. Their thinking was that the few garbage confrontations we initiated would simply go away, disappear. Fall was coming and school was around the corner. Wrong!

We planned and re-planned the next trashing for a hot August, Friday afternoon, strategically deciding to block Third Avenue again, a major vein in Manhattan, leading toward bridges and highways that transported middle-class New Yorkers to their vacation spots on Long Island, in upstate New York, and in Connecticut. This had to be a serious blockade, one that would take hours to dismantle, and it had to be a signature statement, one that had Young Lords written all over it. We wanted city government and the police, especially the police, to know who they were dealing with in East Harlem from now on: a hardcore revolutionary group intent on disrupting and sabotaging their institutional racism and neglect. We took into consideration that with the gargantuan piles of garbage would come criticism from those Puerto Ricans on buses and in cabs, but they'd be the minority. Most of our folks rode the subways, so we took the chance. We also knew that on a hot, hazy Friday late afternoon, news stations would be simply doing weather reports and how New Yorkers would be coping with the heat and the weekend. The blocking of traffic and commerce, the sound bites of angry whites sounding off at being stuck for hours in East Harlem, and then our statement of purpose on camera would be too much for the major channels to ignore.

This time we'd formally introduce ourselves to our neighbors and the press. We'd let Pablo use his formidable skills to get cameras and reporters to certain corners, we'd wear purple berets like our brothers in Chicago, and we wouldn't run and hide after the action. Instead, we'd stand with the people, shouting at the Sanitation and Police departments with chants like, "El pueblo unido, jamas sera vencido [The people united will never be defeated]." Basically, we wanted to stir shit up . . . and that's exactly what happened. We assigned certain Lords different tasks: some to look out, some to move the trash, others to talk to the community. Through street organizing in the projects, we had attracted a few bright teenagers: Mark, a Muslim who went on to teach English in Saudi Arabia; Ramon Morales, who eventually graduated from Harvard and now owns his own consulting company; Benji Cruz, who had so much energy we had to calm him down regularly from cursing the cops out publicly whenever he saw them on the streets; José Diaz, a.k.a. Pai, now teaching t'ai chi ch'uan in Florida; Hui Cambrelen, a student and teacher of the Tiger Claw system in New York City; Muntu, a compassionate Black nationalist; Myrna, a bright, tough, streetwise Puerto Rican sister (now a judge); and Mirta, another Puerto Rican powerhouse of

an organizer and single mother. They were the backbone of the first campaigns, and they took their jobs seriously.

Then there was Carl Pastor (now deceased), a soft-talking Afro-American
who worked his ass off, and Minerva, a thin, fast-talking, energetic Puerto
Rican who took no guff from any of us. We had timed the car patrols, making
sure we didn't telegraph our moves by congregating in any given area, and
then, once the red light stopped traffic, we sprung into action so quickly
that the police were caught totally by surprise. We moved not only trash but
discarded bureaus, beds, shower curtain rods, old valises, cardboard boxes
left near supermarkets, anything that was garbage and left on the streets.
It was a real barricade, in some places four feet high. We just kept piling
shit on, amazed that there was so much debris on our streets. We saw the
Sanitation trucks coming, but we were prepared with a different tactic. We
didn't hate these guys, we didn't hate any of the city services, including,
believe it or not, the police. Well . . . that's not exactly true; our official line
was the police were workers and when armed struggle began, many of them,
especially those of color, would join our struggle. However, we fought them
with a ferocity that was not natural, not composed. They acted like occupying
troops; we struck back, whenever possible, like guerrilla fighters, with curses,
sidekicks, and reverse punches. The objective was to free ourselves from
their grasp, punch, kick hard, and then run our asses away from the scene
of battle. We wanted a prolonged battle, so as the Sanitation guys started
to pull away the bags of garbage from the center of the avenue to allow a
traffic lane, we sent some of our teenagers to casually stroll by, making
believe they were curious rubberneckers, and squirt lighter fluid on the
top of the garbage heaps. Boom, the place lit up like a college homecoming
bonfire.

We heard the fire engines coming and were prepared for them too. When
they scrambled out, uncoiled the high-pressure hoses, and hosed the fire
down, we made sure they got another call of a fire nearby. We'd wait until
the captain called them back into the trucks with the smoldering embers
doused on the avenue, and as soon as they went screaming off, we played
Pony Express and passed more dry garbage, debris, and cardboard boxes
from hand to hand, piling it all up again, in full view of the Sanitation men,
and setting fire to it. When they tried to catch and hold us for the police,
they caught all the punches and kicks we learned from Pai and Hui. Pai was
taught the best side kick, the fastest side kick in the business, by Sifu Ralph
and Monroe Marrow (a.k.a. Abdul Musawwir, now deceased), a Black martial
arts pioneer in Harlem. Hui's blocks and reverse punches, taught to him by
his Chinatown *sifu*, Wei Hung, really hurt. None of us were caught. By the

time the police came, the flames were high, the smoke was thick, the fire trucks were coming again, and we kept on chanting and exhorting the people, this time taking off our shirts and berets, making it almost impossible to be identified by firemen or cops. What the hell, we all looked alike anyway. The cops just stood frozen, their job was not fire; the Sanitation men just stood there like frustrated wooden pegs, their job was not fire. And the fire raged on while we conducted interviews on safe corners giving the reporters great copy and fabulous visuals. The battle lasted for hours. We went home a satisfied lot: We'd gotten our message across, complete with neighbors defending our actions, on television and radio, we got the garbage cleaned up, and we stopped commerce in New York City. There was relatively little criticism from "community leaders," and those who voiced their complaints were shouted down loudly by street people, who would brazenly stand up in meetings and say, "At least they got the garbage cleaned up. What have you done for us lately?"

We heard that irate New Yorkers drove Mayor John Lindsay crazy with phone calls that day and the next. It took a long time for the city to fuck with our garbage pickup again, a long time. They got the message.

Chapter 11

The First People's Church

SUNDAYS HAVE ALWAYS been the days for momentous changes in my life. Whether it was revolutionary actions or spiritual epiphanies, Sundays were the days that allowed my consciousness to receive the ideas and flesh them out.

It seemed that health issues were becoming our organization's focus. The more we spoke to doctors, nurses, and health officials who warned us about the effects of subtle, quiet malnutrition, the more we felt it necessary to do something, anything. East Harlem kids, especially those in the early primary grades, were not receiving the proper nutrition for their first meal of the day. Their attention span, their ability to retain information, was poor; their grades were suffering. A breakfast of coffee and a buttered roll wasn't sufficient to carry them through to lunch, much less the day. We had appealed to several churches to donate space for breakfast programs. We wanted to establish a breakfast program similar to what Black Panther Party branches were doing in Oakland, Chicago, and other Panther locations. They were wildly successful, so much so that FBI director J. Edgar Hoover was doing everything he could to try to destroy them. We lobbied churches with large kitchens to cook breakfasts early in the morning before our kids went to school; we wanted their tummies filled with oatmeal, eggs, bacon, bread, orange juice, and milk. (This was long before we knew anything about cholesterol and starches turning into sugar.)

We visited several churches in El Barrio, but their spaces were either too small or their kitchens inadequate or simply not situated on a plot of land that felt comfortable to the common folk. There was a church close to our headquarters that seemed perfect, The First Spanish Methodist Church on 111th Street and Lexington Avenue, smack-dab in the middle of East Harlem. We knew the sanctuary space was ample, but we knew nothing about their kitchen and seating space. So I paid them a visit and spoke to the church secretary, who invited us downstairs to see the kitchen. It was perfect. The stove was of industrial size and the eating area was spacious.

The secretary believed in our community health campaign and asked us to visit the church office again, apologizing for the absence of the senior pastor. She was excited about the project, and we were excited about the possibilities of fighting less, settling down, and institutionalizing our ideology of serving the people. We scheduled a date for the meeting, thanked her for being so compassionate and courteous, and left the building. The next week I visited the church with two Young Lords Party members and was ushered into the office of the pastor. He wasn't pleased to see us when we were announced by the secretary and gruffly told her he would speak to us outside his office. This was the first insult. Reverend Humberto Carranza was an older, slightly paunchy white Cuban, about 5′6″, with an almost palpable arrogance. His look, his demeanor communicated that he was meeting with inferiors. I had experienced that class/race hatred before, in the Pentecostal church, as my mother would question the exclusion of Black Puerto Ricans and Black Americans from the church and the selection of white Latino ministers to head her local church, Templo Bethel. The Assembly of God officials would listen to and then dismiss her with dulcet tones of piety. You could feel their attitudinal perceptions of her as a single Black welfare mother. I hated them then, and though I've since forgiven them for their insults, these days I quickly put church officials in their place whenever I encounter white colonial attitudes in any Pentecostal church, in any church. While this church was Methodist, the same attitudes prevailed.

He boldly stood face to face with me, almost nose to nose. You could tell he had never had his ass kicked by a Black Latino.

"What is it you want?" he demanded loudly. "Let's get this over quickly. I have things to do."

I just looked at him and knew immediately our petition for space was going nowhere. But I had to try. Maybe, just maybe, if as the Bible says "A soft answer turneth away wrath," it might be possible for the grace of God to change his heart. It was not to be. I tried anyway.

"Reverend, I was raised in this barrio all my life. Went to pre-school in this church and always had a warm spot in my heart for the First Spanish

Methodist. When the roof burned down, all of us in East Harlem contributed toward building a new one. We helped re-build this church."

He looked at me impatiently, tapped my chest, and said, "Get to the point, 'cause I want to give you my answer."

My impulse was to knock him out cold right there, but it would've caused a scandal in our community, not to mention break the secretary's heart. The code in El Barrio is and always has been, never, ever, hurt a holy man or woman, no matter what the provocation.

The two members of the Young Lords instinctively moved to protect me, but my eyes told them step back. I didn't have to say anything. They knew the only real threat was my kicking this "*gusanos*" ass.

"We need space for a breakfast program. We need a large kitchen, which you have, and a large dining area, which you have. Would you allow us to use your space to feed our kids? We'll take care of everything: we'll cook, clean up, make sure the kids don't break anything. We'll take care of everything and we'll leave quietly. You won't even know we were here."

And then I looked at him and almost whispered, "Pastor, we really need the space to do God's work."

He didn't budge, didn't blink, and instead said, coldly, "Are you finished?"

"Yes, sir," I answered.

"This is my answer. NO! Not now, not ever. No! You and your bearded thugs remind me of Castro and his band of Communists. Ten years ago, I had to run from them. They spoke the same way you do, how they want to serve the people when all they wanted was to establish a godless Communist state. And they did it slowly, with programs for the poor like you guys are doing.

"But I see through you. You will not blaspheme the house of the Lord nor impose your thinking on these innocent children. The answer is No!

"Now that I've made myself clear, I will ask you to leave!"

This is when I got scared of myself. I didn't realize it, but my body was trembling slightly, my fists bunched up, my eyes narrowed. I looked at the secretary, incredulously. This motherfucker had just insulted me, Fidel, and the Cuban Revolution I admired, and he called the Young Lords "thugs"?

This white boy had to be hurt, fuck the scandal.

The poor secretary, her hands clasped over her mouth, kept shaking her head from side to side, silently imploring me not to do what she knew I wanted to do . . . badly. I turned my eyes back to the pastor. I was cold-blooded in stare and sound. No more nice guy.

I went street on him, with the thickest, Blackest, South Carolinian accent I could muster. It gets like that when I get riled.

"Let me tell you sumpin', Mister. You don't know how thin the ice is you walkin' on right now. I'm gonna stay in front of yo' face for a few seconds just 'cause I feel like it and 'cause I'm hoping to God you say sumpin' else stupid, so I can lose whatever salvation I have."

A few long seconds elapsed, us staring at each other. He said nothing. He really believed he could win this battle. You ever seen Christians who believe they're right in criticizing "sinners," especially gangsters, even when the gangsters are giving out turkeys for the holidays?

Their bravado doesn't tell you they're shitting in their pants while telling a guy who just shot a nigga the night before that he needs to leave the block. Sucker, he owns the block and lucky he's not making you pay rent or telling you he's doing your daughter after Sunday school and your son cops from him during the week. And then, without taking my eyes off him, I turned toward the door that was already being opened by my two comrades.

At the door I went back to "respectable" English.

"Reverend, you will rue the day you denied us access to your church. You will live to see it. I promise you," I said, and I left.

We knew we had to step up our game. Immediately after, I sat with the Central Committee and worked out a plan for lobbying the church and getting the church fathers to understand how important proper nutrition was for their children and grandchildren. Our organizing was personal, powerful, and persuasive. They'd begin to execute the plan while I fulfilled a longstanding commitment with Rap Brown to undergo survival training in the heavily forested Midwest. We would live off the land, learn how to use long guns properly, how to keep warm in the winter, and how to live in silence without the constant din and distraction of television, screaming voices, ambulances, and police cars.

Rap, a fiery revolutionary Black nationalist, did not believe in the separation of races when it came to survival. Our group was Black, white, and Latino, bucking the popular trend of segregation even within revolutionary circles back in the East. For the next six weeks, men and women of the Young Lords Party attended church services, prayed in their combat boots, sang in their camouflaged jackets, and lobbied outside after church for the breakfast program by establishing trust with the parishioners. There was sympathy, there was empathy, but the theological wall of resistance did not allow the parishioners to go any further. The pastor had effectively scared them with his rantings about Communists.

When I called the office from where I was in the Midwest, they told me there had been no progress on getting the space for the breakfast progam at the church. For me it was now or never.

I told Rap I had to go back to New York City. He agreed and drove me back. Upon my return, I was in no mood for "nice."

The look on my face, my attitude, said it all. No more bullshit.

I convened the Central Committee immediately upon my arrival in the office, sat them down, and ran the plan past them.

No pleasantries, no chatter . . . just business. I launched into the next move. "This Sunday is the seventh Sunday we'll be attending the church. It's going to be Testimonial Sunday, a day when anybody can get up and testify as to what God has done in their lives and what they intend to do to show God their gratitude." Someone asked, "How do you know that?"

"I'm Pentecostal. If there's a law or a ritual in the Protestant faith, in Christianity, Pentecostals know about it. They don't always follow it, they may even rebel against it, but they're aware of it. This Testimonial Sunday, I'm going to get up and declare what God has done for me and how I want to show my gratitude in service to Him. I'll preach about the breakfast program to the whole church."

There was a stunned silence. It took a minute before the smiles appeared on the guys' faces as they began to see the utter simplicity of delivering a direct message to the congregation as a whole.

Sunday came and we marched to the church, this time with a motley crew of Lords, white radicals, and community sympathizers.

I sat in the middle of the pew, toward the back. The others sat quietly in the back. I didn't notice anything strange, anything different. It seemed to be a normal Sunday service. One by one parishioners rose and testified to God's miracles in their lives and their conversions to His will.

At what I thought was an appropriate moment, a long space between testimonies, I rose.

"May God bless all of you," I shouted. "God has been merciful to me and has allowed me health and grace. I was raised in the church and now I want to give back. We ask you, our mothers and fathers, to let us feed the children in a breakfast program right here in this church."

A few members of the congregation tried to shout me down, but I continued. "Why would you refuse your older children from feeding their younger brothers and sisters? This is what God wants us to do." And as I preached, I started walking down the center aisle toward the front of the high pulpit.

I heard a bit of commotion behind me and I assumed it was my support group. It was. But not for support, but for defense. They saw what I couldn't see as I moved forward. About ten cops stood up in the congregation and began to move toward me, some in plainclothes, some in uniform.

They had been planted in the audience by the minister, something I had never experienced in any church.

From a side door came Captain Baller of the 25th Precinct. He was serious and curt.

"Felipe, we can do this inside or we can do it out." I knew exactly what he meant: They could and would beat me up in the sanctuary or drag me outside for the ass-whipping.

I was frightened. I was scared. But I wasn't going to stop. The Lords had waited too long.

"Captain, whatever you're going to do, you're going to have to do it right here, in front of everybody." And that's when the Selma moment happened, when the raw brutality of the police and the indifference of the minister came into full view. It's when they lost the moral high ground.

The first nightstick came crashing down into my Afro, hard. My adrenaline was so high, I felt the thud but not the pain. I turned to the cop behind me and punched him square in the face. There were six cops around me, and they began to whale on my head with their nightsticks. I caught another cop on the jaw, but I was overwhelmed quickly. The blows rained on me like a combo of timbale players all soloing at the same time. Only these weren't thin drumsticks. These were hard wooden clubs tearing through the cushion of my Afro and splitting my scalp. It was all I could do to keep them from breaking my teeth, my nose, my face. I kept my arms crossed in front of me. Pandemonium broke out, women screaming in anger at us and those screaming at the police to leave us alone. In a move right out of an absurd movie, the pastor ordered the organist to play "Onward, Christian Soldiers" as the cops were wading into the pews with their nightsticks. They punched and pulled me from the front of the sanctuary, down the center aisle, to the back. I pulled backward, throwing punches and trying to cover my face, slipping on my own blood. I remember screaming at one of the Lords, who later turned out to be an undercover, to pull the plug on the organ. He did. It wasn't ethereal anymore. I wanted the churchgoers to hear and see the blows, the blood, the breaking of bones, in real time, in real sound, without music, without filters. Let them hear the screams of their neighbors, the crunch of wood on flesh and bone as the cops continued their orgy of violence, cursing us as they connected with our heads. I wanted the congregation to see the Holy Spirit in their young and the evil passivity of their old as they sat looking straight ahead, continuing to sing, ignoring our cries for help.

After about the tenth blow to my head, I felt an intense desire to sleep, to just let go and float. Death was waiting for me, patiently, mask on, arms crossed, right in the middle of the church. I refused to give in and told myself to keep swinging, keep resisting. One Puerto Rican cop jumped on a pew and, with all his weight, came down with his baton, directly onto my head.

They say the blood spewed upward like a geyser. I didn't feel it. I was numb and on automatic. I didn't want to die, not in this church, not by their hands.

Not one Young Lord came to my aid, not one. I say this without rancor after all these years. Most of them were hiding under the pews, including the Central Committee. Thirteen activists were arrested, me and Denise included. No Juan, no Yoruba.

Two non-Lords saved my life. With six cops battering my head and body, it was only a matter of time before I lost consciousness. Out of one of the front pews, a young, tiny, white Cuban woman, Sonia Ivaney, who had been following us from the beginning and loved what the Lords stood for, flung herself at one of the cops, scratching his face and screaming, "Leave him alone, you bastard!" She didn't poke his eyes out, but she happened to grasp his lower lip and, as they say in the martial arts, where the head goes, the body follows. One cop off of me.

Another man in the same pew, Joe Hill, a Black Puerto Rican, just returned from a tour in Vietnam, also a community supporter of the Young Lords, simply stood up and, without saying a thing, punched another cop directly in his eye socket. That cop went down but they kicked Joe's ass viciously.

Those two downed policemen were hurting me the most. I now had only four other cops to deal with, all pulling me toward the front doors on Lexington Avenue and the waiting green-and-white bubble-top police cars.

They had broken my right arm in two places; remarkably, I only needed seven stitches to sew up my scalp. Thank God for bushy, knappy Afros. I considered myself lucky. One white radical, a tall, thick, homely German girl, was targeted by police. They banged her up badly, but she kept on fighting them as they tried to arrest her, cursing them out. Her short blond hair was thin. They cut thirteen stitches into her head. She was defiant even while we were locked up. Courage, like love, has nothing to do with color.

The cops finally dragged us out and threw us into police cars. We were driven to the 25th precinct and herded into basement holding cells. You can discern the character, the revolutionary resolve, of people once they've been busted, once their backs are against the wall. Some stay sullen, regretting their involvement; others continue to resist. Benji was like that, holding onto the bars of the cell, screaming at the cops for being occupying troops, pigs, you name it. It would be only a matter of time before they dragged him out and really laid into him.

Those of us who knew this game stayed quiet, conserving our strength and thoughts. I had to scream at Benji to shut up. We were busted already, I told him. Don't invite anymore violence on the group by your individual anger, righteous though it may be. Thank God, he heard me, understood, and stopped the screaming.

It was a Sunday. In crowded urban court systems, Monday is for backlog, Tuesday is for new arraignments, sometimes. We didn't get to see the judge until Wednesday. My arm was killing me, the pain shooting throughout my body. The cops, as usual, provided no medical attention to the wounded. I knew the cops had broken something. I didn't know then that they'd broken it in two places.

Finally we were hauled into court, a bedraggled, unwashed set of characters facing a female judge who didn't look sympathetic. Appearances can be deceiving. As we stood before her bench, she asked the assistant D.A. what were the charges and why? As the prosecutor droned on about trespassing and violating the right to worship, the judge just stared at this multicolored group of activists who had just wanted to impress upon a church the need for space.

She then fixed her eyes on me and asked why I was holding my arm aloft in such an awkward manner.

"Your honor, I was beaten pretty badly when I rose to speak to the congregation last Sunday. I think they broke my arm. It hurts a lot when I lower my arm to a normal position," I said as clearly as I could.

The judge looked sternly at the arresting policemen and barked, "Has he been checked by a doctor, X-rayed, anything?"

The assistant D.A. turned to the policemen and whispered something, turned back to the judge, and in a business-as-usual voice stated, "No, your honor. These officers just didn't have the time. There were so many of them, thirteen arrested, if I'm not mistaken." He turned to the police for confirmation; they nodded their heads like dummies.

The judge took off her glasses in amazement.

Pointing to the police, she shouted, "You mean to tell me, you've kept these kids in jail for three days, one of whom looks like he has a serious arm injury, and you didn't bring them to a hospital? You guys are utterly ridiculous. This case is dismissed, all of 'em."

Then she turned to us.

"But here's the stipulation, I don't want any of you within a hundred yards of that church. Is that understood?"

We all answered yes without even looking at one another. Hell, we wanted out. And then she looked at me directly.

"Go get yourself X-rayed. Your arm doesn't look good." I wanted to kiss her.

"Thank you, your honor."

She retorted, "Don't thank me, thank the police. They're the ones who blew it." Talk about joy? We left that courtroom in jubilation, hugging and kissing. The Young Lords had confronted an unjust enemy in our community and fought the State in battle. We proved our courage and conviction, and though bloody and scarred, we were still standing.

Afraid that the local police would come looking for us in revenge, we had to find a place for me to hide out and heal. Micky Melendez found us a sympathetic doctor's house on Staten Island where I could whine and cry in pain without an audience. After a trip to a hospital whose name I can't remember, after waiting for the X-rays and waiting to have the plaster cast put on, I was given some painkillers. They didn't work. Whatever nerve centers I had suppressed during the entire ordeal of the church and the jail came roaring back through my arm and body, this time with spears. Iris Morales was wonderful and patient, putting cold compresses on my forehead and sheets over my sweaty body. My scalp burned, my ribs ached, my back throbbed, my arm itched; it was horrible. When you're writhing in agony, revolution doesn't even cross your mind. All you focus on is the pain. And yet we couldn't stop our campaign just because of a few cracked heads and broken bones. This was war. We chose it. We had to fight it. And so we did.

After two days of lying low, Iris and I were driven to Manhattan, where the Central Committee convened again. Five men—Fi, David, Yoruba, Juan, and I, all with different skill sets—sat hunched, squeezed together over a small table in a tiny restaurant called La Cabana, across the avenue from our headquarters, trying to figure out what to do next. Juan, the strategist, suggested we not stop the campaign to feed the kids. But how, with all these injunctions on us preventing us from even getting close to the church? Well, we could demonstrate half a block away, holding signs up every Sunday, shouting slogans, hoping we could embarrass the church elders, wear them down. Nah, too time-consuming and labor-intensive.

Of course, finding another church would be a sure sign of defeat; we couldn't do that. We could have different Lords, undercover, go to the church again and again and continue to lobby after the Sunday service. The injunction was only against me and those arrested. The troops could tell us when they thought it would be the right time for us to stand up again and proclaim our message of feeding the poor. But how many times could we afford to be beaten up? We had a limited number in our cadre; our newspaper sales, our TB and lead poisoning testing campaigns would suffer if most of our organizers were in the hospital or in jail.

Whatever we had to do had to be dramatic, immediate, and impactful; a Hail Mary, a one-shot knockout punch that would show the city and the Puerto Rican community that we weren't playing games.

Then it dawned on us. Why not kidnap the church the next Sunday? Well . . . not kidnap exactly, but certainly occupy the building. They'd be caught completely off-guard. The police wouldn't be standing guard any longer, thinking the beatings we received had taught us a lesson and scared us off. They had already removed the one police car standing guard in front of the building. The church, its congregation riddled with dissent but collectively smug in their assumed victory, would not even conceive of the Lords' returning to declare the First Spanish Methodist the "People's Church." This would be the perfect time to attack; I kept thinking of Chairman Mao Zedong's writings on war and tactics: "When the enemy advances, you withdraw. When the enemy withdraws, you advance." Jumping up, I blurted, "Let's take 'em Sunday after next, let's just occupy the church."

Fi, ever the compassionate one, said, "Chairman, you already have one broken arm. You don't need another."

But I was on a roll, an excited roll. "No, but think about it, Fi. I don't have to be there in the beginning. Our new recruits could do it. No one knows their faces."

Fi continued, "So what are they supposed to do, hold their hands out and tell people they can't leave?"

Fi's father was a Pentecostal minister and a disciplinarian. Didn't work very well with Fi. He still became a respected East Harlem gang leader.

"Man, I'm glad this is not my father's church," he whispered under his breath. And then David, as if in a daydream, looking at no one in particular, spelled out the tactics. "Chains and locks, comrades. Chains and locks. All we have to do is buy heavy chains and thick padlocks, slip the young ones into the service, and at the right time, lock the place up. Nobody leaves."

Yoruba, pensive until then, shouted, "Damn, brother, that's fuckin' brilliant. I can call all the people I know in the press, J. J. Gonzalez, Gloria Rojas, Luisa Quintero, all of 'em, and tell 'em something heavy's gonna jump off at the same church we got beaten up in. Believe me, they'll come with the cameras."

These were the moments when the Young Lords shone, when each member of the Central Committee stoked the furnace of their unique gift (or blessing, as I called it) and applied it to the solution of a challenge or obstacle.

"Whoa, hold up," Fi said. "This is a church we're talking about, a church with elders, man. Suppose somebody catches a heart attack or something?"

I jumped in.

"Simple—immediately once we lock it down, we announce that those who want to leave, can leave. Don't give them time to faint. We don't want to hold them against their will. Those who want to stay, can stay; I bet you a lot of them will. They're already pissed off at what happened last Sunday."

Juan dashed us with a bit of cold water, a reality check.

"But what if the cops are called and decide to bust the doors down . . . and kick our asses again?"

Fi countered: "Not with church members who decide to stay voluntarily. They'd have to beat them up too. I don't think they'd want that blood on their hands."

Yoruba added: "Not with all the cameras around. Even the minister would have to cool out or risk hurting his own people."

God, was I relieved, because I was ready to lash out at the group. None of them had been arrested, none of them had been hurt. I had the cast on my arm and the bandages on my head. If anyone should've been concerned with getting hurt, it should've been me. My self-righteousness was at peak level; I was going to guilt them into action with this plan for a quick counterattack. I had already witnessed their paltry "revolutionary courage" and found it wanting. They copped out at the church, hid when they should've been punching, kicking, scratching, anything, to keep the young ones, and the new ones in our group, safe, to save me from possible permanent injury or death. Though intelligent and articulate, the only ones in the Central Committee I could depend on to fight, hand-to-hand, if need be, were the non-intellectuals, Fi Ortiz and David Perez.

By the group's silence, I could tell we were of one mind, at least regarding strategy and tactics. It was a go. We were going to take the church the next week, ten days away. We didn't know it, but we were about to make history. There is something about a well-planned military offensive with people who know what they're doing. They're aware of their strengths and the enemy's weaknesses, and they play the odds, hopefully to win. It is a chess game, only you're not playing in Washington Square Park with old guys or hustlers, you're playing with lives, your lives, and it's nothing short of exhilarating. That kind of action is a high, and its very addictive.

The Lords immediately went into action. David sent out teams of men and women to several hardware stores in and around El Barrio. We didn't know if the cops were following us, so we ordered the groups to act as if they were buying stuff for their buildings or garages and property. They had to act normally and play the part of married couples in the case of man/woman teams, business partners in the case of man/man teams. It worked, and within a day we had enough chains and locks to restrain Godzilla.

The young cadre was excited to be participating in a full-scale operation; they were chomping at the bit. I prayed they wouldn't telegraph their excitement while inside the church, giving the minister time to call the cops, again. I don't know how they hid those bulky chains and padlocks. What I did know is these were stone-cold barrio kids—they could fight and disappear; lie to the cops with open eyes; hide any guns, drugs, or stolen merchandise; and, most of all, were fiercely loyal.

That Sunday, those of us who were prohibited from being near the church loitered casually between 110th and 111th streets, drinking coffee, chewing buttered rolls, and trying to act normal. Cop cars passed, but they didn't pay us any mind. Within forty-five minutes one of the kids came running toward us on Lexington Avenue with a wide smile on his face. I know he wanted to scream and shout, but his street smarts told him it wasn't the right thing to do.

"Chairman," he exhaled breathlessly, "it's done. We chained the doors, but you better come quick; people are pissed . . . and scared."

I ran the half-block, dropping the coffee and roll, passing even the young man who brought me the news.

There was loud conversational rumbling as the Lords unlocked the chains and let me enter. The elders were confused, understandably.

I launched into my speech without a second's hesitation, walking down the same aisle I was beaten in two weeks before, looking at the same parishioners who wanted me dead, totally ignoring the pastor, who was sitting on the pulpit, silent, pale, and shell-shocked.

"We didn't come here to hurt anybody. We didn't come here to destroy the church. We only came to feed our babies. We love you. We don't want to scare you. Those of you who want to leave are free to go right now. No one will bother you. No one will put a hand on you or speak badly to you. You are our mothers and fathers, our grandparents. You made El Barrio.

"You fought for us, now we're fighting for our kids. Please, do not be afraid. Those who want to leave should leave now. Those who believe in feeding children, who believe that God's word is true, that 'faith without works is dead' should stay and help us. Please!"

Half the congregation got up, including the pastor, and scurried out the doors, leaving church programs and even some personal articles (which we returned). The other half just sat calmly, looking at us with wonderment, and stayed. We had won them over with our love and sacrifice. They stayed, cooking and serving, until the cops kicked us out, eleven days later.

Yoruba was absolutely right: The press, all the television channels and radio news stations, all the dailies, were at the church within an hour. Wisely, Yoruba only allowed those of the media who were union members to interview individual Lords. They never forgot this act; later, in other confrontational situations involving the Lords, these same reporters would press forward, ignoring police commands and the plastic ribbons of the "Do not cross" yellow tape. The press became our greatest allies.

The word was out: free breakfast for children. For the first few days we had our hands full looking for free food from local grocers. We cooked, serving the food on paper plates, and waited for the inevitable showdown with the Lindsay administration. It didn't come the first day nor on the second; we were in heaven. The YLP began to plan cultural events: concerts, lectures, sermons, and poetry readings. The Black Panthers showed up in solidarity, as did Students for a Democratic Society (SDS), El Movimiento Pro Independencia (MPI), the Puerto Rican Students Union, and what looked like the entire leadership of the Puerto Rican community: community activist Willie Soto, my childhood friend; Bronx pastor Raymond Rivera; former light-heavyweight champion of the world Jose "Chegui" Torres; political icon and the first Puerto Rican Congressman, Herman Badillo; and even the Hispanic liaison to the mayor himself, Arnaldo Segarra (who eventually lost his prestigious job for his support of the young barrio rebels). The activists stayed inside; the "recognized" leaders of our community stayed outside, on the front steps of the Spanish Methodist Church, holding their own press conferences and preventing the police from attacking us. We had one major problem. While we had to beg the merchants for the few items of breakfast food for our kids, we couldn't feed ourselves. The troops never complained, God bless 'em, but I knew their stomachs were churning on empty. And then the angel arrived, Evelina Antonetti, head of Bronx United

Parents, with savory pots of rice and beans and meat. With her staff of ladies, she'd push her way through the throngs surrounding the church, holding the pots, wrapped in aluminum foil, high in the air, screaming, "Hot stuff, hot stuff. Outta the way . . . move . . . this is for our soldiers." And the waves parted.

The news stories brought out the progressive elements of New York City: people who rallied for revolutionary causes; people we didn't know or paid any attention to until much later in life; young, vivacious actress Jane Fonda; a bold and brash singer from the male Continental Baths, Bette Midler; one of the stars of a film I saw and loved two years before called *The Dirty Dozen*," Donald Sutherland; the director of some of the finest films in America, *East of Eden*, *Splendor in the Grass*, *Viva Zapata!*, and *On the Waterfront*, Elia Kazan; and the screenwriter for *On the Waterfront*, *The Harder They Fall*, and *A Face in the Crowd*, Budd Schulberg. Mr Schulberg gave us his copy of *The Battle of Algiers*, which the kids loved, hooting and hollering throughout the entire screening. Then there were the muckraker columnists (brought by Chegüi Torres), the critical voices of New York City like Pete Hamill and Jimmy Breslin. Attendance was also very supportive; City Councilman Carter Burden was there.

With all that publicity, one would think we'd have had no problem obtaining foodstuffs. YaYa and Hiram Maristany did their best, but the local *bodegueros* were still resistant to giving us free food even though they were safer from robbery because the local thugs were in the church helping us.

With the increased police presence on the streets, robbery was out of the question. Still, most of the *bodegueros* eked out their daily donations and cursed us out under their breaths.

On one of my sneakouts from the church, one of the hustlers told me, a banana wholesaler on 111th Street, between Madison and Park avenues, wanted to talk to me, ASAP. I tensed up.

Everybody on the block knew the place was a mob front; they ran the business, whatever it was, and they controlled the trucks going back and forth. We didn't mess with them; they didn't mess with us.

The next morning, around 8:00, I walked east on Madison from our headquarters to a three-story, very plain brown building with bricked-up windows on 111th Street. After climbing the outside metal stairs to the second floor, I was buzzed in and walked very slowly through what seemed to be a warehouse of fruits and other foodstuffs neatly piled in wooden crates almost five feet high. It was a surreal feeling being in that place, the sun shining brightly from the tall windows in the back with shafts of light and dust twirling in the room, the front windows blocked, offering only darkness and shadows. Before I closed the heavy metal door, I shouted, "Anybody here?" and saw a small room to my right, the only compartment in this huge 5,000-square-foot loft space. A voice rang out, "Yeah, come on back here." And I did, walking slowly past the piles of fruit, onions, and dried codfish.

Inside, behind a wooden desk piled with papers, was a heavily muscled guy with thick black hair, stern eyes and mouth, and a no-nonsense demeanor. If this was going to be a hit job, there was no better place to do it, and he looked the type.

"Sit down," he ordered.

And I sat my ass down in a creaky wooden office chair. Growing up with Sicilian men in East Harlem, I learned that their gruffness is just their way. Some of them deal in dollars, mayhem, and murder and there's no time for niceties. They don't like too much conversation, and the ones I know tell you what they have to tell you and your job is to shut up and listen. And follow orders. They are loyal, generous, and loving, but in their male-dominated world, you have to be, you must be, a stand-up guy. That means you say nothing no matter what you see or hear.

The man leaned forward and placed his thick forearms on the desk. Said nothing, just stared. I just stared back, not defiant, just waiting.

"How you doin' with your little breakfast program?" he asked softly.

Nervous, I blurted, "Look, if we've done anything to mess with your operation, let me know. It wasn't intentional."

The man looked at me quizzically.

"Hey," he shot out quickly, "take it easy. I just want to ask some questions."

I relaxed a little. Not too much. I still didn't understand why he called me in.

"I hear you're having some problems with getting merchandise. Is that true?"

I had to be careful answering. If one of our people had threatened a reluctant local merchant who was under this man's control, I'd have to answer for it. I didn't know what form that would take.

"Well, boss, we've hit some snags with some of our people. I demand that the Lords speak and act courteously, even if the merchants refuse to give us produce, and there are a few who've been pains in the ass. I'm gonna say this again, we don't threaten anybody, so, if you've gotten complaints . . . ."

He raised his hand.

"Hey, enough. I didn't ask you for all of that. Tell me who's giving you a problem." He took out a small order pad, pen in hand.

Here I am at four years old with my favorite pinto pony in front of the Johnson Projects.

My mom, Aurora, an Afro-Indian Puerto Rican Pentecostal.

My grandma Margo, who arrived in the States from Puerto Rico in 1920. Beside her is her Haitian–Puerto Rican daughter, Albertina.

One of the few pictures of my entire family: me; my sister, Margaret; my brother, Pablo; my father (*seated*), Jose Pepito Luciano; and my mother.

Tito Puente and me.

My three children: Felipe Jr., Ila Amber Hess, and Eric Michael.

Young Lords March for deceased Julio Roldan.

The older Viceroys with Robles in the middle.

Here I am at an outdoor rally.

Me, Piri Thomas, Jose Encarnacion, Ruben Blades, and Felipe Jr.

Me and my mom.

Hui Cambrelen, one of the first Young Lords, guarding the entrance to the Second People's Church, October 1970. (Photograph by Michael Abramson)

The first time a revolutionary group of Puerto Ricans marched in the Puerto Rican Day Parade, June 1970.

Minister of Information, Pablo "Yoruba" Guzmán, addresses supporters on the steps of the People's Church, June 1970. (Photograph by Michael Abramson)

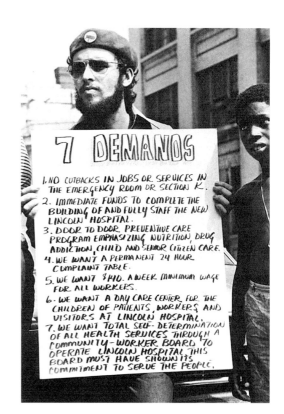

The late Richie Perez at a rally outside Lincoln Hospital, Bronx, July 1970. (Photograph by Michael Abramson)

Pablo "Yoruba" Guzmán with a Remington shotgun. (Photograph by Michael Abramson)

Ja Ja, Black Panamanian Young Lord who guarded our office when we were fighting. (Photograph by Michael Abramson)

Bobby Lemus, serious old-school gangbanger from The Dragons in East Harlem, who converted to the Young Lords in East Harlem, June 1970. (Photograph by Michael Abramson)

Me and my security detail standing guard on the steps of the First People's Church, June 1970. (Photograph by Michael Abramson)

Hui Cambrelen marching in the Puerto Rican Day Parade, June 1970. (Photograph by Michael Abramson)

The first African American woman to join the Young Lords, Denise Oliver, and Richie Rodriguez. There was no color/cultural barrier in the beginning at the Young Lords Party. (Photograph by Michael Abramson)

The family of militant women—Iris Morales, Denise Oliver, Lulu, and Nydia, June 1970. (Photograph by Michael Abramson)

The strategist Juan Gonzalez alongside former light-heavyweight champion Jose "Chegui" Torres on the steps of the First People's Church. (Photograph by Michael Abramson)

Mickey Agrait, Officer of the Day at the East Harlem office, October 1970. Nobody messed with her. (Photograph by Michael Abramson)

The second Central Committee after I was demoted. (*Left to right*) Denise, Yoruba, Fi, David, Juan, and Gloria. (Photograph by Michael Abramson)

The brilliant Iris Morales teaching a political education class, September 1970. (Photograph by Michael Abramson)

Gloria in the East Harlem office, September 1970. (Photograph by Michael Abramson)

The Children's March to the First People's Church—my trusted bodyguard and friend Pai to my right and Fi behind my left shoulder. Mirta, an incredible revolutionary and mother, marching with her daughter. (Photograph by Michael Abramson)

Former gang member Georgie "Little Man," street-smart and courageous, selling *Palante* at Randalls Island, July 1970. He died of cancer. (Photograph by Michael Abramson)

Juan Gonzalez, doing what he did best, explaining the need for revolution at the Lexington Avenue subway, February 1971. (Photograph by Michael Abramson)

Benji Cruz "in your face," revolutionary, loud and proud on 111th Street talking to the people. (Photograph by Michael Abramson)

The home office of the Party on Madison Avenue with Defense Minister David Perez and Aida Cuascut kissing outside, August 1970. (Photograph by Michael Abramson)

Last Poets movie still with the Poets reading poetry for a film called *Right On!* on the top of a Harlem tenement, 1971.

I was flabbergasted. The mob was going to help us? But wait a minute; telling him who the creeps were would be ratting out my own people. Out of the question. "Sir, I don't know your name . . . ."

He barked, "You don't need to know my name. You want us to help you or not? Make up your mind."

I kind of lost it and yelled back, "Yeah, we need help. But I'm not a fuckin' rat. We'll deal with our own in our own time. I don't want you hurting these guys. They're greedy assholes, but they're our folks. I don't want anybody hurt."

The man leaned back for a moment in his creaky chair and stared at me. It was scary. "Let me explain something to you, kid. And listen to me carefully. I didn't ask you to come here to give me names so I can whack 'em. Who the fuck do you think we are? This ain't the movies and we're not amateurs. But let me let you in on something: We like the way you do things. We think you guys got balls. And we know what hunger is. Whether you believe it or not, we remember being hungry, too. Waddaya think, we always had money?"

He paused for a moment, looked away.

"I saw my mother suffer to feed us when my father left. It wasn't a good time." I was dumbfounded. But I had to say it. "You know, I've always admired you guys because you don't abandon your families, no matter what."

He leaned over the desk again and brought me in close with his eyes, formerly hard and impersonal, now amazingly human and vulnerable.

"My mother was Puerto Rican, my father Sicilian. I don't know how or why, but one day he just packed up and left us . . . forever. He was a made guy, you know what I mean?"

I nodded my head, kept quiet. This was not the time to fill the air with ennui. "Who knows? He may have had another wife in Italy, and she came back here to claim him; he may have had an American-born Italian wife here who was connected and wanted him back.

"Maybe somebody threatened my family, who the fuck knows? All's I know is one day he leaves and never comes back. And he was the only breadwinner, so . . . we starved. For a long time.

"I know what it is not to have breakfast . . . or lunch, or dinner. You know what I mean?" he asked, and his voice cracked.

Out of respect, I lowered my eyes, nodded my head. Quiet. Who would've guessed this guy was one of ours and felt the way we felt? If there was ever a God moment in my life, this was one. The man straightened up, cleared his throat, and ordered me to give him the names of those bodegas not giving us food and those who gave us a hard time. I gave him every detail

I could while he scribbled away on his order pad. He rose his head and looked at me squarely. "There'll be no more problems. None. And nobody'll get hurt, ya understand? One thing, though, your people have a habit of not being at places on time. I don't play that! Look at me! Tomorrow and every day after, at 6 in the morning sharp, I want you in front of every one of those stores picking up merchandise. You say nothing to them. Just pick up the food and leave. You say nothing, not thank you, not hello, nothing. You fuck up on any one of these pickups and the deal's off, *capiche*?"

I rose to shake his hand, a huge hand that enveloped mine, a fighter's grip. "Thank you so much, boss. Anything you need from me . . . ?"

He got up, walked around the desk, grabbed my hand again, and told me, "Never make a promise like that unless you're willing to go all the way. Watch what you say and stay out of trouble."

Fat chance, I thought, but I didn't open my mouth. Then he pushed me toward the door. When I turned around, he smacked my face hard, but playfully. "Now, get the fuck outta here. I don't wanna see you again. Good luck."

Don't know what he did, don't know what he said to the grocers, but the next morning we were drowning in food: cartons of milk and orange juice, boxes of bread and bacon, eggs, you name it. The guys who did the pickups told me it was as if the stubborn *bodegueros* had been born-again; the food was neatly stacked outside their storefronts, and they were effusive in their praise and enthusiasm for the Lords and the breakfast program.

As ordered, the Lords said nothing, just made the pickups and left. The mere act of silence scared the merchants, made them want to give us more. We never had a problem feeding our kids again, ever; it's amazing what fear and power can accomplish. Even from places you think are improbable or impossible, you never know where or how your blessings will emerge.

The First People's Church lasted less than two weeks, but it changed the character of El Barrio. Our people participated in and witnessed victory; they started to feel they were worth something. "Famous" and "important" people were coming into their community and entering the church, and news cameras and crews were always milling about. Welfare mothers and numbers runners were sitting and actually listening to the art of the spoken word with poets like Pedro Pietri, who read "Puerto Rican Obituary" for the first time publicly. The Pietri family were stalwart members of the church, and some of them supported the takeover, wholeheartedly.

Though he never joined the organization, Pedro inspired tens of young 'Ricans to join the Young Lords Party with his inspirational readings. The *independentista* singing duo of Pepe and Flora sang patriotic songs like

"Que Bonita Bandera" in front of the altar as we clapped in rhythm and sang along. For the first time in their lives, they heard our history of struggle on the island: the stories of Nationalist leader Albizu Campos and the uprisings in the 1950s, of Dr. Emeterio Betances, who led the first organized rebellion for independence in 1868 against Spain called "El Grito de Lares," of the student movement for independence on the island led by FUPI (Frente Unido Pro Independencia). And they saw a revolutionary coalition: brown, Black, red, yellow, and white radicals working hand in hand to feed children, reading to them, hanging with them. It was a short-lived occupation, but it was glorious. We were free in our own community, on our streets; we were powerful, we could make our dreams come true, if only for a minute.

The First People's Church was our *Battle of Algiers*. We became victors, not victims, the head and not the tail. And every preacher who conducted a sermon in that occupied church confirmed that sin was not only personal; it was institutional as well. Hearts were changed. Beliefs changed. And faith, the faith that everyday struggle produces positive earthly results, burrowed itself into the consciousness of every living being in El Barrio, from daddies and dandies to dealers and dope fiends.

We knew it had to end. We knew the city, the police, could not continue to permit us to illegally occupy the church indefinitely. Eleven days later, they broke the doors down and arrested those Lords who had been ordered to stay. The Central Committee had decided there was to be no resistance, and the arrests proceeded without violence. The Lords marched out proudly, singing and raising their fists in the air. Again, we had won a victory, small perhaps, but significant in that our community learned that if they fought together against injustice, even within our community, we could win and have that win publicized all over the country, inspiring other Latinos to fight for their institutions, for their culture, for their lives.

Reverend Carranza was eventually removed from his post, and, thanks to Herman Badillo and labor lawyer Ted Kheel, the Methodists never filed charges against us. We continued the breakfast program at the Emmaus House on East 116th Street. It was an integral part of our daily activity, and thanks to dedicated Lords like YaYa, a Black Panamanian Korean War vet, and Hiram Maristany, our official photographer, kids were fed as long as the Lords were willing to serve them. To this day, I'm stopped on the streets by Puerto Ricans, now grandparents, who thank the Young Lords Party for those hearty meals. It made a difference in their lives.

Chapter 12

Brothers-in-Arms:
The Miracle of Puerto Rican Love

THE YOUNG LORDS Organization was gaining popularity on the streets of East Harlem. Recruits were starting to come in, young and old. Bobby Lemus, formerly a Dragon, an old East Harlem gang, joined us, as did Husky Willie, a former Viceroy, another powerful gang of the past. I was soon to find out that these two Lords were more than former gangbangers, were more than adversaries, they were mortal enemies. Years before, in a street war between these two East Harlem gangs, Bobby Lemus put a bullet in Husky Willie, crippling him permanently. Husky Willy, a muscular, athletic Black Puerto Rican/Cuban, known for his courage in battle, couldn't walk again, consigned to a wheelchair, and though he always had a ready smile, the brightest teeth, the biggest biceps you could imagine, and the respect of everyone in El Barrio, he had spent a decade vowing to kill the man who had paralyzed him. He and I would spend hours talking about the fight, the moment he felt the bullet, the numbness, the instant realization that he'd never walk again.

He would say, without emotion, "I'll remember that motherfucker's face as long as I live. I'll never forget it. When he dies, when I stab him, 'cause I'm not going to shoot him, I'm not a punk, I'm going to face him and stab him, then tell him, 'Remember me? Look at me good. I'm not going to let you live in shame with piss bags outside your body. You're going to die watching my Black fuckin' face and wishing you had never done what you did. Now, die!'" And then, we'd sit in silence, watching the streets. One afternoon, I asked him, "Willie, with all the street contacts you have, why haven't you put a contract out on the dude?"

He turned in his wheelchair and with more disappointment than disgust, in a voice reserved for the stupid and innocent, said, "That's not the way we do shit here. Something like this, you handle up front, like a man. It's personal, Chairman. I gotta kill him myself. You should know better." I had no idea the guy he was talking about was one of my favorite new recruits, Bobby Lemus, a street-smart, burly, brawling white Puerto Rican, who simply was not afraid of anybody but God. I couldn't wrap my mind around Bobby crippling anyone hurting them, yes, knocking them out and stomping them, of course, maybe even killing in self-defense. But putting someone in a wheelchair, forever . . . never. I just couldn't see it. Especially since Bobby had renounced all gang fighting against other Puerto Ricans. He used to say his penance was serving his people, serving in the early-morning breakfast programs, working on the clothes drives we held and bodyguarding me.

It had to happen, I guess. We had regular political education classes, a requirement for newbies. We held them in shifts so that while some studied, others sold the newspapers we depended on. In one of our evening sessions, as we were discussing the need for unity among all Puerto Ricans, Husky Willie, who usually said nothing, interrupted me loudly.

"All that Boricua unity stuff sounds nice, but if people have personal beefs, it has to be settled between them with no interference."

Willie was staring at Bobby with eyes that wanted to kill. Bobby, sitting by me, didn't recognize Husky Willie. He had gotten much more muscular— his upper body was humongous—he had grown an Afro and a goatee, and, of course, he was in a wheelchair. I thought this was a simple misunderstanding of ideological principles that could be cleared up with a few minutes of historical explanation.

As I launched into the standard rap, Willie interrupted again. Something was wrong. I could feel it now.

"Mr. Chairman, with all due respect, this unity shit doesn't matter to me right now, you know why? Because the motherfucker who put me in this chair is in this room. In fact, he's sitting right next to you, Chairman, nodding his head, agreeing with everything you say . . . bullshit motherfucker!"

The room went cold; everybody was frozen in time; no one moved. Bobby had a puzzled look on his face, then, slowly, began to blush and, in recognition, went cold; his whole look changed, he became an animal with a menacing, no-blink stare and a quiet, coiled, cobra-like presence that indicated he was about to leap to save his life and take Willie's.

Both of them forgot politics, nationalism, unity, everything. They were back on the streets with loathing, do or die.

Willie always had his hand in a bag in his lap when he wheeled through the streets. I knew how sharp his blade was and the lives he was alleged to have taken since his paralysis. He was a small-time smoke and coke dealer—just to pay the rent, he explained—but every once in a while, a youngblood would get the notion he could take the old-timer off and that's where they'd find the kid, on the sidewalk with his guts spilling out. According to legend, Willie would leave him there, money and all, waiting for the police and ambulance so he could explain how he saw the kid try to rob a man and got stabbed. Nobody ever ratted Willie out: His product was good, and his weight was honest. People loved him. In any case, they hated the police and usually the dead kid was from another neighborhood who was given some bad information about the dealer he was about to rob, so no one gave a shit. Bobby spoke first, haltingly.

"Mano, what happened, happened a long time ago. We were different people then, kids. Jesus, if I could do it over, man . . . ."

"Fuck you!" Willie spat out. "If . . .? If I could walk, I wouldn't be in your face, punk. If I had a gun that day, *you'd* be in this wheelchair. But let's settle this shit right here, right now!"

One of the recruits shouted the obligatory "Take that shit outside. This is a political meeting."

I turned my venom on the kid full force. I didn't even know him.

"What the fuck is wrong with you?" I shouted. "Haven't you learned anything? This is precisely the moment to deal with this shit, right here and now."

People started to move out of the way, figuring there was going to be a struggle and a murder. This was a perfect time to divert the energy in the room.

I said, "Look at you ignorant motherfuckers. Wanting to see one of your own killed over a vendetta. Is that what you want? A body left in this office so the police can say we're a bunch of spic thugs? Look at y'all, excitement in your faces rather than compassion for this man who's had to live with this hatred for years . . . for years. And now, he meets the guy he wants to kill, and I understand it."

Bobby looked at me with incredulity; I was throwing him under the bus. He started to rise, but I grabbed his forearm hard and started preaching, looking at Bobby all the time, hoping he'd get it and go along, hoping he would shed a tear and feign regret and sorrow. Thank God, he did.

"Do you know what it is to be a warrior and then find yourself stuck in a goddamn wheelchair for the rest of your life?" I asked.

Husky Willie took it from there. "You need help to climb stairs, to buy food, to sleep, to fuck, to even shit. You're not your own man anymore. You're a fuckin' cripple, dependent on other people." And now the tears started pouring out. "Nobody hires you and everyone disrespects you, thinking they can get over on you. That's what living this shit is like. For all these years of pain, somebody's gonna pay . . . hard." Bobby, his eyes staring into mine, started talking to me as if he were talking to Husky Willie. "I never knew. I swear to God. I never knew you were going through this shit, man."

I gently released his forearm. "Don't tell me, Bobby, tell him."

Bobby stood up, raised his hands to the sky and began one of the most heartrending speeches of forgiveness I've ever heard.

"If there's a way I can say I'm sorry and have you believe it, brother, I would say it. It was crazy that day; I didn't know who I was shooting at. We were all in bunches, man, just stabbing, punching, and shooting. You guys were getting the best of us. Honestly, you were kicking our asses. I wanted to get the fuck out of that street. So I shot and kept shooting. I saw someone go down. I don't know who it was, and I didn't look back. I shot low. I didn't want to hit faces, just wanted to stop whoever was coming toward me. A few of our guys were stabbed, bleeding, and we had to get them and ourselves outta there fast. I never knew who I hit 'til now."

And then he began to cry, silently.

I thought, Thank God for this theatrical mea culpa, only it wasn't phony. Bobby didn't stop. With his eyes closed, Bobby Lemus said calmly, "If you need to kill me now, kill me, if it'll take the pain away from you, brother." And, he just stood there, watching, waiting.

Willie put his head down, grinding his teeth.

"Fuck you, man. You're not getting off that easy. I'm telling you now, you're a dead man. I'm taking you out, somewhere, sometime. And you won't know it's coming. I've waited too long." He backed up his wheelchair and shouted, "I'm finished with all you, now get the fuck out my way. I'm outta here!" And he left.

There was nothing anyone could say; all of us were stunned, speechless. One of the young recruits finally said, "Damn, somebody's gotta do something." David Perez looked at me with that you-know-both-of-them-and-they-trust-you-so-do-something look. I wanted to punch him. Fuck! Why me? This shit is crazy. I felt for them both, the anger, the sorrow, and the compassion.

The meeting ended in some bullshit rhetoric about the need for resolution, blah, blah, blah. I tried desperately to phone Willie the next day; no answer. I knew he was there, stewing, pissed, planning his move. I had to reach him, and soon. Isolation is the worst counselor; you start to mind-fuck and concoct all kinds of vengeful scenarios.

I bumped into his brother on the streets and lashed into him, verbally. Did he want his brother to spend the rest of his life in the joint, did he understand that everything the Young Lords had done in East Harlem (it wasn't much yet, but pride and courage were showing up in people's faces, in their speech) would be destroyed if Willie killed Bobby Lemus? The government wouldn't have to destroy us; we'd destroy ourselves, and isn't that what they wanted, ultimately—to have us kill ourselves with no government fingerprints?

Husky Willie's brother, Wolf, just listened. I admired his style. He could've played his newfound status as the link person, the finder, to the hilt, playing me for days with lies and half-truths, bullshit promises and phony theatrics about his suffering for his brother. Instead, he just listened, looking at me from time to time with emotionless eyes, never saying where Willie was or what his brother intended to do. Finally, after blocks of walking and my cajoling, all he said was, "I'll talk to him. I can't promise you anything. I'll get back to you tomorrow."

Two days passed without a phone call, without any communication. And then it came.

It was Husky Willie, breathing heavily. His voice had a thick, dark, basso profundo quality; it was a death dirge: It was obvious he had made up his mind. It was the end of a long search, this quest to find and kill the man who had crippled him.

"Felipe!"

"Yeah, Willie."

"My house. Tonight. You and Bobby. Nobody else."

"Where do you live, Willie?"

He gave me an address in the East River Projects. I only prayed that I could convince Willie that loyalty to our organization, the love of our people, our community, was as strong as the laws of the streets.

Willie was handsome, but the demons had twisted his mouth into a scowl, his face into a menacing mask. The aura he exuded kept enemies away, for sure, but it also kept love from coming in, a love I felt he needed and wanted desperately. But I also knew this confrontation had to take place. It was the way of the warrior, old school Puerto Rican style; man to man, with one observer pledged to silence, no matter what the outcome.

I called Bobby and told him of the meeting. He listened without saying a word. After my little speech there was silence for a minute or two. I waited, my hands beginning to sweat and tremble on the old black phone receiver.

"I'll be there, Chairman. Meet you at the office at 6. We'll walk there together." And then, he paused again. "Felipe, I trust you and hope this isn't a trap. I don't think so, but I'm bringing my blade, just in case. I promise, I mean it, I promise not to use it unless he tries something.

"And, if he does, I promise not to kill him, but I can't be sure. Shit happens in a tussle, you know?"

Again, silence.

"I promise I'll do my part. I just hope he really wants to talk and nothing else jumps off. Love you, papa; see you later."

Now it was my turn to play the scenario about to happen over and over in my head—the what-ifs.

I had to shake the doubt off; I had told Bobby to bring the light and here I was bringing the rain. Bobby arrived at the Young Lords promptly at 6:00 P.M. He was anxious, avoiding my eyes, and not saying too much. As we walked to Willie's apartment, I chattered away, trying to break his somber mood and my skittish nervousness. It didn't work. Bobby had a heavy load on him, emotionally. He knew all the ramifications of what might happen if things went wrong. We entered the project hallway and knocked firmly on the door. Even the knock on the door had to show strength and no fear. I looked at Bobby's determined face, his granite jaw, and gained confidence.

Wolf opened the door to a dimly lit one-bedroom apartment. Wolf's face and body language showed no sign of betrayal or setup. Willie was sitting in the living room, dressed in an unbuttoned short-sleeved dark shirt covering a sleeveless white summer undershirt.

He smiled, but it wasn't an honest smile, more like a snarl. He was angry, nervous too.

Motioning us to sit down on the couch, Husky Willie took his time to speak, looking away at the first-floor window, stroking his beard slowly like an old Bedouin chieftain. "Honestly, I don't know what to say," he said, softly. "I've been living for this day for a long time . . . a long time. Really, man . . ."—and he looked at Bobby for the first time, hard—"I just want to kill you and get it over with, get this fuckin' demon off my back. All these years, all these fuckin' years . . . ." His eyes teared up. To his credit, Bobby said nothing, looked down at his hands. Then, he slowly started to rise.

"Sit the fuck down, Bobby. Don't even try some shit in here. You're going to listen to everything I have to say, whether you like it or not!"

Startled, Bobby looked at me, he was ready. I motioned for him to sit down and pointed to my ear. Bobby knew my sign language. Time to listen. At this point, he had to trust me . . . and Willie.

Willie's body had stiffened, his eyes wide open, wild.

"You motherfuckers started that shit. We had no beef with you. We were enemies, yeah, but you stayed on your turf, and we stayed in ours. You knew that crossing the lines meant someone was going to get hurt or die. And yet you guys, trying to prove your heart, came into Viceroy territory, looking to start something and we gave it to you good. You knew the rules. No guns. Knives, sticks, brass knuckles, belts, anything, but no guns. And, when our hands were kicking your asses, and we never even took out a knife, a stick, nothing, you faggot motherfuckers pulled the shit out like punks. Why? Why couldn't you take the ass-whipping like men and go the fuck on home, huh? Why? Why, Bobby? I wanna know why. Ten years later, I want to know why. Whenever you kicked our asses, and you have to admit it was rare, we never shot. We had the pieces, but we never shot. We licked our wounds, carried back our wounded, and planned to get back at the Dragons another day. We'd even laugh about the shit. We were warriors, something you white motherfuckers knew nothing about."

Bobby's body, hunched over until now, began to uncoil, his unblinking stare moving up in stages from his hands to Willie's eyes. It was an assassin look, cold and impersonal. If there was anything Bobby was not, it was racist. His family had the most multi-complected faces and hair textures in the Bronx. You fucked with any of his nephews, cousins, anybody who was blood—Black, white, brown—you were dead. He loved his family, Negros and all. Everyone in the Lords knew he was the Blackest white Puerto Rican in the group. He talked shit but backed it up. Had faced many a white Puerto Rican over casual racist remarks, would laugh at the joke, but when it got nasty, when the 'Rican came out of some old racist stereotypes about Black people, Bobby lit them up with hurricane punches and volcanic fury.

Willie, crazy as it sounds in this situation, had stepped over the line.

"Willie," Bobby snapped curtly, "let's not go there. You understand?" And they stared at each other for what seemed, to me, to be an interminable time. Willie, thank God, backed off emotionally, his face and eyes registering that he understood that maybe Bobby was of a different ilk.

Bobby began to look at his hands again as he spoke.

"We fucked up. I fucked up. I got scared. We were holding our ground for a while, you know?

"But, as the fight wore on, you guys, I don't know, it's like you guys developed a second wind or something. It's like you were fighting for your lives, your mothers and sisters. I hit a short guy hard, and it was like I never hit him. Blood came out his mouth and he kept coming, screaming, waving his Garrison belt. It was weird. It was like the Viceroys were on something. Once I saw our guys getting really fucked up and falling, once I saw you guys having no mercy on the wounded, stomping them and shit, I just pulled it out. I wasn't thinking, Willie. I wanted out. Wanted to make you cats split so we could help our guys up and get the fuck outta there. That's all it was, Willie. Panic and retreat."

For the first time, I saw compassion in Husky Willie's eyes.

"But you shot me, man," and then he choked back his tears and put his fist in his mouth, looking away. "You shot me."

Turning to Bobby again, tears streaming down his face, Willie shouted, "I knew it was over, man. I fell and couldn't feel my legs. You know what that feeling is like? I couldn't get up and run. I was helpless. I couldn't help my guys, couldn't help myself. In one flash, in one second, I became . . . this. A cripple." And, then the dam broke—the sobs, the mucus running from his nose, the saliva from his mouth. "Why didn't you just kill me?" Willie sobbed. "Why didn't you just finish the job? It would've been better than living like this. This is torture, goddamnit, it's torture." And then Bobby put his head down and broke. "I would've shot anybody else. I would've shot myself. I admired you, asshole. I thought you were the baddest motherfucker north of 106th Street. We all did. We heard how you fought two and three at a time and got out alive. I would've done anything not to hurt you, man. Even the Italians were scared of you. I didn't mean it, Willie. I swear to God, I didn't mean to shoot you."

And then Bobby uttered the most hideous half-stifled howls and growls, rocking as he kept his head down, wrapping his arms around his chest and crying with Husky Willie. I wish I could've said something, done something. There was nothing to say. Nothing to do. Two of the most amazing men I've known sat and literally plowed through their emotional gauntlet of pain, anger, and guilt while I sat wishing I could pray or preach or punch something. Instead, I put my hands over my eyes, bent down, and sobbed. Bobby, courageous as ever, finally looked up, cleared his throat, and declared, "My brother, you will be my brother 'til we die. Whatever you need—smoke, guns, pussy, or backup in any fight—I'll be there for you. I'll wheel you wherever you have to go from now on. We will not separate until the day they put us in the ground, ya hear me? That's from my heart, and Felipe, you know I don't make promises I can't keep." Willie, tears streaming down his face and beard, smiled the old, beatific Husky Willie smile, reached out his arms, and said, "C'mere, motherfucka." They continued the tears and the oaths of faith and loyalty.

"I'll never leave your side, nigga," Bobby hissed. "Never.

"And, you'll be my brother, until forever, Boricua. Young Lords *hasta la muerte.*"

They stayed buddies for as long as I was in the Party. And they died within two years of each other.

Chapter 13

Dope Fiends and Discipline in the Young Lords Party

THE PEACE PACT between Husky Willie and Bobby Lemus strengthened the Young Lords internally and legitimized us externally. The old Viceroys, whose territory we inhabited, begrudgingly gave us a little more respect. We were not merely young dilettantes playing at revolution. We were serious about uniting Puerto Ricans, serious about defending and protecting El Barrio, serious about social justice and the independence of Puerto Rico. They still wouldn't talk to us on the streets for any length of time, but they would casually stroll past our rallies and listen, without laughing. And then a miracle happened, a miracle called Robles.

He was a drug addict, a serious *tecato* whose glory days of gangbanging were long behind him. He was bedraggled, and the contours of his dark, peasant-flat boxer face were broken only by sad eyes that had seen too much and further darkened by the soot sticking to his skin from sleeping on streets and hallways. He smelled, and his voice was deep and raspy from too much drink and tobacco. It was his hands I noticed first. They were pieces of hardened meat meant to pummel people into unconsciousness—thick palms, muscled fingers, and nails so black and dirty you couldn't distinguish nail from flesh. He was a takeoff artist, a street thug. If you came to cop heroin on 111th Street between the three avenues of Fifth, Madison, and Park and couldn't fight or didn't have a weapon, nine times out of ten you'd get robbed. By Robles.

He didn't like a lot of talk, would just stare at you with unblinking dead eyes, eyes that screamed, "I'm already dead, so I don't mind killing you.

Give me all you got." Squirming was out of the question; his grip was legendary. Screaming got you knocked out . . . quickly. His punches came from the hip and were so quick that even in broad daylight all you would see is a guy approach another guy, a body crumple to the sidewalk, and someone walking away as if nothing had happened. Robles. It's how he made his living, how he survived to buy his shit.

Copping the drugs, cooking them, and injecting oneself was relatively easy. Cops knew who the dealers were and where the open-air drug bodegas were located. Everybody knew. But unless there was a crackdown (usually during mayoral campaigns, Christmas holidays, or when a rich white girl died on our streets), the sales of *manteca* flourished unabated.

Getting high was not the problem; nodding out peacefully was. It was a disgusting contradiction. Police drove by the drug markets and did nothing. But they'd arrest the sick. A *tecato* would shuffle by, scowl on his face, talking to himself, his arms stretched out in front of him, in mid-air, as if pointing to something or someone, stop suddenly, and then in a trancelike dance better than any choreography by Balanchine, bend from the trunk of his body, slowly down, almost touching the sidewalk, and then, quickly, bolt back up, stand erect, and shuffle a few steps ahead, then slowly bend down again, repeating the junkie ballet. That is, if he wasn't beaten by police. The summer of '69 was tough on addicts in East Harlem; cops seemed intent on busting and bashing. Robles made the smart decision that the only safe haven was the Young Lords office. The cops didn't mess with us unless we marched or conducted a garbage offensive. Robles would come in stoned out of his skull and just sit in the front office, nodding out, occasionally asking questions to keep our interest. But it was the nature of his questions that fascinated me. What did we mean by "the state and capitalism"? And how the hell could we win an armed struggle with no guns, no education, and a community full of dope fiends like him? Somehow, through the haze of the high, his brain was working, critically. And he led other dope fiends to our office: Tintan, Cano, Che. Some we threw out. Others we helped to kick the habit, nurturing them for seventy-two hours through the sweat and wracking pain of withdrawal. Some appreciated it. Others betrayed us and themselves. And that's where this story starts. Robles started to change; it was imperceptible at first, little things. He was awake longer, he started bathing regularly, and then he started selling Young Lords Party newspapers, receiving the little money we gave out for lunch. He never robbed us, and every bunch of papers he was consigned was paid for in cash. He was beginning to feel like somebody. He had a support group, a family. He had something to do, somewhere to go every day. He was becoming a Young Lord, and while he still shot up, it wasn't as frequent or as debilitating. He was a functioning addict, and we were satisfied with just that.

Robles's slow immersion into the Party was guided by just two people: Hiram Maristany, our reliable breakfast coordinator and official photographer, and I. He trusted no one else. You had to have barrio pedigree for Robles to confide in you; he had to know your family, your character, your reaction in a crisis, and your love for him. He wasn't about small talk. And he hated the middle-class members of our group, the educated ones, who tried their new nationalistic pride and knowledge of Puerto Rican history on him. He had been in the 'Rican urban trenches all his life, one of those Viceroys who fought fiercely to protect our mothers, sisters, and children in the '50s when Sicilian gangs like the Redwings were kicking our asses every time we crossed east of Third Ave. Robles knew the Maristanys and Lucianos. It didn't matter that many of our surnames were Sicilian and Italian, resulting from the intermarriages of Corsican/Italian immigrant men with Puerto Rican women during the late 1800s. To the dark-skinned Sicilians, Puerto Ricans were "foreigners" and, in their cultural amnesia, treated us as brutally as they had been treated by the Irish Americans fifty years before. The first Puerto Rican families were called *pioneros*, pioneers, and were the first 'Ricans to settle in East Harlem in the 1920s, straight out of Williamsburg, Brooklyn. We struggled through poverty and welfare, abandonment by fathers, addiction and mental breakdowns, jail time and racism. Both the Luciano and Maristany families had survived the deaths and imprisonments of sons, both families had seen a proud people reduced to marginalization, and both families were keenly aware of their Blackness and never backed off their pride in being umbilically tied to Africa. Robles knew this, and when he started attending the obligatory political education classes, his frustration at the ignorance of the new, "educated" Lords knew no bounds.

As we were sitting on an adjacent stoop outside our headquarters one summer evening, Robles turned to me and said drily, "You know your officers don't know what the fuck they're talking about. They don't know shit about El Barrio, but they talk like they've lived here all their lives. They're full of shit."

I knew what he was saying was right, but I had to preserve order and hierarchy in the Party.

"You may be right, Robe, but they've gone to school. They've got some knowledge you may need, brother."

Robles exhaled forcefully through his mouth, a sort of hissing sound.

"What they've got is book knowledge. Book knowledge doesn't give you heart, doesn't teach you how to fight or even the good sense to run when you have to. But what really gets to me is the way they trash each other, especially you. I've told a few of them, why don't they tell you to your face. They never do. And then they want me to take orders from them? Nah. I don't like punks."

Hearing this wasn't shocking; I knew there was jealousy, backbiting, and infighting in the Party. I never gave it too much thought, too busy trying to keep us viable and alive.

"Robe," I answered, "Small-minded people will always talk about their superiors, blood. It goes with the territory. I can't have you going around telling them to go fuck themselves when they order you to do something."

"These are fuckin' kids, man," Robles spat out, "They ain't got no vices. They still pissing sugar. I don't trust motherfuckas who are too straight."

And then he looked at me with those deadpan eyes and laughed, "Half these sapsuckers can hardly do ten push-ups. How the hell they gonna order me in battle? C'mon, Felipe, get real, nigga."

I roared in laughter but then got serious.

"Robe, I need you here, not only for them, but for me. Every damn army has officers who don't know their asses from their elbows. And every army has sergeants who know more than the lieutenants. But you have to trust the vision of the leaders, the strategy, you know what I mean?

"So far, we've done well. We're still alive, people are supporting us, and we're getting shit done. Right?"

Robles looked away and said without turning, "Yeah, but these young-bloods haven't been tested yet. How many will hold up if they get busted and smacked in the face a few times? I've seen some of your 'officers' in battle, and the fear is clear. They don't even leave the office, man. With the exception of you, David, and Fi, I ain't never seen these dudes fight. They're always absent, always got something else to do when the shit is on. They're scared of you, too. You better watch your ass. They'll betray you in a minute." That's how the conversation ended.

That talk came stampeding back to memory a few months later when a drug addict had to be "disciplined" inside our office. The Lords had initiated a program of helping addicts kick the habit, cold turkey. We weren't doctors, nor were we trained medical personnel. All we had was compassion and a burning desire to stop this human devastation we saw before us every day. We knew these guys were smart, we knew they were willing to fight, we knew their souls. They needed help, without the use of methadone, which we saw as another addictive drug.

We put the word out on the streets that we would surround whoever came in with love, soup, food, and hugs if they wanted to quit heroin. For the first seventy-two hours, the most difficult period of weaning one off the drug, we tended to them around the clock, watching them tremble, sweat, retch, and hallucinate as the poison left their bodies. One of them, whom I will call Che, a young, handsome, Tony Curtis–looking Puerto Rican, suffered through the first three days. As I would lift his head and feed him soup, I wondered how he managed to avoid the track scars on his arms, the aging of his face. He had all his teeth, his skin tone was good, lacking the pallor of those who had been in the game for a long time, and he kept himself well groomed, haircut and all. It was obvious he had just gotten hooked. He kept repeating how embarrassed he was to have me see him like this, that he didn't want his family, here or in Puerto Rico, to witness his slide into the streets. I kept telling him that he was being reborn, that the ugly past was over, that he was going to walk out of the apartment, whole, clean. He didn't have to join the Lords (and we meant it), we just wanted to see him live a full, healthy, productive life.

Three days passed and it was like a miracle. After holding him, sometimes pushing him down to prevent him from running out and copping again, after his confessions and tears of remorse, he began sitting up in bed, eating regular food without throwing up and laughing with us as we regaled him good-naturedly about the detox he had survived. He was free to go, and we always advised that brothers check into a rehab or hospital to get some peaceful sober time, some decent food, and some needed therapy. (These were the raw beginnings of the Lincoln Hospital Detox.) Che wanted none of it; he wanted to show his appreciation by joining the Young Lords Party. He felt we would be his rehab, his support system in case he got tempted again. We allowed it, and for the first few weeks Che was the Energizer Bunny, running errands and staying close to headquarters, just in case. His old cronies came by, some motioning for him to come out and get high again, but most, to their credit, praised him and wished him well. He would smile, laugh, take their compliments, shake their hands, and then mutter under his breath, "fuckin' dope fiends." I told him off a few times. How the hell could he condemn those souls still lost, especially since just a few weeks before he was shooting up with them? Hating them meant he hated himself. Che would put his head down, tear up, and then, ashamed, say, "You're right, brother; I have to have pity on them."

"Fuck pity," I would snap. "Love them by serving them. Help them kick. Love them and you'll save yourself. You're not out of the woods yet, blood." And then it happened.

Buoyed by the victory of occupation of the First People's Church, we let our guard down, didn't watch Che, figuring, naïvely, that he had beaten the monster dwelling within. Yes, he had gotten past the acute physical withdrawal, but the real battle, the spiritual struggle, the thuggish mentality, and nihilistic value system were still lurking behind the frenetic energy he exuded.

Morally, spiritually, he was still caught up in individualism and crass survival at any cost, at anyone's expense.

Walking into the front office on a late fall afternoon, I noticed a strange stillness. Things weren't right. Deeper into the office, in the back where we held our strategy and political education meetings, five Lords surrounded Che. He was defiant, jaw jutting out, chest puffed up. They seemed to be asking him questions and he was having none of it.

All I heard was one of the officers asking him, "Why'd you do it, man?" and Che spitting back, "I took it because I needed it. End of story. Now, get outta my face!" The fact that we had pulled him through the acute pain of drug withdrawal, and he was acting like this, angered me. The conversation stopped for a moment as I approached and asked, "What's up?"

Without turning to look at me, keeping his eyes on this short, wannabe tough guy, one of the Lords said softly in an exasperated tone, "We caught him red-handed with Juan's wallet. The money's still there, about $60."

Che turned to me, with a look of relief; he thought he'd get a pass from me and be allowed to leave. With a look of disgust at what he considered quislings around him, he shot back, "Yeah, I took it. So what? I told you I needed the money." I immediately knew he had been talking to Robles about the "frail" nature of our troops and felt he could chump them off and walk away scot-free. Which one of these youngsters was going to stop him?

I still had the cast on my broken right arm from the police beating during a confrontation at the First Spanish Methodist Church a few weeks earlier. I saw no reason to debate any further. Without thinking, without closing my fist properly, I swung hard and caught Che on the right side of his jaw. He stumbled back in shock and then dropped. His eyes said, "Felipe, of all people I thought at least you'd understand. You know the deal."

I was livid.

"Motherfucker, you have the nerve to come into our house and rob the Minister of Education?" As I tried to smash his head into the wooden floorboards with my boot, the Lords held me back. They still didn't get it. This man had to be dealt with. Quickly.

Our rule was "Revolutionary justice must be meted out to traitors, counter-revolutionaries, and reactionaries." Fuck him. Whipping his ass was all I was thinking. The look on the faces of the Lords was one of genuine shock, real fear. Fighting and running from the police was one thing, you could throw a rock or bottle from afar and laugh as you ran, you could scream at a cop's face, knowing that at least for a short while he'd be constrained by police rules of engagement, horrible and racist as they were. But this was upfront and personal, in the office where no violence was allowed. They forgot who I was, the other side of me, the not-so-pretty jail side where robbery was a good enough reason for murder.

I was not composed, I was not being judicious, I was not being "the Chairman." Fuck this dude. He had robbed us in broad daylight, and they were standing around talking to him? Hell no! The fear that registered in their eyes was not fear of Che—they knew who he was—it was fear of me. As they pulled me away from him, I saw their shock at seeing this other side of me.

They must have been thinking, "Oh shit, is this what revolutionary justice means? Suppose I fuck up? Oh, no. This is too real."

They were right.

This was El Barrio, warrior college. And you chose revolution. There was no gray area of commitment. We made the rules, and everybody knew them, we drilled it into them in political education class. You either accepted those rules or left. This was not romance; it wasn't about reading a revolutionary book of gun battles and class struggle. It was about Being and Doing.

Unbeknownst to me, Robles had stepped into the circle and like a gentle father bear pulled me back. I was in pain, my left forefinger was broken, sticking out awkwardly to the left of the rest of my fingers. It was my fault for not having punched correctly, but now I really wanted to hurt this guy.

Looking at my left hand, Robles said, emotionless, "You probably broke it. I don't know why you don't listen. I've told you: Close your fist before you hit." And then he lumbered over to Che, grabbed him by his straight, perfectly barbered black hair, and took him outside. We heard three stomps, head meeting concrete, and three forceful exhalations. Robles broke Che's jaw in six places. Within seconds, Robles calmly walked back into the office and declared. "I'm sorry. It'll never happen again. Now, Chairman, can I speak to you a minute, outside?"

Outside, Robles explained. If he had let Che get away with the thievery, none of us would never trust him or other addicts in the party. Stomping Che had a twofold purpose; it would protect and guarantee the safe haven Robles had developed for himself and other addicts and it sent an indelible message to the surrounding community: Rob anybody else, never family or friends or the Young Lords Party.

There are two schools of thought about the effects of heavy addiction on behavior. There are those who view it as a disease, thus making the individual incapable of making moral, rational decisions unless the addict heals the cause of the behavior through detoxification and rehabilitation. Even after the withdrawal from that lifestyle, there is still the need to rid the mind of "stinkin' thinking," negative thoughts about oneself and the world.

There is another school of thought, one that I have witnessed in myself, my family, my friends. There is always a Third Eye that guides action, no matter the intensity of the addiction. That Third Eye is the God-Force. Even in the midst of the whirlwind of drugs, that voice keeps you to a certain moral/political compass. You may engage in criminal behavior, but there are certain areas that are sacred: family, church, children, and old friends. There are drug dealers who won't deal anywhere near a church or school, who loan money to community residents in need, numbers runners and prostitutes whom I and others have trusted to baby-sit our toddlers or rebellious teenagers.

I learned that addiction is a disease, not the person. There is always another person in that addict. There is also another person in that criminal. You have to dig deep to find the true character.

Chapter 14

Occupying Lincoln Hospital

THANK GOD THERE were people in the Lords concerned with other issues besides violence and police brutality.

Juan Gonzalez, now a writer/professor, television pundit, and former columnist for the *New York Daily News*; Cleo Silvers; and David Perez focused on health issues. We started hearing reports from neighbors and friendly doctors of the treatment accorded our people in city hospitals: long wait times in emergency rooms, misdiagnoses, arrogance, disrespect of our elders, and mistreatment of single mothers with seriously ill children.

But what could we do? We were activists, not medical students. Then the bomb was dropped: Tuberculosis was beginning to show up in El Barrio and the Bronx. This shook me to the core. When I was ten my mother was told I had a suspicious spot on my lungs that would require X-rays and exams. As it turned out, it was nothing serious, but my mother looked and sounded worried. Pops wasn't sending the child support checks, the welfare checks that were supposed to come on the 1st and the 16th were often late, and then this TB scare.

She had a breakdown. She started to scream "I can't take it anymore. I've had it. This is too much. GOD HELP ME!" She picked up the dining room chairs and threw them against the walls, broke bottles and drinking glasses against the floor, thrashing her hands against her body. She had lost it and I was petrified.

Health issues, emotional, mental, and physical, resonated with me, deeply. So did the mere mention of the word *TB*.

Friendly, progressive doctors gave the Lords portable TB tests, little caps with metal prods that pierced the skin with a biological agent that produced a bump on the forearm. Those tested had to be examined to determine whether they were positive or negative for the tuberculosis bacteria, at which point if positive, they'd have to submit to X-rays of their lungs.

Hospitals weren't doing the necessary bilingual outreach, and Puerto Ricans in El Barrio couldn't take the time off from work to spend a day in the hospital emergency room. The solution was to bring the X-ray machines to the community. While there was a portable X-ray truck touring the city, it never seemed to reach the core streets of East Harlem's residents.

Juan Gonzalez made the decision: Kidnap the truck! Bring it right in front of our office and start X-raying our people. To hell with the Department of Health schedules and regulations and to hell with the police. They'd have to beat us while we were caring for our community in full view of the news cameras, cameras that Pablo Guzmán would so brilliantly plant at any offensive we produced, right before the police had the time to react.

It is truly comical, in hindsight, but our dilemma, our real concern, was not physical safety but who among us could drive a stick shift? Thank the Lord, Micky had the skills, so it was decided, once the vehicle was in our possession, that he would drive it. There was a minor incident in making a wide corner turn when he ran over a *piragua* cart, but true to his character, went back later and paid the owner $50, twice what the cart was worth.

Pai and Hui would be the point men and the public relations guys. They'd have to explain to the medical technicians inside why they were taking the truck and why they didn't have to fear for their safety; and hopefully have them stay on board and X-ray the residents of El Barrio.

It worked perfectly. The truck arrived in front of our headquarters on Madison Avenue, between 111th and 112th streets. The mothers and children whom we had contacted earlier were in line, TV cameras were in place, and the most the cops could do was watch while the technicians performed their duties happily. They became part of the revolutionary experience of serving the people, and they felt it. As a group, we were emboldened. If we could take an X-ray truck, why not a whole medical facility, why not a hospital, considering the shoddy, deadly treatment Puerto Ricans were subjected to daily?

The opportunity dropped right into our laps. Micky Melendez and Pablo "Yoruba" Guzmán had opened up the Bronx chapter of the Young Lords on Longwood and Kelly avenues in the South Bronx, an area long known for poverty, hunger, crime, poor housing, and even worse health care than that found elsewhere. There were two reasons for the expansion: Following East

Harlem, the South Bronx had become an area of heavy Puerto Rican concentration. New York City's urban renewal program of the '50s and '60s forced many of them from the area known as Little San Juan, 57th Street to 66th Streets between Amsterdam and Broadway (the area made famous by Leonard Bernstein, Stephen Sondheim, and Arthur Laurents's "West Side Story") in order to build Lincoln Center. Using eminent domain laws, Puerto Rican workers were displaced and shunted to the formerly Irish and Jewish sections of the South Bronx without the corollary services. Schools deteriorated, police became enemies, drugs proliferated, and jobless men abandoned their families, forcing single mothers into welfare dependency. Gangs and heroin, Pentecostal storefront churches, and liquor stores became the panacea for our people. The Young Lords Party had to be embedded in the Bronx.

Also, we simply needed more space. We were bursting out of our seams on Madison Avenue with unsold newspapers books and unused pieces of wood strewn everywhere. We were literally stepping over one another. The Bronx was a chance for a cleaner space, a quieter atmosphere where the *Palante* newspaper could be put together without distraction or constant crisis. If it sounds like a suburban move, it was, kind of. We needed to move up and clean up. Some of our best editions were produced at Longwood and Kelly, with Denise Oliver's artwork, Richie Perez's articles, Hiram Maristany's photography, and an occasional poem by me. As health was a major organizing issue, we had established a coalition with a Lower East Side collective called the Health Revolutionary Unity Movement and a Bronx health workers progressive group called the Think Lincoln Committee, committed to changing the conditions of workers and patients in this century-old building called Lincoln Hospital. The community knew it as a butcher shop and a roach motel where you walked in, but too often didn't walk out.

We had already witnessed first-hand, the deplorable health conditions of the Puerto Rican community around the issue of lead paint. Prize-winning columnist Jack Newfield wrote a series of articles in the *Village Voice* on the poisonous effects of lead paint poisoning on poor children. They developed learning problems, behavior problems, and brain damage that could not be cured; some died from eating the flaky paint chips on the walls or floor of their tenement apartments, paint chips loaded with lead.

After a sit-in at the office of the Deputy Commissioner of Health, the Young Lords were given lead detection kits and we conducted our own block-by-block, door-to-door screenings every weekend. We were genuinely shocked. In the initial survey conducted by the YLP, one-third of the almost sixty children we tested were positive. Doctors in municipal and voluntary hospitals in New York City had always suspected it, but now we had empirical proof. Newfield's articles and the publication of our findings pricked the city's conscience. Mayor John Lindsay ordered the practice of lead paint halted. Landlords were forbidden by law to use lead-based paint in their buildings. We had won.

By focusing on health, we were able to humanize the image promulgated by the church, the FBI, and the New York City Police Department that we were ruthless revolutionaries and totally undisciplined terrorists committed to chaos. We were on the streets, in the apartments, feeling the pain of our folk and doing something about it. And while we sought to enlist the poor and working class in our neighborhoods to rise up, to see their worth, their beauty, their humanity, we were also changed. Fighting for health care sensitized us to the more nuanced and subtle effects of discrimination and marginalization, poverty, and powerlessness: hypertension, heart disease, diabetes, obesity, alcoholism, drug addiction, and violence. And then the shocker: A young Puerto Rican woman, Carmen Rodriguez, had gone to Lincoln Hospital for a late abortion and died on the table. Her death confirmed what we always believed about Lincoln: It didn't care about people of color. Also, from our perspective, Lincoln's affiliation with the Albert Einstein College of Medicine, while providing specialized care, exacted too high a toll on Puerto Rican lives. Excuses aside, Puerto Ricans were used as experimental guinea pigs without their knowledge, to legitimize new drugs.

The YLP focused its media campaign on the grossly incompetent care given by Lincoln Hospital. City cutbacks in funding had left the only public major medical facility in the South Bronx without air conditioning in operating rooms, elevators that didn't work, unacceptably high levels of lead paint on the walls—a building one step away from total collapse.

This was the moment we were waiting for.

I argued against occupying Lincoln: Our people base was in East Harlem and our supply lines for food and materials would be stretched too far. We'd have to depend every day on that damn #6 train to feed and reinforce our troops, from 110th Street on the Lexington Avenue line to Longwood Avenue, a fifteen- to twenty-minute ride. Why not take over Mount Sinai Hospital's community building? It was only a few blocks away from our headquarters.

Mount Sinai was rich, and adjacent to our community and headquarters. Young Lord members could be supported with food, water, and reinforcements. I was outvoted and, in retrospect, the Central Committee was right.

Taking over Mount Sinai would cause panic among liberal supporters and police alike because of its "sterling" reputation. The response would be brutal, and even though our neighbors would fight back valiantly, the issues of health care and the Puerto Rican community would be obscured by the fighting and the protection of a voluntary (white) hospital.

Lincoln had to be taken down; it was a symbol of everything that was wrong with public health care. It was a city hospital that was supposed to serve the people and instead was killing them. So, roughly a year after taking the People's Church in the summer of '69, the Young Lords Party decided to take Lincoln Hospital. It was going to take every ounce of paramilitary strength and science, every molecule of courage and cooperation, and every prayer we still had in us to win this battle. There was the very real possibility that some of us wouldn't make it out alive. We would be attacking and occupying a New York City–owned facility, a health institution, government property, and while it was a symbolic slap in the face to Mayor Lindsay, police strategists had to start thinking, 'What if this group starts to attack and occupy other institutions—schools, firehouses, welfare offices . . . police stations?' We knew this would be our shining moment, our Iwo Jima, where we would plant the Puerto Rican flag of resistance and self-determination. We planned and trained and organized and kept our mouths shut until that day, the day of reckoning. There was no turning back. We had to win this one. Our people were dying in Lincoln Hospital; now, our lives had to be put on the line.

The Health Ministry worked feverishly to obtain the floor plans of the old buildings; we needed to determine what building to hit. Taking over the main medical facility with patients, medical personnel, and machinery might endanger lives. With the help of friendly doctors, nurses, and custodial staff we could probably pull it off, but we'd be bogged down with emergency care, scheduled surgeries, and the daily routine of intake and exams. Anything could happen. A death on our watch would defeat the purpose of exposing the negligence and racism of Lincoln Hospital. We decided to hit the Nurses' Residence, an eleven-story building connected to the main plant through tunnels and ramps.

Occupying an eleven-story building is not child's play; perimeters have to be established, all exits have to be guarded, information has to be relayed quickly from the bottom of the building to the top, food and drink as well. Every warrior has to know his or her role, where to be and when to be there, and close-quarter fighting drills have to be intensified.

We started with cardiovascular training, running around Central Park's Harlem Meer until our members' lungs and hearts were prepared to handle the nine-acre hospital, climb eleven stories effortlessly, and still have the lung capacity to do hand-to- hand combat, if necessary.

We then had to focus on befriending and/or neutralizing doctors, nurses, technicians, and custodial and security personnel; that took months of hard work by the Health and Defense Ministry cadres and anyone else associated with our campaign: Micky Melendez, David Perez, Gabriel Torres, Benji Cruz, Pai Diaz, Hui Cambrelen, Walter Bosque, Cleo Silvers, and The Think Lincoln Committee. They did a fantastic job. Though some "traditional" doctors officially protested our occupation, their concerns about "disruption" were swept away by the passion of the moment and the true frustration of the South Bronx community. There was almost no physical resistance from the security force, with the exception of a reception clerk who was side-kicked by Pai and ran out.

We also put together a list of demands compiled from the meetings we had with all the organizers and medical personnel around the issues affecting Lincoln Hospital: A new hospital had to be constructed, the hospital had to assure the community that doctors would treat them humanely, there'd be no further cutbacks in funding or jobs, a hospital worker/community board would be established to hear complaints, and we would advocate for patient rights. Finally, we demanded the appointment of a qualified Puerto Rican as director of the entire facility.

July 13, 1970. We told the troops we'd be meeting at a Young Lords supporter's apartment on Broadway, on the West Side of Manhattan. I didn't tell the members why. We were going to invade Lincoln the next day, but we had to assemble the players in one staging area. Too much could go wrong if we had people coming from all over the city. Trains could be late, people might not get up on time, parents could demand that chores be done. This offensive had to be timed perfectly, precisely, with no room for error. Everybody had to be in one place at the same time. That evening I announced our plans for the takeover. I made it clear that the cadre would be spending the night in the large apartment and no phone calls would be allowed until we occupied the hospital; there'd be no contact with the outside world. Whoever the police spies were in our group, whoever the informers were, would have to wait until we had established a beachhead before they could rat us out to the police. There was audible excitement among some of the members, quiet concern among others. I could see the worry etched on their faces. Some of it was authentic; they lived with their parents or grandparents and didn't want to worry them with their absence and noncommunication. Others had wives, husbands, and lovers whom they called regularly. The sudden absence would cause problems. It didn't matter. We couldn't take the chance of having our plans revealed and disrupted by preemptive strikes by the police or SWAT.

The hours passed as we joked and kidded one another, somewhat nervously. I was confident we could pull this off; we had done our due diligence, trained our troops, physically, emotionally. We were ready to strike. The only question on our minds was, How the hell do we transport thirty to forty people in one group from the West Side to the Bronx without the cops getting wind?

I had established a warm relationship with Willie Rodriguez, an organizer from District 65, a progressive union, now defunct. We shared many a meal together at his project apartment in Brooklyn, and I had gotten to know and love his wife and daughters. We'd swap movement stories and debate the fine points of socialism and labor organizing. He and his wife, Flo, had an uncommon valor and an unswerving commitment to change. Flo and Willie guided me to an understanding of the need for change for all workers, of all races and ethnicities.

Weeks earlier I had taken him into our confidence by telling him of our plan to rent a large truck, pack the Young Lords into it like a troop carrier, and pile them out in front of the hospital.

I needed somebody to rent the truck and drive us to Lincoln Hospital in the wee hours of the morning, someone who was older, legit, and not being watched by police. I trusted Willie totally and as I was explaining our tactical plan one afternoon in his apartment, he simply asked, "So, who's gonna drive the truck?"

I was a little embarrassed. I was planning to ask him, but I hesitated. Willie was a family man, with a warrior of a wife (who kicked ass better than most men), two daughters, and a decent union job with District 65. He could lose his job, his apartment, his reputation if he were caught. It was a lot to ask of anyone who was not a member of the Party.

I looked at this dark-skinned, curly-haired Puerto Rican man who had befriended us and questioned whether I was using him, exploiting his love for the Young Lords. "Willie . . . could you do it? I mean you could get busted, beaten up, put in jail, anything can happen, you know?"

Willie had these round, childlike, honest eyes that absorbed you with his gaze, took all of you in. When he spoke to you, no matter how many other people were around, you felt you were the only person in the room.

"Bro," he said, putting his arm around my shoulders, "of course I'll do it. I love you guys. Whatever you need; we're comrades. Look at you, all nervous and shit. What were you afraid of? That I'd say no?"

And then he threw his head back and laughed heartily.

"Just tell me when, give me the time, and I'll be there. You guys better be ready when I roll up."

"Oh, we'll be there all right, with bells on our toes." I said, relieved.

Willie paused a moment.

"Make sure no one knows who I am. I don't want any word to get out. Some of the members may have seen me in the office a few times, so they should be sworn to secrecy. You understand? They need to shut the fuck up. If anything happens, I won't say anything. You just bail me out, and fast."

And then he laughed again, almost choking at the humor of the moment. "This is gonna be fun!" he chortled.

Midnight, July 14, 1970. Second-floor apartment, Broadway, West Side Manhattan. Assignments are handed out. The cadre break up into groups based on their skill sets and experience, with group leaders barking out individuals' names and posts. The laughing and kibbitzing stopped. Those Lords who never took their team leaders seriously, who felt singled out because their training seemed to be extra-tough and punitive, who had never experienced in-your-face violence, now saw the raw seriousness in their leaders' eyes, the toughness in their attitude, the military tone of their voices. One or two tried to relieve the tension in the living room with crude jokes. There were a few snickers, but the silence of the mood, and the reprimanding stares the jokesters received from the group as a whole, cured them of any other off-the-wall comments. This was war. We were attacking. No more dreams of negotiating a peaceful hospital settlement between the city and Puerto Ricans, no more standing outside handing out pamphlets trying to organize patients, fire up the community, and sway doctors to our cause. Time for talk was over. Now, it was time to fight back.

True to his word, Willie arrived on time with a large truck and beeped us. We went downstairs in small groups to avoid attention, with larger members sitting in the back spreading their legs to allow smaller comrades to sit with their backs and butts packed tight into the chest and pelvises of the warriors behind them. One would think there would be sexual innuendos or comments. There were none. The Young Lords Party looked like paratroopers loading into the gliders before D-Day and the Normandy invasion. I was so proud of them. Now, I had to oversee without micro-managing, had to trust the trainers and group leaders.

Micky was loved by the progressive doctors, so I knew we had that faction under control. David, the real Spanish speaker in the Central Committee, had convinced enough community residents to join and support us if shit hit the fan. Gabriel Torres, or "T" as he was better known, had the biggest smile and the loudest voice on the streets, and he made it clear to security personnel that one day, justice was coming on a pale horse and they should open the gates or get their asses handed to them. Pai and Hui had trained the shock troops to run quickly, ignore the guards' protests, snatch their walkie-talkies without hurting them, and break open the doors. If there was physical resistance, if a guard tried to be Superman, there was to be no pity, no hesitation, no stop in the flow of action: a sidekick to the chest or knees, a quick reverse punch to the jaw or nose, leg sweep, take the guy down, and keep moving. The troops from behind would restrain the downed worker. If security personnel took out their batons, then and only then would we use nunchakus in a figure 8 motion: once to the head, twice to the knees or shins.

If any of these planned moves took more than ten seconds, we'd be losing. I didn't feel like losing. None of us did.

Benji was the one who would explain to surprised or wounded workers why we were there and what we wanted to accomplish.

Willie drove at a moderate speed up Bruckner Boulevard to the Bronx. I rode shotgun. We arrived in front of the Nurses' Residence, 5:30 in the morning, jumped out of the cab of the truck, pulled up the back gates, and our troops slid out silently. No security outside. As the men and women of the Lords rolled out, they didn't even look at me for validation—a good sign. Soldiers don't need leaders' approval at the point of attack; their training has to kick in and their focus must be on their physical objective. Keep your eyes on the prize. It happened; our training and preparation paid off. We took the first floors of the Nurses' Residence of Lincoln Hospital in seven minutes. We secured the entire eleven-floor facility in fifteen. The operation was flawless. The ball was now in the mayor's hands. Media were alerted, and so were the police. By 9:00 A.M. police tanks, trucks, and snipers were all around us.

Enter the second phase of our strategy: press statements, interviews, negotiations with City Hall and if that failed, preparation for police counterattack. We were ready. The Puerto Rican flag was unfurled on top of Lincoln Hospital and flying proudly in the summer breeze. The hospital was now liberated territory. The press was having a field day; Pablo "Yoruba" Guzmán was doing interviews by the dozens, defending our takeover and laying out the community demands. The Lindsay administration was in panic mode. Church takeovers were one thing; hospital takeovers were quite another. We were stepping over the class and race lines. Puerto Ricans could steal brooms, pull garbage cans onto the avenue, kidnap an X-ray truck, and conduct lead paint poison tests on their congested streets. Taking a city hospital by force was a horse of a different color; we were forging way past our pay grade. City Hall sent two of their best negotiators to stop the rain, Sid Davidoff and Barry Gotterer.

These were hard-core city politicos, versed in the rough-and-tumble world of labor politics, union contracts, arm-twisting, and ethnic polling. Their aura reeked of the city's official enforcement crew, heavy hitters with metaphorical bats in hand. What they didn't understand was that we were a new brand of Puerto Ricans. We weren't the acquiescent old guard. The city was about to face young urban fighters who simply didn't give a fuck about these "troubleshooters or their mission." We knew they were going to bullshit and bray. But we had already been threatened, shot at, beaten, and jailed. Their presence didn't faze us. They assumed we were amateurs. That was their mistake. They thought we would back off in the face of overwhelming guns and armored personnel carriers. They assumed that their values, their worldview, were shared by us. We had no price, and we weren't interested in their validation. Hundreds of Puerto Ricans flocked to the hospital and stood behind barricades for hours to cheer us on: That was our validation.

I knew they wanted to feel us out, to probe. Part of their mission was intelligence gathering. As we ushered them into a large meeting room, we didn't let them see too much, just enough to let them know this was not a small, scraggly band of student activists. The Central Committee had decided not to play too loose with these guys—no laughing, no kidding around, serious faces and direct demands. It was obvious they felt the same way as they sat down opposite us, their faces, their demeanor no-nonsense. They had the weight of city government behind them and firepower in front. After the obligatory handshakes and introductions, they got right to the point.

"What do you intend to get out of this?" Sid Davidoff asked tersely.

I took my time to answer. "Our demands are simple. We want a new hospital, new procedures put in place guaranteed to treat patients humanely, and an administration that comes from our community."

"And you expect to get it just like that?" Davidoff huffed, already sounding exasperated, "Change takes time. You guys don't help the issue through forceful occupation. We're aware of the problems. This place has been in need of repair a long time. The city has been working on it. Again, it takes time."

"We obviously have a different sense of time," I shot back. "You have the time to dilly-dally, to dance with politicians, to wait for studies, and crunch the numbers. We don't. Puerto Ricans are dying here. You read the papers. A young woman just died the other day from a simple medical procedure. It stops here. It stops now. What are you going to do?"

There was no immediate answer.

Sid Davidoff's face looked more haggard than Gotterer's—more lines, sad, rabbinical eyes that looked like they had seen too much. But he noticed everything—every movement, every whisper, our body language, tone of voice, the "feel" of the room. He stared straight at you when he spoke, didn't seem to be afraid of too much. But he had never been to jail. I had. He had never gotten his ass kicked so soundly he wished he would die. I had. And, I was sure, he was never at the point in his life where he simply didn't care, where he was ready to die for something far greater than himself. I was already there. The Young Lords Party was already there, had been there a long time. I knew he wasn't ready to die for the mayor or the city. We, the Young Lords Party, Health Revolutionary Unity Movement (HRUM), the Think Lincoln Committee, were ready to play this drama out as long as we could; if death came, well . . . it would just be that way. Finally, Davidoff began ticking off the "progress" of the negotiations between the Lindsay administration and the hospital organizers that had been held long before the hospital takeover.

Pointing his finger at me, accusingly, he half-shouted, "You already have one of your major demands answered. We hired a well-qualified *Puerto Rican* [he spat this out] to head this place. Listen, just let go, leave and we'll negotiate the rest of the stuff." Weeks before, during bloody demonstrations where organizers were badly beaten and jailed, Dr. Antero Lacot, an OB-GYN doctor, had been hired to oversee the facility. He seemed competent and sympathetic to our cause, allowing a table in the hospital for patient grievances and suggestions, manned by us. But it was only a table, dammit. We weren't in on policy. And how much power had they given him? Did he have the right to hire and fire? Or was he merely window dressing to douse the fire in us, to be cast aside and terminated once the media's eye was off of Lincoln Hospital and onto some other sensational story?

Pressing my hands together and bending over the table, I sharply hissed to the two troubleshooters, "Don't patronize me and don't insult our intelligence. One Puerto Rican doctor does not a systemic change make. We demand more. Rats are running all over the place, people are dying because too many of your medical personnel are incompetent and don't care, workers are being fired because there's no money to run the place, yet you come to my house, in front of my face, to tell me 'Hooray! You won. We found one doctor to fulfill your dreams, to bring heaven on Earth, now go home.'" And then I paused and said, "It ain't happening." I noticed they weren't taking notes. That pissed me off. They weren't taking us seriously. Barry Gotterer's face, once impassive, now became a picture of anger and frustration. I knew the good cop/bad cop game was about to begin. "Do you know the danger you're in?" Gotterer shouted, standing up. "Lives can be lost here; people can get hurt. Those cops out there are not kidding around. You're playing with fire."

For them, the clock was ticking; we were not unions, not wizened, old-school labor leaders with negotiable and non-negotiable demands. They had no frame of reference for us, no visceral connection to the streets. Maybe they had spoken to Arnaldo Segarra, the mayor's Latino liasion, who knew us well. If they had, they obviously didn't take him seriously; they were dealing with hardcore brown and Black revolutionaries.

I leaned back in my chair and looked at these two guys: They didn't have a clue; the cultural gap between us was way too wide. The negotiators were probably working- or middle-class white kids raised in the nice white city away from the real shit. And even though they worked for a likeable, liberal Republican, John Lindsay, their gravitas toward us came from our rebellion against the status quo. Here they were, on our turf facing the threat all cities fear, social disorder. I was pretty sure it wasn't lost on them that they too could be kidnapped and held hostage. They didn't know this, but that chess move was off the table—not from fear, but because I detested the use of kidnapping.

If we utilized terrorist methods, public sympathy in our community would evaporate and slowly slide toward those "poor" city officials being held in Lincoln Hospital. I shot back, "Do you think for one minute, we didn't measure the consequences of our actions? That we don't know those racist police are dying to come in here and kill our asses?

"What you don't know is that we're willing to go all the way to change this disgusting place. I don't think it would be wise to try us on that issue."

Davidoff and Gotterer looked at each other with that sort of we-got-another-fuckin'-dreamer-here-who-has-to-be-taught-a-lesson look. That's when the alarm in my head went off. They were setting us up. Of course, they would try to "talk to these kids, knock some sense in their heads." But, in all revolutionary confrontations, those in power will use negotiations to wear the opposition down, to dilute the rules of engagement, and, finally, to murder the leadership in the room or out of it.

We had decided to play with the Police Department's head by parading Young Lords, male and female, with sticks and two-by-fours wrapped in black tape, in front of the huge, wide bay window on the first floor of the Nurses' Residence. By marching in a circular fashion, they made it look as if we had hundreds of soldiers with guns, ready to repel any attack. It was a comic book move, but it worked. The police, situated on the high ground of the Bruckner Expressway and surrounding rooftops, couldn't distinguish whether these were real guns or taped-up stickball bats.

Davidoff's and Gotterer's body language changed. When their tone went sour, I quickly excused myself, consulted with Central Committee members present at the table, and whispered, "These motherfuckers are going to attack soon. I can feel it. They know now we're not going to give in. Let's initiate the plan. I'll keep talking. Get everybody out. Everybody, including civilians."

The Young Lords Party was always meticulous in its preparations for offensives. My mantra to the leadership and the cadre in any action we planned was simple: "Maximum effectiveness, minimum loss of life."

While we had worked on an effective assault plan, we wracked our brains trying to figure out how to escape in the event of a counterattack by police. No paramilitary tactic works without an exit plan. It's always easy to attack, to get in, to land the first blow; it's quite another skill to get out, to pull back without heavy losses.

Do we negotiate our surrender with the authorities as we had with the First People's Church, allowing them to come in, cuff us, and drag us out for the TV cameras? Should we make a stand in hand-to-hand combat with the very real possibility of a cop's revolver "accidentally" going off and killing one of us? Death in combat is to be expected. Being killed once your hands are up and your body is on the ground is another matter altogether. Since there'd be no camera crews allowed inside, the police could be as brutal as they wanted with no neutral witnesses. Do we just run full speed through side doors, back doors, front doors, toward the crowds, knowing some of us would get beaten and busted, but the rest would hopefully escape?

And then, a "miracle" occurred. One of the workers or one of the doctors, I can't remember which, showed the Health Ministry folks a secret passageway, an underground tunnel from the hospital to the streets formerly used by runaway slaves as part of the Underground Railroad. It was perfect. We could hold out to the very end, trick the city into believing we were going to stay and fight, slip out undetected, melt into the crowd, and let the police smash the place up looking for us.

The plan was to give every activist a white doctor's coat, confusing the police. We'd all leave in groups, mixing in our white progressive brothers and sisters with Latinos and Blacks. How were the cops to distinguish who was a doctor or a lab technician and who wasn't? We'd all have professional-looking lab coats, and we'd throw in a few stethoscopes and clipboards to make it all look "official."

I kept blabbing until Davidoff and Gotterer saw there would be no resolution. They got up slowly and declared solemnly, "Well, whatever happens, we tried. It's on you guys now."

As I walked them to the exit doors, I turned to both of them and said, "Our blood will be on your hands" and walked away.

I knew we had no more than a hour, maybe an hour and a half. I could see the police beginning to stage and tighten up their riot gear. We had to play this escape absolutely perfectly—no one left behind, no one caught.

Everybody got out, everybody except Pablo "Yoruba" Guzmán. We had slipped past the most sophisticated police force in the country; we were free with no injuries except for those of our Minister of Information.

I was incensed, livid. He knew the plan, had been in on the sessions for Lincoln Hospital. We were supposed to melt into the crowds outside, knowing they'd protect us and would not alert the police, then leave the area immediately. How is it that all escaped: doctors, activists, the Lords, including easily recognizable leadership, and only Pablo gets popped?

I was told that he walked slowly to the barricades, almost ensuring identification, and then sauntered through the crowds, greeting people and shaking hands. Was he insane?

I came to the conclusion this wasn't a temporary lapse in judgment. Pablo just chose drama and ego over the collective well-being of our plan and our party. He put his life and his security detail's lives in danger. His personal need for media attention, for the cameras to catch only him being arrested and cuffed, could've ended disastrously. The police let him go fairly quickly, and the Party let him off without criticism. I was really pissed because I had seen it coming. Weeks before, he had walked into the Madison Avenue office, theatrically dressed in Panther garb—black leather jacket, black sweater and pants, black boots, black gloves, and black glasses—berating the cadre for not having the heart, the courage, the militancy of the Black Panthers.

"The Lords have to step up to the plate and fight like the Panthers; those are the real role models," he allegedly said.

It was said in front of street people, ex-cons, dope fiends, and gangbangers who had exhibited extraordinary bravery in confrontations with police during which he was never present.

When I arrived at the office that day, the anger of these Puerto Ricans was palpable. Pablo "Yoruba" had not only insulted their loyalty, he had thrown in cultural seeds of discord by pitting Black militancy against Latino militancy. All this coming from a rail-thin Minister of Information who couldn't perform twenty pushups.

What made matters worse is that no one remembers ever seeing him physically on the line when we had to confront cops or other enemies. The standard excuse was that he was busy writing press releases. Yeah . . . .

Some of the men and women of the Party jumped on me even before I got to the office door.

"Who the fuck does he think he is, putting us down?"

"I don't see his ass out there when we're duking it out."

"If he's so in love with the Panthers, why doesn't he just join them?"

"He doesn't like being Puerto Rican; he wants to be Black."

I listened and took it all in, stopping individual members when they got disrespectful. Pride in being Puerto Rican did not mean we were not Black. Yoruba's actions needed to be corrected—his unconscious divisive statements were just plain wrong—but the criticism that he just wanted to be Black, meaning Afro-American, was way over the top.

America saw no difference between Black Puerto Ricans and Afro-Americans; we were all catching hell. The colonial past had implanted in Puerto Ricans the thought that we were somehow "better" than Blacks. Our grandparents would say proudly, defiantly, "We are not Black; we are Puerto Rican!" ignoring the fact that white supremacists didn't care what kind of "niggers" we were, Spanish-speaking, English-speaking, Dutch, or French.

Calling Yoruba outside, I asked him to sit next to me on the adjoining building's stoop, our unbugged conference room.

"Don't you ever insult or humiliate our people like that again, you hear me?"

Yoruba, genuinely shocked at the vehemence of my statement, raised his hands and feigned ignorance.

"What are you talking about, what did I say?"

"You know exactly what you said, comparing Panthers to Lords. Even the Panthers would disagree with your shit. This is El Barrio, brother. It's a proud place and some of these guys have been fighting cops and each other when you were in grade school. They may not have the political education, but they have the heart. Don't ever put them down again. You'll lose respect and we'll lose morale. We can't afford it, you understand?"

Yoruba tried to open his mouth.

"Don't say anything, Pablo, don't try to explain yourself. *Just don't do it again!* Are we clear?"

Oh, he was clear all right, clear and pissed.

True to form, the police attacked an empty hospital building after we escaped, and they tore the place apart. If they didn't need a new Lincoln

Hospital when we occupied the place, they certainly needed one after the cops got through with it. The place was in shambles.

It took six long years for a new Lincoln Hospital to be constructed on 149th Street in the South Bronx, but today it stands as physical testimony to what struggle can achieve. Lincoln Detox was initiated after the takeover, a clinic within the hospital with an innovative modality that used acupuncture to treat heroin addiction. Led by Walter Bosque Del Rio, now a respected and admired acupuncturist, it became world renowned for its visionary leadership in treating opiate dependency.

Patient rights contracts are now standard in New York City hospitals, and tuberculosis is almost nonexistent in East Harlem and the South Bronx. (To be perfectly honest, we still have the highest rates of asthma in East Harlem and the South Bronx, which we believe are due to car and bus fumes, trash disposal plants, and planes spewing excess fuel as they land at nearby airports.)

The modern father of Puerto Rican independence, Albizu Campos, said it best: *"La patria es valor y sacrificio* [Our country is about courage and sacrifice].

We must remember that!

Chapter 15

My Last Dance with the Party

HAD I PUT a stop to HRUM'S gender-based manipulative tactics on the Lower East Side, had I confronted their racial/nationalistic divisiveness, we might have prevented that same cancer from metastasizing throughout the Young Lords Party later. I didn't.

I believe that the machinations of COINTELPRO and its agents within the Party ate away at the body of the organization until its members began to cannibalize themselves, resulting in defections of our trusted Afro-American comrades and the serious home invasions and beatings of other Young Lord members in good standing. We drank the Kool-Aid mixed by the intelligence community of this country and lost ourselves and our neighborhoods in the process.

Unbelievably, Juan pulled the same crap again, this time with Gloria Fontanez, the head of the same Lower East Side HRUM chapter that had us stumbling in confusion and self-doubt. Shit!! He just didn't get it. For all his political acumen and fervor, Juan had not been raised in the womb of lower-class Puerto Rican street culture. This doesn't make you a revolutionary, but it certainly sensitizes you to what is street-sacred and what is not. On the other hand, had he been immersed in that culture, he might never have read as much, studied that much, or entered Columbia University at sixteen. His was a special intelligence, able to read reams of information and make order of it. But, although he had led the mainly white Columbia student strike of '68, he simply didn't have the "touch," the "feel," nor the value system of the streets.

It seemed everyone else but me knew that Gloria was secretly dating Juan while easing out of her marriage to a Lower East Side drug dealer who allegedly was a police informant. She confessed this later to a filmmaker, adding that she was terrified of her husband. Did he make her inform on us? Was he her handler? Was he provoking the contrived arguments and accusations in the Lords against men and women? We'll never know.

A bearded man came to the office and asked to see me. It was Gloria Fontanez's husband. He sounded angry, but he didn't shout; his was a determined demeanor, hands in his pockets, a firm voice. I didn't feel he wanted a physical confrontation, but he definitely wanted answers.

Those of us in the back of the office that day looked at one another incredulously. What?

We knew Gloria had two kids, but she rarely mentioned a partner or her marital status. We assumed she was a single mother. She spent countless hours in our uptown Madison Avenue office, often going home alone though she lived in the projects way down on the Lower East Side. We didn't make it a practice to follow members and check on their backgrounds. Bad mistake.

As I walked to the front door, I immediately sized this guy up: average build, Puerto Rican, intense eyes, even more intense spirit, fatigue jacket, jeans, no negative aura, just waiting. To her credit, Micky Agrait, the officer of the day, did not let him enter the office. To his credit, he didn't try to rush in. I sensed he knew the street code. "What's up?" I said, offering him my hand from the door. His grasp was firm.

"You're the Chairman, right? Can you step outside for a minute?"

On any street, in any city, these are fighting words, the prelude to hand-to-hand combat. My security person pulled me back and moved forward, but something told me this was a different affair. It wasn't going to be physical—not immediately, anyway.

Pulling my bodyguard behind me, I stepped down into the street, obliquely to defend myself just in case.

His spirit was nonconfrontational. This man didn't want to fight me. He wanted answers.

"Do you guys make a habit of going out with married women?" he spat out. "You're supposed to be protecting our community, defending us, right?"

"Yeah, that's what we do," I answered, still trying to figure out his motive.

"Well, I'm Gloria's husband. I don't know if you know this, but she's never home, she's always here, we have two kids who she rarely sees, and now I hear she's going out with one of your leaders, Juan Gonzalez."

I was taken aback. What I thought was going to be a challenge was, in fact, another damn domestic dispute. And Juan was at the center of it, again.

The shock on my face must've registered in this man's consciousness.

"What?" I sputtered. "Are you serious?" I was really taken aback. Juan involved in another domestic? I stood there, emotionless, embarrassed, with nothing to say. The man, seeing my total confusion, tried to soothe me.

"Look, I didn't come here looking for trouble. It's obvious you don't know anything about this. This whole thing just stinks."

And then he stopped, waited for me to pull my eyes up to his, and said, "I'm a street guy: a bit of a fuck-up, but I know what you guys are doing is the right thing. I thought of joining you, but it's not me. I like making money on the streets, you know what I mean? I deal and do my thing. I think maybe things could've been different years ago, but this is what I chose, you dig?"

I just looked and nodded my head, dumbfounded at the revelation and the man's brutal honesty.

"I just thought the Lords had more honor than this. I thought you knew this."

I lowered my eyes again and just stared at the concrete sidewalk.

"We do. We know it. I swear to you I never knew this was going on. I would've put a stop to it, immediately. If you know me, if you know our style, we don't play that shit. We respect marriages, brother, and I'm so sorry you've had to go through this. Your wife never told us about you. I assumed a grandmother, or someone, was taking care of the kids while she worked for us. And she does spend a lot of time here. I should've known something was up. I thank you for being man enough to come to me with this rather than Juan. I really thank you."

Juan must've had angels on his shoulders and a lot of prayers around him because I know what could've happened if this irate husband had decided to take the law into his own hands.

"Bro," Gloria's husband continued, "you know how this shit goes down. *La calles son las calles.* [The streets are the streets.] If you got a problem with someone in the crew and you don't want a full-scale war, you go to the leader and have him deal with the asshole, right?"

I nodded my head and we both stayed quiet.

I broke the silence.

"This will be taken care of immediately."

I had to admire the man's courage, walking into unfamiliar territory and confronting us with the indiscretion of one of our members.

Before he turned to leave, he said, "For some reason, I do trust you. And I hope you go through with it. Nobody should be meddling in our shit. You agree?"

I nodded my head. "Definitely."

And then he walked to the end of the block and turned the corner.

We talked to Juan again about his dangerous liaisons, but the Central Committee did nothing about it. He continued his relationship with Gloria and she grew in power and influence within the Party.

Juan seemed powerless to stop her. It seems he was wrapped up in her, on her. Using her relationship with him, Gloria worked her way to the top echelons of power in the YLP, dropping hints that only "real" Spanish-speaking, island-born 'Ricans could be trusted to be loyal members of the Party. This was in direct contradiction of our initial recruiting mantra, *"Tengo Puerto Rico en mi Corazon* [I have Puerto Rico in my heart]," meaning all you needed was the love of the island to be a Lord. You didn't have to speak Spanish or know the history or have been born in Puerto Rico or even be Puerto Rican. You didn't need straight hair or white skin or a degree. The love and the willingness to fight for the island's independence and social justice for Puerto Ricans and people of color are what counted. Very few of us spoke Spanish well; most of us had been born in the States. While speaking Spanish was important, basing ethnic authenticity on language or birthplace was a false criterion for nationalism, inclusion, or eligibility. It was your commitment and service to your people, your ability to stand up and be counted.

African American comrades, with us from the start, began to feel alienated and started to leave the organization. It was Puerto Rican nationalism at its worst. Throughout this period of relative calm, the Lords had conducted a successful clothing drive and attracted the admiration of cops, who would offer us tips on when the heat was coming down. We enjoyed the admiration of celebrities like Bette Midler, Jane Fonda, Donald Sutherland, and Miriam Colón. Writers and directors came to our aid, like Pete Hamill, José Torres, Elia Kazan, and Budd Shulberg. We also had the good fortune of being financially supported by wealthy benefactors like Ellie Guggenheimer and City Councilman Carter Burden, who, along with Herman Badillo and Arnoldo Segarra, Latino liaison to then-Mayor John Lindsay, helped in the negotiations for withdrawal from the First People's Church takeover.

Kids and grandmothers hugged us on the street. What really gave the Lords credibility was the support of local Puerto Rican leaders like Evelina Antonetti of United Bronx Parents, a local tenants' rights group, who brought food for us while we occupied the First People's Church and stood guard on the front steps every day until they arrested party members eleven days later.

"Yoruba" Guzmán had established personal relationships with several journalists. His brilliant media strategy literally saved our lives. Whenever the police were ready to attack, whenever we felt their rabid paramilitary spirit of "kill 'em all," Yoruba would have the journalistic cavalry arrive right on time: Luisa Quintero, a columnist for the most important Spanish daily, *El Diario-La Prensa*, and grandmother to us all; Jack Newfield of the *Village Voice*; Jimmy Breslin of the *New York Post*; Pete Hamill of the *Daily News*; Gloria Rojas and J. J. Gonzalez of Channel 2, the local CBS affiliate; and the nobleman of all TV journalists, Gil Noble of the ABC local affiliate, Channel 7. There was also Vic Miles and Chris Borgen of Channel 2 plus Jeff Kaiman of Channel 11, a radical in his own right.

Former Viceroy gang members who thought we were dilettantes began to talk to us seriously; some even joined. We were heroes.

What I also loved was the pride, respect, and counsel we received from the National Lawyers Guild, a progressive group of lawyers committed to defending those fighting for social justice. Three of those lawyers I became enamored of: Mary Kaufman, Dick Ashe, and Dan Myers. But the lawyer I kvelled over was Mary, a handsome, no-nonsense, white-haired bubbe who would sit for hours with me and the Central Committee, discussing the legal ramifications of our "offensives," be it garbage, church, or hospital takeovers. Whenever we would delve into violence, she would look at me sternly and say, "I don't want to hear it. I'm here to help you stay out of jail, not put you in it. The movement has enough of that."

She had parted front teeth like me, and her smile was beatific. I knew when we hatched a plan whether it was going to be successful or not, just by that smile; it was like the sun coming out.

Dick Ashe was a Princeton man, very serious, intense, tightly wound, but very thorough, a finisher. No loose ends. You had to have a reason, an answer for your actions, or he would be against it and say so.

Dan Myers had an activist's enthusiasm; he was down for anything that would highlight political contradictions and move the revolution further down the road. His energy and assertiveness were so fierce I often thought he would have liked to join us. He came from a proletarian labor-organizing family, and upon meeting his father, I knew whence his militancy emanated. His father had a serious face and strong working hands, and he was used to violence in the labor movement, ready for anything, totally fearless. His son was the same way.

Then there was Geraldo Rivera, a Manhattan Legal Services lawyer who crashed into our office one day, saying he wanted to help his people by legally representing us. Legally defending the Young Lords Party was his entrée into the reality of Puerto Rican life in New York City: poverty, racism, police brutality. His mother was a wonderfully engaging Jewish woman, embracing, loving; his father, on the other hand, was a bit stern, taciturn. I deduced that he had spent his entire life trying to run away from the Puerto Rican ghetto and its dysfunction, tried to give his family a different life on Long Island, tried to achieve the American Dream.

Whether Geraldo Rivera was attracted to the core principles of a Puerto Rican group committed to armed struggle for self-determination in the United States and the independence of Puerto Rico or was struggling with a post-adolescent identity crisis, we'll never know. What I do know is that during his brief foray into our movement, he displayed courage when confronted with police and authority.

While demonstrating against Governeur Hospital's treatment of poor people, the Young Lords Party and the Health Revolutionary Movement found ourselves face-to-face with a detachment of New York City police called out to monitor and restrain us if a takeover were imminent. Most of the cops were calm and professional. Except one. He kept pushing me back with his nightstick. I didn't move, so he decided to poke me in the stomach, repeatedly. I told him to stop. We had the right to demonstrate and had made no threatening moves. He continued to poke, harder. Finally, I knocked the stick away and pushed him back, harder. That pushed his button, and as he raised his baton, the melee started with cops swinging and our hitting back and running. The young cop I'd pushed singled me out and ran after me, screaming, "Halt!" Hell no! If he wanted me, he was going to have to work for it. No policeman ever caught me in a chase. But this guy was a distance runner. He stayed on my ass, wouldn't let up. The streets were blocked by police cars and men in blue, waiting to beat and arrest anyone who tried to slip through. My only option was the nearby project building. This guy was gaining on me.

I ran into a six-story project building and started knocking on doors, screaming I was a Young Lord and the police wanted to beat me up. In East Harlem, we always had at least one family in any building who would open the door quickly, put us in a closet or under a bed, and lie to the police when asked if they knew our whereabouts. Even brown and Black Pentecostals would harbor us with the kids being the best of actors when questioned by police. Not this time. No sounds from inside the apartments, no open doors. I ran to the second floor: nothing. The third floor: nothing. The fourth and fifth floors: nothing, no beckoning hands motioning silently for me to rush in and hide. Desperately, I ran to the sixth floor with the sounds of that same cop in pursuit. It was now just a matter of time. I pounded the doors and still no one opened. It was over. I knew it. I was at the far end of the hallway, on the opposite side of the staircase. As he reached the last step of the sixth-floor landing, this guy started to pull out his revolver. I figured rushing him would give him a clear shot, so I turned sideways. Hopefully, if I caught a .38 slug it would enter and exit without hitting any vital organs.

Miraculously, out of nowhere, Geraldo appeared at the top of the stairs and screamed, "Don't shoot! He's my client." The cop holstered his gun, looked angrily at me and Geraldo, and backed off, cursing. Realizing he had broken ranks to chase me, he ran back down the stairs to join his comrades. I was never so glad to see a lawyer and I'll never forget that act of bravery.

I've had several occasions to criticize Geraldo: his alleged drug incident at WABC-TV when a courier was arrested for bringing drugs to his office. Ordering the drugs and getting high didn't bother me, even during work hours. In those days, many reporters were drinking and drugging, on the job and off, including me. (During the mid-'70s and '80s I was a TV reporter, but that's for another book.) What bothered me was that Geraldo blamed it on his girlfriend. Definitely not something Puerto Rican men do. When he found another gig as a TV talk show host, he asked me to provide him with active drug addicts to discuss the ravages of addiction and the cost to society, promising me he would cover their faces. I found two guys I'd known for years on the streets of El Barrio. I felt like a pimp, and while my soul kept whispering to me that this was wrong, my old gang loyalty kicked in. Geraldo was a brother in need. It was the only way I could rationalize my actions. I caved to the pressure of bonded warriorhood rather than ethics (which I thought I had mastered) and morality. During the subway ride to the *Tribune* Times Square studio, the two street guys kept asking for assurances that their faces would not be shown. Their mothers watched Geraldo's show daily, proud that a Puerto Rican had made it to the media national stage.

I brought them into the studio, past the security guards and into Geraldo's makeup room. You could see their star fascination, their admiration of him, their pride at being part of anything this man wanted to do. Geraldo told me he wanted to speak to them alone. So I left the room. I lost contact with them until the audience was seated and the cameras started rolling. But something was terribly wrong. Their faces were being shown: no masks, no attempt to hide their identities.

The two addicts confessed to having robbed for money to feed their habits. His interview was more degrading than informative. I was in the audience and enraged. At the point at which audience participation was requested, I stood up and told Geraldo I was appalled at his degradation of these men in public.

"You didn't keep your promise to me to hide these men's faces. Their mothers are watching. It could kill them. They know what their sons do and so does the community. But do you have to televise it like this, to humiliate them like this? You promised me you wouldn't. But what really pisses me off is your hypocrisy. I've seen you high several times and now you have the damn nerve, the gall, to criticize these guys? How dare you, Geraldo?"

Everyone was in shock: the audience, the heroin addicts, the stage manager, the cameramen, the crew.

Geraldo stood flat-footed and dumbfounded, stammering to find an answer. "I . . . uh . . . never used drugs. You're wrong. Ahhh . . . I may have experimented with marijuana a few times, but I stopped that." His lack of a strong comeback, his phony excuse, was so corny and so transparent.

I roared back. "I saw you at Channel 7 several times, in your office, stoned out of your mind, and it wasn't pot. Give me a break. You're lying and I can't stand it or you." Finally, someone shouted, "Cut tape" and I knew our confrontation would never be seen in public.

I went to the lobby and waited for the guys to finish their session, to take them back to El Barrio. The taping resumed. I never heard what Geraldo asked them or stated in the aftermath of our standoff. Tired of waiting for them to finish, I started toward the exit doors to wait for my guys. Geraldo rushed toward me with his hand outstretched in the most patronizing way. Refusing to shake his hand, I just bleated out, "I can't believe you did this. This is beyond sell-out, this is the lowest; your own people. Stay away from me."

It took decades for us to even look at each other again. The death of a mutual friend, Basil Paterson, in 2014, brought us into the same space. For me, the anger wasn't there any longer. I tapped him on the shoulder during funeral services at Riverside Church, gave him my card. Later in the year, we were both speakers at Herman Badillo's memorial at Hunter College. He was not effusive with me, barely cordial. We both know that we were simply not part of each other's lives anymore. While I still keep in contact with the warriors of the Party, Geraldo remains a skeletal memory with no flesh attached. What matters was that we shared a time in history, we shared the good fight when it was right to do so, and we gave the Puerto Rican community a legacy of self-defense, self-esteem, self-pride, and the power to dream, sacrifice, and achieve victory. What we did after, what ideological paths we chose to follow after the Young Lords Party, was a matter of individual decision. Individual decisions make for individual consequences.

I, too, made some horrible turns in life that affected me and the Party. I never took the time to think of responsibility in relationships, faithfulness, truthfulness. Sacrifices in a relationship were not uppermost in my mind when it came to women. I never saw those traits in my father, who also had myriad relationships, hadn't been raised with those values. Even though I witnessed loyalty in other marriages and relationships, some with men who also came from poor, female-headed households, those values and behaviors didn't resonate with me. In the poor Puerto Rican and Black communities I was raised in, having a "main squeeze" was part of your masculine image; so was having a Plan B, another woman on the side. It was part of street tradition, and men rarely questioned the practice. But tradition is no excuse for using women, going from bed to bed, from having three children from three different partners.

While in the Party, Iris and I began having problems. We were growing apart. I was into war, planning attacks, new tactics, public speaking; she was into education of the cadre and the strengthening of Party infrastructure. Though I was married to her, because of my warped ideas of relationships I never felt an iota of guilt about sleeping with other women. I had left Joan Meinhardt, my former Queens College English teacher, after the Martin Luther King assassination, to live with Iris in her apartment on 168th Street in Washington Heights. It was, as I remember it, a lovely, stimulating relationship in the beginning with long conversations about armed struggle, how to achieve independence for the island of Puerto Rico, racism, colonialism, and the histories of her family and mine.

Both of us had devoted mothers and philandering fathers, the difference being that Iris's dad lived with his family, albeit in a separate room, and my father just split when I was three. It didn't occur to me until much later in life that Iris and I had severe abandonment issues such that any ripple in the façade of this young marriage, any doubt, any perception of unfaithfulness, would cause a major disruption, a tsunamic rupture. It did.

I was still into my spoiled, selfish "frat boy" (though I never joined a fraternity) behavior: calling old girlfriends, making quick pit stops, fucking furiously, then leaving to do the work of the Revolution. An easy, pseudo-pyscho excuse would be that I was under stress, street stress. The government, the cops, some dealers were out to kill me, and I had to release pent-up nervousness.

Bullshit. It was my way of having my way with no regard for the feelings of the women I lied to, lay with, and later waited with in abortion rooms for them to shred the three-month-old fetus to pieces. And those women, who will not be named, were so much in love with me and so not in love with themselves, they complied with my wishes and demands. I have three children, two boys and a girl, all men and women now. I would've had at least ten had my lovers' pregnancies had gone full-term.

The usual liberal response is to say, "I now see the error of my ways and how I hurt those I loved and who loved me . . . blah, blah, blah."

Again, bullshit. I was steeped in arrogance, ego, and the dangerous mixture of feeling that since I did some things right, made some courageous decisions in the Lords, had survived gangs and jail to become a member of the Original Last Poets, and now was the elected Chairman of the Young Lords Party, I had the right to go off the grid, "off the res" from time to time, to push the envelope past the tear mark and always be forgiven.

"Without impulse control, there is no emotional growth. If the self is not conquered, the external conditions will not change." I thought this was Christian or Zen blather. I've discovered that it is also an inviolable warrior code. Take control of yourself, first! Though I was married to Iris, I had not gotten old loves out of my system. Judy Thropp was a brilliant student, well read, passionate about social justice and making love. I had met her as she tutored SEEK college students on the Queens College campus. Everyone loved her ebullient spirit, her gutsy laughter, her scholarship, her sense of right and wrong. She was a short, well-muscled, slightly buck-toothed Jewish girl who said what she felt about the Vietnam war, about racism in America, about left- and right-wing conformity with ideas that were old and rancid, and it didn't matter whether it was male chauvinism or the newly emerging radical feminism. She believed that sexual repression produced an armoring of the psyche, resulting in disease and war.

Judy's father had been a top student of Wilhelm Reich, whose theory was that all matter is connected by orgone energy. That energy, if channeled properly, could make people healthier and our Earth cleaner and less polluted. Through a device that was called an "orgone energy box," Dr. Reich cured cancer patients and coaxed acres of desert into blooming fields of flowers. An Austrian Jew, Dr. Reich was hated by the Nazis and later condemned by the Communists for his theories of free sexual expression and contraception.

Fleeing to the United States after the war in Europe, he discovered that America's medical elites were just as dismissive of any radical theories as the Austrians and Nazis were, if not more so. Deeming his theories quackery, the U.S. government banned his works, burned all of his research papers, and removed "orgone energy" from the official lexicon of psychiatry. What scared them? Dr. Wilhelm Reich died in prison on charges of fraud for his alleged "false claims" about the curative effects of the "orgone box."

Neither the government nor the medical establishment ever officially tested Reich's theories; they just denied his results.

Judy was immersed in the Reichian psychology of unrestricted sex. Booyah! A white girl who had no inhibitions about sexual intimacy, who advocated fucking with no guilt. Shit, I was on board . . . totally. But during the breaks in our lovemaking, Judy would gently probe into my past, my ideological convictions, my spiritual convictions, my parents.

She began to peel away my layers of anger toward women, of insecurity with true intimacy, the feelings of abandonment and how it didn't allow me to make any real emotional commitment.

I left relationships early rather than go through the pain of being left alone. Judy suggested therapy, two to three times a week. Since I was in street battle, it was important to make decisions based on fact, not feeling, she advised. She was right. I was primed for it since my first college lover, Joan, had also implored me to seek therapy. I did for a while but argued with the psychiatrist about armed struggle and the need to defend Puerto Ricans and people of color. He droned on about my using external violence and revolutionary activity to divert my attention from the real issues raging within me.

I agreed to some extent, but the suggestion that I stop all politics to focus attention on my angst sounded like typical liberal bullshit. Was I supposed to sit back and watch my people die while I "worked on myself"? Hell, no!

And then the tenor of the whole relationship changed when I brought up German Jews and the Holocaust. Had they seen the writing on the wall after Kristallnacht in 1938, had they realized the Nazis detested them and wanted them burned, gassed, raped, dead, they might have fought back with force. Thank God for Polish Jews in the Warsaw ghetto who decided, "Fuck it! If we're going to die, let's die fighting these bastards. Some of us might survive and that's worth every drop of our blood." The psychiatrist's face blanched and he shifted uncomfortably in his chair. "You can't compare the Holocaust to the struggle for civil rights," he intoned in his most professional manner. "And you're changing the subject. It's about *you* right now."

I shot back, "I am them. They are me. They die, I die. They feel pain, I feel pain. There is no me without them. Can't you understand that? You don't see the similarities?"

I could feel his exasperation with me. He thought I wasn't sophisticated or educated enough.

I left the sessions soon after, convinced that this doctor had forgotten his people's litany of pain, death, and rejection. For him, cultural amnesia was the easy way out. I would argue in parties and political meetings that while Jewish America perceived this country as the New Jerusalem, America was only a superficial "friend." The United States had provided wondrous opportunities for those fleeing the madness of fascism. But underneath the political epidermis there was an ugly hatred of Jews and Blacks.

I reminded them constantly of the betrayal of Polish Jews by their very own neighbors during World War II. When the Nazis invaded Poland, denouncing Judaism and the Jewish people, too many Polish "friends" turned them in. I would argue the same thing could happen in the United States if the economy fell. For me, the raw face of racism and anti-semitism was just a few lost paychecks away.

Once the bulk of American whites begin to lose white-skin privileges, begin to experience political and economic deprivation, lose their "constitutional rights," as it were, that ugly, lynching spirit will emerge. It was always there. Still is, as far as I can see.

I finally asked the therapist, "How much more do you need to see before it dawns on you that there are Americans who hate you as much as they hate me? Putting Jewish heads in the sand is not going to make it go away. If they're coming for me now, they're coming for you tomorrow, regardless of your money, your professional status, your contributions to the nation."

I left therapy.

Judy understood all of this but still strongly urged that I seek help. I searched and found two therapists: a Cuban male psychiatrist, Dr. Martinez, raised in Puerto Rico and aware of my activism, and then, subsequently, an Afro-American male psychiatrist, Dr. Hugh Butts, steeped in Black history. They helped immensely. They both allowed me to peek into my upbringing, my culture, to sift through the anger without condemning my rebellion against America or my Black Puerto Rican maleness.

I discovered that with my mother throwing my father out when I was three because of his affairs, I was left with a severe dread of abandonment. I couldn't be alone for any length of time, certainly couldn't live alone without a strong female connection who would play mother and housekeeper, whether we lived together or not. And because I was terrified the woman would ultimately abandon me, I would never commit to her, never trust her fully, never marry her, and always have an "active reserve player" in the dugout.

Both psychiatrists gently led me to understand that when confronted with my promiscuity, I would dodge and weave; I would lie.

With white and Black women, I would decry their lack of Puerto Ricaness, their inability to serve and cater to my needs, from washing my clothes to cleaning house to cooking pernil properly. To Puerto Rican women, I would bemoan their lack of intellectual stimulation and their unwillingness to let my soul soar to explore and experiment sexually. There were exceptions, women who fit all the insane criteria I set up. With those women, I would simply end the relationship, declaring I wasn't in love with them any longer.

Through all of this, Judy Thropp and I remained lovers. She never let my personal dysfunction get in the way of her politics.

Once, after punching a cop involved in the beating of a drug addict on 111th Street, I was forced to go underground. The police had an all-points bulletin out on me and they weren't going to be civil if they caught me on the streets.

I called several of my Black/'Rican friends to hide me. Nothing doing. So much for being "down with the revolution."

Desperate, I called Judy. Without hesitation, she told me to rush over. She lived in a large one-bedroom on 110th Street between Columbus and Amsterdam, and for two weeks, with police cars whizzing by and cops patrolling the streets, Judy fed me and my bodyguard, Pi, five blocks from where the incident occurred, while regaling us with stories to calm our anxiety as we peeked out of her first-floor blinds to see if they were going to search her building. It was rented by white students, mainly. The police never came in to question the tenants.

Judy's courage, her honesty with me, her tolerance of my immaturity and demands on her time endeared me to her.

Judy eventually became embittered with me. She wanted marriage, children, a family. And, while she didn't press hard for these things, she felt I eventually would calm down and stay home with her. I didn't. It hurt her, deeply.

Judy Thropp saw me as a leader who could guide all people, but especially people of color, into an honest probing of self-defeating, self-destructive thinking and behavior. Instead, I became a poster boy for it.

Judy died of cancer, bitterly disappointed with me, the drugs I was ingesting, my career meandering.

I had lost contact with her long before she passed. She taught at Sarah Lawrence, lived a block away from me on Columbus Avenue, but our paths rarely crossed. When they did, it was a cordial hello, a smile and goodbye. After the Lords I became immersed in the Latin music world, fascinated with its rhythms, its hypnotic dances, its eclectic musicians, its secret drug world, and the sheer genius of its bombastic sound. I heard Judy was ill, heard she had a son, but never reached out, never asked for forgiveness and never thanked her for saving my life. I was focused on one person: me.

I was thoroughly in love with Iris Morales, whatever that meant to me in the late '60s.

I heard her speak at a SEEK student rally in Albany protesting proposed cuts in the CUNY budget and was immediately beguiled. She was pretty, intelligent, militant, and articulate.

After I spoke, she seemed to be attracted to me, too, so we sat next to each other on the bus ride back home to New York City. We connected immediately, speaking feverishly of societal contradictions, our lives, our dreams, our upbringing, our desire to change this country by any means necessary. At the end of the bus ride, I was more than beguiled; I was swooning. I was in love.

We decided to make a date to see the movie *Black Orpheus* the next week, playing at a theater on Bleecker and Thompson streets in the West Village. The movie left both of us breathless, and for a long time we walked silently in a snowstorm from the Village to Harlem. Only two young people in love can do that. The love-heat, the fascination of discovery with each other, the connection with another intellect capable of understanding a Puerto Rican worldview, our sense of tribe and the need to fight injustice kept us warm. When we did speak, it was to laugh at how far we had walked, holding hands as we sloshed through the snow. It is one of the few truly romantic memories etched in the back of my brain.

Iris was working as a counselor in an Upper West Side after-school center named ABLE. Having been one of the privileged Puerto Rican youngsters to have been given a scholarship to Fieldston, a tony rich kids' school, she was well prepared to tutor those who needed academic remediation. I would often pick her up after rehearsals with The Last Poets and she'd introduce me to her mom and sisters, her college friends, and I'd bring her into my world of Black poetry and activists. We became close to Gylan Kain and his wife, June; Rap Brown and his wife, Lynne; and Amiri and Amina Baraka. She loved the passion of the poetry, recoiled from the danger and the hypocrisy of revolutionary politics, said she wanted nothing to do with it. As I became embroiled in the machinations of building the Young Lords, Iris made it clear that she would not become a member:

"You're going to have enough to deal with without worrying about my safety and whereabouts."

She would often say, "Plus, I don't trust a lot of those people. Who's going to stand beside you when the pressure gets intense, when the slaps get harder? Me!" (As it turned out, Iris became my worst enemy.)

The only people Iris felt truly comfortable around were Rap and Lynne Brown. They didn't judge her, enjoyed her agile mind, and loved her stories. Rap, a hardcore revolutionary, was particularly patient with Iris, answering all her innocent questions with the sagacity of an old, seasoned warrior.

I argued against Iris's staying out of the Party. I needed her partnership, her intelligence, her discernment in knowing true allies from foes. I was also afraid of our growing apart as I organized on the street. Organizing is labor-intensive. There is no substitute for plain old hard work: pounding on doors, standing on street corners, and bringing the issues of social injustice and revolutionary solutions straight to our neighbors. There is no clock. So if I was going to spend that much quality time with the Lords, why not work side-by-side with the woman I loved?

Iris gave in and joined the fledgling organization. Big mistake. I was now not only embroiled in working out the kinks and challenges of building a fighting unit, I was also facing having to build a love relationship with very little alone time, time to work on ourselves, on myself.

Something was bound to break. It did.

The Central Committee received information that a promoter was planning a major rock concert, summer '69, on Randalls Island. Buses and subways would leave concert-goers in East Harlem because the only way to get to Randalls Island was through our neighborhood. Hordes of smoked-up, zonked-out white rockers who never gave a shit about our neighborhood would come tramping through our streets oblivious to the poverty, the people, the children. We had our hands full with our junkies; we didn't need middle-class imports. So, we called the promoter.

He ignored us for a week, refusing to take our calls or simply slamming the phone down once we identified ourselves as Young Lords. We simply wanted him to respect our community by educating his throngs about what not to do: no racist remarks, no lighting up joints on the street, no ogling Puerto Rican women, no public urination, etc.

Frustrated with his superior attitude and not taking us seriously, we let his secretary know that his bringing those kids onto our streets was an act of war. We would attack them at every bus and subway stop, warning them to go home or face the wrath of every gang member and addict who lived within our borders. We couldn't guarantee what the street people would do, but robbery was the obvious danger. Immediately, we got a call-back from the promoter.

"Are you fuckin' guys crazy?" he screamed over the phone. "Are you fuckin' serious? I'll have cops all over the place, watching."

I picked up the receiver.

"Listen, asshole. I don't give a fuck how many cops you call out. You expect thousands; the cops can't protect all of 'em. All it takes is a bold headline in the *Post* or *Daily News* that one li'l white girl was punched in her face, knocked to the pavement, and robbed for your dream concert to be smashed to smithereens. We demand a meeting or fuck you and your concert."

And then I slammed the phone down.

It didn't take more than ten minutes for him to call back.

He still sounded like an arrogant fuck, but just a mite contrite. "Meet me downtown. Now! I know you have my address," he ordered. I still didn't like his attitude. Now I played tough.

"Hey," I barked. "We got things to do. You expect us to jump because you call? We'll call when we're ready. We got people to talk to, papers to sell. I gotta go." As I took the receiver off my ear, I heard him screaming, "Whoa, whoa . . . whoaaa. Hey, I'm sorry." Sounded like he meant it.

All of us crowded around the receiver, afros and hair in one another's faces, bursting with silent, hysterical laughter, holding our sides, some of us falling to the floor and rolling on the ground.. I motioned for them to shut the hell up. There were tears in their eyes as they nodded their heads in agreement.

"Look, I'm not your enemy. I like what you guys are doing, what you stand for. I understand your passion; hey, I was young once. But I'm running a business. And this sounds like extortion."

His change of attitude was nauseatingly liberal and patronizing. I just stayed quiet. "Let's take a step back and calm down. I'm not tellin' you, I'm asking you to come down to the office. We can work this out, okay?"

All I replied was a curt, "Yeah, OK." And I hung up.

The Central Committee—me, Juan Gonzalez, Pablo "Yoruba" Guzmán, Juan "Fi" Ortiz, David Perez, along with Denise Oliver—immediately began to work out different scenarios and strategies.

Our primary concern was that this guy would try to talk us to death, weaken our resolve, offer us a few bucks, and "politely" shove us out of the office. He thought we were community hustlers, poverty pimps.

We decided I would use language that was neutral and nonthreatening just in case the promoter was taping the meeting to give to the police or FBI. We would let him offer suggestions as to how to end the impasse. And, regardless of how good a deal he might offer, we wouldn't agree to anything until we got back to home base and talked it over.

There'd be no laughing, no smiles, no acceptance of any food or drink, and only one speaker. The discipline had to be tight and military-sharp. No breaks, no cracks, no looking at one another for confirmation. This was serious negotiation and there had to be a "win" for us and our folks. One thing we were absolutely clear on: He was not going to pull off a concert on our turf without paying a price: money, food, clothing, or jobs. He was going to have to give up something or hit the wall of disruption. And we knew how to disrupt, street-style. Every action we had taken—the garbage offensive, Lincoln Hospital, the kidnapping of the TB truck, and the takeover of the People's Church—had prepared our troops. We were ready. And prepared for him to say no. Two days later, we filed into his relatively small Midtown office and into a room cluttered with posters, charts, legal pads, and notes all over the walls. The promoter looked haggard and tired. I felt we weren't the only obstacles in his life "So whadda you wanna do?" he asked wearily, looking at some papers, not looking at us.

I didn't feel we were being disrespected; he was just overwhelmed. I kinda felt sorry for him. I looked at him for a long time, kept silent, waiting for him to lift his eyes and connect with us.

He did, finally, his thin, hunched body, his unkempt Beatles-style hair, bleary eyes, his lined face almost pleading for us to understand his predicament and see his side of it. If we capitulated and came in soft, he'd probably see the group as a bunch of chumps and find a way of dismissing us. If we came in too hard, he'd simply close the mental gates and refuse further negotiation.

Once we locked eyes, I began.

"Our mission is service. Serving our people is all we do, all day, every day. We serve breakfast to our kids, find clothing for those who don't have it, and attack those institutions that hurt our folks. We're not afraid of getting caught. We're not afraid of being jailed. We're not afraid of being beaten."

The promoter perked up and narrowed his eyes, but he didn't speak. It was us and him now. With all the busy activity in that Midtown office—all the phones ringing, all the loud conversations, the air conditioner noise, the muffled traffic noise outside—this moment was ours.

"What can we work out?" he answered softly after a short pause.

The Central Committee had already worked out a plan; we wanted these white kids to know who we were and we wanted them to buy our newspaper, Palante. (Frankly, we needed the money.)

"Most of your attendees are not political; they know something about the Panthers, nothing about Latinos and the Lords, and less about why the Vietnam war has cost our country lives, money, and credibility. We want to sell our papers in the stadium. That's all. If one-eighth of these kids learns about Puerto Rico's colonial status, the condition of Puerto Ricans here in their own country, and why we fight for social justice for all Americans, we will have done our job."

The man's scowl turned into a smile, not patronizing, not liberal, just admiration. "I think you fuckin' guys are crazy. They'll kill you! Don't you know that? Aren't you afraid?" I didn't even think when I answered.

"Nope." And we stayed staring at each other.

He hung his head for a minute, looking at the wooden floor of the office, touching his earlobes, And murmuring "Hmm" to himself several times. This guy listened to his own counsel.

"I believe what you stand for. I admire that kind of courage. Yeah, I'll let your papers be sold for as long as the concert lasts. And I'll go a step further. I'll pay you guys to pull security for me inside Randalls Island. You patrol the aisles, you protect the stage and equipment, you watch for the druggies, you stop any fights in the audience. You know the terrain and it's obvious you guys know how to take care of yourselves. And I'll give you $5,000 on advance right now and more after the concert. I'll pay well. I won't gyp you. You guys don't show up, it'll be on you. I won't say anything to the cops. No contract, no nothing. I can't think of a better solution. Agreed?"

The Central Committee had agreed not to answer immediately, but I instinctively felt this was a great deal and that seizing the moment was crucial.

I answered curtly, "Agreed." He took out a checkbook, signed one, handed it to me, I handed it to Denise, we shook hands, and we walked out of the office, dazed. We had won.

And we got much more than we expected from the concert: two streams of revenue, selling Palante, and acting as security.

We shook hands and slapped five once we got a few blocks from the office, but we were quiet. Oh shit, we were really in the big time now. All I could think of was how important it was for us to train our Defense Committee to patrol an area as huge as Randalls Island. It was time to memorize our political education mantras and internalize our martial arts training. This was the real thing; we had to take our duty seriously. We had to become professional.

The Defense Ministry sprang into action, going over and over the "what to dos," the "ifs" . . . .; what to do if someone was openly smoking pot, what to do if the cops wanted to make arrests within the stadium, what to do if the kids rushed the stage and tried to touch the performers, what to do and how to treat groupies, drug overdoses, reporters, parents, and kids?

David Perez, a quiet, humble, island-born Puerto Rican, was up to the task. His quiet manner belied his courage. Once while on an elevated subway platform in Queens, we were confronted by a squad of uniformed policemen. We were chanting and laughing, on our way to a Panther 21 rally in Queens. We weren't drunk, we weren't high, we were not obstructing, we were not harassing or bothering passengers; we were just a group of happy, energetic young people not unlike those groups of college students one sees on the subways on their way to a school basketball game.

One white policeman approached Tintan, a tall, dark, black-haired, ruggedly handsome Taino-looking Young Lord and ordered him to the middle of the platform. It was pure harassment. Tintan was a foot away from the edge and no New Yorker stays in the middle unless they want to stand for the duration of their ride. It must have been Tintan's lack of fear, maybe his attitude or emotionless answer that riled the cop. Tintan, a former Viceroy gang member, was a heroin addict. He never embarrassed us, was always courteous, never ran from a battle, and always shot up before we had confrontations.

He hated the police. It was a seething, deep-down-in-the-gut hatred born of watching too many of his friends beaten to a pulp for nothing other than being Puerto Rican and staring cops in the face when questioned.

I was about three feet away when Tintan turned to the cop, with cold eyes, and simply stated, "I'm okay right here, thank you."

The other policemen stayed away, just watching. They knew their comrade was off the "res" and trying to start some shit, but rather than pull him back, call him off, they just stood there.

I knew the syndrome, the code of loyalty, backing your comrade up whether the person initiating the conflict is right or wrong. And I knew we were in for it, right there, on an outdoor elevated subway platform with trains screeching in and out at high speeds.

This cop was crazy.

But so was Tintan.

The policeman was a bit shorter than Tintan, but well built. He moved closer to Tintan, almost nose to nose.

"I asked you to back the hell up," the cop barked.

"And I told you I'm fine where I am. I ain't breaking no laws and you know it."

The cop reached behind his back for his handcuffs and that's when Tintan executed the smoothest, the most perfect close-range right cross I'd ever seen. Boom, dead on the cop's left cheek. The wise guy stumbled back, dazed and confused. I was surprised he didn't fall straight down on his face, the punch was so powerful. I screamed, "Everybody out, now!" and the Lords scrambled. Even as I was running, I marveled at how the cadre performed. They instinctively knew not to run toward one stairway. It would create a choke point; they'd stumble and the cops could arrest them en masse. Instead, the Lords ran toward the stairways in the front and back of the platform while others took the wider middle stairs, diverting the small group of policemen who had to zigzag past commuters and chase in different directions. Downstairs, there was another platform for trains going into Manhattan. Luckily, there was a waiting train and some of us took off our berets and jackets and calmly sat down, waiting for the car doors to close and the train to move out. I chose to stand, holding onto a subway pole, my back toward the open doors so as not to be recognized quickly. That's when I saw David, looking like a factory worker with his sneakers, a work shirt, sleeves rolled up, and chino pants. We both smiled and just when I was about to open my mouth to greet him, his eyes, his face told me to stay quiet. The cops were right behind me, huffing and looking to kick ass, anybody's. One went to the left of the subway car while the other pushed past me and stood right in front of David, his nightstick at ready. "You thought you'd get away, huh?" he said, too calmly.

David, in his thickest Puerto Rican accent, asked quizzically, "Wha jou seh?" The policeman ordered him to stand up.

"You're under arrest"

David stayed seated, stayed in character, playing his role of unsuspecting Puerto Rican worker to the hilt.

"Offeecer, why jou bothering me. I deen do nohtheeng."

As the officer raised his nightstick to crush his skull, David whipped out his nunchakus in a swirl motion, hitting the officer directly in the mouth. All I saw was blood and teeth spurting out. David and I ran out of the subway car and down the stairs. The other cop had already entered the other car so we had a few seconds to clamber down the stairs to safety.

It was incredible. I had rarely seen someone react so quickly to oncoming danger and physical violence.

After a few minutes of nervous silence, labored breathing, and furtive glances checking for cops, I asked David if he knew what he did as we walked half a mile to another Manhattan-bound subway line.

He turned to me, giggled a bit, then, while continuing to dart his eyes all over the place for police, said, with a surreal calm, "I just didn't want to get hurt. I didn't want to die that way." I never doubted David's courage or warrior spirit again. I saw this courage time after time in the Young Lords Party.

A few Lords were arrested that day, including Lulu, one of our loyal members, who slipped while running down the wide middle stairway, spraining her ankle. She ended up in the Women's House of Detention on Greenwich Street in the West Village. We were concerned because Lulu had been raised in the church. She was quiet and humble and had not one iota of tough street girl in her appearance or aura. You looked at Lulu and thought piety and motherhood. It was difficult even cursing around her. She survived those few days inside jail. Having the reputation of being in the Young Lords helped inside the joint. But, as I discovered when Geraldo snuck me in as his legal assistant to visit Lulu in the antiquated jailhouse, this young woman had an interior toughness, a core of strength and ideological belief that shone through her wide eyeglasses.

"I'm fine," she asserted, jutting her jaw out when we visited her, "Nobody's messing with me." Lulu, a short, thick, pretty, brown-skinned Afro-Indian with saucer plates for eyes and hair so thick you could fantasize braiding it and sliding down the outside world to freedom, simply told us to get her out. No drama, no tears. I remembered thinking if it ever came to an armed showdown between the Young Lords and the police, I would want her at my side, to win or die.

We got her out quickly. She never bragged about it.

David and Lulu, Mirta and Myrna, Robles and Tintan, Gabriel Torres and Bobby Lemus, Pai and Hui, Georgie Little Man and Mike Rivera, Husky Willie, Cano and G.I., Iris Benitez and Connie, Cleo Silvers and Carl Pastor, Minnie and Muntu, green-eyed Gene and Mark, Robert Ortiz and Marlene Cintron, Lou Garden Acosta and Pelu, Alcides and Eddie Figueroa, Aida Cuascut and Doolie, Nydia and Larry, Felix Resto and Benji Torres, Bobby Lemus's brother George, Frankie Maldonado, Mickey Agrait and Larry, Lou Perez, YaYa and Ramon Morales, and my man, Huracan. These warriors were the personification of Young Lord bravery and dedication. I knew the Randalls Island security would be handled well; very well.

The concert came and went with no major incidents; we sold hundreds of papers and educated hundreds more on the history of Puerto Rico and the need for independence.

A month later, two young, average-looking white women appeared at the Madison Avenue headquarters claiming they were planning a similar concert in the coming months. We didn't allow them into the back of the office. Instead, Yoruba and I sat with them on an adjoining stoop. They didn't seem to have a clear plan; they were not specific about bands or funding. What they were clear about was their need to have the Young Lords Party pull security for them at their future venue on Randalls Island.

We politely questioned their project and told them they needed to put more meat on the bone—where was the money coming from, what bands did they intend to hire, how were they going to pull off getting past all the New York City regulations and insurance for large-scale open-air music productions? Their answers were hazy. They praised our "vast knowledge" of the scope of the problem and asked, in the most innocent of voices, "Could you guys come to our apartment and help us in the planning? You could be co-producers of the concert."

Rising from the stoop, pushing my chest out in the corniest manner, and offering a hand to one of the young girls, I declared, "Of course, we'll help you. It'll cost you, but we'd be glad to help you plan the concert." Little did I know the sequence of events that would lead to the breakup of my marriage and my departure from the Lords. In hindsight, all the signs were there: They had no office, no money, and no clear strategy for pulling this huge promotion off. And we had no female Lords to observe and give us their "wisdom" about these "wilting lilies" who just "needed" our help.

We decided to meet that night at their apartment in The Apthorp apartment building on Broadway, near 79th Street.

When Yoruba and I arrived, the doorman gave us a strange look before he called up to confirm our appointment and allow us unto the premises. His attitude, his eyes said it all: two Black Puerto Ricans with huge Afros, dressed half-military/half-street, meeting two single white girls at night in an exclusive building on the West Side meant one thing to him: jungle fever.

The apartment we entered was sparsely furnished, with old pieces that looked second-hand. All four of us sat in the living room for a minute, during which nothing serious was discussed. I can't speak for Yoruba, but the concert these girls were allegedly planning was the last thing on my mind. I hadn't been seduced like that by white girls since Queens College. It felt good. Eventually, one girl took Yoruba to a back bedroom, and I stayed in the living room with a chunky, dirty-blonde girl who seemed to be the spokesperson/dealmaker and leader.

Again, no talk of concert or security concerns. Without asking, the girl lit up a joint; she didn't roll it, just took it out of a box. I didn't think I was in danger, didn't think that just maybe it was a setup. I forgot I was Chairman of the Young Lords Party. I was just a guy having a good time with a strange female like in the old college days. One big difference: I was married.

The girl passed me the joint; it was strong. After the first pull of smoke, I was dizzy. After the next two, I was totally stoned. But I didn't feel the giddiness or the pleasurable sense of all is good in the world with the accompanying giggles and laughter. Instead, I started to hallucinate as objects began to move around the room. I felt a deep sense of dread and negativity.

The woman leaned forward, as if studying me, peering at me intensely. I noticed she had only taken one drag of the joint; the rest of the time she had just put it to her lips as if she were inhaling, but never really took the smoke in.

"How do you feel?" she asked coldly.

"Not good," I answered. "This joint doesn't feel right. Did you put something in it?"

"Nothing," she said and leaned back on the couch, watching me.

I suddenly felt suicidal. I wanted to jump through the half-opened window and just end it all. Not my style.

I couldn't move. My body wouldn't respond to any of my mental commands. It was as if I was stuck in an invisible spiderweb. My thoughts were horrible, dark. I didn't want to kill anyone; I just wanted to destroy myself.

I asked the girl to please close the window, that I felt I wanted to throw myself out.

She started to play head games. "Which one, this one, that one?"

"The one right behind you," I said, "Please close it."

"Ohhh, this one," she said breezily and rose.

Instead of closing it, she opened it wider.

The old lampshade started to sway from the wind. The screw had not been tightened. I asked her, in a hoarse, weak voice, to please tighten the screw on the lampshade because the motion was making me nauseated.

From the window, she walked a few feet toward the lamp table and took the screw off. Finally, finally, I knew I had been drugged and this woman in front of me was dangerous. I somehow knew her job was not to kill me, but to have me kill myself or go stark raving mad.

From a frozen seated position in an old chair, I mustered enough strength to turn my head toward her, look at her, and state, "I know what you did! Now, let me tell you something. You're not leaving this room. You got me this high, you better get me down."

Her face changed. Her body stiffened. Whatever she saw in my face scared her. And for the next ten hours, we stayed immobile and quiet, she on the sofa, me in that chair. And I began to pray, hard.

At some point, Yoruba came out from the back bedroom, looked at me, and asked if I was okay, saying that I looked sick and did I want to leave? I just shook my head vigorously and said no, emphatically, continuing to stare at this girl.

"You okay?" he asked again.

"Yeah" was all I could whisper. And then he left with the other girl, back to the rear bedroom. I kept praying. I didn't want to die this way.

"Father, I'm in trouble. I'm sick and want to throw myself through that window right now. Don't let the devil win, please. Get me out of this. I don't know what's in me but, get it out, 'cause if I go, I'm taking her with me."

I was powerless . . . powerless and angry with myself. Suddenly I felt a wave of sweaty nausea, doubled up, and vomited all over the floor.

It was over. Whatever poison was in me had worked its way through my system and been expelled.

My mother and the Pentecostal Church had taught me about the process of spitting up demons, so I wasn't shocked. I was relieved. The self-destructive thoughts disappeared. I was free, back to normal.

The strange woman said nothing, did nothing, just sat watching.

But here's the strange part. Instead of leaving, I felt an incredible lust. I don't know why. To this day, I've tried to figure it out. Why would I want to touch or penetrate someone who just tried to kill me? The lust was animal-like; there was no love or like associated with it, only anger and conquest.

I bolted up from the chair, walked toward her, grabbed her hand and told her to lie down and take her clothes off. With a quixotic smile, she complied. Her body was thick, shapely. I hardly looked at her. I still don't remember her face. Without my asking she opened her legs and grabbed her knees, waiting. I took off my pants, left my shirt on, and plunged into her, repeatedly. She was wet and panting. I remember her looking at me, as I pushed in repeatedly. She'd close her eyes from time to time and whisper, "Yes."

She started to moan loudly. Her legs were spread even wider now, her arms around my back, hands gripping my lats, no more smiles, no more words, her pelvis thrusting upward as my pelvis pummeled her down.

This sex act was about power, my power and taking it back.

I stayed in that mindset until the glass door opened and Yoruba walked in with his partner. There was shock on his face, not revulsion, not disgust, not male agreement with the act taking place before him, just shock.

He stood there for a few seconds until I told him to leave and close the door. He couldn't take his eyes off me. Here was the Chairman of the Young Lords Party furiously fucking a stranger. He looked like a child catching Mommy and Daddy in the throes of passion, innocent and bewildered. Don't know what he did in the back room, never asked him, and later, when I was brought up on charges and had to face the members of the Party, the same way Juan Gonzalez had faced charges, no one ever asked Yoruba what he was doing in the other room. They focused on me. It was explained to me decades later that since I was married, I was held to another standard. Yoruba backed away slowly, until he turned the corner of the wall and returned to the other room with his strange partner.

I quickly pulled out, peeled off the woman's body, jumped up, put my underwear and pants on, stepped over the vomit, went to the door, shouted for Yoruba to meet me and left the apartment. Never looked back at the girl, said nothing to her. We were at 79th and Broadway. Iris and I lived on 81st between Amsterdam and Columbus, two blocks away. It was going to be a short walk for me but a long time explaining to Iris my stupidity and indiscretion.

We walked in silence for a very short while until we hit Amsterdam Avenue. I broke the uneasy quiet.

"Listen, this is my problem," I said, turning to Yoruba. "I'm the one who's married. I'm gonna catch hell from Iris. Just do me a favor. Don't say anything to Party members about where we were or what we did. Tell them I'll explain when I get there. Promise me that, okay?"

Yoruba nodded his head in agreement and then said, "But they're gonna ask why we didn't check in like we're supposed to. What do I say, man?"

"You say nothing," I barked. "Tell them you promised me you wouldn't talk until I got there. They're street people. They'll be pissed, but they'll understand. Now, do you understand?" Yoruba nodded his head again and continued walking east. Don't know how far he walked, don't know if he took the train or bus. Hitting me gently on the shoulder, he said softly, "Good luck."

It was the last time Yoruba and I would ever be close again.

As soon as I knocked on our apartment door and heard Denise Oliver answer rather than Iris, I knew all hell was going to break loose.

Denise opened the door and with a deadpan expression said drily, "You're in trouble."

"Yeah, I know," I replied and barged past her into the apartment.

As I came in, Iris came rushing out of the bedroom toward me, screaming. "Where were you? Where the hell were you? You didn't call, nothing. We thought something happened to you."

I didn't want to talk in front of Denise. This was a personal matter between Iris and me; there was no need to confess in public. Though Denise and I were friends before I met Iris, and knew the streets, the sexual misadventures of most of the guys in the party, she didn't have to hear all the shit I was about to reveal. This was a husband-and-wife conversation.

I turned toward Denise and half-shouted, "Denise, you should leave." Iris went ballistic.

"No, hell no. She's here and stays here. This is not just your house. It's mine, too." I knew I couldn't win this one, so I grabbed Iris's forearm and pulled her toward the living room, away from the kitchen area, immediately facing the door of the apartment.

Iris resisted, pushing my hand away, but she followed me into the sunlit living room facing 81st Street.

Denise stayed watching, her arms crossed, her face expressionless.

"Two girls invited us to their apartment last night to discuss another rock concert." I looked into Iris's face, bloated from worry and no sleep, eyes brimming with tears. "I smoked a joint with one of them, got very high, very stoned. Something was in it. Something. I don't know. I wanted to commit suicide, wanted to jump through the window. And then, after . . . ."

I paused. Iris's body was trembling, her arms shaking. I knew I had to stop the bullshit and get it all out, quickly.

Iris grabbed my jacket and said, "And then what?"

"I fucked her. I don't know why I did it. It just happened." I heard Denise mutter, "Oh, God."

Iris's shoulders slumped, her face went pale.

And then she went off, flailing at me with punches and screaming.

"How could you? How could you do this to me? How could you do this to yourself, you asshole" The whole Party was worried that something had happened to you, and you were fucking some bitch!" She proceeded to lay into me, fists flying, trying to scratch my face, pull my hair.

I had heard Iris raise her voice in anger before. But the screams she emitted that morning came from a place deep inside, heartrending screams, from the pit of her soul. I had never heard these sounds before from her. They were horrible. I remember forgetting about my fuck-up and thinking, "Oh Lord, she's on the verge of a nervous breakdown."

"Iris," I screamed back, holding her arms tightly and pushing my butt back to avoid being kicked in the balls. "Calm down, calm the fuck down. You're losing it. Stop for a minute."

It didn't help. In fact, her screaming and punching got worse as I tried ducking to avoid getting hit.

"You bastard," she continued. "You have no respect for anything, for anybody. Get the fuck out." And then, she stopped screaming and hitting and with her face flushed, her body shaking, she bellowed, with a blood-curdling intensity, "Get the fuck out of my house."

That's when I smacked her. Don't know why. I had the image in my mind of James Cagney smashing a woman's face with half a grapefruit. Obviously, I had lost it. I was being thrown out of the home I had built with her, my home.

It was a nuclear explosion. Iris went even more crazy, throwing punches, my blocking and trying not to hit back. I never hit back. I had already put my hands on her. I knew it was over—the relationship, the marriage, our living together, everything. I pushed her away and she stood in the middle of the living room, on a beautiful, sunny morning, sobbing. I didn't even look at Denise. Just turned my back, opened the door, and left. As I walked down the hallway toward the stairs, I could hear Iris's sobbing. I don't know where I went after that. What I did know was that my life was never going to be the same, again. Ever. And I did it to myself.

I don't know where I went, what I did. It's all a mishmash in my head. For some reason, I can recall past events with clarity—what was said, who said it, the actions that occurred—but I can't remember clearly what happened that day.

I do know that eventually I ended up at headquarters. The expressions on the faces of my comrades made it clear they all knew. Yoruba had blabbed before I got there, spilled it all, bowed to the pressure of the group, contrary to what he had promised me hours earlier. I had to face the music.

The Central Committee decided I had to face charges for failing to report my whereabouts that night and for having slept with someone other than my wife. The first charge I understood; the second was none of their business. However, previously we had brought Juan Gonzalez up on charges of endangering the welfare of the YLP by sleeping with married women and/or single women in committed relationships. Their husbands or lovers could've attacked Juan, thereby attacking us, and the ensuing violence could have gotten people seriously hurt or killed and would have tarnished the Party's reputation and certainly torn us away from our mission of serving the people.

I had slept with a strange woman, probably an informer for the police or FBI, allowed myself to be drugged, and, while I gave up no information, could've been photographed or even attacked and killed. I placed the Party on the chopping block with my lapse in judgment.

For the women in the Party who had been clamoring for equal treatment and representation in the leadership of the Young Lords, there was a not-too-subtle subtext: I, a married man, the "national" leader of the Young Lords Party, had been unfaithful to my wife. Adultery was the unspoken charge and untrustworthiness was the feeling floating around the YLP offices. There had to be a trial.

Within the next few days, the cadre was called in. We all sat in the back office, some on chairs, others just plopped themselves on the floor, in nervous anticipation of what was about to occur. I, the elected Chairman, the orator, the "charismatic leader" and point man between the streets and the Party, was found to have feet of clay. I had fallen from grace. Those who had constantly gossiped about my leadership of the Party could now smirk and openly ignore me in the office. Those who were "friends" couldn't look me straight in the face. They were embarrassed for me, for themselves. Yes, I had the outward look and behavior of warriorhood, but, I surmised, they felt I didn't have the internal fortitude or discipline to resist temptation, something I had lectured about constantly.

It felt like I was in the Pentecostal Church again with all its repressive trappings and catechisms of dos and don'ts. And, as one of the architects of that repressive structure, I had to pay the price.

Chapter 16

Revolutionary Machismo?

THE TRIAL STARTED with the Central Committee stating the charges: unclear politics and male chauvinism. Though it was never brought up in the trial, the "unclear politics" charge was a direct result of my relationship to Black nationalism. I did not subscribe to the notion that one could be a true socialist of color without having passed through and lived the lessons of cultural nationalism and Afrocentricity. Touting the rhetoric of an integrationist socialist ideology without understanding the history of virulent racism in the United States toward Black, brown, red, and yellow people was an exercise in ignorance, hypocrisy, and self-hatred. Puerto Rican activists in particular had to study Black history because of the lessons to be learned from blindly following, imitating, and loving the Spanish conquistadors and now the American ruling class, all while being exploited, marginalized, and killed.

I kept a very close relationship to the architect of the Black Arts Movement, Amiri Baraka. The Last Poets owe him a great deal of gratitude for his support and encouragement. Amiri and I spoke about forming a mutual defense treaty between the Young Lords Party and the Committee for a Unified Newark during the campaign to elect Kenneth Gibson the first Black mayor of Newark. After discussions with the Central Committee, we formalized the agreement and it became a precedent-setting relationship between a Black and a Latino militant organization in the United States. If CFUN was attacked, we would come to their aid in New Jersey; if the YLP was attacked, they would cross state lines and assist us. That intimate/family relationship exists to this day. Oh, we argue, we disagree, but the umbilical connection of deep respect and love has held for more than fifty years.

During the time of my Chairmanship of the Young Lords, I also had a deep and close relationship with Minister Louis Farrakhan, meeting with him regularly and discussing the politics of the time, both national and global. We bandied about the idea of a mutual newspaper publication, combining the best of the YLP newspaper *Palante* and the Nation of Islam's organ, *Muhammed Speaks*. That idea didn't go over very well with the Central Committee, and for a long time there was a simmering residue of suspicion on the part of some doctrinal Marxists, inside and outside the Party, about my refusing to part with cultural nationalism and my lack of commitment to scientific socialism and class struggle.

The facts belie the charge: Most of the African American members of our original group had joined precisely because I and the others made it publicly clear that we were Black Puerto Ricans and identified with the tenets of Black art, Black history, and the Black liberationist struggle, both in America and in Africa. Muntu, Carl Pastor, Troy, YaYa, Cleo Silvers, Denise Oliver, all African American Young Lord members in good standing, joined because of their deep connection to Blackness and the Puerto Rican struggle, their love for the Puerto Rican people in general, their friends in particular. Malcolm X, The Black Panther Party, the Republic of New Africa, the Black Liberation Army, and the Last Poets featuring Gylan Kain, Abioudun Oyewole, David Nelson, and I were the Afrocentric poets and revolutionaries who inspired many of the YLP to fight in the first place.

Who was kidding who here? Yes, the Nation of Islam philosophy of hating the white man, the mad scientist and the legend of Yakub, was simplistic and historically incorrect, but their mantra of "Black man, Love yourself, Do for self" resonated with many young men of color of my generation. Yes, their anti-semitism was repugnant, but I felt they would eventually move to a more thorough understanding of Marxist-Leninist dialectics and the traditional Islamic code of brotherhood as time progressed. I believed what they preached in terms of preserving Blackness. Forgetting your roots and the history of your race, however, was a path toward destroying your legacy, your ancestors, and your children. Puerto Ricans had an African cultural and historical foundation that underlay our food, our sense of family, our music, our belief systems, and our skin color. To be healthy and successful, I felt it necessary to embrace our Blackness with no apologies.

With respect to the charge of "male chauvinism," they were right. However, those women on Iris's side decided to make me the target of their anger. They smelled blood; they could discredit me and push their agenda for equal treatment. Their position was that the "revolutionary machismo" principle of our original thirteen-point program was a contradiction in terms: You couldn't be a revolutionary *and* a macho male.

They had forgotten or didn't know or understand the way the original Central Committee had strategized a program to get the men in El Barrio to join our ranks. The history, the culture of the Puerto Rican community was replete with examples of men who stood up for their community, their families, their mothers, sisters, and daughters, stood up for us and exacted justice; machismo equaled chivalry. Granted, these same men never questioned the violence they perpetrated on their own women, not to mention their own Puerto Rican male counterparts. In fact, it was considered "unmanly" and "not cool" to intervene in a Puerto Rican domestic dispute, even if the male was almost killing the female. That was not chivalry, by any stretch of the term or imagination.

The older warriors would stand by and watch as the police harassed, beat, and arrested members of the Young Lords. At that time there was no revolutionary consciousness in El Barrio, with very few exceptions. Hardly anyone spoke of the independence of the island of Puerto Rico or self-determination for Latinos and people of color. Apathy reigned supreme. You couldn't blame the street folks. Their ideology was survival, by any means necessary; jobs, family, church, that was the credo, and you never questioned those pillars of existence.

How do you get men to change behavior within a traditional cultural matrix? How do you motivate them to want to change and be proud of that change? You change the definition of what it is to be "macho." "Beat the system, not your wife" is how the Young Lords Party redefined the new male code.

"Defend your children and us, against the new white gang, the police."

"Stand up for Puerto Ricans as men and hold that flag up: defend the values of our people, be 'revolutionary men'!"

We took the old meaning of machismo, reworked it within the context of our own culture so that our uncles and fathers could understand it, and then prodded them to help us fight for and defend East Harlem through "revolutionary machismo." I would often cajole them, sometimes screaming at the men in street rallies, "There are no punks here; ain't no cowards. We fought for the streets you stand on in hand-to-hand combat. We know the heroes who are in jail now for not allowing bullies and racists to run our streets and businesses. And yet we're still poor and still discriminated against. Where are my older brothers, my uncles? Where are my fathers, my god-fathers? *Donde estan los machos?* Where are the men, 'cause we are dying, being slaughtered in Vietnam, being assassinated here in America, being drugged and beaten right here on 111th Street."

"Where are the men? I need you, my brothers! Viceroys, Dragons, we need you! Join our cause, join our struggle."

And then I'd hit them in their hearts and balls. "And if you don't want to get hurt, if you feel you're too old for this shit and don't want to do a bid again, then let us fight and don't interfere. Help us help you. We, your kids and nephews and cousins and neighbors, will kick whatever ass we need to kick to defend these streets. You've seen us battling out here and you just fold your arms and watch as the cops bust our asses. Be men again. Be proud of being Puerto Rican again. Hide us when we run, feed us when we're hungry, arm us when we need to shoot back, defend us against the punks who say we're a bunch of crazy Communists. We can win. We are winning. *Que viva Puerto Rico Libre!*"

The roar that would emanate from those rallies sometimes scared me; it came from the bellowing lungs of a pride of sleeping lions. And that's how we got old gang members, hustlers, dope fiends, numbers runners, and factory workers to join the Party: revolutionary machismo! Use what you have to get what you need. Today, that concept, that terminology, that thinking wouldn't work; however, I put forth the question of how do you get Puerto Rican boys to become productive men? How do we define manhood? Women can care, educate, and nurture male children and in many instances raise models of success, but women aren't men. Boys need men as role models, as fathers, uncles, grandfathers, and mentors. All studies have pointed to the crucial role positive fathers and men play in boys' lives. We need to stop the put-down of men in Puerto Rican society and stop the gender war. It's killing our kids, male and female.

I've heard Black and Puerto Rican women rail against the men of their culture in such degrading ways. It's a miracle not more of our men are misogynists. The road to building a man who hates women is to talk about his father like a dog, constant criticism, and negativity.

My mother didn't have the information or the education. She'd beat me when I showed signs of intelligence and/or independence, screaming, "You're just like that father of yours. Just like him. Think you know it all." And the blows would come raining down me, a child who wanted to explore the world and stretch the envelope of authority a bit.

She never mentioned how she loved my father, how she preened when he walked into our project apartment, how she loved his looks, his touch, his gregarious personality. The beatings continued until I was fourteen and a gang member. Male children who endure that gauntlet of pain will usually end up being the man the mother hates. And the daughters, very often, find solace and betrayal in the arms of those same guys, the "bad boys"—that is, if they don't end up dressing and acting like the "bad boys" themselves.

The trial became the Waterloo, the decisive battle for gender equality. It worked for some of the women; it almost destroyed most of the guys who ended up being led by Gloria Fontanez. The men, street men most of them, raised and nurtured in gang battles and prison, had an umbilical connection to every block, every building, every apartment in El Barrio. They knew the numbers runners, the working girls, the welfare mothers, the ministers, the priests, the mob, and the straight-up working-class men and women. By leaving them leaderless, rudderless, the trial became a test case of culture versus intellect and destroyed the healthy, necessary connection to our community. The Young Lords died a slow, ignoble death.

But let's get back to the Young Lords Party courtroom.

Not one Lord defended me. No one. A few got up and criticized my abandonment of Party principles, some because they felt a need to ingratiate themselves to Party leadership; others spoke sincerely of the heartfelt disappointment in and anger at my intemperate, impulsive behavior. I mounted no real defense. They were right. Days later, in an attempt to gain favor with the Party, to explain that I was drugged by an informant, I went back to the Apthorp building with two trusted male Lords. Didn't even have to speak to the daytime Puerto Rican concierge; he knew us and waved us upstairs. When we got to the door there were two open holes where the locks used to be. Peeking inside, I saw some strewn papers, clothes, and nothing else. The women had obviously split within days of the incident.

The trial lasted three days. Accusation after accusation. Since this was called in socialist circles "criticism/self-criticism" sessions, I was required to stand up and verbally enumerate my sins and sorrow. I didn't do much of that. Just hung my head, agreed that I had fucked up, endangered the Young Lords Party, and betrayed my wife. Iris said nothing. It was obvious the relationship was over. I was dead to her. I didn't know how dead until I tried contacting her by phone to no avail, trying to patch things up, trying, beyond hope, to keep the marriage alive.

I was used to my mother's compassion, always forgiving my father even after repeated infidelities. As a child I witnessed older Puerto Rican wives, after a period of arguing and separation, accept their husbands back once they agreed not to stray again, not to rule with iron fists again, and even to attend church with them on Sundays. Some wives relented because they had children and didn't want their kids brought up without a father; others took their men back because their husband's paycheck, though paltry, allowed them to squeeze out a living, put food on the table, put clothes on their children. There were other women, more than the gossipers would admit, who truly loved these guys and felt that going on without their partners would leave a gaping hole in their hearts. This often happened with women who had been with their partners since childhood; their identities were intertwined. Walking the streets, shopping, worshipping, visiting neighbors and relatives, and holiday activities that were a vital part of life in El Barrio would be tainted and lonely without their men at their sides.

The unspoken cruelty was the stigma attached to women with no husbands or partners; something "had" to be wrong with them. Often, they were abandoned by the same community that had once shouted out how beautiful they looked together. The other wives, afraid of the potential threat the new single women posed, would demand that their husbands not even look at the newly separated women. The men, afraid of their own transgressions' being made public and losing the family unit they had in hand, would not go looking for any woman nearby, particularly if she was attractive. So, unfortunately, those women who threw the unfaithful men out were them-selves severed from the lifeline that kept El Barrio superficially cohesive and humming.

Neither of the above cases was true of Iris. She was educated, could make her own money, had no children, and was angry as hell. The door was shut, permanently. Every time I called to plead with her, Richie Perez would answer. He was cold and impersonal. He simply wouldn't give her the phone and told me so. The venom he issued over the phone curdled my blood.

"Look, you're not going to talk to her. Stop trying. She doesn't want any-thing to do with you, man. Get over it." There was no empathy, no under-standing embrace in his tone.

We hadn't been separated more than a month. I needed to hear her voice. No matter what, we were close friends, or so I thought.

Richie reveled in his newfound power. I had been warned of his jealousy and his destructive gossip about me and my leadership by the street guys who felt that Richie, a former high school teacher, displayed an arrogance, a subtle swag, that he hadn't earned. That didn't bode well with them. They pointed out that he would stay in the Bronx office, on Longwood and Kelly, working on the paper and pontificating. Whenever it was time to rumble, to lock and load, close the office, and come to help us on the streets, he disappeared or would claim he had to put out the paper. He learned this behavior from some in the original Central Committee. Yoruba and Juan would mysteriously fade away when there was fighting to be done. To their credit they all gained some notoriety and, in Richie's case, some courage after the Lords era; Richie became a Brooklyn College teacher and a prominent activist against police brutality. He passed, too soon, from cancer several years ago. Yoruba went to federal prison rather than be drafted; that took a lot of heart. He went on to become a celebrated New York City television reporter. Juan became a prize-winning progressive columnist, TV pundit, author, and teacher. But everyone in the Party knew that as "intelligent" as they were, they couldn't fight to save their asses. It was a standing joke with us. It took all my might not to burst into the office, pull Richie out of his chair, and whip his ass soundly. We were never buddies, never close, but he would've never disrespected me in person. I don't know whether he was following Iris's orders or exhibiting his personal animosity toward me, but it hurt terribly not being able to even hear Iris's voice, if even to curse me out.

I was demoted to cadre and though stunned, I accepted the decision. Several of my revolutionary friends outside of the Party suggested I fight the demotion or leave and start a new Puerto Rican militant organization. Some Young Lords suggested the same thing, but I was too weak emotionally to even think about it, and, if truth be told, my "baby," the YLP, would have been riddled with in-house conflict. Though no one stood up for me, I knew there were still strong elements within the group who would've gladly left. And I knew those street folks were the backbone, the loyal fighters who had branded the Lords as tough, courageous, smart, and resilient. The Young Lords, I felt, would have been left defenseless. It wouldn't have been fair to use my hurt to hurt the Party.

But the hurt was there, deep down, burrowed in my head, my heart, my body. My soul ached from the contradictions lurking inside: I loved the Young Lords, but I wanted to kill some of them. I almost did.

Three months after my demotion and subsequent resignation, a party member I trusted told me that Iris and Yoruba were now lovers. This was my chance to strike back. I now know all the pent-up rage centered on my ego, my jealousy, my sense of possessiveness, and the old Barrio code of pride and masculinity.

Three months had elapsed since Iris and I had separated. I was inconsolable . . . and angry. Angry at myself for having fallen for the oldest sexual trick in the book with a strange white woman, angry because I was guilty of sexual misconduct as charged and there was no one else to blame, angry at Iris for not taking me back, and angry at those "comrades" who just a few weeks ago were laughing and hugging me and now were passing me by in silence with scowls and nasty looks, men and women in the Party who bared their fangs at me for failing them.

The affair between Iris and Yoruba was a bombshell. Of course, I never thought of the shock Iris must've felt when I told her about my dalliance. I tried to justify my rage by thinking that my indiscretion was with a stranger, a one-time thing; I didn't love that person, didn't even know her. Yoruba, however, was my friend, I thought, Iris was still my wife. How could he? How could she?

As an old school Puerto Rican man, I had only one solution. Kill him, up front and personal. I mulled it over day after day until I decided to confront him on the streets and plunge a knife into his neck, watch him bleed out. At that point, nothing else mattered, not my mother, not my brother or sister, not jail. I had to take Guzmán out, now and forever. The only pang of feeling I harbored was for his mother, whom I loved and who always showed me lots of affection. But the pain of loss and betrayal buried whatever nugget of rationality I had.

I had put some close street Lords on notice, Robles, Huracan, Bobby Lemus. They were waiting for word. While they felt the killing was going to have horrible implications for the collective, they'd been brought up in the same Puerto Rican street warrior cultural matrix. To them, to me, it was the right thing to do. Someone snatches what is "yours," you don't go to the police, you don't spend too much time crying and feeling sorry for yourself. You take them out.

I was three years out of jail, and all the feelings, all the reflexes, all the coldness came flooding back to my brain. The dam had burst, and the restraining barrier of politics and love for my people couldn't contain the tsunami of mud and emotional sewage. I was a wounded animal, like Husky Willie, who wanted to kill Bobby Lemus. I reverted to the gang instincts of five years before, the sixteen-year-old Bushwick kid with promise who found his brother beaten and unconscious in 1964.

But how would I escape once I'd killed him? I stupidly thought I would stab Yoruba and go into hiding via Micky Melendez's network of underground connections. Thank God, I didn't. Micky never finished that crucial part of our revolutionary organization. I would've been out in the cold.

I picked the day, a sunny, brisk autumn day, and selected a fighting knife with good balance, a sturdy handle, and a very sharp, very pointy blade. The steel had to puncture the neck easily and then had to slice through tissue quickly. I called my guys. They were ready.

There was no turning back. I had to do this. I felt nothing; all I focused on was getting the job done. I don't remember who transmitted the message to the couple that I wanted to meet with them. They agreed and on that early fall day, I walked toward them as they were sitting on the stoop of a building on Madison Avenue, across the street from the YLP headquarters. I saw the guys who were supposed to whisk me away casually standing almost in formation from the middle of the block between 112th and 111th streets. I made believe I didn't see them, didn't nod, exchanged no pleasantries. This had to be quick and fast.

I do remember standing in front of the seated couple, Yoruba with his head down, Iris looking up at me, emotionless.

"Of all the people you could've chosen, why him, Iris, why him? He's a punk, never stood up and fought for anything," I muttered.

Yoruba raised his head and attempted toughness. He didn't stand up, just sat there. All I felt was disgust.

"Hey, man, wait just a minute . . . ." was all he could shout, feebly.

I shut him down quickly; this was taking too long already.

"Shut the fuck up, don't say a fuckin' word," and I started inching the blade down my right coat sleeve, working it into position so it would slide into my open palm, thumb up, ready to thrust.

"Look at him," I declared to Iris. "I tell him to shut up and he shuts up like a fuckin' mouse. Is that the kind of man you want, Iris, 'cause that's what you got right now, a punk!"

For one brief second, Iris's eyes turned defiant.

"Yeah, well I'd rather have that than a tough Mr. Macho guy around me all the time. He's softer, more sensitive than you."

This was the moment to strike, and just before I jiggled the knife into position, I looked up at the sky and couldn't believe my eyes.

Against a clear blue sky there was a *New York Post* headline in bold black type, "YLP Destroyed by Love Triangle."

I immediately sensed the setup. I was doing it again, falling for the same bullshit I did when I slept with a government informer. He was not worth it, and neither was she. Getting caught never occurred to me. Had I been caught it was going to be an easy twenty-five to life sentence. The sky message was an immediate epiphany; it was God. It had to be.

I turned my head right. The guys were getting impatient, the car was idling on 111th Street, ready to screech off to the West Side. I turned to face Iris and Yoruba. "You guys deserve each other," I said flatly and walked quickly to 112th and turned left toward Fifth Avenue.

I didn't see Iris or Yoruba again for almost twenty years. My friends, the street guys, were enraged. All that setup and adrenalin for nothing. They eventually forgave me, though it took a year. I miss them. All three are dead now.

There were a lot of infrastructural changes once I was demoted. Cadre who had not proved themselves in battle were suddenly promoted; people I had personally rejected as psychopaths or simply wanting in the courage and/or natural street intelligence department were suddenly accepted as Young Lords.

Julio Roldan, the cousin of one of the members, was one of them. I had rejected him as a recruit earlier in the year even though he was a Vietnam vet. He burst into the office one day, bragging about his ability to turn lightbulbs into bombs.

It would've been a comedic moment had he not been dead serious about his plan. I told him to keep his voice down, that if the government was listening in, the conversation would be a perfect excuse to arrest all of us. He continued, speaking at a rapid pace, almost unintelligibly, making me think he was on some sort of medication or high. I remember telling him, firmly, that he was either a government agent or a fool. Either way, we didn't want him as a member.

He looked at me, fire in his eyes, and declared, "You're going to feel sorry for this. I'm a soldier and I'm ready to die for my people."

I sat back in the chair, just staring at him for a few moments. I was always suspicious of sudden conversions, spiritual or political. Leaning forward, looking intently at him, I replied, "Brother, this conversation is over. I said no and I mean no. You're not coming into this Party. Not while I'm Chairman." It was a prophetic statement because as soon as I was demoted, he was inducted into the Young Lords. That's when I knew the leadership was desperate to give the impression that the Party was stronger than ever, had more members than ever, and could conduct even bolder street demonstrations and police confrontations without me at the helm. For weeks after, I was in a daze. Confused, embarrassed, and hurt, I simply walked the streets and stayed by myself. I couldn't bring myself to go into the office too much. My ego, my sense of self, was wrapped around being the "Chairman." I had organized, fought, bled, had bones broken, and for what, I thought. Self-pity was the blanket I wrapped myself in, self-pity and remorse.

Someone introduced me to a SoHo artist named Peter Dechar and his wife, Reeva. Peter painted pears, beautiful pears, sensuous pears that seemed to leap out of the canvas. We were introduced to each other in his second-floor loft on Prince Street in SoHo. The bonding was instantaneous, both personally and politically. We spoke for hours, me droning on about what happened, him listening and wisely shifting the conversation away from me to the madness that was occurring in our country and government, the Vietnam war, the war on the Panthers, whether armed struggle in New York City was feasible, and the artist's role in revolutionary consciousness. I recited some poems. He showed me some canvases and was impressed with my minimal knowledge of art history and aesthetics.

He was thin, pale, almost frail, had long, stringy, curly brown hair, a long nose, somewhat sunken cheeks, firm chin, and very clear, curious, smiling, friendly, but serious eyes. He wore paint-splattered denim shirts and dungarees and he used his hands, though extremely strong, in an almost feminine manner as he described things. The tone of his voice shocked you. It was in complete contrast to his appearance. It was a deep baritone, full-throated, clear, masculine, and confident. He believed in his political convictions, and when he spoke, you knew he believed it, totally, and would be willing to do whatever was necessary to defend them. I believed him. To my amazement, he had followed the Young Lords in the news, made me feel I was part of a whole body of consciousness and progress in America. He didn't care about the demotion.

Finally, after four hours of spirited discussion, he simply said, "Why don't you stay here? Nobody will know where you are. You can nurse your wounds and find yourself again. Art is great for that. You can hang with the silence and the paintings. If you want to talk, you can come out of my back studio and talk; if not, you can stay by yourself and just think things out. I understand. It won't bother me or my wife. Artists understand solitude. You need time to heal. Don't worry about food or rent. You'll eat what we eat and you'll meet my friends. I think you might like them. Deal?" I nodded my head and gave him my hand and my heart. God had provided me with an angel. I was close to a nervous breakdown. I could feel myself losing control of my thoughts and just fleeing from sequential thought patterns, the logic of daily reality. I was losing my grip on life. I had no one, didn't want to go to family, couldn't seek solace from folks in the Lords, didn't have a church or a fraternal organization I could run to, and I had lost my wife. I had already burned the bridges of most of my female relationships and was too proud, too chagrined to go back to them. And then came Peter Dechar and art.

For weeks I slept on a pallet in Peter's workshop, the air suffused with the smell of acrylic paint and machine oil. It was heavenly: no stress, no pressure, no accusations, no standard to bear. All I had to be was me. Didn't have to argue a political point, didn't have to try to "convert" anyone, didn't write a poem or essay, just got up in the morning, ate with my new "family," napped, sauntered into the living room whenever I wanted to, and discussed . . . whatever. It was paradise.

SoHo was a fascinating mixture of working artists, small grocery stores, Italian old folks, and eccentric bars frequented by eccentric people. On any given night, you could meet Fred Brown, a Black Chicago transplant and masterful oil abstractionist (the van Gogh of the twenty-first century), whose gigantic *Last Supper* and *Ascension* of Christ canvases followed by his Pink Fox paintings, left me breathless. His genius portraits of Black folk heroes like Stagger Lee, John Henry, Native American chiefs like Geronimo, and the strength and pathos of jazz musicians Louie Armstrong, Thelonius Monk, and Muddy Waters made you stop, stare, breathe heavily, and cry.

Willem de Kooning was a painter who refused to stand still, constantly changing his aesthetic vocabulary within a thirty-year period, from *Excavations* in 1950 to *Police Gazette* in '55 to the stunning, colorful *Untitled V* in 1980. De Kooning shattered my sense of "sensible" art. Then there was Romare Bearden, whose collages exposed the joy and current and past brutal treatment of Black Americans; Leroy Jenkins, another Chicago transplant who played an avant-garde jazz violin as if possessed, leading a group called the "Revolutionary Ensemble"; Ornette Coleman; who had already flipped the jazz world on its ass by playing a plastic alto sax in a harmonic manner that even Coltrane viewed with awe; or Anthony Braxton, alto sax visionary who once talked to me about recording an album from the moon to the Earth and computing how long it would take for the call and response to take place. I laughed and blurted, "Obviously there'd be some long spaces between notes." He didn't see the humor and sat me down and explained, in detail, mathematically, the way the recording could take place with notes bouncing off the moon and coming back.

I was fascinated with the new thinking, the new paintings, the new music, the new poetry, some of which I was writing and reciting. Peter Dechar loved watching me interact with artists as I dove into political conversations above the din of the bar crowd. They'd listen carefully and then explain how real revolution involved art, a searching of the soul, a quest to manifest the best, and/or certainly the most advanced aesthetic forms to bring man to the next step in intelligence and beauty. For the SoHo crowd, God was art. Art, like nature, was the manifestation of God. I can't remember who told me that the moment our government started arresting artists would be the moment the second American Revolution would begin. Though the emotional pain was constant, it was beginning to ebb. I was laughing again.

And then a jagged rock came through the glass house, shattering the crystal-clear windows, the blue skies, the brilliant sun, and the peace. David Perez, the Young Lord Defense Minister, called, saying he had to talk to me in private, urgently. He sounded desperate, depressed, like a condemned man who has only hours to live. I don't know how he got my number and, though I was pissed that he hadn't stood up for me during my Young Lords trial, I truly loved this urban *jibaro*. After getting him to agree not to divulge my address or the details of our conversation, I agreed to an immediate meeting the next day. Didn't sleep well that night.

He arrived the next afternoon, and it was so good to see him. We hugged each other hard and sat down on the sofa of the brightly lit living room area of Peter's loft. It had been a month since I last saw him. I was in my other element, the art world, SoHo, canvases all over, the smell of paint, Peter and Reeva, two white people, passing through to the kitchen, ever so often, smiling, nodding hello to him and nothing urgent other than breathing and creating. I felt relaxed. David could feel it. There was no crisis, no deadlines, no screaming, no overt politics. It was too early in the day. This was not East Harlem and certainly not the headquarters of the Young Lords Party.

As the delivery trucks rumbled by, David sat, a bit uncomfortably, and looked around. I knew what he was thinking. "Where the hell am I? You mean this atmosphere exists in the city?"

He couldn't look at me for any length of time, his eyes darting from me to the paintings on the wall, back to me. I thought he must have been saying to himself, "I thought I knew this guy. Who is he really?"

But there was no judgment in his spirit. In fact, he seemed a bit contrite. Uncomfortable with long silences, I usually am the one who initiates conversation. I didn't feel that at all. It was at that moment that I knew I had changed considerably. I could let others be without forcing them to become.

I sat, waiting for David to let out whatever he had on his mind. He might express some personal remorse, might ask for forgiveness, he might be seeking advice on how to leave the Party, I really didn't know. What I did know is that he was already forgiven, just for having the courage of meeting me, face to face, that afternoon. He began . . . slowly.

"The Party doesn't know I'm here. But I had to come to explain the trouble we're in." My immediate reaction was to feel vindicated. Good, I thought, they demoted me, disrespected me, and now they're suffering, crawling back. And then David dropped the bomb.

"We took over the church, again, this time with guns."

"What?" I screamed. "Are you out of your fuckin' mind? How the hell did you get in?"

"Pai, Hui, and Ramon Morales climbed up the wall, broke the window, and slipped in."

"Was anybody inside?"

David started laughing. "Yeah, one security guard. They fucked him up a little and he split." For me, this was no laughing matter. Fear replaced ego. It enervated every nerve cell in my body. I was aghast, totally shocked.

Granted, I was angry at the Party, filled with my false sense of entitlement and pissed that they'd treated me shabbily, but I didn't want them to die. This was not supposed to happen. You don't retake a Latino holy sanctuary . . . with firearms. You lose the support of the people who love you and give the police more reasons for murder. We had done this already, took and occupied the church, without guns, almost a year before. Why do it again? What insane reason would make the Lords do this? David was talking, but I was drifting far away.

David, still standing in the loft, looking at me strangely while I was day-dreaming. He must've realized that while I was hearing him, I wasn't really listening.

"Felipe! Are you here? I'm trying to tell you something, man."

"Dave, forget about it. I forgive you. Not sure if I can forgive the others, but I forgive you. You're a good man, a great fighter. I won't forget you."

Reaching over the length of the sofa I hugged him hard. We just stayed like that for a few seconds. It was an awkward moment, an awkward hug, a bit uncomfortable, but it's what I wanted to do, what I felt I had to do.

"I'm gonna miss you, brother," I said. "Really. It's gonna be rough for a minute, but we'll both make it. Good luck."

David, looking a little shell-shocked, grabbed my hand, held it hard, twisted his mouth and looked at me straight. It was his soldier face. I had seen it before when he had something difficult to say and I knew what it meant. He hadn't told me everything. He wanted me to do something.

I jerked my hand back quickly.

"No fuckin' way, David. Don't even try it with me. Fuck them." David just stood there, pale, worn out, looking as if his body had been compressed.

"Chairman, just listen to what I have to say."

This bastard was using my title to get to me, I knew it. It was a fuckin' setup to get me to go back and help their funky-punk asses out in their ill-conceived second takeover of the church. Their impulsive actions had them with their backs against the wall and now they had nowhere to go, strategi-cally. They had shot their whole load with the guns, guns I had bought, guns I told them never to use unless attacked, guns I had them hold in the attic of Professor Arthur Adlerstein's house out in Westbury, Long Island, guns they didn't even know how to clean and load properly. They had no heart, so they sent David to recruit me again. Hell no! Fuck 'em. No way. My ego was running wild. So were my hurt and feelings of humiliation at the hands of those I thought were family.

"I know what you're thinking, Felipe. But they didn't send me. They think they really know what they're doing. Things are so fucked up uptown, new Central Committee, a lot of women who hate your guts and don't know how to shoot . . . I had to come down here and talk to you. They didn't send me. I need your help. Me! Felipe . . . we need more guns. We only have the few you hooked up.

"I don't mind dying, but if I have to die, let me die shooting back with some decent firepower. If you don't help, we're like sitting ducks. The cops are all over the place, outside the church, sharpshooters on the roofs, God knows who they got inside undercover. We're in bad shape, man. I don't want to go down that way." Looking at this dear friend of mine, hearing him say those things, saddened the hell out of me. I'd never seen him afraid, never saw him back down from any challenge. But even he realized this situation was untenable, unworthy of a valiant death. This was suicide.

Which brings me to the second reason for the second church takeover: The first was an attempt to consolidate the party and the community through service, to infuse the troops and the public with a new confidence; the second was an understandable, albeit impulsive, not-well-thought-out reaction to the suicide of Julio Roldan, the same man I had rejected as a member who had been arrested for one of our regular garbage offensives. The Lords labeled the death a police murder. I just stood and stared at David. I was going to lose this warrior to bullshit. "David, don't you see this is madness? It's a no-win situation. Do you have trained shooters inside?"

David Perez shook his head. "Nope!"

"Do you have enough ammo for the guns we bought?" Again, Dave shook his head. "Well . . . have you at least wire-meshed the windows in case they start firing in?" David just looked at the floor and shook his head.

I tried to be understanding of his situation as a faithful soldier, but I was livid at the stupidity.

"Goddamn, David. You know better than this. Why did you put yourself in this situation? Did you tell them how ridiculous this standoff is? We were lucky the first time. The mayor had some sort of compassion for us. Maybe the informants told him we were simply activists looking to feed kids; I don't know. But this? Bringing guns into a church? You're asking to get killed and David, you fuckin' know better. Who's gonna fight with you, what leadership is staying with you?"

When David looked up at me from the couch, I saw the death mask, a look that warriors have when they know their time is up. It is not noble, and it isn't the Hollywood it's-a-good-day-to-die look. It's a gut-wrenching, bowel-loosening, nauseating, depressing spirit mask. The body excretes a foul, rotting smell and exudes a feeling that on this day, at this moment, you will die for nothing.

I've experienced it once or twice and I've seen it in others, mainly in crime situations with cops surrounding the culprit and the realization there's no more negotiating, no way out, and the very clear conclusion that you fucked up, made a poor decision, and few will remember you once you die riddled with bullets. Having goaded you on, those who convinced you to die needlessly will go on living, laughing, loving. And you? You'll be dead!

"That's when you start the remorseful backtracking of how you got into this mess, how you could've avoided it. Could've stayed in bed with your lover, could've visited your mother, could've taken the kids to the zoo, but now you're in the cage, in the zoo, guns pointed directly at you and there's nothing you can do 'cause you bit somebody, made them bleed. Or worse, you're Black or brown and dangerous; you got guns and you can shoot. You hear the sirens, the bullhorns, and you hear the natural sounds of the streets and the city. Your stomach churns because you'll never hear them again and 'Oh, God, if I could just do this day over.' You want to live . . . but it's too late. Your number's up and you did it to yourself. So, you'll just keep firing until you're out and their bullets are in . . . you. Fade to black."

I had felt that "no exit" emotion the first time I was arrested for murder at sixteen. And again during the Young Lords period when I discovered there was a contract on my head . . . to be cashed in by anybody.

I barked at David, "Who's standing with you, where will the leadership be?"

"Outside," David said softly. "They'll be watching from the outside."

I knew then my days in the Young Lords Party were over. They had copped out and left this guy to die.

Weirdly, I had an urge to die with my buddy, even if it was suicidal. Soldiers, warriors, gang members will understand what I'm saying. The male bonding that glues men together in battle also commits them to die with one another, if need be. The thought of life without your "band of brothers," without your family, your life-giving support system is unbearable. The guilt of not being with them, especially when they're in danger or not having been there when they were killed, leads to alcoholism, drug addiction, violence, and isolation. The nice term for it is Post-traumatic stress disorder, but in simple terms, it's this: Having found your niche, your purpose, your importance in a group, to leave it is devastating to the psyche. It's why soldiers go back to active war zones when they've already been discharged. It's also part of the reason released inmates go back to jail. The world is a different place when they re-enter society, having survived the stress of war on a battlefield or in prison. In their universe, warriors make their own rules. And everyone knows the protocol, knows where the lines are and when not to cross them. Some are born for perennial battle. And sometimes those lines have to be crossed, changed, or dismantled. Sometimes the lines are crossed inadvertently, sometimes consciously. Men have to do what their code demands. Their fellow soldiers, their fellow inmates, their fellow gang members, their fellow cops are comrades, flesh of their flesh, and they would rather die than betray or abandon them in time of need, even if they made a mistake, even if they're wrong. This country institutionalizes that innate male instinct in the armed forces. What we refuse to understand is that the same instinct, that same warrior-bond group feeling, exists outside of the army paradigm.

You see it utilized in sports, in Boys' Clubs and the Boy Scouts, in unions, in police departments. But what about those young men who don't have those opportunities available or simply don't fit into those nice peg holes, young men of color, for example?

American society emasculates these men; they deconstruct the definition of man in an attempt to defuse the potential for violence and social disorder. Any young Black or brown urban male who talks back, who pushes back, who simply stands tall and declares his manhood is shot down or jailed.

We say we govern ourselves by the rule of law. Ultimately, however, that rule of law is backed up by violence. Our history is rife with the organized state-sponsored terror meted out against those who fall outside the perimeter of what America considers "regular folk." We've done it to Native Americans, African Americans, Latinos, Asian Americans, Communists, activists, revolutionaries, whistle-blowers, anyone who doesn't toe the line.

In this regard, the state and society are in collusion, consciously or unconsciously. They fail to recognize the primal need for men, especially men of color, to be men—physically, mentally, emotionally, psychologically, culturally—and they don't allow for expression of that instinctive need to be a warrior. The need was taken away by slavery, colonization, and in today's society jail, addiction, and unemployment. Boys need gym and recess, sports teams and contact sports, something urban public schools have increasingly abandoned. They need to figure out their socialization patterns through teamwork. Roughhousing is natural, bullying is not. Women are leaders, just as capable as, if not more capable than, men.

They've had to step up their game. They need to feed their children, feed their families, and lead their communities. They need to aspire, to actualize their individual dreams. When vacancies are created in the home, vacancies created by men who abdicated their positions as fathers, husbands, leaders, and mentors, people of color can attribute it to institutional/systemic racism, and they would be right, but it doesn't give men the right to attack women, nor does it give women, be they liberals or feminists, to condemn men as the enemy, incapable of praise, pride, and courage. As I sat back down, exhausted, going through all these thoughts, David stayed seated, scrutinizing my every eye and head movement.

I had to think this out, but I was out of ideas; nothing creative popped up. I was empty. I don't know why I said it. It burst out spontaneously.

"David, let me visit the church. Let me check some things out with Pi. I want my two best friends, Bobby Lemus and Huracan, beside me to check some things out downtown. I'll give you my answer then."

David's face shone again. His smile was beautiful, lit up the room. He bear-hugged me hard, almost knocking me down, murmuring. "Love you, brother. I'll set everything up and call you."

And before I could reset my thoughts, he rushed toward the door and ran down the stairs, shouting, "Wait for my call. And answer the fuckin' phone!" I heard the downstairs door slam, and he was gone.

I stood there that fateful afternoon, in the middle of Peter's loft, thinking, "What the hell did I just do?"

Peter and Reeva walked slowly into the living room, worried looks on their faces, and saw me standing there, dazed.

"What happened, what's wrong?" Peter asked.

Reeva, the ever-practical one, asked, "How'd they find out where you were?" Without looking at them, I assured Reeva there was no danger. Turning to both of them, I explained it all:

"They want my help; they've taken over a church with guns. I don't know if they can get out of this one without people getting hurt."

"So, what do they expect you to do?" Peter shouted. "They demoted you, didn't they? They made their bed . . . ."

"It's not that easy for me, Peter. Part of me feels the way you do. But there's another part of me that loves them, demotion or not. I don't know what to do. The truth is they need more firepower. I look at it the way David does, if you're going down, might as well go down fighting. They do need more guns."

Peter walked straight toward me, grabbed my two arms, bent down a little, and looked up at me.

"Felipe, wake the fuck up! Whatever they're trying to pull off, one thing is clear. They want to die. And they want you to die with them. Can't you see that?" Letting my arms go, he ran his fingers through his hair, muttering, "Jesus, this is ridiculous. So, now, what the hell do they want you to do? Buy guns for them? With what money? This is fuckin' crazy. The whole thing is crazy."

"I know. I know," was all I could say.

Finally, I sat down and tried to reason my way through the ambiguity. "Maybe the first thing to do is to find out how this Roldan guy died. He was off when I met him. Didn't look like he was playing with a full deck, so I threw him out. Maybe the cops did kill him. The first thing I gotta find out is how he died. It'll make my decision to help the Lords easier."

Peter grabbed Reeva by the hand, helped her with her coat, put his on, and said in a tired voice, "Brother, that sounds logical. It's a first step. We'll talk later. We're going shopping. Want some Rum Raisin ice cream?"

David's call came that same evening.

"It's all set. Bobby and Huracan are happy you're helping and they want to know where to meet, where and when?"

"Tomorrow morning, 10 o'clock at 100 Centre Street," I answered, "in front of the entrance to the courthouse."

The next morning, I saw the duo from a block away, berets on their heads, short-sleeved shirts with massive forearms, combat boots, loose-fitting chino pants, looking mean, looking focused. No one got in their path as they diddy-bopped and swaggered toward me.

I ran to meet them like an ecstatic puppy seeing his owner. I didn't realize until that moment how much I missed my family, my brothers, my fighting buddies. Huracan, a huge chunk of a man, 6′3″, a little overweight, but fast with his hands and powerful with his punch, ran a few steps toward me and picked me up like a baby, both hands on each side of my ribs, in the middle of the sidewalk, screaming, "What's up, my pretty nigger?" Huracan said it so proudly, so confidently, so lovingly, no bystander turned around. Now, both Huracan and Bobby were white Puerto Ricans, but they had more African spirit in them than three-quarters of the Blacks and browns I knew. They could dance, fight, think, and talk shit. And they believed in the code of brotherhood.

"I miss the shit out of you, Chairman. You miss us, *papi*? All we do is talk about you and what went down."

"Man, forget about that shit. And would you mind putting me down?"

He finally placed me gently on the sidewalk and I rushed into Bobby's outstretched arms and embrace.

The hug was powerful and as we kissed each other on the cheek, he murmured, "I missed you, *papi*. Whatever it is we have to do, we're ready!"

Once we separated, we just stood there holding each other's shoulders, misty-eyed. Anyone walking by might have misinterpreted our sexual orientation, but we're Puerto Rican. We show love physically. Lot of hugging. Lot of kissing, male or female.

Doesn't matter. The love is profound, especially the warrior love.

I had to break up this love fest quickly before we got into the nostalgia of the old fighting days and the embarrassing situation of my demotion.

We were on a mission; that's all that mattered at that moment.

"Look, Bobby! You were with this kid before he got busted. What happened?" Bobby launched into the narrative: "Remember the last garbage offensive a month ago?"

I nodded my head.

"Well, after we put the garbage cans across Madison Avenue, we took off our berets like we were trained to and split to the safety house around the corner, right? That's when you told me to watch this guy who you didn't want in the party in the first place because you thought he was off. I remembered."

As I was listening to him, the memories came flooding back. Iris had been given command of the offensive on Madison Avenue, and when the cops came and it looked like shit was going to hit the fan, she froze. I thought it was a temporary lapse, but it was taking too long. Even though I'd been demoted, I jumped right in and started giving loud orders on how to retreat once the garbage cans were lit. That's when I told Bobby to watch Julio. He was too skittish, too nervous, and trembling after the offensive. I thought it best to keep an eye on him.

"But how did he get busted?" I asked. "Did the cops break down the door?"

"Mano, no. This fuckin' guy couldn't sit still in the pad. Kept on pacing and looking out the window. Finally, he just opened the door and ran down the stairs. Said he wanted to see how much damage had been done and how the cops were handling it."

Now, I was irritated. "Bobby, the rules are you don't leave the safe house until the next day. You know that!"

"Yeah, Chairman. I know that. But this guy was a new jack, and you did order me to watch him."

"Bobby," I said, with all the patience I could muster, "The code is you stay upstairs, period. And if a guy breaks discipline and splits, you are not to follow. That's his ass."

"I know, *papi*, I know. But this guy was like a kid, man, and I knew if the cops caught his lightweight ass, he'd be broken up."

"Bobby, look at me. He's dead now. Better for him in the fuckin' hospital but alive." Bobby put his head down and muttered, "Yeah, I thought about that too. I fucked up."

"You didn't fuck up, brother, you just loved on him. You were watching his back, that's all. What happened after that?"

"As soon as we hit the streets, someone, I don't know who, pointed us out to the police, and they cuffed us. They brought us to Central Booking downtown. He seemed okay.

"I was pissed at him for breaking discipline, but getting popped meant a three-day holiday for me, laying up, watching TV all day, seeing all my boys, and three hots and a cot. I needed a vacation. I didn't worry. I know how the Lords work. We weren't going to stay in longer than a week. The brothers inside told me he was acting out, but I figured that was just his first-time jail jitters.

"Once the Lords came to bail us out, they found him hanging, dead."

I stayed quiet. I wasn't sure how the death occurred. Was it murder or suicide? The only way to find out was to go straight to the source, the inmates themselves. How? You go right around the corner to White Street, where the inmate windows face the streets and scream out the name of the detainee. If he's not there, they find another detainee, who will give you a pretty blow-by-blow account of the inmate's state of mind and body. That's the way it was in those days.

What never ceased to amaze me was how the authorities never seized on the idea of having an undercover listen to all this intel from upstairs in the cells to downstairs on the street and vice versa. They could've solved a lot of crimes.

The warrior code in those days was very simple. Whatever you heard in those street/jail verbal encounters, you didn't repeat to anyone.

And forget the faces of the people next to you. If you see them on the streets, make believe you don't know them, unless they greet you and then a quick greeting and you jet outta there.

Girlfriends and wives would come and pull up their dresses just a bit, pointing their pelvises in the direction of their lover's voice coming from the upstairs cell window. Those of us downstairs would respectfully turn away to let the lovebirds do their thing for a minute.

Dope deals, murder contracts, robbery plans, weddings and births—all were discussed in loud voices on White Street. And to my knowledge, nobody ever ratted anybody out.

Bobby, Huracan, and I waited patiently for the sisters ahead of us on the White Street verbal telegraph line to finish talking to their partners, but before they finished, someone upstairs shouted, "Hey, isn't that that nigga reads poems and shit . . . what's his name . . . ? José Fleepiano, right?"

Seizing the opportunity to bring a laugh and some information from the guys locked up, I shouted back, "See, that's why y'all need to be in school. Can't pronounce Spanish to save your fuckin' lives. It's Felipe Luciano, ma'fuckers, in the flesh." There was loud laughing and a collective cacophony of "What's happening, nigga" and "You know my cousin. Tell her to bail me out" and "I used to see you at the East Wind reading that poem 'my pretty nigger' and 'Yo, those some big ass Puerto Ricans you got next to you.' Y'all come to fuck somebody up?" to which everyone upstairs laughed heartily.

"Naw, man," I shouted. "What I'm here to find out is how one of my guys was found hanging in his cell. What happened? The truth now, no bullshit."

First, there was a sorrowful silence, not eerie, just a kind of reverential quiet for a fallen brother. One voice pierced the quiet, his tone authoritative, firm, balanced. He must have been the jailhouse leader.

"Brother Felipe," he intoned, "I'd like to tell you the pigs killed him, I really would. I hate these motherfuckas."

Then, he waited a few seconds and spilled it.

"Your boy bitched up as soon as they threw him into the cell. The motherfucka was screaming and carry'n on like he never been to jail befoe. Now, y'all supposed to be revalewshunaries. Y'all should be used to this shit. Why'd you let that boy come to jail? He weren't ready. All screamin' and shit, saying what he was going to do when he got out, kill the guards, kill the poe'lease. He was screamin' so loud we wish they had hung his ass and shut him the fuck up. But we would've known if the hacks had hung him. Nobody sleeps long in this shithole. We woulda heard them skirmishing, 'cause the way he hated these ma'fuckas, they would've been rockin' and rollin' just to string him up.

"Naw, man, they did something more sneaky. Knowin' he was a head case, they left him with sheets, his shoelaces, and his belt. They knew sooner or later the boy was gonna hang up . . . which is exactly what he did." And then the brother paused. "Sorry for your loss, brother. Later." And we didn't hear from him again after he stepped away from the window and went about his jailhouse business.

The three of us stayed motionless, like those subway performers who don't move, posed in one position, staring straight ahead like statues. I didn't need anymore corroboration. The brother spoke the truth and no one contradicted him. And they all hated the police. If there was a scintilla of foul play by the police or correctional officers, they would've blurted it out.

No. Julio hanged himself. My take on it is that he simply couldn't take being confined in a small space, severe claustrophobia. It can lead to suicide. Now that we heard how Julio died from the inmates on White Street, the challenge was how to tell the new leadership of the Lords the real deal and call off the madness of guns and occupation in the church on Lexington Avenue. The move to occupy the church again was undertaken because the new Central Committee decided to label Julio Roldan's death a police murder rather than a suicide. They knew he'd killed himself, but they decided to lie. In doing so, they hoped to gain community support, support I had been told by friends was waning. The social justice "offensives" had slowed considerably. The umbilical connection between the streets and the Party was deteriorating as the leadership began to lean toward a more dogmatic socialist ideology. My demotion and absence began to weigh heavily on the new Party leadership. While the Lords were functioning, there was dissension within the ranks and a questioning attitude on the streets. The street folks were loyal to those who came from their blocks, people they knew, people whom they had grown up with and who had proved themselves in battle, whether in gangs or in revolutionary action.

Something had to be done to offset the turbulence within. The Lords had to concoct a new plan, re-invent the collective, and re-energize the community and progressive allies with a tale of murder, even if it wasn't true.

The new Central Committee, larger and with more women members, could have used the suicide to rally for prison reform: more in-house observation and vigilance for inmates who appear fragile and emotionally unstable, less crowding and quicker turn-around time from arrest to arraignment to sentencing, more lenient sentencing for simple drug busts, a thorough investigation into the violence perpetrated by correctional officers on detainees in city detention centers including Rikers Island, etc. Instead, they decided to march Julio's body in a wooden coffin through the streets of El Barrio, hiding the guns inside the death box as they took over the church again. This plan for an armed takeover of the church was ignorant, impulsive, cynical, mean-spirited, and manipulative. And while it incorporated revolutionary allies from different ethnic communities—the Black Panthers, I Wor Kuen (Chinese American radicals), and white radicals from the Young Patriots Party—it was the beginning of the alienation from an East Harlem community that was simply not ready for armed struggle and certainly not prepared to see guns in a holy sanctuary.

"I began to suspect that the FBI's COINTELPRO had already begun to infiltrate and influence the leadership of the party. I was almost assured of it when the Young Lords decided to start organizing in Puerto Rico, based on some ill-conceived nationalism that reeked of arrogance. We, the mainlanders, would bring independence to the island and free the populace from the corporate/military chains of colonialism? That move failed miserably, and those brave souls who risked their lives to bring revolution to the masses on the island were lucky they weren't killed by police or the islanders themselves."

I knew I had to help those ordered to stay and fight it out.

Now that the few guns were in the church, now that armed Lords were guarding the coffin and the entrances, David Perez was asking me to bring more guns to at least make it "an even gunbattle." There was nothing "even" about this, but if they were going to die, I felt they should take their leave of this life as warriors, not martyrs. Back in the SoHo loft, Peter and Reeva Dechar looked at me wearily as I explained my reasons for wanting to help David and the other Lords in the church.

"So, you want to get more guns to help your friends in the church who are choosing to die in a suicide mission?" Peter asked incredulously.

Reeva screamed at me, screamed at the absurdity of it all.

"Felipe, this is insane. No one's gonna win this. And people are going to die, needlessly. Shit, can't you see that?"

"Yes, Reeva, I can see that. And I can't explain why I feel compelled to help David. All I know is, he's going to die. It's going to be a shoot-out, Reeve. And he's got four or five guns, that's it. If a man chooses to die honorably for a cause he believes in and asks you to provide him with weapons so he can at least have a fighting chance, and he's not going to kill innocent people, he's simply going to defend himself, what can you do, Reeva, how do you answer him?"

"You tell him to ask somebody else!" Reeva screamed. "You tell him you will not participate in his own suicide mission. That's what you tell him."

Reeva had tears in her eyes as we stood silently on a winter afternoon in that quiet loft in SoHo. We just stood there, three of us, staring at the walls and floor, but not at one another.

Peter broke the silence.

"I think I understand, kid. You can't just leave them there to die, though they're going to die anyway. I understand."

Reeva whirled and bolted toward the bedroom.

"There's too much testosterone in this room," she declared and slammed the door. I was embarrassed. I was in their home, bringing my problems into their living room and now slowly immersing them in emotional whirl-pools of life-and-death decisions. They were artists and all they were trying to do was help me gain some balance again. Not get me killed.

Turning to Peter, I muttered, "Peter, am I getting you into trouble with your wife? Man, that's the last thing I want."

Peter, kindly but firmly, looked at me and said. "Felipe, in any relationship there's compromise—you give, you take. But there are some things you must do for you. This is one of those things.

"Reeva knows that about me. She knew it before she married me. When I believe in something, I believe in it. I believe in you, and I believe you need help. Now, we can stand here and debate or go look for firearms. Which will it be?"

A sudden peace came over me.

"You know what my answer is, brother."

"Good," Peter shot back as he put on his denim jacket. "Let's go get some guns, but let me tell you something. None of this, none of this, can be traced to me, understood? I mean it, Felipe. You gotta promise me, no one will know of my involvement. As far as the Young Lords are concerned, you got the guns."

As he stuck out his hand to seal the deal, I told him, "It will never happen. Nobody uptown will ever know. This I promise you." And we left, clambering down the stairs, without a plan. My faith was in Peter. He seemed to know where to go, what to do. I never doubted him, and as we walked briskly through SoHo, I made no sounds, asked no questions.

First stop, a Midtown gun shop hidden among discount stores and pharmacies. I was amazed at how easily Peter bought a 30 caliber hunting rifle—no suspicious looks, no questions, nothing, even though I was standing near him. White skin privileges are real, I thought to myself.

The man placed the piece in a pretty case, Peter paid him, and the clerk handed it over, just like that. I was in shock. Even with credentials and a solid credit rating, I would've been questioned and probably made to sign all kinds of papers.

The next few stops were at friends' lofts, friends who loved to hunt and had two or three rifles. Peter would sit with them, discuss the crisis uptown, say he would be responsible for getting the guns back, and basically pull the "How ready are you to support the Black and Puerto Rican liberation struggle" speech. It worked. They gave up their guns and at the end of the day, I had six or seven new and used automatic rifles, with ammo, all in working order, in a green duffel bag, ready for delivery. I knew I needed to get them uptown as soon as possible, so I called Pai, the Lord closest to my heart, to tell him I was coming to the church the next day; there was something "important" I had to tell him.

He understood the code and said he'd be waiting. He sounded tired and fatigued; that worried me.

Pai was a gift from God to me. He had a boyish enthusiasm and passion that emanated from his being. And a disarming candor when it was needed. One day, while walking through East Harlem, we came upon a young man hawking our paper, *Palante*, on Third Avenue.

As we approached him, I asked Pai if he recognized him. "Naw, I never saw him before. Maybe he was just recruited?"

"No, Pai. No recruits sell papers until they've gone through political education classes. You know that. This dude doesn't smell or look like us. Let's check him out."

"All right, Chairman, but do me a favor," he laughed. "Don't go off on him. We've got work to do and your arm is still healing." And he laughed again. It was true, but it pissed me off.

I greeted the stranger warmly.

"What's happening, man? How you doing?"

Without even looking at us, in a uninterested tone of voice, he said, "Hey, what's happening?"

He didn't know who we were, why we were in his face, ignored us, looking past our bodies as he shouted to passersby, "Get your Young Lords paper, here."

Wrong move. I knew from his hustler spirit he was looking for some money to get high. Cool, but not with our papers.

Pai got serious and challenged him.

"Brother, you know who this is? He's the Chairman of the party whose paper you're trying to sell."

I hated that opening gambit from people introducing me because it almost always invited a disparaging or humiliating remark from street guys, like "So what?" or "What does that mean?" I was already behind the eight-ball with this dude.

"Where'd you get those papers?" I demanded.

"Hey, I bought them from somebody, maybe I found 'em. What the fuck is it to you? My man, you're in my face and I'm trying to make some money. Step aside." And he actually moved to his right toward a man coming up Third Avenue. It was clear what had to be done.

Pai started to chuckle. But I knew that little giggle. It usually came before a barrage of face-swelling blows and broken knees.

Pai continued to reason with the dummy.

"Look, just give us the papers and we'll call it a day."

The man whirled on Pai and spat out, "I ain't giving you shit. These are mine and I'm gonna sell 'em!"

From his stance, I knew Pai was going to side-kick the shit out of him, probably break a rib, so . . . I quickly left-crossed the sucker on the right side of his face, protecting the cast on my right arm. It was an awkward punch, off-balance, and the guy held on to the papers. Pai stood there, embarrassed, hands on hips, smiling wanly. "You finished, Mr. Chairman?" Then he twirled around with a spinning side-kick that caught the fool dead in the middle of the solar plexus, knocking all the air out of him. Before he hit the sidewalk, Pai adroitly snatched the papers from his hands.

"Asshole." He muttered, "C'mon, Chairman. Let's get the fuck outta here." But he continued laughing.

". . . fuck are you laughing at, nigger?" I snapped.

"Look at your finger, bro. Broke it again. I told you," and he laughed all the way to the office. "You got heart, Chairman, but you ain't got no sense."

Pai lived for this stuff. So did Hui.

Pai had been trained by Sifu Ralph, a Vietnam vet and a hardcore street warrior and teacher. Soon after, he was mentored by Monroe Marrow (known as Abdul Musawwir), who had fought full contact against all of the major karate stars on the circuit: Ronnie van Clief, Owen Watson, Ron Taganashi, Louie Delgado, Chaka Zulu, etc. Both teachers taught Shotokan, a hard, linear Japanese form of empty hand fighting. Their sidekicks were more than just pretty and picture-perfect; they could break knees, ribs, and thigh bones, if done correctly.

Pai saved many a Lord's life by teaching and re-teaching the basics, day after day, until we could flick out a powerful sidekick and crunching reverse punch in seconds, enough time for us to stick it to arresting cops and run away. Before he joined the organization, Pai's mother came to the office looking for "the Boss." She was a short, stern, handsome woman who alone had raised two daughters, a son, and the "baby," Pai (another son was born later). I stepped out of the office onto the sidewalk in front of the door.

"*Tu ere el jefe?*" she asked, dispensing with the usual formal greeting and apology of "*Como esta Ud. y perdona la molestia.*"

She launched right into her narrative, straight, no drama.

"My son wants to join you. He loves you," she said in almost a whisper. "*Ahora . . . el sufra de asthma.* It's been cured a little by his karate training and I love his teacher, but I'm still concerned about his health . . . and his life."

She wouldn't take her eyes off me and moved closer. The woman simply wasn't afraid. She was on a mission. Some Lords were looking from the doorway, but Pai's mother's aura was so strong, no one came near.

"I cannot mold a man. He thinks he's grown at fourteen and I'm scared. *El es un hijo bueno*. He listens to me, never joined gangs, never gave me a problem. I could probably hold him back from joining you, but I don't want to."

I was moved by this wise, brave Bronx woman who had traveled all the way from the housing projects near the Saint Raymond cemetery in the Bronx to see me. I gently took her hands in mine.

"Señora, que tu me quiere decir? Dimelo! [What do you want to say to me? Tell me.]." It was the only time she turned her eyes away, only for a minute. When she turned to look at me again, her lips were pressed hard, her jaw was firm, her eyes were piercing.

With a clear voice though tears were welling up, she said, "*Te lo voy a dar a ti*. I will give my son to you, but you must promise me something."

I answered quickly, putting my head down, "Yes, ma'am, anything."

"Don't say 'anything' so quickly. You don't know what I'm going to ask."

I kept my head down, respectfully.

"*No quiero que me lo matan*. Promise me, right now, that you will never put him in a situation where he could get killed."

This was too much to ask. We were all putting our lives on the line, and as much as I wanted to accede to her heartfelt wishes, in effect I'd be saying other young people's lives were less important than her son's life. They were all in harm's way. I was in a quandary; how do you say no to a mother?

"Mrs. Diaz . . . ," I started and then looked into her eyes. They were deep pools of pain and fear. She tightened her grip on my hand and just stared at me.

"Please . . . please, say yes. He's all I've got. I don't know what I'll do if he . . . . Just promise me you won't let him die. I'll give him to you. He's your son, now. *El es tuyo, ahora*. Protect him . . . please."

I looked at her eyes again, tried to gather the courage and discipline to refuse her request as nicely, as politely, as respectfully as I could. But there was no stopping this woman. She gave me her son—what more of a sacrifice could she offer the Young Lords?

"Okay, I'll take him, he'll be my bodyguard. I'll watch over him. But I don't ever want you to say anything to him about this meeting. I won't either. You promise me that." She nodded her head vigorously, backed up quickly, turned around, and left the block. Pai is alive today; he took care of his mother in Florida until she passed in 2015. He escaped gunfire with his pal

Hui, another fearless fighter, and he often got mad at me for not putting him in some of our more dangerous situations. After the Lords' experience, he castigated me for treating him like a child, screaming he was not my son, he was a man. I took it all in and said nothing.

He's alive today. That's all that counts. I kept my promise to his mother without making him any less of a fighter. He fought well. He protected me well. I have my sons, Felipe Jr. and Eric Michael, two wise, profoundly intelligent, sensitive, and spiritual men, but in a metaphysical sense Pai was my first son (along with Khalil Kain and Sarael Martinez, my nephew). We fought together, laughed, hugged, and cried together as we suffered broken hearts and broken bones.

He was and still is my heart. But his mother's words rang in my ears as I brought the guns to the church and placed the duffel bag of rifles into Pai's waiting hands. How was I going to keep my word to his mother when, at any minute, the church might turn into a kill-zone? He looked tired, mainly sad, hugged me, thanked me perfunctorily, grabbed the weapons, and hurried off to do a security check.

As soon as Pai ushered me into the church, as soon as I handed him the weapons, I knew something was off. Too many kids milling about, no reinforcements on the doors or windows, a general atmosphere of normalcy rather than one of discipline and vigilance. I didn't feel a fighting spirit but rather one of resignation.

David approached me, and I recoiled at his demeanor. He had accepted the fact that only he and a few others were going to fire away and die in that church on 111th Street and Lexington Avenue. Other Lords had already begun to leave, not wanting to die needlessly. The veteran Lords were not there; neither was the leadership. While there was a buzz of activity, the place felt desolate.

The fact that I had brought more guns to the church didn't register with our Minister of Defense even though it was he who had asked me to bring them more arms two days before. I deduced he felt his sole purpose for being in that church was to die. Taking him to the back of the church, I asked him, "David, is there any method of escape before the gunfight, any way of getting out of here?"

And this is when I really knew all was lost.

David looked at me sadly, seriously, and announced, "We're going to drill our way through the wall of the church into the subway."

The wall was five feet thick and while the Lexington Avenue line was directly underneath, it would take weeks, even with modern equipment, to drill though.

"With what bit, David? You'd need a bit the size of a man to get through this concrete, not to mention the chance of explosion when and if you cut through." David reached for an old-fashioned hand drill with a wooden handle. "If we work hard, little by little, we can bust through."

At that point, I knew David was delusional. He had drunk the Kool-Aid.

"Let me show you around," he muttered, and as we walked toward the front, I saw a kid dropping a single 30 caliber shell into a double-barreled old-fashioned shotgun and wondering aloud why it didn't fit. The air was thick with martyrdom, predestined death, all for what? A poster image? I was sick with despair, with anger, with guilt. They would've never pulled this charade if I were still Chairman, I thought. And each step I took, each interaction I witnessed, got me sicker.

What was worse was that it was too late. I was out of the leadership loop with no power.

I made up my mind. I had to leave this madness, this chaotic infrastructure of so-called warriors who would order people to die for a lie, for nothing other than to show the world they were "revolutionary" and would shoot it out to prove that they were "down," to get some press coverage for a dispirited organization and shoot some life into their public image. I was totally disgusted. There was no "win" here. I stopped in my tracks, turned to David, and said, "I need to make an announcement to the troops. As soon as possible."

First, I had to grab Pai and try to convince him that he didn't have to take this path. I would do anything to get him out of this murky death dance. He was not going to be killed this way, not this day or any other. Not on my watch.

Then, a miracle took place in the strangest of ways, something that on the surface was horrendous but that forced my friend to make a decision.

Unbeknownst to me, Pai's girlfriend, Ana Jones, had tried to commit suicide the night before. She was a beautiful, Afro-Indian Puerto Rican with sculpted Asian features and a nervous energy around her. Though she was a parent of two young children and older, she loved Pai like a junior high school girl, all giggles and shyness and effusive public displays of affection. I didn't trust it. But I liked her and I loved Pai, so I never criticized.

Earlier in this narrative I explained that each one of the HRUM collective was having an affair with key members of the Young Lords party. The guys were enmeshed in all kinds of domestic squabbles: ex-husbands, rebellious kids, you name it. It was hurting our effectiveness as a fighting unit.

But there was something very innocent and touching about Ana. Brutally honest and physically brave (she was never afraid to throw down), she suffered from depression. Any criticism, any life-challenge, would thrust her into a downward spiral of tears, anger, arguments, and subsequent sadness. She had no money, was on public assistance, her husband was in jail, she was poor, a Black Puerto Rican and she couldn't see a life outside the housing projects. This was not unusual in our communities. She just showed out differently. When Ana had the blues, everyone saw it, everyone felt it. She made attempts to disguise it with makeup or a forced joke, but it never worked. She was a tortured soul.

Pai had decided to end the relationship. He had explained to me that the emotional baggage, his and Ana's, was too much to bear; it was taking a lot out of him. She was jealous, possessive, and domineering, according to Pai. He was now fifteen, and to be tied down like that was just too much. So he left and told her it was over. He was going through his own turmoil what with the church, the guns, certain Lords confessing to him that they didn't want to die and slipping out of the church, the death dirge. In her eyes, the relationship was the only thing keeping her sane. When that ended, the dam broke. Ana tried to take her life.

Pai must've already heard the news. When I found him again, he was staring into space, his arms crossed.

"This is madness," I announced to Pai as I approached him. "These fools are wasting lives with this bullshit. And none of the Young Lords Party bigshots are going to be here when the bullets start firing." Pai looked at me forlornly, nodded his head, and said softly, "Yeah, you're right."

Then he looked and murmured, "Did you hear about Ana?" I got cold. "What . . . what happened?," I asked nervously.

"She tried to commit suicide, cut her wrists real bad. I guess she really wanted to take herself out."

"Oh, my God" is all I kept saying. "Oh, my God, oh, my God" as I turned in circles.

"Why," I screamed at him, "why'd she do it? What happened?"

I didn't mean to sound accusatory, but that's exactly what I sounded like. It wasn't Pai's fault, I knew better than that, but by the look on his face, those huge orbs looking at me, I saw he blamed himself because of the breakup.

"Felipe, I never wanted this to happen. I still love her and . . . ." His voice trailed off. I grabbed and hugged him hard.

"I'm so sorry, *papi*. Sorry for her, sorry for you, and sorry that I screamed at you the way I did. Pops, it's not your fault. Suicide never is anyone else's fault."

I pulled him away, looking at him with all the love I could muster; fifteen years old and he's got to deal with all this stuff, my God!

"Pai, what do you want to do, right now? I'm with you, no matter what!"

Pai's eyes were welling up; it was breaking my damn heart.

"I want to see her. I want to be by her side." Pai declared. "She shouldn't be alone now. I'm cutting out right now."

I straightened up.

"Why don't you wait until I finish talking to the troops. David is getting everybody inside together. Soon as I finish, I'll go with you."

"Felipe, you don't have to do this; it's my problem."

"Stop," I said sharply. "I'm not gonna argue this. Don't you understand, it's my problem too. I'm not gonna let you go down there alone. Just wait until I finish speaking."

The Lords assembled in the large basement room of the church, a few steps down from the main worship area. I waited until the buzz died down and then launched into my speech.

"I joined the Lords a year ago to fight for self-determination for Puerto Ricans and the independence of Puerto Rico. We fought well; we took over this church and started a breakfast program. We succeeded. We liberated a TB truck, brought it to El Barrio, X-rayed our folks and proved to the city how many of our folks tested positive for signs of tuberculosis, something they had ignored for years. We succeeded. We won." There was loud applause and hooting.

"Then, we struck at the heart of the city health system, the hospitals. We took over Lincoln hospital and made them change the way they do business with Puerto Ricans. We forced them to admit that Lincoln was a racist death trap that had to be restructured and had to be run by Puerto Rican administrators. We won."

The applause grew louder and the shouts of "Right on" and "*Despierta, Boricua*" rang off the walls. They weren't prepared for what came next.

"This armed takeover is a failure and it's built on a lie. Julio Roldan wasn't murdered. He killed himself. I never thought I'd see the day when we started to lie to our own people. That's not how we started this organization."

The Lords in the room looked at one another in shock. What the hell was I doing? Where was I coming from? I took notice of the looks and raised the decibel level, standing in the middle of the circle of Lords, some whom I knew and many I had never seen before.

"But let's say the cops killed him. Let's say, for argument's sake, that we had a right to take out the guns and declare war against these racist bastards. Let's say we're willing to die to defend our right to live, to be treated as human beings, not to be murdered once we're arrested.

"Then it seems all of us should be prepared to pay the price and all of us should be down to shoot it out and face the consequences, no matter what. That's not what I see here and I'm disgusted." There was a dead silence in the room. No one moved. No one opened their mouths. Real quiet.

"You are facing annihilation. And your leaders will be outside watching the battle and preparing to identify the dead bodies, yours.

"There are kids here too young, too inexperienced to be handling weapons safely. We're supposed to be defending our future, not putting them in harm's way. I realize that the party has lost its way, lost its heart, lost its character. I can no longer be part of this organization." And then I took off my purple beret and threw it to the floor.

Pai did the same. And then he made his speech.

"I believe in revolution. I believe in armed struggle. But this situation is ridiculous. I don't mind dying and I'm only fifteen. I haven't really begun to live. But if I must die, let it be for something. This is not it. What makes matters worse is that the Central Committee, with the exception of David Perez, is outside while we face the fire. It's wrong. I don't know if it's that they're scared or what. All I know is that they're not here with us and that I can't deal with it. Goodbye and good luck."

And with that we walked out of the church. No one moved. No one said anything. Pai and I said very little to each other as we took the subway to the hospital downtown. We were immersed in our own thoughts and fears and some guilt. We had divorced ourselves from an organization we had built, fought for, and loved. Where do you go from there?

(We came back from time to time to check on things, Pai to help David with security, me to make a speech or two or participate in a press conference, but for all intents and purposes, it was, sadly, over.)

The staff at the hospital was supportive and courteous as they ushered us into Ana's room. They must've felt our dazed, angry spirits; we were in no mood for hospital regulations of who could visit her and who couldn't at that time of night. Ana smiled as Pai walked into the room. He cooed to her as you would a baby, stroking her hair, kissing her cheeks, ignorning the swaths of bandages covering her arms from wrists to elbows.

His affirmations of love to her touched me deeply. He kept saying, over and over, "Ana, I love you, baby. I'll always love you." He would ask if she was comfortable, if there was anything he could do for her, change the bed angle, the pillows, put more covers over her, to which Ana would only respond with huge teardrops rolling down her cheeks. I stayed near the door just watching them. They never took their eyes off each other. It was hard to keep my tears inside. Who has the right to judge love, who? Who has the right to tell you whom you can love and whom you can't? This was a mother in her late twenties in total love with a fifteen-year-old. Forget the Freudian shit with all its theories of dysfunctional behavior.

They were in love.

That moment taught me to stop judging people based on age, gender, color, or culture. It was transformative.

Eventually, Ana was released and though they didn't make it as a couple, they remained friends.

The fighting family of the Young Lords Party had provided me with an emotional village of like-minded people. Being alone was shocking, terrifying. I had no one to bounce my ideas off, my dreams, my visions, my fears. I was forced to look at myself to hear the criticism of those "I told you so" folks about how I had messed up my chances for a career.

I had no money, no motivation and very often I thought of ending my life. Without the adrenalin of revolutionary activity, what was I to do? I stopped calling Iris, stopped talking to the Young Lords, and stopped visiting my family.

I had had spent six gratifying months with Peter and Reeva, but my soul and my pride told me I couldn't continue using their compassion and love to buoy me into a new reality. I had to leave.

With the money I had and with Peter's contacts I rented a pretty one-bedroom apartment on St. Mark's Place between Second and Third avenues. And I began the tortuous process of stripping away old thoughts, old behaviors, old acquaintances.

There was nothing for me to do. Broke, depressed, and angry, I roamed the streets of SoHo and the East Village, sometimes sober, definitely disoriented, high on Fridays, drunk on Wednesdays; no purpose, no mission. Thank God for Victor Hernández Cruz, who would come by my apartment and bring long-playing records of Johnny Pacheco and Pete "El Conde" Rodríguez, explaining the Spanish lyrics to which I had never really paid attention. And thank God for Slugs, the jazz club on East Third Street between Avenues C and D. With whatever monies I made from lecturing or consulting with the Urban Coalition (thank you, Arthur Barnes and José Ferrer), I'd spend many an evening nursing a single beer and listening to the genius lyricism of alto saxophonist Jackie McLean backed up by that smiling percussion master Billy Higgins, thumping bassist Scotty Holt, and jumpin' pianist Lamont Johnson. I'd close my eyes and ride the musical thermals with the punctuated blasts of brass with master trumpeter Lee Morgan or the happy tunes of vibraphonist Roy Ayers.

I can't forget the magical music matrix of Sun Ra, who would enter jazz clubs with a single-file parade of musicians singing, "If you find earth boring, just the same old, same thing, c'mon and join us with outer space waves, incorporated." Damn if that didn't lift your spirits.

No matter what shape I was in, the place to be for breakfast was the Ukrainian diner on Seventh Street and Avenue A, Leshko's, where poets and laborers, musicians, and writers congregated for a cholesterol-rich meal of eggs and sausages, potatoes and rye bread, coffee, and orange juice.

Lunch, and sometimes dinner, was reserved for Verta Mae's sprawling two-bedroom garden apartment on Houston Street between C and D. It was the artistic and gastronomic international watering hole for artists and intellectuals: Amiri and Amina Baraka; Puerto Rican poet Victor Hernández Cruz; Sun Ra; actress Hattie Gossett; one of the founders of The Last Poets, Gylan Kain; poet Quincy Troupe; trumpeter Olu Dara; tenor prodigy David Murray; Miguel Algarin, founder of the Nuyorican Poets Café; master storyteller Ntozake Shange; the stinging humor of Steve Cannon's poetry; the creative seriousness of writer and social critic Ismael Reed; the painter Joe Overstreet; painter and sculptor Ellsworth Ausby; writer/poet/coalition builder David Henderson; blues singer Taj Mahal; and loads of others, including me and Verta's mom.

To define the late Verta Mae as simply a chef is to insult the memory of my nose, my palate, my ears. A tall, strong, dark-skinned, wide-smiled, loud-singing South Carolinian Gullah lady, Verta Mae had just published a book titled *Vibration Cooking*, and if she wasn't famous before that tome (and she was), she was certainly certified platinum after it. While we argued the politics of revolution and the sonority of Ornette Coleman with Verta Mae chiming in from the kitchen as she orchestrated her culinary compositions, we feasted on fried chicken, candied yams, collards and okra, porgy and whiting fish, boiled cabbage and string beans, corn on the cob, and Coltrane.

To add a bit of heaven, her two daughters, Poochie and Koli, attracted a bunch of crazy Black, white, and Puerto Rican kids to the place. They ran around the house, asked questions, ran through the backyard garden, asked questions, jumped on the beds calling questions from their room about the strange poetry words they heard from the living room, curses and all, and would ask me to come to the back yard and help bury whatever birds or pets had died in that cacophonous salon of love and music. I knew the animals died mad, but they died happy. There were times I wished I could have died with them. I saw no reason to go on. My skills, I thought, were fighting, not writing. How would I validate myself? Why did I need to validate? Why couldn't I just live a humble, uneventful life, find a job, maybe marry, raise some kids, and die?

Chapter 17

Art Must Be Honest, or It Is DOA

IT WAS THE summer of 1970, and in the midst of all this hurt, angst, and brain fog, in stepped Ronnie Brown, walking like a funky 4/4 blues. I remember the phone ringing in that sunny one-bedroom apartment I rented on St. Mark's Place in the East Village and wondering who the hell was calling. "I don't like the way I'm feeling," she said hesitantly on the phone. It was Ronnie Brown from Queens College. "I sense you're not doing well, and I want to see you." I brightened once I heard her voice. We had fallen in love at Queens College, dated, and slowly drifted away from each other as I continued my revolutionary work and my nonrevolutionary sleeping around. Ronnie was as liberal as God made them: a Jewish American dentist's daughter from Bayside, Queens, whose moral compass was straight out of Harlem and whose political wisdom was straight out of S.D.S. (Students for a Democratic Society). She was never a member of any radical group, but her insights into how Americans worked and thought and how best to approach them were impeccable.

"Ronnie, how great to hear your voice," I said gaily, trying to hide the pain. "I'm doing fine. How'd you get my number?"

"Old mutual friends of ours," she said warmly.

As I held the phone, I flashed back to my Harlem episodes with Ronnie during my Last Poets/Queens College days. During that time, I lived on 132nd Street between Fifth and Lennox avenues. Up the block, going west, was Club Baron, where I would sit and discuss life and music with Johnny Hartman, one of the greatest singers America has ever produced; down the block, going east, was dope fiend alley, where the youngbloods would steer taxi drivers under the trestles of the Metro-North train and rob 'em in the isolated darkness. Few cops roamed there, and nobody cared as long as no shots were fired and nobody got hurt . . . badly. My third-floor neighbor was the Imam who had tutored Malcolm X, a simple, kind man with a wonderfully happy family who thought I was a little insane, coming in and out at all kinds of hours with different sisters and loud sounds coming from my bedroom. He was not part of the Nation of Islam; he was a true Sunni, traditional, peaceful, respectful. And when I introduced him to Ronnie, he didn't betray me with his face or attitude but simply looked at her lovingly and said, "Very happy to meet you. You know I love this boy."

She greeted him warmly and somehow this Jewish-American college student and this Black American Sunni Muslim took a liking to each other. So much so that when I couldn't or wouldn't call her during the week, she would come looking for me, walking the streets of Harlem between 125th Street and 132nd Street, without fear, asking for me by name. The street folks loved her, loved the way she loved me, the way she didn't care about ego or whiteness but would come looking for her man. Sisters identified with her; they often had to do the same with their men, dragging them out of drug dens or some woman's house. And some would capitulate to her inquiries, telling her where I was without telling whom I was with, thank God. She'd scream my name from the streets, "Felipe . . . Felipe . . . FELIPE . . . . I know you're up there so you'd better come down" until I'd appear at the door of whatever tenement I was in, sheepishly, tail between my legs, grabbing her hand and walking back home as the older sisters in front of the building laughed raucously, screaming, "That's right, girl, come get yo' man. He don't have no sense. Good woman like you, and he's out here running the streets. Kick his ass, baby! We'll hold your schoolbag. And he better not raise his hand, 'cause he knows what we'll do. He's stupid, but he ain't crazy." Ronnie would double up with laughter, waving good-bye to them while I kept my head down, laughing too, as we'd walk home to explore bodies and politics. When she couldn't find me, she'd knock on the Imam's door, his wife would let her in, and they'd discuss politics, culture, and theology until I arrived. He loved her intellect and she loved his compassion. They became good friends and through him, I learned to love Ronnie even more.

Gylan Kain took a liking to her, too. She was the first white person to visit the East Wind. Ronnie would stand in a dark corner of the loft as we ranted on about crackers, racism, and our love of Black women. He admired her guts and how she repelled all the evil looks of most of the chanting, gele-wearing Black women and the dashiki-clad Nationalist brothers. Ronnie just stood her ground laughing and singing along at all the right intervals; shouting out all the call-and-response chants to our poetry, "Ungawa, Black Power, Ungawa, Black Power!" She damn near memorized almost all our stuff, leaving many with their mouths open in amazement as she jumped up and down and clapped to the rhythms of Nilijah's hypnotic conga beats. Imagine a well-dressed, middle-class, pony-tailed white girl, with a stack of textbooks, in the midst of a poetry concert whose theme was Black and brown revolution against a white system. I'm talking 1967, way before rap and white kids' love affair with it. (Actually, The Last Poets were the seminal foundation stone for rap.) She wasn't a self-hater; she wasn't a guilt-ridden, wilting, white lily. Ronnie was proud of being Jewish. And God, was she beautiful: a short, brown-eyed Semitic beauty with long hair, small lips that felt full when you kissed her, a long, angular nose on a delicately defined oval face, and a perfectly rounded butt like a Black or Puerto Rican woman's. She never wore clothes that accentuated her curves or backside, nor did she strut like some women do to make you notice them. Her simple, quiet grace drew my attention. Just her walking got me excited. And, though her face was always serious, she was nothing like that. She loved to laugh; she was smart and accepting. She knew that the metaphors we threw into the air were historical/political truth, as we saw it. She loved Black history, was proud of my being a Black Puerto Rican. The relationship clicked. It just worked.

Her brashness earned Kain's respect.

I knew he had given her my new number.

The poetry of the Original Last Poets was intensely militant and promoted an all-encompassing Black Nationalist ideology. Kain, however, believed that being pro-Black did not have to mean we were anti-white. We allowed whites to attend our shows and suffered intense criticism by the more orthodox Nationalists. Ronnie came often. I started to feel guilty and wanted to ingratiate myself with the anti-white feelings of those Harlem warriors who felt we were living and espousing a total contradiction. Their belief was you were either for Black people or for the continuation of white supremacy. They could not/would not accept Kain's class argument that being for Black folks did not mean you severed ties with progressive white political allies. I wrote a vulgar, profane poem called "Pig Woman" attacking white women for their seduction and destruction of Black men. I remember calling Abiodun, David, and Kain to the stage area of the loft and screaming the piece out like an Albert Ayler sax solo. I finished reciting the piece and stood before my poetic family, slumped and sweaty. There was an ominous silence, not a word, not a sound.

I waited . . . and waited, alone on that East Wind stage. Finally, out of the dark came Kain's voice.

"Do you love Ronnie, Felipe?"

I was taken aback.

"Of course I do. I love her very much."

"I never want you to read that poem again, here or anywhere. Are we clear?"

"Yes," I answered, "but the reality is still true of other white women and Black men." Kain's response was bellowing, so loud, I stepped back a few steps from the force of the outburst.

"You're being a fuckin' hypocrite. Poetry without honesty is death. You're not being honest. I would rather you sing odes to this white woman you love than stand beside me on stage and spit a lie. Never, ever read that poem again. Now . . . what else do you have?"

I never forgot that lesson. If art is not honest, it's dead on arrival. Kain was correct. I was being a total hypocrite. Ronnie had proved her love and commitment by her actions. With me on the passenger side, Ronnie reluctantly put her safety on the line several times, transporting guns in Harlem to radical underground cells in her little pewter-colored Mustang. She stood firmly for social justice, for Black self-determination, for the independence of Puerto Rico. She never wavered publicly or privately; her love was total.

This woman tutored my mother privately, day after day, in math and English, as my mother prepared for her Statewide Practical Nurse test. Mom was in her late fifties and didn't feel she had the brains to pass; she was too old, she would say to Ronnie. And Ronnie would stroke her hair and build her confidence with affirmations. "You can do this, Aurora. You have to believe you can do this. This is where your faith in God has to kick in. God will give you the strength. I'll give you the knowledge. Now, let's go over these test questions again."

My mother passed at the top of her class, thanks to Ronnie Brown.

The bark in her voice on the phone brought me back from reverie to reality.

"Are you there, Felipe?" she asked angrily. "You're not saying anything, something's up."

"I'm doing okay, a few challenges, but such is life," I said weakly.

I heard Ronnie breathing hard, an exasperated breathing. You can't hide what you're feeling from someone who knows you, someone who really loves you. There was a small, nervous interval; I was a little embarrassed to let her know everything.

"Don't bullshit me, Felipe," Ronnie blurted out. "You're hurting and I can't sleep. I heard what happened in the Young Lords. I read your phony resignation in the *Times*. It didn't even sound like you. My God, after all the work you put in, shit!"

"Yeah, well . . . shit happens" was all I could muster.

"Oh, shut up, Felipe. You don't even sound like yourself. I'm coming over right now. I know where you live. Peter and Reeva told me. They're worried, too. I'm coming right now and you'd better be there!" and then she hung up.

She must've been speeding because she drove from Bayside, Queens, to the East Village in forty-five minutes.

As soon as she opened the door, we threw ourselves in each other's arms, kissing and hugging in front of the open door. We just didn't care who was watching. No one was, but it didn't matter. I broke down completely. I cried so hard, so loudly, Ronnie kicked the door closed with her foot and pulled me inside.

I started screaming hysterically. I could hear myself screaming as if I was outside my body. I realized right then that I had been close to a nervous breakdown.

"Why'd they do this, Ronnie? Why? I love them. I would die for them. They hurt me so much, Ronnie. Why'd they do this to me?" And as I pummeled her sides with my fists, Ronnie just kept my head on her shoulder and caressed it, over and over again, whispering, "It's all right. You're not alone anymore, I'm here. We'll build again. Remember who you really are."

For half an hour, I cried and slobbered and felt sorry for myself, never telling her the reason for my demotion or my departure from the Young Lords Party. Every few minutes, I'd raise my wet face and ask Ronnie, "What do I do now? I don't know who I am anymore. What do I do?" Ronnie would hold my face firmly in her hands and say, "You are more than a revolutionary, Felipe. You're a great poet, an artist. And I will not allow you to question that. There is much more for you to do, to write about. Don't let them rob your spirit, your mission, your art. You're going to write, dammit. You're gonna write new poems, new essays, and people will hear your voice again, you hear me? You hear me?"

All I could do was collapse into her shoulder again, trembling violently, until she dragged me to the bedroom, laid me down, and stroked my face to sleep, watching me, kissing my cheeks and head. I slept like a baby, for hours. We were inseparable from then on.

With all her revolutionary courage, Ronnie yearned for a family of her own, complete with me and children.

She didn't care that much about marriage; no one did in those days, but the thought of children between us made her very happy.

Fall 1971. The day came, it had to. We were not protecting ourselves during our lovemaking.

Ronnie rushed into the apartment as I was writing, threw her law books down, flushed and excited, and kissed me and made the announcement.

"I'm pregnant, Felipe. We're gonna have a baby!" and she literally jumped for joy. I wanted to be happy. I wanted to please this woman who had literally pulled me from the abyss. But I knew I wasn't ready to be a father. I was just starting to readjust to a new life and Ronnie was in her first year of law school at St. John's. To me, the timing was all wrong. Though I knew and liked her brother, Mitch, I had never met her mother or father. Her mother was lukewarm about the relationship. Her father was dead-set against it and threatened to disown her. This was not the the time for us to have a baby.

Ronnie stiffened when she saw my face and stood ramrod straight in our dining room, shaking. I had to say it. I couldn't feign joy and hit her with the truth later.

"Ronnie, I love you," I said, "But, having a child now . . . is just not right. A baby takes money and I'm not making any right now. And you got two years before you graduate. How do we pull this off, honey? A baby takes money . . . and time, time we really don't have."

It was like I'd stabbed her in the heart. She just stood there, staring at me, hurt, angry, disgusted. She saw me as a warrior, and now I was acting and sounding like those middle-class white men she called "boys" who always thought of themselves and their careers first, not their wives and children. She used to regale me with stories of these men with small, selfish minds who bought little homes in Queens so they could save for the future, whose children were starved for attention and affection (she personally knew many of them) and whose wives suffered silently in mini-surburbia with nervous conditions that turned into drinking, pills, or extramarital affairs.

Their husbands rarely came home on time, and when they did, they ignored the women who arranged their daily lives and kept them afloat.

She walked toward me slowly, disappointment in her eyes.

"Maybe I was dreaming too much. Maybe I thought there was more to this relationship.

"You see, Felipe, as much as you talk about revolution and God and miracles, I really believe in those things. I wanted to have a child with you when I first met you. My womb jumped. I never told you. I had never known anybody Black or brown or radical. Nothing. But when I saw you, when I heard you speak, I wanted to be with you forever and have your babies. I loved your fire, your dedication. I guess, for you, the revolution is for the outside, not to change the inside.

"I'm going to lie down. What you've said has hurt me deeply 'cause I'm ready to sacrifice. I can do law school pregnant. I'm tough and you know it. I'm not so sure you are." And she walked away toward the bedroom and lay down, no tears, no phone calls to friends, just the heavy feeling of sadness. I stayed sitting at the dining room table, near the legal writing pad, for hours, until nighttime.

For days, we walked around each other like ghosts, hardly saying anything to one another. Finally, at breakfast, Ronnie turned her chair toward me, held my hand, and said, "Felipe, if I give up this baby, we'll be over; I know it. The hurt in me will be too great. I just want you to know that." And with that, she picked up her law books and left for school.

We spoke after that, laughed after that, but the feeling of Light and Love left the apartment. The place became an empty shell we just happened to inhabit. I knew Ronnie did not want to raise a child alone. She wanted two committed parents to raise a little person, happy parents, filled with the joy of being blessed with a miracle called baby.

Once she realized it was not to be, she resigned herself to finding a doctor to perform the abortion. The doctor was upstate somewhere and since abortions in New York were illegal in those days, the details had to be kept secret. The day arrived and we drove upstate, not saying much to each other as we held hands. It was like being in a funeral procession. It was a funeral procession. We were going to kill the promise of our future as a couple, and we knew it. Snow began to fall lightly as the car crunched its way through the highway. I remember looking at the pine trees, the sky, the rolling hills and feeling nothing. It began to thunder. I could hear the crackle of lightning behind us. Suddenly, a flash of lightning hit the front end of the bumper, shaking both of us and the car. Ronnie screamed and grabbed me.

"Felipe, please stop. Turn back. Don't you see that's God's way of telling us that what we're doing is wrong? Let's turn around, please. He could've killed us. That was a direct hit, a warning sign. Please listen to it."

I gripped the steering wheel hard and pushed the pedal down harder, barreling the car to our destination. My insensitivity at that moment, my cruelty, my unwillingness or inability to see what Ronnie was trying to tell me broke whatever shred of hope existed in our relationship. Ronnie slipped her hand out of mine and stayed silent the rest of the trip.

The doctor was coolly professional, no small talk; he knew he was in danger too. We signed some forms, Ronnie went inside a room, and in a few hours it was over. So were we.

I took care of her for a few days, until she felt strong enough emotionally and physically to fend for herself.

Then, one day, she packed a few things–her books, underwear, pajamas, and toiletries—kissed me goodbye, and left . . . for good.

The last thing I heard about Ronnie devastated me. She had married an Orthodox Jewish fellow and died after giving birth to a child. For the next year, I carried the guilt of the world on my shoulders, thinking that complications from the abortion had killed her as she tried to bring a new life into the world. For a year cocaine and liquor became my escapes, that and doing odd jobs just to pay the rent and buy a little food and a lot of drugs. Revolution was over for me. All I had was me, whatever that was. Years later, I found out it was a faulty heart valve that killed Ronnie. It had nothing to do with the abortion. Still, as in so many other cases, I had never asked her for forgiveness.

Chapter 18

From the Taino Peoples
to the Young Lords

THE STREET VALUES of the Black and Puerto Rican community in New York City during the '50s and '60s were major factors in my survival on the streets and during my period in the Young Lords Party. The Black community, mainly South Carolinians from Charleston, Gullah people, instilled in me the ability to confront white authority with a loud, unabashed, righteous indignation. Their stories of humiliation and cruelty during the antebellum Southern days of slavery and the Jim Crow segregated societal aftermath of daily insults, dehumanization, beatings, whippings, mob lynchings, disrespect, and the violation of women filled me with an unfathomable rage. I'd sit at the feet of the elders, listen to their stories, told with laughter and a disarming resignation, and blurt out that I wouldn't have taken any of it. I would've killed the master or the sheriff or whoever hurt my family. How could they say these things so calmly? They spoke about these Southern whites with an intimacy I couldn't understand.

Miss Kathryn would regale us with incredible stories of greed and lust. And racism. "You remember that man owned the store in town, who'd turn red, get all nervous, and start stuttering soon as Marybeth walked in? Couldn't control hisself and he was married. He tried everything to sleep with that girl and when nothing else worked, threatened to raise the rent on the little shack her and her husband rented from him and told her she wouldn't get no more credit."

I'd look up at Miss Kathryn and ask, "So what did she do?" And the whole living room erupted in raucous laughter, her church friends slapping their

273

ample thighs and pudgy hands, exclaiming "He so sweet. Thank God for innocence. Thank you, Jesus."

But it wasn't only Southern whites they sat and talked about. As domestics they saw the rawness, the madness of white power and supremacy right here in the "liberal southerness" of New York City.

I remember their stories.

"Listen, girl. The rich white lady I work for downtown hardly ever comes home, doesn't cook, and doesn't buy groceries for her chi'ren. I have to spend my money to buy food, and then beg her for it at the end of the week and she never gives me all of it. Those children so scared of that big ole drafty apartment, they come into my room and crawl into my bed at night. When the missus has them big parties, she gives her kids' rooms to the guests, and I have to sleep in the twin bed with the girl. And, if there's a cousin or friend sleeping with her, I have to sleep with the boy and he's damn near thirteen now. It's sickening. I wish I could leave. Can hardly take care of my own kids."

How could they laugh at the cruelty of these white men and women whose kids they raised and fed and nurtured and tucked into bed at night? What kind of Christianity did they believe in?

Kathryn Keeles, a handsome satin-Black, portly woman, my second mother, would look at me as she sat on her bed after reading her Bible, and with the kindest of eyes, say, "Baby, you don't understand. There was nothing we could do but pray. Pray to God to protect us, pray for their ignorant souls, and pray to save enough money to leave. Anything else down South, would've gotten us all killed."

Slowly, imperceptibly, I learned the essence of Black patience and faith in God. In the face of insurmountable odds, with white men lusting after them, with Black men being rendered powerless and sometimes taking it out on themselves and their families, these women cried out to God . . . and waited with incredible elegance and grace. And so, they came North, filled with a seething anger that was loud and confrontational.

They simply weren't having it anymore. Black people taught me the power of faith. They taught me not to be afraid to scream and shout for justice. I don't know where I heard it, how it seeped into my bones, into my brain, but I believe it is essential to pray and . . . pass the ammunition.

Puerto Ricans had a different take on justice because they had a different take on race and colonialism: ambivalent, confusing, confounding. The Spanish and the Portuguese were the first to introduce African slavery to the Western Hemisphere; they controlled the seas, they controlled the slave trade. Their murderous mantra was "God, gold, and glory," not necessarily in that order. But since the Catholic Church wanted converts, wanted to save the Black and brown heathen from eternal hellfire, they demanded of their conquistadors that they convert and marry the women they raped so that the children would be legitimized in the eyes of the State and the Vatican. Thus, your master could also be your father and as my mother would intone often, "You can't kill your father. It's a sin."

British African slaves were totally marginalized; Spanish slaves were sold the lie of inclusion. Their most macabre strategy was how they kept the slaves divided by color classification: one drop of white blood in a Black slave made him or her better than other slaves. The more one looked like the slave owner, the more social privileges one was accorded, thus light skin, straight hair, straight noses, and thinner lips were the validating factors in Spanish slave society.

Large lips, kinky hair, wide noses, and dark skin were reminders of "primitive" Africa, and as such, stratification based on hair texture, facial features, and skin color became the way the Spaniards controlled slaves' minds, making them hate themselves. Puerto Ricans have a popular song about the embarrassment of Afro-Ricans with regard to their African features and Black skin; "El Negro Bembon."

To this day, most Puerto Rican/Latino media champion white skin and its privileges in movies, telenovelas, print and television advertising, and, of course, political candidates. Afro-Ricans play the roles of servants, slaves, and *santeros*, rarely leading men and women, rarely lovers. Yet the core of our culture is Africa-based. Our *bombas* are African via Haiti, our *plenas* are African-inspired, our cuisine is African, our greatest composers, musicians and athletes are Black. With the exception of the Black chained hands breaking free at the entrance to the town of Ponce, the statue of Roberto Clemente and the busts of Rafael Cortijo and Ismael Rivera and Tito Puente, in Puerto Rico nothing honors the contributions of Blacks. Add to this the fact that every Spanish word beginning with "al" is Arabic, a people who aren't in the least European white and you have a Puerto Rican culture that is in severe denial.

What we do have, what I have learned to love, admire, and treasure, is our incredible adherence to family: the blood code. Fathers abandon us, mothers beat us, uncles violate us, aunts criticize us, but no matter what, when trouble brews, when crisis erupts, we stick together, almost fanatically. Woe to outsiders who mess with family. It's a beautiful thing to watch, a beautiful thing to witness, a beautiful thing to experience.

The Puerto Rican cultural value of compassion, the "*ay bendito*" syndrome of sympathy for abuses of personal or political power, for dysfunctional individuals on our streets or in our homes, has allowed the cancer of apathy, disengagement, and resignation to metastasize to the extent that too many Puerto Rican children feel their culture and contributions to America are meaningless or nonexistent. In Puerto Rico we are prohibited from voting in stateside elections even though we are U.S. citizens. In the mainland's urban areas, Latinos are the swing vote. We decide who is elected to office, be it mayor, governor, or president. We need to wake up, read up, arm ourselves with education, and fight for our right to stand in the sun as proud Puerto Ricans and Latinos. Absent that, we will disappear into the bland porridge of assimilation with no cinnamon, no sugar, no salsa, no hot peppers. We will disappear into the white hole of American homogenization that criticizes loud anything: loud music, loud Spanish, loud behavior. We will die in our colonized desire to assimilate . . . and we'll be ignorantly proud of it.

No one will remember that Mexico was right for not allowing slavery and beating the Texans at the Alamo. No one will remember it was Tito Puente who composed "Oye Como Va"; that it was Cuba that gave millions to the radicals of the American Revolution; that Chano Pozo and Dizzy Gillespie, Mario Bauza, Rene Hernandez, and Machito founded Cuban Bop; that Mongo Santamaria and Willie Bobo popularized "cool" Latin jazz with Cal Tjader; that Mario Bauza discovered Ella Fitzgerald while working with the Chick Webb Orchestra and gave Dizzy his first break with the Cab Calloway Band, that Herman Badillo was the first Puerto Rican U.S. congressman, that Puerto Rican soldiers took Latin music all over the world, popularizing the Afro-Cuban musical form we call salsa and the dance form we call mambo. The mis-match clothing of our impoverished childhoods, the different cloth patterns of stripes, polka dots, shiny beads, and cartoon characters, the reds and pinks and yellows we wore at one time because we had nothing else have now become fashion statements for young children, adolescents, and runway models. We are the fashion. We just don't know it. And in the same way, the Spanish and English robbed our sugar cane, processed it, and sold it back to us, in the same way they do with some fashion styles.

Somehow, the Young Lords Party knew all that in 1969. Some of us were reading. We were not a group of homogeneous beings. We had different outlooks and personalities, different upbringings. There were those who joined the Party based purely on their ideological beliefs: Puerto Ricans were an oppressed people. As such, we had a right, a duty, to fight for the independence of the island of Puerto Rico and self-determination (social justice) for the Puerto Rican communities here in the continental United

States, even if, and especially, if that meant armed struggle against the government of this country.

We knew the history: the brutal Spanish domination of our island since 1493, a year after the dark Moors of Andalusia in southern Spain were defeated by the white Catholics in the north after 750 years of relative peace and development and advancements in science, engineering, medicine, and philosophy. We had read about the imperialist military takeover of Puerto Rico in 1898 and the subsequent expulsion 30 years later of island 'Ricans to Hawaii and to the mainland 20 years after that. We knew that the history books lied about our "ignorant, uneducated passivity" and our love for oppressors.

Upon investigation, we learned that the Tainos fought the Spaniards on the beaches, in the savannas, in the mountains with stone clubs against superior firepower. We read about the trauma of experiencing an advanced weapons technology and things we had never seen before . . . horses, steel swords, armor, white skin, blond hair, dogs that ate human flesh, and long sticks that spit out little balls that tore through skin, put bloody holes in your body, made you lose blood and die.

They also brought an invisible disease, smallpox. We could fight against a visible enemy. Tainos had no immunity against smallpox, and they died in the tens of thousands. Cristóbal Colón invaded Borinquen in 1493. Within thirty years they were almost all wiped out through murder, maltreatment, and disease. All of this we knew.

We knew how the Americans brought warships to Guánica Bay 400 years later, took over our ancestors' *bohios* and the *jibaros'* little plots of land to build sugar *centrales* with accompanying asphalt roads, paving over the homes and history of a valiant people, infecting them with everything from the common cold to a virulent racism to greed and materialism. We knew this.

We knew that patriots and leaders sprang from our loins to hold the banner of independence high: Agueybana, Guarionex, Hatuey, Emeterio Betances, Albizu Campos, Lolita Lebron, Rafael Cancel Miranda, Irving Flores, Andres Figueroa Cordero, Oscar Collazo, Blanca Canales, Griselio Torricelo and Filiberto Ojeda, Oscar Lopez Rivera and Dylcia Pagan, Vidal Santiago Diaz, and Carmelo Alvarez, and we knew the prison sentences, the torture, the price they paid with their lives. And we knew if this generation didn't fight, if we didn't stop the leviathan, kill the beast, we as a people would be no more. We knew this.

Then there were those of us who weren't as familiar with history or socialist ideology; we didn't go to college; we barely finished high school.

But we knew El Barrio. We knew the Bronx, had been raised by welfare and solid working-class parents. We knew we were Puerto Rican and we faced discrimination daily by policemen, by teachers, by city agencies.

We felt the racism and we knew those who resisted, who fought back. We knew the gangs that defended our honor and our streets: The Viceroys, the Dragons, the Turbans and Copasetics of East Harlem, the Sportsmen on the Lower East Side; the Chaplains, the Roman Lords, Spanish Romans, the Bishops, the Jolly Stompers, The Frenchmen, the Corsair Lords, the Buccaneers, all out of Brooklyn; the Savage Skulls, the Savage Nomads, the Ghetto Brothers, and the Black Spades in the Bronx.

We joined the Young Lords Party to protect our land, our families, our brothers and sisters, our children. Ours was a war of heart and soul more than intellect. There was another type of Young Lord, a small minority; some from mixed-race marriages, raised in cultural confusion, who wanted to "feel more Puerto Rican." And, within those ranks were many who had been taught to denigrate their culture, to avoid being labeled "Latino," to reject any association with brown people because they were inferior, to admire, seek after, and emulate white American culture and to identify with European Spain, *la madre patria.*

To the extent that these strains within the Young Lords Party intertwined and fed off one another, we succeeded. To the extent we allowed myopic nationalism and false criteria to determine who was a true revolutionary and who wasn't, we failed. Add to this the insidious, murderous nature of the FBI's COINTELPRO program and you understand why the Young Lords were destroyed from within and without. Street men and women made the Young Lords Party. They were the blood, the bodies, the substance of our group. Our fame was built entirely on their shoulders, their exploits, their quick-thinking intelligence, and their unimaginable bravery. This is not literary hyperbole.

In the fall of 1969, at the 110th Street and Lenox Avenue subway station, two of the youngest of our members, Pai Diaz and Hui Cambrelen came across a policeman roughing up a man. In these situations, YLP policy was to ask the police what the offense was, and if it was a clean collar to make sure the arrest proceeded without brutality. If it was a bogus charge accompanied by a beating, we were trained to do all we could do to free the person, screaming to attract a crowd, pulling the person out of the cops' grip, and doing anything to distract the cop so the person could pull away and run.

The cop was taken aback by the boldness of the two Lords and let go of the man he was beating to reach for these interlopers, banging Hui's head hard with his gun. Pai twisted the cop's wrist, stepped into his body perfectly, flipping the cop on the edge of the platform, right near the tracks. He told me later his mistake was holding onto the cop's arm for fear the guy would roll onto the third rail and be electrocuted or get hit by an oncoming train. Though stunned and on his back, the policeman had the presence of mind to pull his revolver and point it at the chest of this boyish-looking teenager. Pai just stared at him. He didn't shoot, thank God, but he did peg a shot at Hui, who upon seeing the .38, realizing that Pai was not going to be killed, took off. Here's the amazing part: Hui said he could almost feel when the cop was going to pull the trigger and immediately jumped as high as he could.

Sure enough, the bullet whizzed underneath him. He escaped without a scratch. Pai was released without even being charged. The embarrassment would have made the Police Department look ridiculous and, more important, ineffectual and dangerous.

We were lucky, maybe blessed. Had Pai let the brother's arm go, the cop would've been killed, and he would've faced a murder charge. It would've destroyed his life. It would have also destroyed the Young Lords Party. There are those who might argue that the cop's murder would've put us on the map nationally, would've given us revolutionary credentials and support worldwide. But I saw how lengthy court trials, fundraising, increased surveillance, and arbitrary, vengeful police raids depleted the Panther Party because of the media's portrayal of them as "cop killers." These brave men and women were slowly bled to death and murdered by COINTELPRO and local police because of a concentrated, distorted media campaign of negativity, keeping them from creating new strategies and programs in their communities. The Young Lords Party didn't need it. The Black Panther Party, born before us, suffered severe consequences for defending themselves and the Black community from wanton police violence. They paid for our right to life with their lives. The YLP made a conscious decision to focus on martial arts rather than on guns; the NYPD could not come at us with the thought that we would pull out a gun at any moment and use it. It made a difference in their aggression and tactics. Our community, still basically a law-and-order group, would not have to harbor divided loyalties in the event of a confrontation. It was clear: We were unarmed, the cops had the guns.

Pai and Hui were just some of the youngest of the streetbloods. There was Bobby Lemus, Georgie, and Mikey (all part of one family), Huracan, Georgie Little Man, Husky Willie, Muntu (now known as Faisal), Carl Pastor, G.I., Frenchy, Ramon Morales (another fifteen-year-old who eventually graduated from Harvard), Eddie Figueroa, Mirta, Myrna, Iris Benitez (three women I'd go into battle with any day of the year), Lulu, Betty Perez, Connie, YaYa,

Robles, Tintan, Robert Ortiz, Alcides, Eugene, Fi, David Perez, Denise Oliver, who might as well be called one of the co-founders of the Young Lords Party, Iris Morales, Micky Melendez, Gabriel Torres or "T" as we called him (the courts gave him twelve years in prison for what they say was participation in an armed robbery for the Black Liberation Army), Benji, Carlos Rovira, Cleo Silvers, Larry, Hiram Maristany (our official photographer), Cano, Lou Garden Acosta, Micky Agrait and Doolie, Frankie Morales and Louie Perez and Pelu, who had the biggest Afro in the Lords and would stand up to cops anywhere, anytime, take an ass-whipping by police and not complain as he came limping back into the office. These were just a few of the street folks who put their lives on the line, day in, day out.

Our fame was built entirely on their shoulders. Everything I am today in politics and what little wisdom I possess is attributable to them. The Young Lords story is really their story, a tale of how young people of color came together, some educated, most not, around the issue of community self-determination and the independence of Puerto Rico even though most had not been born there, and others could not claim Puerto Rican as their nationality. It didn't matter.

Ours was a shining example of truth, as we saw it, multicultural celebration, and revolutionary ideology superseding crass nationality, racism, and class myopia. Their confrontations with police, with reactionary bullies, with gangsters, are almost comic book heroism, now the stuff of legend, but it did happen.

I often told the members, "It's not that we can't die, it's that they can't kill us." It was a dangerous axiom to live by, immature and, in retrospect, downright stupid, but some of us really believed it. I certainly did.

Coda: A Voice for Our People

I DISCOVERED I had a knack for analyzing music, for being able to explain subtlety and nuance to others of musical arrangements. My musical preferences were jazz and Latin music, and I would regale those who visited me about Miles Davis, John Coltrane, and Tito Puente.

Someone suggested I be interviewed on a political program hosted by a young white radical woman named Chris Millier on the now-defunct WRVR-FM. Chris gently probed around the edges of my relationship to the Young Lords Party, the Black Panthers, The Last Poets for two hours. She would bore into me with layer upon layer of questions about race, revolution, and ideology. At the end of the program I was sweating, laughing heartily, and feeling I had purpose in the world. Upon ending the interview, she told me to follow her into program director John Wiklein's office. She knocked and, before he could answer, pushed open the door, declaring firmly, "I've got the next host for that empty spot from 12–5 A.M. on Sundays; his name is Felipe Luciano. He's amazing, hire him."

He did without a whimper. And radio became my next adventure. I remember sitting in that studio the first time, in Riverside Church, feeling completely at home. I could preach, pontificate, debate with listeners, and play the music I loved. I became a student of music, interviewing musicians like Tito Puente, Machito, Mongo Santamaria, Chico O'Farrill, Ray Barretto, La Lupe, Charlie Palmieri, and Willie Colon; musicologists like Rene Lopez, Bob Sancho, and the Gonzalez Brothers. Researching the music, I read everything I could on the African, Spanish, and Arabic origins of Latin music and how this mélange of sound traveled with the slave trade from the continent to the Caribbean and finally to the United States.

I used the same warrior instincts I had in politics to fight the battles of disrespect and discrimination on the part of radio stations toward Latin music. Eventually, I was promoted from the midnight shift on Saturdays, to Sundays from 1–5 P.M. The show, "Latin Roots," became an instant hit during the '70s. You couldn't go anywhere on Sunday afternoons and not hear the rhythmic joy blaring through boom boxes and car stereos. Inadvertently, I happened to stumble into the golden age of salsa, an exhilarating time of concerts, travel, club life, love affairs, and dreams. I had finally made it from street battles and garbage offensives and taking over institutions to hosting concerts and drinking champagne in penthouses and Madison Square Garden.

It took years before I lost the guilt of having left my revolutionary comrades, but in the end I knew the Young Lords Party had left an indelible mark in the Puerto Rican consciousness and in the minds of America.

I lost the visceral anger and forgave my comrades even though many felt I had abandoned them. I had to live with that.

Today, I know the Young Lords Party is inscribed in the annals of history. We fought, we bled, we cried, and we shouted out heartily in our victories. I will never forget them and will continue to dream of a Puerto Rico free and independent.

ACKNOWLEDGMENTS

I FLUNG THIS manuscript at friends and "frenemies."

I especially wanted to hear the reactions of those who simply didn't like me too much, who tolerated my pontificating on politics and my arrogance based on my insecurities. Each person had a unique perspective, and I could tell by the way my body tightened whether the criticisms were authentic (meant to make me feel good and draw me closer to the other person) or just plain cruel.

Flattery and passive-aggressivity are the worst snake bites to a writer, to an artist of any kind. Those who cannot construct an ideology or develop an aesthetic that is uniquely theirs insidiously work at chipping away at your confidence—sometimes through "humor," sometimes through outright hostility, and sometimes through noncommittal statements. I had to learn to construct the armor of self-confidence and faith in myself.

I like being flattered, I like being accepted; however, as Frank Sinatra once said, "Flattery can be as deadly as arsenic."

There are those who stood by me through moodiness, depression, "high-ness," and immature rants. I would spend hours reading them passages of this manuscript, and they never wilted. They got tired, to be sure, but somehow through the torrent of words they'd reach into the whirlwind of verbosity and pull out the nugget of the idea I was trying to convey or scrape out the contradiction of the bullshit I was writing.

Lydia Nicole, for example, exhorted me to tell the truth without adorn-ment. "This is your legacy," she would scream, "and you cannot let others interpret your life or your contributions to the world. It's gonna hurt some people, but you have to be authentic. History is not always nice." So I thank Lydia Nicole profusely for her uncompromising love and honesty.

But first there is this man named John Coles, a prolific television director and dear friend who had the patience and creative intelligence to read the narrative and offer suggestions on how to improve the clarity and sequence of events. John always motivates me to greater heights in my writing. He knows the euphoria of acceptance and the pitfalls of rejection. Because he had become acquainted with some of the Young Lords through a film project that never came to fruition, he could discern what were the elements of truth and the blather of nonsense.

Professor Gary Dorrien of Union Theological Seminary read the entire first draft and egged me on even before I found a publisher. His is a unique compassion, and may God bless him profoundly.

Megan Bowman Brown, my friend of fifty years, was always excited about the "poetry" of this book. She wasn't raised in poverty or violence, but after listening to excerpts of *Flesh and Spirit* she would call to tell me how much it allowed her to see the other side of life in America.

In the beginning of the final phase of the manuscript a young editor, Yvonne Washington, sat at my kitchen table for hours, offering me advice on how to prune the literary branches from this tree of memoirs.

Then there's my namesake, Felipe Luciano Jr., who suffered through years of my mood swings and my blabbing to strangers about my childhood experiences. He is a quiet soul, more reserved, more elegant, and during my upward spirals of grandiosity he would respectfully bring me back to Earth.

My daughter, Ila Hess Luciano, and her mother, Maya Hess, would also ride herd to my stampedes of anger and depression. Ila has morphed into my mother, reminding me of appointments I'm supposed to make and medicine I'm supposed to take. Her reason: She wants me around for a long time and wants her daughter, Eva, to know her grandpa.

Then there is Melinda Ledesma, who suffered through my betrayals and rode shotgun with me through my early adulthood until she got tired of the abuse. Our son, Eric Michael Luciano, is a shining example of Puerto Rican manhood. He's married, and he has a home and a beautiful wife and son, Lennox. One hopes this book serves as a springboard for a new life for the next generation of Lucianos.

My gang consists of some Blacks and Puerto Ricans who are exemplary in art and in battle. They are Abiodun Oyewole and Umar Bin Hassan of The Last Poets, who would listen to my poetry and my chapters; Jamal Joseph, former Black Panther, jailed for nine years and now a filmmaker and professor at Columbia University, and Aaron Dixon, former captain of the Panther Party in Seattle, Washington, both of whom are brothers from another mother; Abdul Musawwir, formerly known as Monroe Marrow, who recently passed and left me with a hole in my heart. Ramon Morales, computer wizard and former Young Lord, let me stay in his apartment in Puerto Rico whenever I needed a shot of tropical sun. Writer/poet Quincy Troupe's admonishment was "Fuck the editors and those in control of the publishing industry. Say it the way you saw it."

Former Young Lords José "Pai" Diaz and Hui Cambrelen felt that the chronology of events was correct, though Hui felt there were things I shouldn't reveal. Harvard grad and lawyer Ramon Jimenez, now deceased, goaded me in his South Bronx office when I procrastinated and felt like giving up. Painter Fred Brown, before his demise, told me I had a responsibility to the children of the future to break through the wall of mediocrity with regard to people of color. Micky Melendez is the dude who started it all by enjoining me to the Young Lords. He was the first of us to write a book, along with boxer José Torres, titled *We Took the Streets*. I was pissed and jealous. Finally, I realized I was angry only at myself for not having written my version of events. Thanks, Micky, for motivating me.

During the beginning phases of this book there were two women who literally cared for me by feeding me, allowing me quiet times in their homes, and hugging me through tears of guilt and anger as I went backward in time through the writing. They were Barbara Weinstock and Kristie Velasco. We lost Barbara to cancer a few years ago. Her sense of balance became my literary sextant. Kristie is still one of my best friends whose love and loyalty astound me. I still see her children, Amanda and Danny, as my own.

Reverend Mark Rivera of the Primitive Christian Church read my master's thesis for Union Theological Seminary and would listen to excerpts from this book, serving as a cleansing balm during the times I became too critical.

Reverends Sam Cruz and Ray Rivera, both raised in the Pentecostal tradition (Sam is now a Lutheran minister), would guide me through the finer points of Pentecostal faith and practice.

Sheila Williams, a dear friend, would listen with a metaphysical ear and a knowledge of the "softness" of my character, asking pointed questions about what I really felt.

Marta Lichenstein and Harry Mule brought out salient points about the contradictions in my habits and behaviors.

Then there's the Lower East Side gang, like the late, great Puerto Rican poet Tato Laviera, who made me promise before he died to turn *Flesh and Spirit* into an audio book. Community activist Herson Cabrera did the same and still picks me up for breakfast from time to time to discuss God and politics.

Gabriel and Sara Moreno are my secret family, and whenever I felt there was no hope in our community they would provide me with a circle of faith and excited expectancy about the future of Puerto Ricans and Latinos.

Then there's the late Hiram Maristany, the official photographer of the Young Lords Party, who passed on and lovingly fought me every step of the way with regard to art, culture, and politics.

My cousin Cynthia Lopez bolstered my voice as a writer.

I also have to give credit to Gail Badillo, widow of the first Puerto Rican congressman, Herman Badillo. As a former junior high school teacher and a lover of the English language, she offered support in the framing of the narrative and grammar. She was inspiring.

Shidoshi Ronnie van Clief (the Black Dragon) told me he loved the action sequences. He told me it was the stuff of movies.

Professor Mark Naison brought me into the academic world of Fordham University and introduced me to Fordham University Press.

"Tonka" Lindsay went to great pains to help me stay aloft during the last part of this book by prioritizing my speaking engagements and handling my finances.

Two childhood friends, Hector "Frenchy" Rivera and Sebastian "Sabu" Sinclair, were combat Vietnam veterans who were invaluable guides in the inner workings of war and personal combat, PTSD, and recovery.

My younger brother, Pablo Luciano, is one of the wisest persons I know. Through his experiences on the streets, he developed an inner ear and a god-fearing spirit. I called him several times in South Carolina and he always gave me the "real."

My sister, Margaret Luciano, is an indomitable woman whose church musings sometimes enraged me but often dissipated the mind fog.

Professor Johanna Fernandez, who wrote a definitive history of the Young Lords Party called (what else) *The Young Lords*, has served as a literary Velcro backdrop. I would know when I was on point by what facts stuck and what facts didn't.

Finally, after much gnashing of teeth and casting about for editors I was introduced to Randall Williams, a hard-core, working-class white radical who had a brain, an understanding of the contradictions in American society, and a real feeling for activism. He and I completed this tome; he cut my lines, cut my distracting stories, and got to the core of the story: me, what I saw and what I experienced. I will forever be grateful to him.

I must thank the late Jackie Onassis, who befriended me while I was a reporter at WNBC, New York. I was introduced to her by the great journalist and writer Pete Hamill, and we became instant friends. As an editor at Doubleday, Jackie would push, plead with, and cajole me to write this book. During that time of immaturity and getting high, I never did. She stopped calling because I didn't follow through. In a sense, this book is my apology to her, my way of letting her know I grew up and finally pulled it off.

Jackie, my family and I will never forget you.

Each person mentioned was a necessary step in the completion of this manuscript. We may think we can do it alone, but the truth is we need each other. And even as we reach that plateau of confidence within ourselves, we still look to connect.

INDEX

Felipe Luciano is an Emmy Award–winning journalist, news anchor, and former adjunct professor at Fordham University. He is the founder and chairman of the Young Lords Party, a member of The Original Last Poets, an advocate for inter-ethnic communication, and the host of "Street Talk." A talented diversity speaker, Luciano is committed to community empowerment, ethnic pride, and civil rights. He is a regular contributor to many New York–area newspapers and magazines, including *The New York Times* and *Essence.* His poetry has appeared in anthologies such as *Puerto Rican Poetry: An Anthology from Aboriginal to Contemporary Time.*

William Seraile, *Angels of Mercy: White Women and the History of New York's Colored Orphan Asylum*

Daniel Campo, *The Accidental Playground: Brooklyn Waterfront Narratives of the Undesigned and Unplanned*

Joseph B. Raskin, *The Routes Not Taken: A Trip Through New York City's Unbuilt Subway System*

Phillip Deery, *Red Apple: Communism and McCarthyism in Cold War New York*

North Brother Island: The Last Unknown Place in New York City. Photographs by Christopher Payne, A History by Randall Mason, Essay by Robert Sullivan

R. Scott Hanson, *City of Gods: Religious Freedom, Immigration, and Pluralism in Flushing, Queens.* Foreword by Martin E. Marty

Dorothy Day and the Catholic Worker: The Miracle of Our Continuance. Edited, with an Introduction and Additional Text by Kate Hennessy, Photographs by Vivian Cherry, Text by Dorothy Day

Mark Naison and Bob Gumbs, *Before the Fires: An Oral History of African American Life in the Bronx from the 1930s to the 1960s*

Robert Weldon Whalen, *Murder, Inc., and the Moral Life: Gangsters and Gangbusters in La Guardia's New York*

Sharon Egretta Sutton, *When Ivory Towers Were Black: A Story about Race in America's Cities and Universities*

Britt Haas, *Fighting Authoritarianism: American Youth Activism in the 1930s*

David J. Goodwin, *Left Bank of the Hudson: Jersey City and the Artists of 111 1st Street.* Foreword by DW Gibson

Nandini Bagchee, *Counter Institution: Activist Estates of the Lower East Side*

Susan Celia Greenfield (ed.), *Sacred Shelter: Thirteen Journeys of Homelessness and Healing*

Susan Opotow and Zachary Baron Shemtob (eds.), *New York after 9/11*

Andrew Feffer, *Bad Faith: Teachers, Liberalism, and the Origins of McCarthyism*

Colin Davey with Thomas A. Lesser, *The American Museum of Natural History and How It Got That Way.* Forewords by Neil deGrasse Tyson and Kermit Roosevelt III

Lolita Buckner Inniss, *The Princeton Fugitive Slave: The Trials of James Collins Johnson*

Jill Jonnes, *South Bronx Rising: The Rise, Fall, and Resurrection of an American City, Third Edition*

Barbara G. Mensch, *A Falling-Off Place: The Transformation of Lower Manhattan*

David J. Goodwin, *Midnight Rambles: H. P. Lovecraft in Gotham*

Maximo G. Martinez, *Sojourners in the Capital of the World: Garifuna Immigrants*

For a complete list, visit www.fordhampress.com/empire-state-editions.